IDEAS IN HISTORY

IDEAS IN HISTORY

ESSAYS PRESENTED TO

LOUIS GOTTSCHALK

BY HIS FORMER STUDENTS

EDITED BY RICHARD HERR

AND HAROLD T. PARKER

DUKE UNIVERSITY PRESS

DURHAM, N. C. 1965

PRINTED IN THE UNITED STATES OF AMERICA
BY THE SEEMAN PRINTERY, INC., DURHAM, N.C.

CONTENTS

INTRODUCTION

Harold T. Parker

One of the more attractive traditions of the scholarly world is the dedication of a collection of essays to an admired teacher. It is followed not from the mistaken belief that such a collection can add stature to a man whose reputation has long been established but out of the realization that the interchange between a gifted teacher and his students is one of the most cherished intellectual experiences life offers. For the authors of these essays the teaching of Louis Gottschalk has been such an experience. In offering him this volume, they wish to speak not only for themselves but for his other graduate students who have given this venture their enthusiastic support, as well as all persons who have enjoyed his teaching and friendship over the past forty years.

From their association with Gottschalk his graduate students carried away the memory of sustained kindness and professional excellence. He is a professional historian, who was educated by professionals and who always works at the current problems of his occupation with intelligence and professional skill. Born in 1899 in Brooklyn, he graduated from Cornell University with an A.B. in 1919 and with a Ph.D. in history in 1921, at the age of twenty-two. Indeed, honors and associated responsibilities—for men honor their fellows by giving them work to do—came to him rather early. After a stint of teaching at the universities of Illinois and Louisville, he became associate professor of history at the University of Chicago in 1927, chairman of its history department for a five-year tour of duty in 1937, and president of the American Historical Association in 1953.

In the years 1919 to 1921 the history department at Cornell University was a good place to study. The number of history graduate teachers at Cornell nearly equaled the number of history students, and the members of both groups were first-rate. The professors of the graduate staff included Carl Becker, George Lincoln Burr, Charles Hull, and William Westermann. The graduate students were George G. Andrews, Leo Gershoy, Gottschalk, Harold Hulme, Ernest Willian Nelson. . . . The members of the graduate staff complemented each other. For example, Hull, who had been educated at the University of Berlin, taught in the best traditions of the Rankean historical seminar the intense, critical scrutiny of evidence. "I learned technical historical method from Hull," Gottschalk would later remark. Meanwhile, across the hall in his office, Becker, no less scrupulous, was leading young men to question the pseudo-Rankean preconceptions of Herbert Baxter Adams and his school. Becker thus gave his students a direction of attention that lasted the rest of their lives. "Cornell meant Becker to me," Gottschalk later observed. To understand the implications of that remark, it is necessary to go back a little, at least to Herbert Baxter Adams.

Adams rendered immense services to American historical scholarship. When he started his influential career as a teacher of history at the Johns Hopkins University in 1876, there were not more than eleven history professors in the United States. Adams introduced the Ranke-type historical seminar at Johns Hopkins, and sent out young history Ph.D.'s to staff history departments throughout the country and to train other students. He and his disciples, for the most part, were aglow with the noble dream that if they searched the mountain of documents that has come down from the past and if they allowed their minds to follow the evidence, they would attain a thorough and impartial historical description that would correspond to what had actually occurred. They would test each document for its authenticity, appraise the reliability of each author, and compare the statements of several witnesses; when they had two independent witnesses not self-deceived agreeing to the same historical circumstance they would have a historical fact, to be placed with other historical facts in a narrative that would offer a sure description and explanation of the movement of historical events. So assured were they of their method that they would have approved the celebrated remark of the great French medievalist Fustel de Coulanges to an admiring audience: "Do not applaud. 'Tis not I who speaks, but History,"

which speaks through me.   In accord with the dominant historiographical tendency of the nineteenth century, history for Adams
and his disciples was largely political history—the narrative of
reigns and ministries and, more profoundly, the evolution of political institutions.   Through their efforts Adams, his associates,
and his students established the study of history as an independent,
self-respecting discipline in American universities, inculcated
respect for the methodical search for historical truth through
tested procedures of bibliography, scrutiny, authentication, and
verification, and deepened political history through emphasis on
the continuity and growth of political institutions.

However, to a degree the reputation of Herbert Baxter Adams
and his associates was the victim of their success.   Once their
battles had been won, people forgot that there had ever been any
enemies to fight.   Forgotten were the absence of history instruction in colleges and universities, the unmethodical handling of
evidence by amateur historians, and the tendency of political
narrative superficially to recount the intrigues and exploits of the
court and army.   Also, some of the mottoes of the Adams group
easily lent themselves to caricature.   The phrase, to write history
wie es eigentlich gewesen, when lifted from the context of Ranke's
thought, seemed to betray epistemological naïveté. The dictum
of E. A. Freeman that history is past politics and politics are
present history, which was placed above the doorway of the Johns
Hopkins history seminar room and which was intended to convey a
sense of historical continuity, seemed to show a shocking disregard
for perhaps 80 per cent of history's content.   Nevertheless, caricature is only the exaggeration of the truth.   The solution of Adams
and of some of his disciples to the problem of historical investigation did have severe limitations and shortcomings. Although he
allowed his graduate students complete freedom to follow their
interests in their main research, for the most part they did write
monographs about political, constitutional, and legal history.   In
developing their themes, they tended to use events that could be
observed externally by two independent witnesses not self-deceived
and thus established as historical fact.   They tended to shun the
shadowy, treacherous world of thought and motive. Stringing one
external fact after the other, they were naïvely sure that the state-

ment of each fact and sequence corresponded to what actually occurred.

As early as 1891, Frederick Jackson Turner, a Johns Hopkins Ph.D. but one who was aware of multiple English and German historiographical tendencies and who had a mind and imagination of his own, took issue with some of the tenets of Adams and his disciples. To be sure, Turner observed, the historian is honor-bound to be as scrupulous and exacting in his search for truth as any scientist. Yet the historian is operating in the present, and his mentality and hence his historical account will be affected by present conditions. In an age of political agitation, such as the early nineteenth century, it was natural for historians to be interested in political history. In a period of growing technology, scholars such as Wilhelm Roscher in Germany, Thorold Rogers in England, and (Turner might have added) Karl Marx would be concerned with the economic interpretation of historical events. Actually, Turner remarked, a historian who wishes to understand and be self-conscious about how the complete present came to be must know something about the complete past. History is not simply past politics or past economics; it is past religion, past art, past everything. The historian must also seek the vital forces that lie behind institutions, such as thoughts and feelings, advance multiple hypotheses to explain sequences of events, and enlist the procedures and knowledge of allied investigators in related disciplines.

With this enlargement of the dimensions of historical investigation, Becker, one of Turner's students, was always in sympathy. "By all means," he wrote in 1912, "let the historian learn all he possibly can about the newer sciences of mankind, and about philosophy, about literature, about art, about everything that is under the sun."[1] However, while most of Turner's students and Turner himself sought the vital forces that lay beneath events in social and economic circumstance, Becker tended to seek them in thoughts and sentiments, in the unsubstantial realm of internal events whose reality could not be established by any number of witnesses. In 1898, at Columbia University, he enrolled in James Harvey Robinson's seminar in eighteenth-century thought, and in

1. Quoted in Burleigh Wilkins, *Carl Becker* (Cambridge, Mass., 1961), p. 93.

preparing a paper on the Physiocrats he "acquired an abiding interest in why people think as they do."[2] He became less and less concerned with the record of events, "of what men have done," and more with "the state of mind that conditioned those events."[3] Documents he valued less as reports of what happened than as revelations of the ideas and impulses of those who made them. In his dissertation on the formation of revolutionary parties in New York, 1760-1776, he became "absorbed in the mental processes by which the revolutionist was gradually differentiated from the loyalist."[4] In his *Eve of the [American] Revolution* (1918), he sought to convey less a record of what men did than "a sense of how they thought and felt about what they did."[5] His *Declaration of Independence* (1922) was an essay in formal ideas, popular philosophy, and revolutionary psychology. The last two books were being prepared while Gottschalk was at Cornell, and Becker may have read chapters of them to his seminar. By precept and example Becker was leading a personal crusade for the involvement of ideas in the average historical account. He was interested in all sorts of ideas, from the formal ideas of abstract speculation to the images, common prejudices, and half-spoken notions of everyday life. However, he was not interested in ideas apart from the individuals who held them. In these years he was concerned with defining delicately the subtle interplay of ideas, events, and personal temperament in the ongoing narrative movement of history. At the same time he was also conducting another crusade against the naïve assumption that there was a one-to-one correspondence between the statement of the historian and what had actually occurred. Becker's subtle, intricate mind seems to have been outraged by such simplicity. With irony and wit he observed that even our notion of a historical fact, "Caesar was stabbed in the Senate house," was shot through with present images and ideas, while our selection of facts was affected by our present interests, needs, and concepts. Anyone who attended Becker's seminar in those years could not fail to emerge with a lasting

2. *Ibid.*, p. 62.
3. Carl Becker, "The Memoirs and the Letters of Madame Roland," *American Historical Review*, XXXIII (1927-1928), 784.
4. Charlotte Watkins Smith, *Carl Becker: On History and the Climate of Opinion* (Ithaca, 1956), p. 169.
5. Carl Becker, *The Eve of the Revolution* (New Haven, 1918), p. vii.

interest in the role of ideas in history. Anyone who had the seminars of both Hull and Becker could not fail to have an abiding concern with the practical and theoretical aspects of historical method. The two teachers gave Gottschalk questions to ask of history, and some of the means for answering them. They endowed him with an initial philosophy to exploit, before he developed one of his own.

Gottschalk initiated his first two studies, of Jean Paul Marat and of the Marquis de Lafayette, while he was still under the dominating influence of the Cornell experience. Although in these years Becker was still writing United States history, he was teaching modern European history, and specifically the history of the eighteenth century and French Revolution. For his doctoral dissertation Gottschalk examined the development of the political theories of Jean Paul Marat. However, as the development of Marat's ideas could not be explained apart from his character and outside circumstances, the dissertation was expanded for publication into a biography, *Jean Paul Marat: A Study in Radicalism* (1927). Previous biographies of Marat had been warped by rancor or adulation and overlaid with legend. Gottschalk's narrative was distinguished by its non-partisan tone, the cool, competent appraisal of contradictory evidence, and lucid exposition. It was in essence a discriminating delineation of the interplay of temperament, events, and ideas in the evolving career of a popular leader. In this evolution, temperament and circumstances counted for somewhat more than ideas. In the decade before the French Revolution, Marat was a successful physician who had little cause for complaint on the material side of life. However, he was also an amateur scientific investigator embittered by his failure to be elected to the Academy of Science for his publications on fire, electricity, light, and optics; always prone to be suspicious, he blamed his "enemies" for his exclusion. With the opening of the Revolution, he started with a basic loyalty to the monarchy and a desire for reform. But by temperament preternaturally suspicious he began in his newspaper, as a friend of the people, violently to denounce counterrevolutionary plotters and plots. In time several of these plots of Mirabeau, Dumouriez, and others came to light. Marat was justified and acclaimed. Ideas, curiously, tended either to exercise a restraining influence (his belief that a republic could not succeed in a country as large as France delayed his rejection of the monarchy) or to suggest the elements of a positive program of revolutionary clubs, tribunal, and dictatorship that was largely ignored. In the flow of events he became a radical by virtue of his temperament rather than his convictions, and a leader by reason of his denunciatory actions rather than his ideology.

A successful one-volume biographical study of radicalism in the person of Marat suggested to Gottschalk the preparation of a similar one-volume biographical study of liberalism in the person of Lafayette. However, events involving the hero of two worlds were so numerous and the sources so voluminous that a one-volume essay burgeoned into a monumental multi-tomed enterprise that is still in progress. Four volumes, carrying Lafayette from 1754 to 1789, thus far have been issued. The book on Marat had been aptly dedicated to Carl Becker. Although the work, when necessary, displayed that technical address in handling sources Gottschalk had learned with Charles Hull, its dominant interests were Becker's—the interrelations of personality, formal ideas, and events. A volume of the Lafayette series was dedicated to Hull, and justly so: the series smoothly fused the thoroughness and skills of technical historical method with the interests of Becker. The Lafayette story abounded in technical historical problems—the authenticity of documents, the dating of letters, the accuracy of memoirs, the question of intent, the reliability of oral tradition. These problems were solved in the Lafayette volumes with professional assurance and proficiency, in the best traditions of the Rankean school. One reviewer observed that the manner in which Gottschalk managed to gather his material and sift it "by the most enlightened processes is a model for all research historians."[6]

However, the verity of historical statements was not established simply from delight in establishing verities. The statements were used to present a full-bodied biographical narrative and to define delicately and subtly the moving interrelations of ideas, character, and events in the evolving destiny of a historical personality. In

6. Bernard Faÿ, reviewing *Lafayette Joins the American Army* in *The American Historical Review*, XLIV (1938-1939), 393.

his memoirs Lafayette had represented himself as having been
brought to America at the age of nineteen by his love of liberty
and of the rights of man; thereafter, devotion to liberal causes
had explained all his public conduct. Gottschalk suggested that
historical reality was far more complex and nuanced. Reared in
rural isolation by the adoring women of his family, Lafayette had
emerged from childhood into the larger world of adults with a
personality that needed outside approval but did not always have
the means to secure it. He desired to please but did not always
know how to do so. Awkward, diffident, and unhappy at the
court of Versailles, the young adolescent dreamed of glory. The
Paris agent of the United States, Silas Deane, was recruiting French
officers for service in the American army. The Comte de Broglie,
Lafayette's former commander, hoped to become the stadtholder
of the rebellious colonies, and encouraged Lafayette to enlist;
Vergennes, the French foreign minister, was not averse to weakening Great Britain by encouraging the rebellion of its wealthiest
colonies. And so, encouraged by a few friends, not really opposed
by the French government, hungry for glory and hating the
British, Lafayette embarked for America. However, as soon as he
had signed the contract with Deane, he began to talk about fighting for liberty, without really understanding the meaning of the
phrase. Upon arrival in the United States, he was pleased by the
simpler and freer manners of the Americans. He became a friend
of Washington, who seemed to personify republican ideals, and
adopted him as a model and guide. He succeeded in the American
army as an active and effective major general. He came to be
identified in France and in the United States and in his own
mind as a generous champion of freedom. He came to admire
many American institutions and to believe that he had always
been a defender of liberty. After the American Revolution his
admiration for the United States and his new, sincere devotion to
liberty led him to espouse in France various liberal ideas and
causes: the negotiation of a Franco-American trade treaty, abolition of Negro slavery, toleration of Protestants, summoning of a
national legislative assembly, and drafting of a written constitution and bill of rights. But always there was this hunger for approval and an outward glance—What will other people think?—

and now a new inward glance—What would Washington do? Becoming and being a liberal were with Lafayette infinitely complex processes.

While Gottschalk was working on the Marat and Lafayette volumes, he was having as a scholar a series of maturing experiences that led him to qualify, develop, and deepen the philosophy about history he had absorbed at Cornell. From 1923 to 1926 he prepared six booklets on the history of the French Revolution, which were later expanded into a textbook, *The Era of the French Revolution* (1929). Preparation of this general work, along with his own research and teaching, led him to reflect on the causation of the French Revolution. The results of these reflections were published, notably, in four articles: "The French Revolution: Conspiracy or Circumstance?" (1931), "Some Recent Countersocialistic Literature" (1945), "Philippe Sagnac and the Causes of the French Revolution" (1948), and "The Place of the American Revolution in the Causal Pattern of the French Revolution" (1948). In the 1920's and 1930's the Russian Revolution was a live issue and provoked him to study the problem of drawing analogies between it and the French Revolution and other revolutions. Reflections on the comparative study of revolutions and the generalizations that might be derived therefrom were scattered throughout his writings but appeared notably in four articles, "Revolutionary Analogies" (1926), "Leon Trotsky and the Natural History of Revolutions" (1938), "Revolutionary Traditions and Analogies" (1939), and "The Causes of Revolutions" (1944).

In 1933 he began to collaborate with several colleagues in teaching at the University of Chicago a "Laboratory Course in Historical Method." Several years later he took over a course in modern European historiography. In the 1940's and 1950's he became associated with the Social Science Research Council in various capacities. For its Committee on the Appraisal of Research, he helped prepare Bulletin 53 on *The Use of Personal Documents in History, Anthropology, and Sociology* (1945). As member of the Committee on Historiography he participated in the preparation of Bulletin 54, *Theory and Practice in Historical Study: A Report of the Committee on Historiography* (1946). Most recently, as chairman of the Committee on Historical Analysis, he edited a report on *Generalization in the Writing of History* (1963). The fruits of this teaching and committee discussion appeared in the above publications and also in remarks at a Round Table discussion on "Generalization in the Social Sciences" (1939), in a manual for apprentice historians, *Understanding History* (1950), in his presidential address to the American Historical Association, "A Professor of History in a Quandary" (1953), and in three articles, "The Scope and Subject Matter of History" (1941), "The Historian's Use of Generalization" (1955), and "Categories of Historiographical Generalization" (1963).

In all these writings Gottschalk has quietly and intelligently articulated the working eclecticism of the modern American research historian. In so doing he altered some of the questions that have been traditionally asked of historical writing. Instead of asking, "Is history an art or a science?" he assumed that writing history is now a profession and inquired, "How can historians maintain high professional standards?" With apologies to the Dutch historian, Johan Huizinga, he offered another definition of history: "History is that intellectual form whereby each individual renders unto himself an account of his past (in the widest sense, including the past of his civilization). Some accounts will naturally be better than others."[7] To assure that a historical account was the best possible and met the highest professional standards, Gottschalk recommended the acceptance of what seemed most useful of the Ranke–Herbert Baxter Adams tradition: the intense scrutiny and validation by well-tested procedures of each source and each statement in it. He also adopted the fundamental observations of Becker and other relativists that the historian writes in the present, and that in selecting and arranging his validated statements he is necessarily affected by present conditions, including his own biases. However, to minimize the distorting effect of the present, the professional historian "will try to give to each piece of testimony in his collected data its full and no more than its full weight"; he "will also make a conscious effort to lean over backward against his own national, religious, racial, party, class, professional, or other biases"; "in cases where the testimony is un-

7. "The Scope and Subject Matter of History," *University Review*, VIII (1941-1942), 83. Two passages from the original article have been combined to form this single definition.

available or, if available, inadequate for a definite conclusion, he will be careful . . . to suspend judgment"; "finally, he will studiously avoid gratuitous assumptions or inferences and will endeavor to present only such conclusions as logically proceed from the evidence."[8] Gottschalk also adopted the view of Turner and others that history is not only past politics and past economics, but also past literature and past religion, in fact, past everything. In reconstructing this comprehensive past, the historian will seek the aid of social scientists. He will check their generalizations against his data and utilize them when they seem valid and relevant. Indeed, he himself will "attempt contrasts and comparisons of historical episodes, situations, and institutions and advance generalizations of his own."[9] A comparison of the major revolutions in Western civilization would seem to reveal that back of each one lay a class or classes that were dissatisfied with the existing order, ideas about what a new order might be like, and a government incompetent for discipline or reform. Gottschalk would contend that of the three conditions, formal ideas are the least important. "Though intellectuals usually have a role to play in causing revolutions, it is seldom decisive."[10] They are primarily critics. They do not "father new intellectual attitudes but work upon the raw material of independent hostility" around them.[11] They stimulate, energize, verbalize, and organize this material, and only secondarily add to it. The American Revolution obviously aggravated all three basic conditions in France. The example of a freer society intensified dissatisfaction with the Old Regime; the state constitutions suggested measures of reform; the expenses of French participation in the war rendered unmanageable the recurring deficit and the royal debt and thus weakened the royal government. All these ideas about history and the writing of history were developed by Gottschalk with an amplitude and a sense of nuance impossible to represent here.

8. *Understanding History: A Primer of Historical Method* (New York, 1950), p. 279.
9. Louis Gottschalk, "A Professor of History in a Quandary," *The American Historical Review*, LIX (1953-1954), 279.
10. "Some Recent Countersocialistic Literature," *Journal of Modern History*, XVII (1945), 224.
11. "Philippe Sagnac and the Causes of the French Revolution," *Journal of Modern History*, XX (1948), 142.

In preparing a volume to honor Louis Gottschalk, it seemed appropriate to center it on the theme of ideas in history. To the delicate definition of the changing position, nature, and function of ideas in the historical process, he had devoted much of his scholarly life. In preparing their separate essays to illustrate the theme, the contributors to the volume naturally sought to attain the professional standard that their teacher had exemplified and exacted. Otherwise, they allowed themselves considerable latitude of subject matter and approach. Each contributor might define ideas as he pleased, to include only the formal concepts of philosophy or to embrace any object of the mind existing in thought. The essay might pertain to the history of any country and of any century, and relate to any category of historical investigation. From this freedom, it was hoped, would emerge variety, an illustration of the richness of the theme, and perhaps data for a few tentative generalizations.

IDEAS IN HISTORY

THE GREAT INVERSION: AMER-
ICA AND EUROPE IN THE
EIGHTEENTH-CENTURY
REVOLUTION

Robert R. Palmer

I

No contributor to this volume can owe more of a debt to
Louis Gottschalk than the present writer, who was his student for
only a year, and who, upon his advice and initiative, then went off,
in 1932, to seek his fortune and his Ph.D. with Carl Becker at
Cornell. The Gottschalk "influence" remained very strong, even
when merged with others, for it was by him that I was introduced
to two problems that I have been living with off and on ever since.
One was the relation between America and Europe at the time of
the American and French revolutions. A paper on this subject,
written in his seminar and at his suggestion, was enlarged into
a Cornell dissertation, which in turn (fortunately remaining unpublished) proved of use some twenty-five years later when I was
writing the first volume of the *Age of the Democratic Revolution*.
The other problem, or rather conundrum, was the "role of ideas"
in history. My first full awareness of this question came from an
essay which he published, as it happened, in the year of my graduate study at Chicago, in a volume in honor of another Cornell
professor, George Lincoln Burr. The essay was called "The
French Revolution: Conspiracy or Circumstance?" and it set forth
that dichotomy by which some have found the causes of the
French Revolution in practical circumstances and real problems,
and others in the development of the ideas, ideals, and militant
ideologies of the Enlightenment.

ROBERT R. PALMER *is professor of history and Dean of the Faculty of Arts and
Sciences at Washington University, St. Louis.*

The role of ideas in history and the relationship between the American and French revolutions are distinct and separable matters; but they can also be closely connected, since the latter can be used to illustrate the former in time and place. I shall try in the present essay to say something of both in the belief that, whatever else may or may not be accomplished, no combination of subjects could be more appropriate to a volume in honor of Louis Gottschalk.

It is not at all clear exactly what the expression "role of ideas in history" actually refers to. The issue seems clearest when an antithesis is perceived. There is the familiar antithesis associated with the names of Hegel and Marx: on the one hand, ideas have a life of their own, are produced out of other ideas by a kind of internal logic, and are then institutionalized or actualized by an effort of mind and will (if one may so interpret Hegel); or, on the other hand, it is real or "material" conditions of society or technology which are primary, and from which the ideas are generated, so that the ideas seem to be the product of conditions, or even an outgrowth or superstructure. Closely related is the question whether ideas are always expressions of self-interest, or whether some ideas, at least in contrast to others, may represent a general good or a body of universal values above the arena of group conflict. Another antithesis, familiar to all students of revolution or sudden change, takes another form. We may incline to believe— of the French or the Russian Revolution, or of the anti-slavery movement or the New Deal in the United States—that it was either (at least up to a certain point in time) a "natural" outgrowth of circumstances, a sane and reasonable attempt to deal empirically with inescapable problems; or that it was imposed by "men of theoretical views" (in Burke's phrase), representing an irresponsible incursion of abstract ideology, in which little groups of wilful men, or fanatics, by concerted action (or in the extreme form by conspiratorial action) set out to undermine a social system which, except for such interference, had been going well enough or was in any case susceptible to more moderate reform or improvement.

Or again, "ideas" may mean images in individual minds, or climates of opinion characteristic of whole generations or periods.

They may refer to concepts, beliefs, doctrines, and programs consciously formulated in words; or to vague *états d'âme*, emotions, attitudes, or purposes, colorations of personality, moods and feelings, incentives and drives, predispositions to thought and behavior arising from the depths of the unconscious. The problem of the role of ideas in history turns into a series of problems of epistemology and of psychology, problems of human nature and human behavior, which are by no means limited to history, and with which the historian is not especially well-equipped to deal.

The difficulties can be seen, for example, in attempts to assess the Idea of Progress of the past three hundred years. It has been both a pure idea contributing to bring about improvement in the material world, and a derivative notion itself brought into being by anterior changes and material improvements. It has expressed the particular group interest of certain Western elites and been a meaningful conception for mankind at large. A sense of progress was both a "cause" of the French Revolution, as Condorcet held, and also a rationalization and excuse for its violence. It has been an intellectual concept and an optimistic emotion. It has been a thought and a form of energy; it has operated both at a conscious level, and in an unconscious zone in which attitudes of confidence in the future are formed. Or to take a more specific example: Robespierre in the spring of 1794 decided to institute the Worship of the Supreme Being. We can think of the ensuing festival as an idea peculiar to himself and a few followers, or an idea characteristic of the Enlightenment as a whole; as a manifestation of general ideology, or an immediate constructive policy arising from the religious breakdown of the preceding months; as the conscious formulation of certain propositions concerning God and immortality, or the surging up of deeply felt emotional and mystical needs; as the reflection of pious sentiments in men who expected to benefit materially from the Revolution, or the genuine effort to give a purified religion to mankind.

The role of ideas in history is, in short, elusive. We know of no human behavior without mental activity of some sort. The antithesis of ideas and conditions seems like the antithesis of heredity and environment; it may be a useful tool of analysis, but it is difficult to employ since neither term of the antithesis is ever observed without the other.

The other problem, as already mentioned, is the relation between Europe and America, especially during the time of revolutions at the close of the eighteenth century. To this problem much of Professor Gottschalk's work has been devoted, notably in his intensive volumes on the Marquis de Lafayette and in his broader ventures into world history. On the whole he has aligned himself with a group—which has come to include Professor Jacques Godechot of Toulouse and myself among authors of recent books— by whom the American and French revolutions, along with more or less revolutionary troubles in Holland, Italy, Poland, Ireland, and other places at the same time, and Latin America a little later, are seen as aspects of one great disturbance or upheaval in the world of Western civilization. In this connection some of the problems of the role of ideas in history are posed very forcibly: questions of the influence of ideas upon action or of reading upon behavior; of the effects of growth of the press, of communications, of public opinion; of the influence of ideas first developed in one country upon the people of another; of whether the same formulas of words, such as "liberty" and declarations of rights, really mean the same thing when used in different countries or social contexts; or whether peoples with different social structures, or different national and historical backgrounds, can share in the same ideas in any significant way. This is in turn to pose again the question of whether ideas are determined by and suited only to specific social conditions or specific social groups, nations, or classes.

Bringing the two problems together, the role of ideas and the relation between Europe and America, we propose to examine in this paper the relationship of certain ideas to certain identifiable groups in Western society during the revolutionary era.

II

While the notion of one general eighteenth-century revolutionary movement has been well received, it has also evoked much criticism and doubt. The doubt rests on an awareness of national differences. Many French scholars believe that in the conception of a "world revolution" (if the term may be accepted when admittedly applying only to the Western or European world) the specific features of the French Revolution—its peculiar causes and problems, its violence and its struggle, its exaltation and its qualities of fanatical commitment—are minimized or lost. There are some in England who believe that in such a broad pattern the true character of England in the eighteenth century is distorted or misconceived. So much was made clear, for example, by Professor Steven Watson of Oxford University in a session at the Mississippi Valley Historical Association at Milwaukee in 1962.

In America the adverse criticism has been more muted, but the same considerations must obviously apply. The differences between America and Europe are evident, as are those between the American and French revolutions. It is hardly to be denied that the United States has long possessed a distinctive national character. The special peculiarity of American civilization has been the theme of much thoughtful review of our history, notably by such writers as Louis Hartz, Clinton Rossiter, and Daniel Boorstin. As Hartz puts it, American development has been characterized by the absence of the "feudal factor" without which European history cannot be understood. Or, in another of his phrases, where Europe has been the land of the frustrated democrat, America has been the land of the frustrated aristocrat.[1] The logic of such a position militates against the thesis of an Age of Democratic Revolution in which, in America, France, and elsewhere, similar causes had similar effects, similar problems led to similar attempts at solution, or similar people and similar social classes developed similar ideologies and ideals. There is much in the thinking of Hartz, Rossiter, or Boorstin with which one must agree. There must be some grounds for a conciliation of what appear to be opposite positions. If so, they cannot lie in a fatuous idea of a mere misunderstanding, or the feeble notion that truth lies in splitting the difference. What we need to do, to quote the sociologists, is to modify the conceptual framework. We must find

1. Louis Hartz, *The Liberal Tradition in America: An Interpretation of American Political Thought since the Revolution* (New York, 1955); Clinton Rossiter, *The First American Revolution* (New York, 1956); Daniel Boorstin, *The Americans* (New York, 1958). On the whole matter, see also my recently published *Age of the Democratic Revolution*, Vol. II, *The Struggle* [1792-1800] (Princeton, 1964).

a level of abstraction from which differences yet seem to be manifestations of the same thing.

One observation suggests itself. It has been seldom made, yet
the more it is considered the more obvious it seems to be. If we
look at Europe and the United States at the close of the eighteenth
century we see a Great Inversion—a grand intercontinental trans-
vestitism, in which the parties on the two sides of the ocean seem
to be wearing highly inappropriate clothing and speaking in unsuitable tones of voice.

We must accept, as a fact, that a great many Europeans, especially in France, adopted the language and ideas of the American
Revolution in the 1770's and 1780's. We must accept as a fact that
a great many people in the United States adopted the language
and ideas of the French Revolution in the 1790's. There were
Frenchmen who identified psychologically and emotionally with
the revolutionary Americans. There were Americans who identified psychologically and emotionally with the revolutionary
French. What then is the inversion? It is this—that in each case
the people who thus "identified" were not of the kinds that one
would expect, at least from the point of view of an uncomplicated
analysis by social classes.

America in the eighteenth century was rural, France already
relatively urbanized. In the United States in 1790 only a little
over 2 per cent of the people lived in towns having a population
of more than 10,000. In France the corresponding figure was 10
per cent. The French urban population, thus defined (and many
smaller French towns were sociologically "urban"), was almost as
large as the total population of the United States without the
slaves. To put it another way, for every American farmer then
alive there was a French bourgeois or petit-bourgeois or urban
workingman walking the streets as his counterpart.

If only because towns were small, few, and far apart in America, most of the people who carried out the American Revolution,
to speak very generally, were farmers, either small ones working
their land by their own labor, or large ones who worked it by the
use of slaves. Yet it was the middle-class French townspeople who
saw in the American Revolution a lesson for themselves. The
French Revolution, after the first months, and for ten years on

through the Terror and the Directory, was the work of towns-people, among whom the well-to-do bourgeoisie generally took the lead. Yet many American agrarians, slave-owning gentry in the South and small farmers in various parts of the country, saw in the French Revolution a kindred movement to their own. The same paradox holds for counter-revolution and conservatism, which in Europe drew strength from the great aristocratic landowning interests or from the apathy and traditionalism of the agricultural masses. But in America in the 1790's, it was certain mercantile and banking circles, as personified in Alexander Hamilton, that most heartily detested the French Revolution and agreed with the spokesmen of European conservatism.

There is a certain sense in which contemporary Americans profoundly misunderstood the French Revolution. This is an old observation, implicit in the monograph of Charles Downer Hazen of 1897 and going back to the old Federalists themselves, who thought that American sympathy for France, or the wild reception given to Citizen Genêt, was no more than concocted propaganda, or a fad or frenzy among the ignorant, making a great to-do over matters that had no relevancy to the United States. This is not what is meant here. The principles of the French Revolution, which can still be summarized as Liberty, Equality, and Fraternity, were not without relevancy to the United States. It does seem, nevertheless, that there was something that the Jeffersonian democrats or republicans misunderstood. The same is at least equally true of the Hamiltonian Federalists, and of the more moderate or John Adams-type Federalists as well.

III

What Americans failed to understand, if one may so far agree with Karl Marx, was that the French Revolution was a bourgeois revolution. Even the best recent Marxist writers in Europe, and others who by preference have studied the revolutionary role of the true lower classes, often with loving care, insist that the Revolution was mainly a middle-class development. For the true lower classes they claim no more than that they were worthy and decent people, that they had much to suffer, that their insurrectionary up-

heavals proved useful to middle-class leaders, that they provided
the manpower which filled the armies, that they had aims of their
own which presented the middle-class Revolutionary governments
with serious or insoluble problems, and that by their pressures
they pushed on the middle-class leaders to acts of courage or
audacity of which they would otherwise never have been capable.
In all this there is nothing with which one need disagree. The
official leadership and the stated objectives of the French Revolution, even at the height of the Terror and of lower-class initiatives
in 1793, remained in the hands of men of the French middle
classes.

To argue that the Revolution was "bourgeois" it is hardly
necessary to go to Marx or the modern Left, since European conservatives of the time were of the same opinion. Edmund Burke
put it with his usual vividness. For him the French Revolution,
which he hated, was the work of "economists and calculators,"
of "Jews and jobbers," of persons who lived "in cities"—"tradesmen, bankers, and voluntary clubs of presuming young persons:
advocates, attorneys, notaries, managers of newspapers, and those
cabals of literary men called academies"—surely a delightful catalogue of the "bourgeoisie," with the bankers thrown in between
the tradesmen and the clubs of presuming young persons![2] The
Swiss Mallet du Pan, writing in 1796, by which time revolution
was breaking out in Holland and Italy upon arrival of the French
armies, found the revolutionary sympathizers in much the same
classes. They were, he scornfully and sarcastically said, "those
foresighted people with their little investments, those sagacious
men of business, those second-hand shopkeepers of every description who in most of the commercial cities of Europe continue to
show themselves as auxiliaries of the French Revolution."[3] In
Burke and Mallet du Pan we hear the voice of true European
conservatism, for which it was not enough to be wealthy but
necessary for wealth to be hereditary and invested in immovable

2. *Reflections on the French Revolution* (Everyman ed.; London and New York,
1910 ff.), pp. 40, 46, 73, 101, 291-293. The last reference is to the *Thoughts on
French Affairs* (Dec., 1791) as printed in this volume.

3. J. Mallet du Pan, *Correspondance politique pour servir à l'histoire du
républicanisme français* (Hamburg, 1796), p. 5. The phrase "people with their
little investments" is used here to translate Mallet du Pan's single word *rentiers*.

assets, as the foundation for a "permanent landed interest" from which the bulk of the governing elite should properly be recruited.

It is a question, of course, how much truth there was in this allegation of the conservative publicists, that the business and banking classes of Europe were sympathetic to Revolutionary France. It is a subject on which constructive research in some detail can yet be done. Men of the banking and business classes were naturally divided, according to the circumstances or temperament of each person, but anything above a low percentage of sympathizers with the Revolution would be significant in such a case. It is important, too, to examine the individuals hidden in the general categories, for the terms "banker," "financier," and even "merchant" could be ambiguous. As Alfred Cobban has asked, "What kind of merchants were these who are said to have rioted in the streets of Amsterdam?"[4] If care is not used, we may misinterpret the significance of men who were not engaged, so to speak, in legitimate business, but were merely adventurers, speculators, opportunists, intriguers, get-rich-quick operators, or simply rich men or their sons with a taste for radical politics.

The evidence that we have, nevertheless, shows a significant sympathy with the Revolution on the European side of the water among men of real substance in commercial affairs. This was true in some degree even in England. Both James Watt and Matthew Boulton were less than pleased with the ruling parliamentary and ecclesiastical elites of England, especially after the church-and-king mob made a wreck of their friend Priestly's house in Birmingham, while the local gentry, squires, parsons, and justices of the peace took no action. James Watt, Jr., was a pronounced "Jacobin," as were the sons of Boulton and Priestley. Young Watt's later career with the firm of Boulton and Watt suggests that he had been no flighty ideologist in his youth. Other individual cases point in the same direction. Thomas Walker was of the early generation of cotton manufacturers who were bringing about an industrial revolution at Manchester. Unlike most of his business associates, he was a man of inherited means, an Anglican and not a disgruntled Dissenter, and sufficiently wealthy and socially estab-

4. A. Cobban, "The Age of the Democratic Revolution," *History*, XLV (1960), 238.

lished to have his portrait painted by Romney. In politics he favored the parliamentary reformers of the type later called radical, and he looked with favor on what the French were trying to do in France. He was caught up in the treason trials of 1794, and, though acquitted, was financially ruined by the legal expense and subjected to an extreme case of what we now call character assassination. Or there was the famous ironmaster, John Wilkinson. A self-made industrialist with a fortune of £80,000, he invested £10,000 in French government bonds between 1791 and 1793, all of which was repaid with interest to his estate in later years. At the end of 1792, six weeks before England and France went to war, Wilkinson, needing a local scrip in which to pay his workers, used small denominations of French *assignats* countersigned by his cashier. The government not unnaturally regarded this operation as a piece of Jacobin propaganda.[5]

On the attitudes of businessmen on the Continent, Jacques Godechot five years ago wrote a paper that was translated and presented to the American Historical Association in New York.[6] He found that merchants and bankers, in Belgium, Holland, Switzerland, and Italy, while they seldom took any revolutionary initiative, in many cases accepted and welcomed the new regimes, such as the Batavian and Cisalpine republics, or the incorporation of Belgium into France, which followed upon the victories of the French armies. They did so for good reasons having to do with the modernization of their respective countries, to get rid of discriminations based on religion, to remove the social differences between themselves and the aristocracies, to acquire landed property formerly belonging to the Church, to have the benefits of a new bankruptcy law more favorable to those who took business risks, to obtain uniform decimal systems of coinage, weights, and measures, to overcome the restrictiveness of the trade guilds so as to have more freedom in the employment of labor and the development of new enterprises, or to abolish local tariffs and tolls

5. E. Robinson, "An English Jacobin: James Watt, Jr.," *Cambridge Historical Journal*, XI (1955), 349-355; also by Robinson, "New Light on the Priestley Riots," *Historical Journal* (1960), pp. 73-75; Frida Knight, *The Strange Case of Thomas Walker: Ten Years in the Life of a Manchester Radical* (London, 1957); W. H. Chaloner, "Dr. Joseph Priestley, John Wilkinson and the French Revolution, 1789-1802," *Transactions of the Royal Historical Society*, 5th series, VIII (1958), 21-40.

6. "The Business Classes and the Revolution outside France," *American Historical Review*, LXIV (1958), 1-13.

and create wider trading areas through territorial unification. In addition, among Continental men of affairs there was a good deal of opposition to England, at a time when British interests had long been encroaching on the Dutch colonial empire, insisting on the continued closure of the Scheldt River, and penetrating Italy through the commercial depot at Leghorn. In these circumstances it was often the large businessmen of modern outlook, not the small ones protected by older arrangements, who showed the most definite sympathy for France and for the Revolution. In Belgium, for example, it was the newly rising industrialists who wished to develop the port of Antwerp by opening the Scheldt River and in other ways to widen their markets; they are found, therefore, first among the Democratic or Vonckist party in the Belgian Revolution, and later among those willing to accept annexation to the French Republic. In Germany east of the Rhine the great commercial city of Hamburg was one of the warmest centers of sympathy for the French Revolution, and the most prominent Francophile in Hamburg was Heinrich Sieveking, a man of great wealth, and head of one of the leading commercial establishments in the city.

IV

There is really no mystery in the fact that the French Revolution, or general European revolutionary agitation, considering the whole revolutionary decade, and with exceptions for the period of the Terror, which after all lasted little more than a year, should have proved attractive to persons engaged in commerce and industry in Britain and Europe—as well as to professional men, journalists, lawyers, and doctors, and to others of lesser social position not here mentioned. The mystery is in the inversion of opinion that characterized the United States.

The Federalists in America, when they took form as a party, drew their strength from business circles in Boston and Philadelphia, and from the rural population in the areas of older settlement, who had farms near the seaports or along the rivers and were in touch with outside markets, with townspeople, and with the world. Such is the distribution found upon close statistical study in the work of Manning Dauer some years ago.[7] The Jeffersonian democrats, on the other hand, while drawing some support from competitive business groups in the cities, and some from the town artisan class, relied mainly on Southern plantation owners, and on farmers who lived out toward the frontier or in other places isolated from the main channels of trade and communication. Indeed, a dislike of town life and suspicion toward businessmen lay deep in the psychology of many American democrats. It is well known how Jefferson feared and disliked really large cities, with their rabble as well as their moneyed men. The Federalists, though many of them were agrarians and suspicious of banks, like John Adams, had nevertheless a certain positive attitude toward what we would call modernization, while the Democrats (if the word may be used) extolled the supposedly more simple and ancestral virtues of the old agricultural America.

In Europe, close statistical study shows exactly the opposite. Outside of France, it was only among the people of cities, together with a few rural landowners in close touch with city life, that the principles of the new democratic order made any headway. That the same was true in parts of France itself is confirmed by the work of Charles Tilly now in progress.[8] He has made a detailed analysis of western France, the region of the Vendéan rebellion. He finds that it was by no means a solid or uniform region in which provincials rose against the domination of distant Paris. Looking more closely, he distinguished dozens or hundreds of small urban communities with a population of a couple of thousands, each with its immediately surrounding rural area forming a nucleus in which patriotic, revolutionary, or republican sentiment predominated. These nuclei were islands in an agrarian ocean. The people in this ocean, living away from the towns, isolated from the channels of trade and communication, remote from the action of government, were not susceptible to the idea of the rights or responsibilities of citizenship in a large modern state, and provided the mass backing for projects of counter-revolution as devised by

7. M. M. Dauer, *The Adams Federalists* (Baltimore, 1953).
8. C. Tilly, "Civil Constitution and Counter-Revolution in Southern Anjou," *French Historical Studies*, I (1959), 172-99; Tilly, "Some Problems in the History of the Vendée," *American Historical Review*, LXVII (1961), 19-33, and his book, *The Vendée* (Cambridge, Mass., 1964).

big landowners and manorial lords.   In America one suspects that they would have been Jeffersonian democrats.

Let us simplify by posing the question in terms of the classic dualism between Hamilton and Jefferson.   Why was Hamilton so enamored of the British constitution?   Who or what did he think really ruled in England?   Interested in economic development or modernization for America, he might have known that important men with these same ideas in England did not share his admiration for British society or his aversion to the Revolution in France. He should have heard of the Dutchman Isaac Gogel, whose career and ideas resembled his own.   Gogel worked to reform the old taxes and revenues, and to assume and consolidate the debts of the old Dutch provinces so as to create a unified Dutch state and nation; he was a vehement revolutionary in 1794, a founder of the Batavian Republic in 1795, and a radical democrat in 1798, and continued nevertheless to be respected as a financial expert by all governments for twenty years thereafter.

As for Jefferson, why was he so enamored of the French Revolution?   Who or what, in the way of social classes or forces, did he believe gave it momentum?   How could he so warmly approve of it, when it was so much an affair of cities?   Why is it that, where John Adams had four copies of Rousseau's *Social Contract* in his library, Jefferson had apparently never been impressed by the book at all?   Jefferson did not see that one of the chief principles of the Revolution was to turn the individual into a citizen of the state, and to define and rationalize the authority of the state over the individual.   He did not understand the centralization of power in the Revolution, which was so apparent to Burke as later to Tocqueville.   He could have learned something of Europe from the Italian economist, Melchiorre Gioia, a supporter of the revolutionary Cisalpine Republic of 1796.   In that year Gioia wrote a famous essay, in which he proposed a single unified and republican government for all Italy, and pointed to American decentralization and states' rights as an example to be avoided.

v

There is no time to do more than suggest answers to the questions raised by this inversion.   One of them is certainly, in Louis

Hartz's words, the absence from America of the "feudal factor." In Europe, the middle class and business groups had to oppose a variety of interests, aristocratic, corporative, localistic, that were all vaguely "feudal" in background. They found themselves in a revolutionary conflict after 1789. In America these business interests and the Federalists generally were not exactly conservative, since they were the ones who most wanted to change the character of the country, but they could enjoy the pleasure of a conservative posture because there was no one of higher prestige with whom they had to contend. Similarly, in Europe the "feudal factor" meant that the rural masses, left to themselves, might go along with lords and gentry. They were not "naturally" democratic. In America the corresponding rural populations, among whom were many property owners in fee simple, with few habits of deference or obligation to a class that they regarded as higher, were in truth quite different from the country people of Europe. Equally conservative they might be, suspicious of cities and with little interest in modernization; but what they wanted to conserve was an older America whose people, as Hartz and Tocqueville have said, were in an important sense "born equal."

It must be added, in explanation of the "great inversion," that there was much in the French Revolution, and still more in what happened in Holland or Italy, that the Americans of the 1790's simply did not understand. They are not to be blamed; the historian should be the first to admit that one of the gains of the twentieth century, in matters of research and education, is a more effective comprehension of contemporary problems. Nor must we forget, among these explanations, the continuing American dependence on a somewhat intractable mother country. American economic development, as Hamilton saw, did in fact depend on the maintenance of tolerable relations with the financial, commercial, and naval power of England. In the circumstances the American business interests could not be, and did not have to be, as anti-British as those of Europe. Even more important, in the sphere of images and ideas, was the American dependence on England for information, on the English newspapers that were brought into American seaports, and on the English books and English translations which American publishers for their own purposes chose to import or to reprint. What began as war propaganda or class propaganda in England, understandable enough in the circumstances, might seem in America to be serious philosophy or sound information on current affairs. Even so, in recognition of the intelligence of the English and the freedom of their press under trying conditions of war and domestic disturbance, one has the impression that the Americans would have understood Europe better if, each year, they had simply read the pages of the *Annual Register*.

It seems probable that the first generation in New England had had more direct intellectual contact with the European continent, and more fellow feeling with it, than the generation alive during the wars of the French Revolution. When Elder William Brewster died at Plymouth in 1643 he possessed 393 books.[9] About fifty of these were recent works, chiefly in Latin, by Calvinists and Reformers in Holland, Switzerland, the German Rhineland, and Italy. It would be interesting to know whether even John Adams, a century and a half later, possessed so large a proportion of recent works written in or dealing with these countries. They were precisely the European countries, outside France, which saw the most serious movements of political revolution in the 1790's. The first generation of New Englanders understood perfectly well that a religious revolution had been attempted on the Continent in their lifetime, and that it had succeeded in some places and failed in others. In the America of the 1790's there was no such perception of a movement of political revolution in the regions lying east of France. What was seen was hardly more than French conquest and exploitation. Sheer ignorance compounded the other difficulties of understanding.

Lastly, it must be remarked that, in a sense, this "great inversion" is of limited importance. All it shows is that Europe and America were opposites in the relation of social classes to a given body of principles. Or perhaps it suggests that rural people in America, for reasons that need not be detailed here, resembled the middle-class and urban people of Europe in their outlook. If

9. G. Spini, "Riforma italiana e mediazioni ginevrine nella Nuova Inghilterra puritana," in D. Cantimori (ed.), *Ginevra e l'Italia* (Florence, 1959). Spini cites H. M. Dexter, "Catalogue of Elder Brewster's Library," *Proceedings of the Massachusetts Historical Society*, 2nd series, V (1889), 37 ff.

so, the force of the alleged inversion tends to disappear. In any case, while it is important to study the "social structures," as French historians of the Revolutionary period so frequently insist, it is well to do so with both caution and open-mindedness, and to avoid reducing politics, ethics, or psychology to a form of sociology with a class angle. The success or failure of an idea, the degree of realization of a program, will depend on the identity, strength, and numbers of those who favor it in comparison to those who oppose. The political wisdom or ethical content of a program, or the psychological reasons for its appeal, are less easily equated with particular interest groups. It has long been observed, and rightly, that the ideas of the eighteenth-century revolution were "abstract." This diagnosis, which originated with eighteenth-century conservatives, was understood by them to mean that the ideas in question were irrelevant to real problems, or unworkable in practical politics. On this matter there is ground for legitimate argument, but the revolutionary ideas were abstract also in another and less debatable way. They were transferable; they had a "universal" appeal; persons of many kinds, classes, nationalities, and races, when faced by wholly different difficulties or problems, could find in them a message and application to themselves.

The ideas, as everyone knows, expressed themselves in demands for liberty and equality, citizenship and fraternity, law and constitutionalism, the sovereignty of the people and the rights of man. Their point is more clearly seen in the negative formulation. The bad things were held to be special privilege, hereditary legal advantage, unjustified discrimination, group exclusiveness, unfair treatment, unnatural and unnecessary barriers, as they were thought to be, that stood in the way of individual merit, liberty, and achievement. The actual practices or institutions charged with these forms of badness have varied with circumstance, time, and place. Or in other words, persons of different kinds, differing in class background or other background, have been able to share in the same positive affirmations. In the United States today it need hardly be said that the issue is very much alive, that "desegregation" is the old mystic triad of liberty, equality, and fraternity; that the demand for racial justice is a repudiation of racial privilege; that equal rights cannot be perpetually refused to persons who are accepted as fellow citizens and fellow men.

As for the eighteenth century, and the "world" or "Atlantic" revolution of that time, the inversion that has been the subject of this paper helps to explain the differences between Europe and the United States. It supports the view taken by Hartz, Rossiter, and Boorstin. But the inversion need not lead us on to denying that there was any similarity at all. Sympathizers with the French Revolution tended to be agrarian in America and urban middle-class and business-class persons in Europe. Both held that they were somehow not yet adequately integrated into the existing order. "Integration," or the demand for equality of treatment and social participation, whether it be called a principle or a psychological need, goes beyond the differences between races, classes, or countries. The role of ideas is undoubtedly to meet human needs. But the greater ideas, like the most broadly human needs, do not remain the special property of any one kind of human being.

UTOPIA IN MODERN WESTERN THOUGHT: THE METAMORPHOSIS OF AN IDEA

Leslie C. Tihany

Few Western literary forms are as irrevocably dead and extinct as the political utopia; few Western ideas are as mischievously rampant today as political utopianism. We appear to be living in an age of moral pessimism and scientific optimism, without firm critical justification for either attitude. Technological progress, we hope, will land us on the moon and on the planets; but on our socio-political horizon loom, we fear, Brave New Worlds and Nineteen Eighty-Fours. Contemporary authors still write of distant or future commonwealths, but their imaginary states are dismal projections of communal depravity and degradation, not ideal societies. No longer does Western man look, as he did in the eighteenth century, to the noble savage and the wise Chinaman as models of attainable virtue and statecraft; nor can these discarded models of perfectibility now agree which camp of the divided West, capitalist or Communist, is worthy of emulation.

A confrontation of the European with the noble savage during the eighteenth and nineteenth centuries resulted in lost political illusions for the former and in envy to imitate for the latter. Utopia then shifted from an extra-Western to a Western-centered position. The eighteenth-century West thought of itself as morally and politically underdeveloped; today the term is applied usually to areas originally beyond the pale of Western civilization. During the seventeenth and eighteenth centuries it was the West which sought social and political perfection in faraway isles; in the twentieth century it is these once far-flung lands which are rebuilding their societies and institutions under the impact of a

LESLIE C. TIHANY *is First Secretary of the American Embassy at Beirut, Lebanon.*

Western utopia. But which Western utopia? ask the latter-day noble savage and wise Chinaman. The tragic intra-Western schism of our century has produced in non-Western minds a clash of two competing Western utopias: today's free and affluent society in America; tomorrow's stateless and classless society promised by the Russians. The very idea of utopia has been bisected and revolutionized.

Probably all ages have groped for the perfect and the ideal. The utopian tradition in the West is as old as Western thought. A glimpse of it appeared in the *Odyssey*, where Homer conjured up the vision of a godlike people, the Phaeacians, dwellers on a blessed isle under a wise government. Plato's portrayal in *The Republic* of the ideal commonwealth, the just and perfect society, where kings are philosophers and philosophers kings, was the classic formulation of the Greek search for political perfection. In Thomas More's *Utopia* (1516) public felicity was assured by utilitarian laws and practices, and the framework was set for the modern Western utopia. Campanella's dream of the perfect state in the *City of the Sun* (1643) was another monument of utopian writing in the West at the end of the seventeenth century.

The rebirth of political utopianism in the West coincided with the intellectual quickening during the sixteenth and seventeenth centuries, probably in reaction to the geographical discoveries and the political turbulence of the era; in any event, it occurred in a crosscurrent which Paul Hazard once described as "the crisis of European consciousness."[1] The medieval mind had turned to the city of God for perfection; the spirit of the Renaissance had sought it in the remote and fabulous arcadian past; the groping founders of the scientific age meant to find it in imaginary states distant in space or in the future. The early modern tradition of utopianism, beginning with the sixteenth century, was an incipiently and increasingly romantic delineation of the ideal commonwealth which was alleged to have already been established in some temporarily inaccessible part of the globe. The classical utopian made little or no attempt to render the existence of his imaginary commonwealth more credible by enveloping it in a realistic literary form. The early modern utopian resorted to

1. Paul Hazard, *La Crise de la conscience européenne* (Paris, 1935).

realism, the substance of which was placed at his disposal by a scientific and information-rich civilization. It was this note of literary realism, absent in prediscovery and present in postdiscovery utopias, which distinguished these two chronologically continuous waves of utopian literature from each other.[2]

In the further development of utopianism in Western thought from the late seventeenth century to the present, the utopian mentality[3] changed from a non-empirical to an empirical frame of mind. The non-empirical utopian mentality appealed to the authority of the classics, reason, the sentiments, or to the doctrinal inevitability of progress in presenting the desirability of utopian antitheses: peace for war, plenty for penury, liberty for despotism. Since it was non-empirical, it did not clearly distinguish between the desirable and the possible, and failed to perceive that the possibility of peace, plenty, and liberty may at a given time depend on the external situation. The empirical utopian mentality, on the other hand, related its ideas to observations, data, and statistics collected from contemporary experience; distinguished between the desirable and the possible; and assumed that it had discovered the inexorable laws which are pushing society toward the establishment of utopia. As Western utopianism became more empirical, there was an increasing disposition of utopians to translate their ideology into political action. The utopian mentality was transformed into the utopian will of a minority to impose its dreams on the majority. When this effort succeeded, utopia lost its etymological and philosophical denotation of "nowhere" and became a well-defined geographical reality for millions of totally controlled people inhabiting utopias in construction. In three centuries there has been a metamorphosis of the utopian idea itself.

The French Utopia of the Pre-Revolution

France, not England, became the country where political utopias proliferated after the seventeenth century. England had produced and all but abandoned utopianism, while France

2. P. B. Gove, *The Imaginary Voyage in Prose Fiction* (New York, 1941).
3. For an exhaustive but different treatment of the utopian mentality, see A. Kolnai, "La Mentalité utopienne," *La Table ronde*, No. 153 (Sept., 1960), pp. 62-84.

adopted and developed it as a discreet and sophisticated vehicle of political agitation. By the end of the seventeenth century the English had fought and won their long battle to make parliament an accepted part of their government; the French constitutional struggle was still distant. Yet, by the end of the seventeenth century, royal absolutism in France was beginning to prepare its own destruction. From 1672 on, when Louis XIV first sent a French army across the Rhine into the Low Countries, the national resources of France were to be used and exhausted in dynastic warfare. The War of the Spanish Succession and the cruel winter of 1709 produced unprecedented misery and popular discontent among the French; more and more minds sought to escape to happier climes where government did not embroil the state in useless dynastic wars but maintained the prosperity of the subjects.

Political utopianism, the use of the descriptive method for subtle political protest, had its heyday in France between 1676 and 1790. The former date marked the publication of Gabriel Foigny's *La Terre australe connue*; the latter witnessed the final deterioration of the literary medium in Nicolas-Edme Rétif de la Bretonne's *An 2000*. During this period the French utopian was a *philosophe* who expressed his disapproval of the existing state of affairs by describing society and state as they could be or as he hoped they someday would be. He was not a political activist and, as a rule, only a literary mediocrity, although utopianism as a vehicle of political dissent was not disdained by such towering figures as Fénelon, Montesquieu, Voltaire, and Rousseau.

A historical postmortem of the French prerevolutionary utopia, as described in twenty-two published works between 1676 and 1790, reveals a composite commonwealth which is monarchical in form of government and has a social structure conceived in liberty, equality, and fraternity, and an economic structure based on some sort of collectivism. The religion of the citizens is usually deism. The existence of this superior society may be due to wise laws, reforms, or revolution, either violent or peaceful. After 1750 utopia rests upon a belief in the natural and irrepressible progress toward perfection. The utopian authors represent all strata of French society, from dethroned king (Leszczynski) to printer (Rétif de la Bretonne), but the majority belong to the bourgeoisie. Beyond this composite picture, the evolution of the ideological content of these utopian writings appears in the changing image of the perfect government. This is the only component of the utopian ideology which shows some volatility and gradual unfolding. The other components, social structure, economic organization, religion, and education, remain more or less static, although in the educational field a shift occurs toward the middle of the eighteenth century from "rational" to "natural" upbringing of children.

The evolution of the French idea of a perfect government starts in an abstract philosophical sphere at the end of the seventeenth century and ends in a concrete and actual political frame of reference on the eve of the Revolution. During the last quarter of the seventeenth century Cartesian rationality is the criterion by which the authors determine the superiority of a given utopian government. Among the austral hermaphrodites of the ex-priest Foigny's *La Terre australe connue,* for example, government is almost invisible and the citizens live in geometrical anarchy. (As a matter of fact, Foigny's Australia anticipates by almost a century Rousseau's ideal democracy which Rousseau was to define in the *Contrat social* [1762] as the state in which government is delegated to all the people and in which there are as many citizen magistrates as there are individual citizens.) In the lawyer Vairasse's *Histoire des Sévarambes* (1677) the idea of a perfect government is an early form of Montesquieu's tripartite system of checks and balances; it consists of an executive who is responsible to the legislative and is assisted by the judicial branch of government. The political system of the fabulous Avaites, described in the barrister Gilbert's *L'Histoire de l'isle de Calejava* (1700), resembles Vairasse's scheme but is more in keeping with Rousseau's than with Montesquieu's future political ideas. The frame of mind which dominates these three utopias written during the closing quarter of the seventeenth century is a belief in the absolute superiority of reason over all other human faculties.

During the early eighteenth century the idea of a perfect government emerges from the philosophical void and becomes a vehicle of concealed political and economic protest. The mythical Naudelians described in the noble Lesconvel's *Relation historique et morale du Prince de Montbéraud dans l'île de Naudely* (1709), and the spurious austral aborigines and the nebulous Greenlanders projected in Tyssot de Patot's *Voyages et avantures de Jaques Massé* (1710) and *Le Voyage de Groenland* (1720) enjoy the blessings of a benevolent government which does not sacrifice the welfare of the citizens for the dynastic ambitions of the king. Such a government, as a rule, comes into existence as a result of revolution. Montesquieu's Troglodites, whose history is narrated in Letters XI-XIV of the *Lettres persanes* (1721), search for a perfect government and, after much suffering and bloodshed, opt for an elective monarchy. The monarchical form of government still holds the allegiance of early eighteenth-century utopians; however, they appear to believe that a purge, usually of blood, is a necessary forerunner of the ideal monarchy.

There is evidence in this utopianism to suggest that French political thought during the first half of the eighteenth century was dominated by aristocratic writers who advocated governmental reform in the form of restrictions upon royal absolutism by the nobility, but whose political objectives did not include a republic. Until 1750 the French idea of a perfect government is predominantly monarchic; of all the utopias published between 1700 and 1750 only the lawyer Gilbert's Avaites and the Abbé Desfontaines's mysterious Letalisponians, described in his *Le Nouveau Gulliver* (1730), live in a republic. But a slight change in emphasis begins to appear. The utopian writers of the first half of the eighteenth century begin to register their dislike for that type of royal rule which wastes the substance of the state in waging needless wars abroad while the common people starve at home. The idea of a constitutional monarchy appears to be coming more into the open, though the faith in monarchy as such remains largely unshaken.

The French utopias written during the sixth and seventh decades of the eighteenth century reveal a minor ideological trend toward republicanism. At the middle of the century the republican form of government receives powerful publicity from the obscure Morelly, author of the *Basiliade* (1753) and *Code de la nature* (1755), and from Rousseau's *Contrat social*. It is also championed by the anonymous author of the *République des philosophes* (1768). Both Morelly (in his *Code de la nature*) and the anonymous author of the *République des philosophes* project a federal republic as the ideal form of government. In his *Contrat social* Rousseau is tacitly in favor of the republican idea. But Rousseau's political thought is characterized by a note of relativity. According to him, monarchy, aristocracy, and democracy may each be the best form of government for various peoples at the same time, or even for the same people at various times.

But even after 1750 the democratic trend is still restrained by the dominant current of monarchistic utopianism. In contrast to the republican proclivities of Morelly, Rousseau, and the anonymous author, four other utopians who published between 1750 and 1765—Leszczynski,[4] a reigning prince; Villeneuve,[5] a financier of noble birth; Beaurieu[6] and Roumier[7] (both of whom prefixed a *de* to their names, but whose nobility is open to question)—all subscribe to enlightened despotism as the ideal form of government. The chief aim of this enlightened despotism is to maintain peace and to insure the prosperity of the subjects. Thus, republican sentiment among the mid-century utopians is voiced only by a minority; it cannot be considered representative of a significant body of opinion, because it includes two misfits—Morelly, an anachronistic phenomenon, and Rousseau, who candidly admits in his *Confessions* that he is not like anyone else. The majority of the mid-century utopians are firmly in favor of monarchy as the desirable type of government, but of that type of monarchy under which the subjects do not starve—as did the French in 1753—and which does not embroil the nation in dynastic and futile wars—as did the French government in 1740-1748 and 1756-1763.

On the eve of the Revolution the republican idea disappears completely from French utopian thought: not one of the four utopias[8] published between 1770 and 1790 advocates the republi-

4. Stanislas Leszczynski, *Entretien d'un Européen avec un insulaire du royaume de Dumocla* (1752) (Paris edition, 1825).
5. Daniel de Villeneuve, *Le Voyageur philosophe dans un pais inconnu aux habitans de la terre* (Amsterdam, 1761).
6. Gaspard-Guillard de Beaurieu, *L'Élève de la nature* (Amsterdam, 1763-1771).
7. Marie-Anne de Roumier, *Voyages de Milord Céton dans les sept planètes* (Amsterdam, 1765).
8. Louis-Sébastien Mercier, *L'An 2440* (London, 1770); Guillaume Grivel, *Isle inconnue* (Amsterdam and Paris, 1783-1787); Nicolas-Edme Rétif de la

can form of government. All three utopians of the last two pre-revolutionary decades describe constitutional monarchy as the ideal form of government. Mercier, a professional writer, in his vision of the year 2440 pictures France as a monarchy under a wise *philosophe*-king, who himself was the author of the revolution which reinvigorated the French state. In the year 2440, according to Mercier, the government of France is based on Montesquieu's principle concerning the separation of powers; the executive, legislative, and judiciary or administrative branches serve as checks and balances upon one another. A similar but less profoundly elaborated dream government is presented by Rétif de la Bretonne, a printer, in his description of France at the second millennium. The future government is based on the achievements of 1789, and the country is supremely happy under the wise and philanthropic rule of its peerless sovereign, Louis-François XXII. Constitutional monarchy also remains the political ideal of Rétif de la Bretonne when his utopia is placed in the newly discovered austral land. There a proposed republican form of government is expressly rejected by the subjects; these scientifically bred supermen place limitless trust and confidence in their reigning monarch, who himself will promulgate the reforms necessary in state and society. On the conservative lawyer Grivel's unknown isle, the hereditary monarch is assisted and advised by a general assembly of citizens. When the republican form of government is proposed by some malcontents, an overwhelming majority votes down the motion and metes out severe punishment to the agitators. Up to the very outbreak of the Revolution, French utopian thought mirrors more a royalist than a republican frame of mind.

The idea of an ideal social structure is constant throughout the 1676-1790 period. The great watchwords of revolutionary France are precociously present in utopian literature at the end of the seventeenth century: Foigny in 1676 describes a society characterized by liberty, equality, and fraternity. The same ideals dominate the social thinking of nearly all the French utopians. Where pronounced class distinctions are permitted in the

---

Bretonne, *La Découverte australe par un homme volant* (Leipzig and Paris, 1781), and *L'An 2000* (1790) (Strasbourg edition, 1905).

utopian social pattern—as among Vairasse's Sevarambians and Lesconvel's Naudelians—the upper classes enjoy a privileged status not because of heredity or riches but because of excellence in virtue. Rousseau, during the second half of the century, is careful to distinguish between "natural" and "civil" (or "moral") equality. This "civil" or "moral" equality of Rousseau, however, is not tantamount to a classless society, for distinctions, riches, and the privileges of genius will be maintained even in Rousseau's democratic state. Grivel, the conservative lawyer who wrote on the eve of the Revolution, restates Rousseau's views concerning physical inequalities placed upon man by nature at birth. In his ideal society such distinctions are recognized and properly utilized. Robust individuals with weak intellects are not exposed to as much book learning as are less perfect physical specimens with strong intellects. The former are expected to serve the state through the use of their physical powers; the latter, through their intellectual ability.

Liberty and fraternity are on the whole less enthusiastically championed than equality by the French utopians. In nearly all of the French prerevolutionary utopias the liberty of the citizen is subject to restrictions of varying severity. In Rétif de la Bretonne's imaginary austral society the citizens voluntarily surrender some of their liberties to the royal authority, but in exchange enjoy the benefits of what later becomes the Napoleonic doctrine of carrières ouvertes aux talents. Fraternity is the least precisely expressed social ideal in the works of the prerevolutionary utopians; it consists mostly of communal living in geometrical housing projects. Foigny's androgynes address one another as "brother," and Leszczynski describes his Dumoclans as giving the impression of being members of the same family. Beyond this, little indication is given by any of the utopians how the ideal of fraternity is translated into a working social reality.

The idea of a perfect economic structure is also constant throughout the prerevolutionary utopias. Only one of the utopians fails to adopt some sort of collectivism as the economic basis of his superior society. The non-collectivist is the conservative Grivel, an ardent champion of physiocracy. State socialism and pure communism dominate the economic thought of the other prerevolutionary utopian writers. At the end of the seventeenth century this frame of mind is probably a continuation and imitation of the classical utopian tradition, for Plato, More, and Campanella had all advocated pure, non-dictatorial communism. After the privations of the War of the Spanish Succession and the cruel winter of 1709, however, the idea of economic collectivism, whether conceived with or without state ownership and management of resources and means of production, assumes a more concrete shape and is described as a panacea to prevent misery and starvation.

By 1755 this collectivist doctrine finds a precise formulation in Morelly's *Code de la nature,* an early communist manifesto. No private property is permitted in the ideal society of the *Code* except for actual use, and each citizen is a "public man" sustained, supported, and employed at public expense. Durable goods are kept in public warehouses and are distributed among the citizens according to need. All citizens are obligated to practice agriculture before entering an *atelier* to work at a trade or profession. Behind Morelly's public warehouse and *atelier* loom the periodic famines and the increasing unemployment of the *ancien régime.* These are the historical factors which evoke and resuscitate the philosophical heritage of Plato, More, and Campanella, much as the Industrial Revolution during the next century was to lead Marx to revive and refurbish the heritage of prerevolutionary utopianism.

Perfect political, social, and economic structures depend on human beings who have already reached or will eventually reach a state of perfection. The idea of human progress, which is lacking in classical utopianism, makes its appearance in the French utopias about the middle of the eighteenth century. The ideal commonwealth and society of the late eighteenth century are to be attained through natural progress, which is inevitable and practically unlimited. In his *Découverte australe* Rétif de la Bretonne outdoes other utopians in his search for human perfection; he suggests a cross-breeding of Europeans and gigantic Patagonians in order to create an improved and superior race with a greater capacity and potential for intellectual and social progress. Progressivist optimism reaches pathetic heights on the eve of the

Revolution. Mercier, writing in 1770, senses the coming change, but his optimism is so great that he expects it to take place without any upheaval, as a result of royal magnanimity. The doctrine of revolution, which first appeared in French utopianism toward the end of Louis XIV's reign, is retained but transformed by the late eighteenth-century utopians into a royal revolution or—as in Grivel's *Isle inconnue*—into a peerless code of wise laws bestowed upon a deserving people by royal grace. If the utopian authors are to be believed, the Revolution finds the French monarchy buttressed by a climate of opinion which hopes for and fervently believes in the regeneration of institutions, dictated by the prevailing idea of inevitable and unlimited progress.

This firm and fervent belief probably accounts for the diminishing discretion shown by the utopians. The inhabitants of utopia, the beneficiaries of the perfect society and state, fall into three distinctive and successive categories. During the early part of French utopian writing down to the middle of the eighteenth century, utopias exist only for strange and fabulous races inhabiting vaguely remote lands. At mid-century a change takes place; in the hands of Morelly and Rousseau, utopia becomes a scheme of communal living, not for mythical creatures beyond the seas, but for real men everywhere. Finally, after 1770, utopia reaches its destination; it turns into a political and social blueprint for the French. The three utopian writers who published between 1770 and 1790—Mercier, Rétif de la Bretonne, and Grivel—describe utopias inhabited by Frenchmen. Mercier and Rétif de la Bretonne (in his *An 2000*) draw the picture of a future France. Grivel and Rétif de la Bretonne (in his *Découverte australe*) fancy an overseas France where the goal of perfection either has been attained or is near attainment.

The most graphic illustration of this evolution is the gradual change in the plans for geometrically designed cities. From 1676 to 1752, from Foigny to Leszczynski, these symmetrical cities have already been built and are inhabited by such startling races as the austral hermaphrodites, Sevarambians, Naudelians, Mercurians, Dumoclans, and their ilk. From 1753 to 1770 the dwellers of these cities on the whole remain fabulous creatures—Selenites, Abadians, and Ajaoans—but the plans that Morelly draws for his perfect city in the *Code de la nature* are designed for no folk of mist but for real men. Then, after 1770, the mask drops and Paris itself becomes the geometrical city, even when it is cunningly called *Sirap*, as in Rétif de la Bretonne's *Découverte australe*.

The spirit of prerevolutionary French utopianism is thus characterized by a homeward movement, which starts on an unexplored austral continent and ends on the banks of the Seine. This is a symptom of increasing boldness and conviction. Foigny and Vairasse at the end of the seventeenth century were too timid and too impressed with the stability of the status quo to build a utopia anywhere but in Australia. Mercier and Rétif de la Bretonne at the end of the eighteenth century are so bold and so aware of the impending transformation of their milieu that they construct their imaginary commonwealth on French soil. With this daring innovation, which could not have come about without a weakening of the censorship, the homeward movement of utopia comes to an end. The utopia in space yields its function as a vehicle of political protest to the utopia in time. Future rather than distant environments will henceforth serve as subjects for Western imaginary commonwealths, and pessimism will finally replace optimism.

From Ideology to Action: Babeuf

The Revolution temporarily inhibited the vogue of utopian writing in France. After 1789 obscure French intellectuals could try their skill at drafting constitutions for France rather than titillate minds by writing about non-existent islands. But ideas, it is said, are immortal, and revolutions in societies are conditioned by preceding revolutions in the minds of men. If so, what was the influence of the utopian writers of this intellectual revolution upon the events and acts of the revolutionary epoch? How, if at all, was the utopian ideology translated into action? The Taine school of French historiography has long held that the influence of the prerevolutionary utopias was sufficient to "seduce a multitude of enlightened men."[9] To this asserted influence are attributed the discarding of the monarchic idea, the establishment

9. A. Le Flamanc, *Les Utopies prérévolutionnaires* (Paris, 1934), Preface.

of the Republic, the execution of Louis XVI, and even Bonaparte's Egyptian expedition.[10]   On the other hand, a dissenting school of historians believes that the prerevolutionary utopias were but *jeux de l'esprit*, "whose diffusion is mediocre and whose influence, even when they are sincere, is almost nil."[11]

"Almost" is the key word in the preceding sentence.   Not counting Rousseau's *Contrat social*, which lacks the outward trappings of a utopia, it is indeed impossible, with one exception, to establish a documented causal connection between French revolutionary action and utopian stimulation.   This single exception is the case of Gracchus Babeuf (1760-1797), leader of the conspiratorial Society of Equals, whose members plotted an attempt in 1796 to replace the "bourgeois republic" of the Directory with a "democratic republic" on the Robespierrist model.

Babeuf is an important link in the transmission of European revolutionary thought.   His writings and activities provide a clear illustration of the metamorphosis of the utopian mentality into utopian will.   He was the first activist to translate into revolutionary action the utopian ideas analyzed in the preceding pages. Babeuf's utopian mentality was transformed into a utopian will under the impact of Thermidor and the misery of French workingmen during the Thermidorean reaction.   He and his *sansculotte* followers looked back upon the Terror under Robespierre as a paradise lost and a Republic of utopian virtue.[12]   For Babeuf and his followers the abrupt overthrow of their short-lived utopia constituted a violation of "the will of nature."[13]

The details of the conspiracy of 21 *floréal* An IV (May 10, 1796), have been too well reviewed[14] to need repeating in this es-

10. *Ibid.*

11. D. Mornet, *Les Origines intellectuelles de la révolution française* (Paris, 1933), p. 472.

12. Jean Dautry, "Le Pessimisme économique de Babeuf," *Annales historiques de la Révolution française*, XXXIII (Avril-Juin, 1916), 224.

13. Excerpts from Babeuf's correspondence and writings, quoted by Dautry, pp. 215, 226.

14. For narrative accounts of the conspiracy or conspiracies of 1796, see the classic Buonarotti, *Conspiration pour l'Egalité dite de Babeuf* (2 vols.; Paris, 1828); V. Advielle, *Histoire de Gracchus Babeuf et du Babouvisme* (2 vols.; Paris, 1884); E. B. Bax, *The Last Episode of the French Revolution* (London, 1911); G. Javogues, "L'Affaire du camp de Grenelle," *Annales historiques de la Révolution française*, II (1925), 23-32; P. Bessand-Massenet, *L'Attaque de Grenelle: Les Communistes en 1796* (Paris, 1926); J. Godechot, "Les travaux récents sur Babeuf et le babouvisme," *Annales historiques de la Révolution française*, No. 4 (1960), pp. 369-387; Claude Mazauric, *Babeuf et la conspiration pour l'égalité* (Paris, 1962).

say. The aim of the conspiracy was to replace the Constitution of
1795 (the Directory) by the Constitution of 1793 (the Republic of
Virtue of Robespierre). The *Manifesto* of the conspirators proclaimed that "the French Revolution was only the precursor of
another, much greater, much more solemn revolution, which will
be the last revolution." It threatened that "the People, which
had trodden on the bodies of kings and priests allied against it,"
would do the same to the new tyrants of the "Republic of the
Rich" (the Directory), and promised to end private ownership
of land.[15]

Where did these ideas come from? Their provenance poses no
problem for the intellectual historian. As early as 1793 Babeuf
referred to Diderot as "our sage, our principal precursor."[16]
During the second half of the eighteenth century and well into
the nineteenth it was generally believed that Diderot had used
the nom de plume "Morelly" for his more radical writings, including the *Code de la nature*. Babeuf shared this error and
repeated it in his speech to the jurors during his trial before the
Cour de Vendôme in 1796. He cited verbatim the three "fundamental and sacred laws" of Morelly, namely, that "nothing in the
society shall belong singularly and exclusively to any person, except the thing of which he makes use either for his own needs,
pleasures, or his daily work," that "each citizen shall be a 'public
man' sustained, supported and employed at public expense," and
that "each citizen shall contribute his part to the public authority
according to his ability, talent and age...."[17] Then, with a
sarcastic thrust in the direction of the public prosecutors, whose
list of accusations he was attempting to refute, Babeuf exclaimed:
"Do we not find even in the exposé of the *accusateurs nationaux*
such statements, less applicable to these...alleged conspirators
than to the author of the *Code de la nature*?... In the eyes of the
same *accusateurs* Diderot [*sic*] should appear as the supreme chief
of all the conspirators. It is upon him that the most flaming
passages of the fulminations should fall."[18]

15. Advielle, I, 185 ff.
16. Letter from Babeuf to Chaumette, May 7, 1793; quoted by Dautry, p. 215.
17. "Défense générale de Babeuf devant la Haute-Cour de Vendôme (An V),"
in Advielle, II, 58.
18. *Ibid.*, II, 59.

Diderot, of course, was dead in 1796 and could not protest. If the mysterious Morelly was still alive—forty-one years after the publication of his *Code*—it would have been too much to expect of him to step before the court, acknowledge his authorship of the *Code de la nature*, and mount the guillotine[19] with Babeuf as co-chief of the conspiracy. But Babeuf's testimony is sufficient evidence that the Society of Equals had accepted the ideas of an obscure utopian who published the *Code de la nature* under the name Morelly, and that subsequently it plotted a desperately impractical attempt to translate these ideas into political reality.[20] One might say that Babeuf was a frustrated minor Lenin, who stood in the same relationship to Morelly as Lenin would one day stand to Marx.

The Utopian Will Prevails

The success of the Marx-Lenin combination in making the utopian will prevail in Russia took place one hundred and twenty years after the failure of the Morelly-Babeuf synthesis in France. Why did Marx and Lenin succeed where Morelly and Babeuf had failed? Babeuf believed that he had failed because of treason and "the bad composition of the General Staff of the plebeian phalanxes."[21] The real answer to the question is provided by the accumulation during the nineteenth century of empirical data not available to Morelly and Babeuf, which enabled Marx and Lenin to draw certain practical conclusions from the fuller unfolding of the Industrial Revolution, from the failure of European working-class revolutions, and from the proposals of utopian socialism. The difference between Morelly-Babeuf and Marx-Lenin is empiricism: the former represent the non-empirical, the latter, the empirical utopian mentality and will.

19. Babeuf attempted suicide by stabbing himself upon being sentenced.
20. The writer, who composed this essay as a tribute to Professor Louis Gottschalk during a Foreign Service assignment in the Eastern Mediterranean, away from great libraries and archives, wishes to express his gratitude to his friend and colleague, M. Hugues-Jean de Dianoux, *Conseiller d'Ambassade*, who found time in the course of a busy Parisian schedule to check in the Bibliothèque Nationale and in the Archives Nationales the chronology and other obscure points of the Babeuf episode.
21. Letter from Babeuf to Hésine, Dec. 16, 1796, published in *Annales historiques de la Révolution française*, XXXV (Janvier-Mars, 1963), 79-82.

Historically the utopian socialists of the nineteenth century—most of them French—are important for an over-all study of the development of utopianism.   For the most part they were zealous eccentrics and impractical dreamers, who nonetheless went beyond their eighteenth-century precursors by offering prescriptions to cure existing ills instead of giving descriptions of alleged perfection.   Most of the prescriptions were bizarre and ridiculous and yet suggestive.   Saint-Simon (1760-1824) and his disciples practiced a "new form" of Christianity and recommended the abolition of inheritance.   Fourier (1772-1837) and Cabet (1788-1856) proposed the organization of phalansteries and icarias, in which work would proceed joyfully.   Owen (1771-1858) tried communal living in co-operative cities.   Louis Blanc (1811-1882), echoing Morelly, elaborated a scheme for "social *ateliers*" or workshops.   The United States in the nineteenth century was a tolerant host to experimental utopian communities at New Harmony, Brook Farm, Oneida, and elsewhere (though less tolerant of the unconventional morals displayed in some of them).

All these nineteenth-century prescriptive and small-scale experimental utopian ventures were doomed to failure.   For historians of the Western intellect their failure should confirm one of the contentions of this essay, that, until our century, the utopian ideology was more remarkable for its facility to transform itself than for its ability to turn ideology into reality by "sweeping away the non-utopian world."[22]   It would be difficult to avoid concluding that, until the Russian Revolution, the historic function of utopianism was mainly to perform a type of intellectual trick photography, either to show the white-and-black negative of imaginary perfection as a foil to existing black-and-white imperfection, or to make imperfection ridiculous by focusing on it the distorting lens of satire.

The Marxists, always aware of utopian continuity, have always acknowledged, though at times scornfully, their indebtedness to utopian precursors.   The *Communist Manifesto* refers to "the writings of Babeuf and others" (the "others" may include the pre-revolutionary French utopians from Foigny to Rétif de la Bretonne), and also to the "critical-utopian socialists" Saint-Simon,

22. Kolnai, p. 79.

Fourier, and Owen.[23]   The French Communist party has enshrined Babeuf in its hagiology; the babouvian legend was recently
resurrected for literary purposes by Louis Aragon.[24]   In the USSR
there is a special archival collection devoted to Babeuf and babouvianism.   Indeed, in Russia the origins of the Soviet Communism
are now being traced back not only to centuries before Babeuf but
also to "the presentiments and thoughts of such ... forerunners
as Thomas More, Tomasso Campanella, Claude-Henri Saint-
Simon, Charles Fourier and Robert Owen ... brilliantly transformed by Marx and Engels into the science of the construction of
socialist society."[25]

To the non-Marxist student (and perhaps even to some Marxist students) of utopianism the transformation of the utopian doctrine into the empirical science of the construction of socialist
society by Marx and Engels explains only in part the pragmatic
success of Lenin and his successors.   Kolnai, a profound non-
Marxist analyst of the utopian mentality, explains the process
leading to the success by stressing the concept of the *utopian will*,
which "confirms the system by imposing it," or "verifies perfection by realizing it."[26]   But is the *utopian will* alone sufficient
for this?   Babeuf, the utopian socialists of the nineteenth century,
the communards of 1871, and Lenin in 1905 possessed the will,
but still failed to accomplish their objectives.   Clearly, the evolution of the utopian mentality into the utopian will must be followed by a favorable constellation of external factors if success is
to ensue.   The history of the twentieth century in Russia, China,

23. *The Communist Manifesto* (Centenary ed., published by Socialist party of
Great Britain, 1948), pp. 88-91.   For the most recent appraisal of Saint-Simon and
Fourier, see Frank E. Manuel, *The Prophets of Paris* (Cambridge, Mass., 1962).

24. Aragon, *La Semaine sainte* (Paris, 1959).   This unusual and, according to the
author, non-historical novel presents a panoramic view of French society during
the chaotic Easter week of 1815.   The underground babouvian organization has
survived and in a nocturnal meeting debates the party line to be adopted in the
new situation created by Napoleon's return.   In a choice between the fleeing
Bourbons and the arriving Emperor, the latter offers more hope for a socio-economic
leveling of French society, provided that he choose the proletariat as his new power
base.   Napoleon, however, snobbishly refuses to become "emperor of the *canaille*."
He thus seals his own doom and perpetuates the fatal schism left in French society
by Thermidor.

25. *Kommunist*, No. 7 (Moscow, 1959), pp. 38-50.   English translation in *Soviet
Highlights* (Washington, Oct., 1959), p. 2.   See also V. P. Volgin, *Frantsuzski
utopicheski kommunizm* (Moscow, 1960) and *Sen-Simon i Sen-Simonizm* (Moscow,
1961).

26. Kolnai, p. 69.

and the Communist satellite countries suggests that two of these factors are the weakness of existing authority and the availability of other power centers upon which the utopian will can draw.

Conclusion: Utopia in Construction

The attempt, which is this essay, to trace in broad outline the metamorphosis of the utopian idea in modern Western thought is now concluded. Three fundamental observations can be made. The first is that utopianism, originally an aristocratic doctrine (in *The Republic* of Plato, it seems, only the Guardians of the State were thought fit to practice communism), became after Babeuf a "plebeian" (today we would say a "proletarian") program. The second is that utopianism, originally a passive, escapist idea, was gradually transformed in its French phase into a revolutionary doctrine and was transmitted as such by babouvianism to Marxism-Leninism. The third is that utopianism emerged from the French Revolution with a dictatorial determination to substitute, by force if necessary, the preconceived ideal for the persistent real. Later, in the sweeping and irresistible crosscurrent of nineteenth-century laissez-faire capitalism, the strategic objective of frustrated European utopianism became a revolutionary dictatorship of the proletariat.

During the two and one-half centuries which separate the publication of Foigny's *Terre australe* from the establishment of the Communist state in Russia, three distinct, major forms of utopianism succeeded one another. The first type, which appeared before the French Revolution and harked back to the classics, was descriptive and fictive, an instrument of discreet protest in the hands of intellectuals excluded from the governing elite. The second form, which left its mark during the interval between the French and Russian revolutions, was prescriptive and experimental, a blueprint for organization and action which, in reality, was unsuccessful. With the victory of the Russian Revolution the third, palpable, and coercive utopian form emerged. Reality became subject to governmental fiat, in accordance with which citizens first of one country, then of additional states, were compelled to live in and work for what was officially declared to be utopia in construction.

If the eighteenth century witnessed the end of the utopian homeward movement in the fictive sense, the twentieth century has seen the grounding of the idea itself: the appearance of the self-proclaimed ideal commonwealth on earth, not in the happy future but in the dismal present. Utopia, as we said, thus loses its etymological and philosophical denotation of "nowhere" and becomes a well-defined geographical reality for millions of totally controlled populations. The process of transformation is complete. However, an element of make-believe persists because descriptive and coercive utopianism all have pretense—the assertion that the ideal can be or has been substituted for the real—as their common base.

TOWARD THE HISTORY OF THE COMMON MAN: VOLTAIRE AND CONDORCET

Karl J. Weintraub

During the third quarter of the eighteenth century it was not uncommon for aspiring intellectuals to undertake a pilgrimage to the oracle of Ferney. Thus, in September, 1770, Voltaire received his old friend D'Alembert, who introduced the young secretary of the Academy of Science, the Marquis de Condorcet. The seventy-six-year-old warrior of the *philosophes* and the twenty-seven-year-old recruit liked each other immediately. The cordial correspondence exchanged during the remaining eight years of Voltaire's life attests to Condorcet's reverence for the "illustrious master" and to the latter's respect of the young "citizen-philosopher."[1] They were joined by many ties, the bonds of an intellectual fraternity fighting for enlightened civilization, the shared admiration for Turgot, and such common friends as D'Alembert and Diderot. The young man acknowledged Voltaire's position as head of the "party" but retained his independent mind. Voltaire, usually impatient of criticism, could accept it rather graciously from the young philosopher and geometer.[2] Upon Voltaire's death, Condorcet assumed some responsibilities as his literary executor. In conjunction with the playwright Beaumarchais he was responsible for the famous Kehl edition of Voltaire's works which he also supplied with critical annotations.

KARL J. WEINTRAUB *is associate professor of history at the University of Chicago.*
1. Condorcet, *Œuvres*, ed. by M.F. Arago (12 vols.; Paris, 1847-1849), I, 1-164. The *Correspondance entre Voltaire et Condorcet* from 1770-1778 contains eighty-six letters.
2. *Ibid.*, I, 151-155 (*Correspondance ...*); Condorcet refused, politely but firmly, to publish an attack by Voltaire on Montesquieu as unwise and unworthy of Voltaire's reputation. Voltaire graciously answered that he, the "Mathusalem," without blushing, was willing to listen in such matters to the younger man.

His *Vie de Voltaire*³ was the first popular biography of the great poet and *philosophe*.

Voltaire was for Condorcet the pioneer of the Enlightenment. "It has been the fate of this great man to precede his age in everything and to force his century to follow him."⁴ By Voltaire's works and good offices Europe has been stirred to humanitarian and rational activity. Enlightened men owe it to Voltaire that the priesthood has lost some power and riches, that greater freedom has been granted to the press, that tyrannical intolerance wanes in some societies, that through inoculation some men escape illness and unnecessary death, that feudal servitude has been seriously undermined in some eastern European countries, that reform of absurd and barbaric laws has become more widespread. Voltaire's influence can be found at work where reason overcomes prejudice, where charlatans are exposed and men are introduced to their rights, where the love of humanity has become the true concern of government.⁵ "As a philosopher he presented the first model of a simple citizen embracing in his work and his purpose all of Man's interests anywhere and at any time; raising himself against all error, against all oppression; defending and expanding all useful truth."⁶

Condorcet also attributed to Voltaire a revolution in historical writing. He thought the *Essai sur les moeurs* truly a philosopher's history and "une lecture délicieuse."⁷ The *Siècle de Louis XIV* was in his opinion the only readable history on that reign.⁸ The eighteenth century could best be understood through the *Précis du siècle de Louis XV*.⁹ Voltaire had focused historical vision on matters worthy of enlightened attention: the peace and happiness of nations, their prejudices and their moments of illumination, their virtues and vices, their arts and manners.

Yet, despite Condorcet's praise of Voltaire the historian, striking differences in outlook are discernible in the two men's treatment of history. Hardly a trace of disagreement on such matters

---

3. *Ibid.*, IV, 1-186. It was published in 1789 and has often been included as a part of Voltaire's collected works. In the annotations to Voltaire's works ("Avertissements insérés par Condorcet dans l'édition complète des Œuvres de Voltaire," *ibid.*, IV, 187-315, and the "Notes sur Voltaire," *ibid.*, IV, 319-635) Condorcet often added new knowledge, but also subtly expressed his differing opinions.

4. *Ibid.*, III, 576 (*Éloge de Pascal*).   5. *Ibid.*, IV, 176-177 (*Vie de Voltaire*)
6. *Ibid.*, IV, 175 (*Vie de Voltaire*).   7. *Ibid.*, IV, 97 (*Vie de Voltaire*).
8. *Ibid.*, IV, 79-81 (*Vie de Voltaire*).   9. *Ibid.*, IV, 143 (*Vie de Voltaire*).

appeared in their mutual correspondence. It was never an open controversy. But in a few critical remarks made after Voltaire's death, Condorcet consciously differentiated himself from unacceptable views of the late master.

In the center of Condorcet's disagreement with Voltaire lies the problem of "the history of the common man." In the few criticisms he allowed himself of Voltaire's work, Condorcet remarked that Voltaire too frequently and too freely praised rulers and powerful men.[10] The great *philosophe* had failed to come out strongly against one-man rule. His enthusiasm for Louis XIV clearly seemed a prejudice from which even such a model of enlightenment had never freed himself. When Condorcet, during the Revolution, projected his great plan for public instruction, he examined all the available works for teaching history.[11] He then felt compelled to reject Voltaire's histories because they did not sufficiently decry despotism. A "completely new kind of history" was therefore needed which would give special attention to the problem of social equality.[12] In his chief historical work, the *Esquisse d'un tableau historique des progrès de l'esprit humain,* Condorcet made the same point but without specific reference to Voltaire.

Up till now, the history of politics, like that of philosophy or science, has been the history of only a few individuals: that which really constitutes the human race, the vast mass of families living for the most part on the fruits of their labor, has been forgotten, and even of those who follow public professions, and work not for themselves but for society, who are engaged in teaching, ruling, protecting or healing others, it is only the leaders who have held the eye of the historian.[13]

Condorcet attributed Voltaire's weakness for great men and his esteem for cultured elites to the peculiarities of life under absolutism. The ardor for Louis XIV "is the only prejudice of his youth which Voltaire retained."[14] Some of his "mistakes" could be written off as the natural errors of a somewhat less enlightened generation.[15] And since Voltaire had to fight two

10. *Ibid.,* IV, 136-138, 153, 183 (*Vie de Voltaire*), and 468, 619-620, 627 ("Notes sur Voltaire").
11. *Ibid.,* VII, 417-419 (*Sur l'instruction publique*).
12. *Ibid.,* VII, 419 (*Instruct. pub.*).   13. *Ibid.,* VI, 232-233 (*Esquisse...*).
14. *Ibid.,* IV, 183-184 (*Vie de Voltaire*).
15. *Ibid.,* IV, 235, 236, 247 ("Avertissements...").

tyrannies simultaneously, the oppression by the Church and by
secular despotism, he had been forced to employ the tactics of
praising one while striking the other.[16] By inference, therefore,
Condorcet's explanations ascribed the difference in historical outlook to the disparity between two generations of *philosophes*.
And he left the impression by his remarks that Voltaire might
have shared the more radical position had he only stood at Condorcet's point in time.

To be sure, many differences between these two men can be
traced to the fact that the older one was a pioneer of the Enlightenment while the younger could build upon the foundations laid by
an earlier generation.   Other differences can be attributed to
historical events which either no longer moulded the world view
of the older man or occurred only after his death.   A more ambitious treatise in the history of ideas might try to explain Voltaire
and Condorcet in terms of a changing climate of opinion and the
impact of events upon the minds of men after 1778.   This paper,
conceived in a more limited sense, merely wishes modestly to suggest that the differences in attitude toward a "history of the common man" depended also upon great divergences of world view,
personality, interest, and temperament.   The study seems to indicate that there are differences in the thought of men which are
somewhat less touched by the flow of time and events.

In the center of Voltaire's life was his love for a truly civilized
existence.   In a relentless and a meaningless universe man could
save himself only by creating and maintaining the highest form
of culture.   Voltaire's concept of history was thus shaped under
the impact which the culture of the *grand siècle* made on him as
a thinker and artist.   In his opinion, man had acquired an un-
equaled level of cultural development at the time of Louis XIV.
The arts, in general, had been cultivated, and the literary arts,
in particular, had been perfected.   The French language had become a refined and noble instrument.   All forms of social intercourse had been endowed with a degree of *politesse* and taste so
that cultured men now had a home in this earthly wilderness.
Paris had become a civilized metropolis with paved streets, adequate lighting, and all the marks of true urbanity.   With the help

16. *Ibid.*, VII, 419 (*Instruct. pub.*).

of such capable ministers as Colbert, the king had unified the nation and developed its great resources. In spite of the hardships of wars, the reign had been marked by an active concern for the welfare of the people. France had become a respected nation and the school of Europe. If her religious and trade policies were still less enlightened, and the growth of science and "sane philoso-phy" somewhat less spectacular, a refined modern man found these perfected in post-Stuart England and the Dutch republic. So that the "age of Louis XIV," in a wider sense, had introduced Western Europe to genuine civilization.[17] And the remarkable example of Peter the Great demonstrated that cultured existence lay now within the reach of all.[18]

Voltaire broke through the confines of political and ecclesiasti-cal history toward a history of civilization by proceeding from his concrete experience of a decent human existence. He could un-dertake his assault upon the chronological and spatial framework of Judeo-Christian historiography because he thought of man as the creator of civilization, and not as a pawn of Providence. As Candide found refuge from the perversities of life in a little garden, so man saved himself by creation of his culture. With the exception of the early work on Charles XII, Voltaire pursued in his histories man's labors on behalf of civilization. The attain-ment of enlightened culture was the theme of the *Siècle de Louis XIV,* the *Précis du siècle de Louis XV,* and the *Lettres phi-*

17. These points are made eloquently in the *Siècle de Louis XIV,* the *Précis du siècle de Louis XV,* the *Essai sur les mœurs et l'esprit des nations,* and in Vol-taire's correspondence. He thought of the *Siècle de Louis XIV* as his life work to glorify the greatness of that age; see Voltaire, *Lettres choisies,* ed. by L. Moland (2 vols.; Paris, 1883), II, 233. For biographic accounts concerning Voltaire, see G. Desnoiresterres, *Voltaire et la société du XVIIIe siècle* (8 vols.; Paris, 1871-1876); H. N. Brailsford, *Voltaire* (New York, 1935); P. de Vries, *Voltaire, burger en edelman* (Bussum, 1951); R. Mahrenholtz, *Voltaires Leben und Werke* (Oppen, 1885). On special aspects of his works and thoughts see the following: J. H. Brum-fitt, *Voltaire Historian* (Oxford, 1958), the best book on Voltaire's historical method and thought, although it concerns itself very little with Voltaire as a historian of civilization; P. Sakmann, *Voltaires Geistesart und Gedankenwelt* (Stuttgart, 1910); I. O. Wade, *Voltaire and Candide* (Princeton, 1959); P. Gay, *Voltaire's Politics* (Princeton, 1959); R. Naves, *Le Goût de Voltaire* (Paris, n.d.); W. Dilthey, "Das 18. Jahrhundert und die geschichtliche Welt," *Deutsche Rundschau,* CVIII (1901), 241-261, 350-380; and F. Meinecke, *Die Entstehung des Historismus* (Munich, 1959).

18. Voltaire, *Histoire de l'empire de Russie sous Pierre le grand* in *Œuvres historiques,* ed. R. Pomeau (Paris, 1957), pp. 339-602. See especially the last sentence: "Les souverains des états depuis longtemps policés se diront à eux-mêmes: 'Si dans les climats de l'ancienne Scythie, un homme, aidé de son seul génie, a fait de si grandes choses, que devons-nous faire dans des royaumes où les travaux accumulés de plusieurs siècles nous ont rendu tout facile?' " (*ibid.,* p. 598).

losophiques (although it is difficult to regard these letters on English conditions as a strictly historical work). The *Histoire de l'empire de Russie sous Pierre le grand* detailed the tsar's exertions to lift his nation from barbarism onto a plateau of civilized existence. And the magistral *Essai sur les mœurs et l'esprit des nations* contained Voltaire's extensive search for the few moments of civilization to be found among the vast deserts of barbarous life.

This first historian of civilization had no carefully elaborated concept of culture or civilization. As a matter of fact, the two nouns "culture" and "civilization" did not appear in European languages until the last years of his life.[19] But, through his encounter with the age of Louis XIV, Voltaire knew in concrete detail what constituted a good life, a civilized existence. As a historian of civilization, he therefore treated all those cultural matters which he knew to be significant. His histories contain lengthy investigations of the political conditions of societies. With few exceptions these inquiries are dominated by such questions as: In what measure did this or that state create the conditions for civilized life? To what extent was power exercised on behalf of human welfare? How well did the state maintain the order so necessary and conducive for the growth of culture? In such connections Voltaire gave considerable attention to the wisdom or failure of economic measures and the effectiveness of laws and judicial procedures. He included large parts delineating the influence exerted by religious convictions and institutions upon the health or malaise of society. Interlocked with these is a concern for man's varied conceptions of the universe. In some chapters Voltaire outlined the condition of the arts, of languages, of customs and manners. His irrepressible interest in any civilized act of man fixed his prospecting eyes on an array of details such as the cost of cannonballs, the quality of textiles, the size of windows, the logistic problems of the Crusades, the fluctuating value of money, the interrelation of coarse linen and the spread of leprosy, the reform of the calendar, or perhaps the development of Gregorian chant. Voltaire construed the content of cultural

19. Joseph Niedermann, *Kultur, Werden und Wandlungen des Begriffs und seiner Ersatzbegriffe von Cicero bis Herder* (Biblioteca dell' Archivum Romanicum, serie I, Vol. 28; Florence, 1941); and *Civilisation; le mot et l'idée.* Centre International de Synthèse, Paris. Première semaine internationale. Deuxième fascicule, 1929.

history broadly. He neither reduced it to an antiquarian's curiosity shop of peculiar customs, nor did he truncate it to a history of letters and arts, nor did he condense it to an account of the progress of the human mind. Amid the crime, folly, and misfortune composing the bulk of history, Voltaire looked everywhere for man as the creator of a civilized oasis.

Throughout his search for civilization in history, Voltaire stressed certain preconditions for the growth and preservation of culture. Men must possess a correct conception of the basic nature of the physical universe and of mankind's position within it. They should combine the courage of ignorance toward unanswerable metaphysical questions with the certainty that two and two make four. Their morality should be founded on a few simple verities which can be derived from the study of human nature. They must be free to cultivate toleration, good manners, and refined taste. This requires a stable political order in which wise rulers devote themselves to the material, social, cultural, and intellectual welfare of all.

Voltaire's historical studies strengthened his conviction that civilized existence was more threatened by anarchy than by tyranny. Tyranny is rarer than generally claimed since "everywhere a restraint is imposed on arbitrary power by the law, or by customs (*usages*), or by morals (*mœurs*)."[20] Surely, he admits, all too often power has been miserably abused, and it is saddening to see how poorly man has been governed.[21] Seldom have the laws been in harmony with morality, and rarely have good laws been justly administered.[22] For centuries Europe lived in total anarchy; the age of feudalism was an age of sanctioned robbery and ceaseless civil strife. "Envisage deserts where wolves, tigers, and foxes kill a weak and timid beast: that is Europe's picture for many centuries."[23] Even so, history had heroes; and not all of them scientists like Newton, philosophers like Locke, or superb dramatists like Racine. Mankind had also been blessed with a Solon, a Marcus Aurelius, a Julian, an Haroun-al-Rashid, an Alfred the

20. Voltaire, *Œuvres complètes*, ed. by L. Moland (52 vols.; Paris, 1877-1883), XIII, 181 (*Essai...*); cf. also XII, 113 (*Essai...*).
21. *Ibid.*, XI, 405 (*Essai...*).
22. *Ibid.*, XI, 67, 424, XII, 66 (*Essai...*); XIX, 319, 624 (*Dictionnaire philosophique*); and *Œuvres historiques*, pp. 390, 571 (*Pierre le grand*), 848, 861 (*Louis XIV*).
23. *Œuvres complètes*, XI, 269 (*Essai...*).

Great, an Elizabeth, a Henry IV, a Peter I, a host of good Chinese
emperors, and a Louis XIV, who all labored for the good life.
Many less benevolent rulers also did spadework in man's cultural
garden. Alexander built more cities than he destroyed; Augustus
brought peace to a strife-torn world; Frederick II of Hohenstaufen
protected the arts; Philip IV of France admitted the bourgeoisie
to a participation in national affairs; and Louis XI, concerned for
postal services and uniform weights and measures, "proved that a
méchant homme might perform the public good when personal
interest was not in the way."[24]   Indeed!—even popes like Alexander III, Leo X, Gregory XIII, or Sixtus V advanced man's
well-being in some respects.

Under any circumstance, the form of government mattered
less to Voltaire than that its powers be employed for cultural tasks.
He could be rhapsodic over republics and free states.   The freedom of the Greek citizens, the virtues of free burghers in medieval
towns, the free and simple Swiss, and the liberties of the Dutch
elicited his favorable historic judgment.   In more speculative
writings he occasionally extols those societies where man only
obeys the laws.   If such a land does not exist, "we must search for
it."[25]   But as one critic of Voltaire's political thought has said:
"A few scattered opinions, playful and carefully hedged, do not
add up to a position.   They reflect a mood and the aged Voltaire's
flexibility.   Voltaire did not become a convinced democrat. . . ."[26]
His misgivings about republican life were strong.   Free towns are
either incapable of defense against strong neighbors, or they fail
to control the egotism of private persons, or they become the
possession of a patrician aristocracy which is seldom less oppressive
or more enlightened than monarchy.[27]   Voltaire consistently de-

24. *Ibid.*, XI, 121 (*Essai* . . .).   25. *Ibid.*, XX, 34 (*Dict. phil.*).
26. P. Gay, *op. cit.*, p. 237.   Of interest also are the following comments: "A
brilliant, learned, versatile French critic once pointed out that Voltaire was the
best representative of the French spirit because he was of all men the most absolutist, and because Liberalism, the opposite of absolutism, is not French" (John
Morley, *Critical Miscellanies* [4 vols.; London, 1904], IV, 296).   And the judgment
of a revolutionary observer: "Le bandeau qui nous cache l'aristocratie de Voltaire
tombera. . . .   Rousseau eût été bien grand dans le jeu de paume de Versailles;
Voltaire y eût été bien petit.   Voltaire aurait dû naître cent ans plus tôt" (J. de la
Vallée, *Tableau philosophique du règne de Louis XV* [Strasbourg, 1791], pp. 282-
286).
27. Among many possible citations see: *Œuvres complètes*, XII, 172, 179, 248,
284, 305, XIII, 76, 118, 178 (*Essai*. . .); XX, 238 (*Dict. phil.*); and *Œuvres historiques*,
p. 234 (*Histoire de Charles XII*).

nied Montesquieu's contention that republics are characterized by greater virtue.[28] He considered the tyranny of one preferable to the tyranny of the many.[29] How could he have sanctioned, as Condorcet did, the disorders of the Revolution when he felt physically ill in recounting how the mob slaughtered the brothers De Witt?[30] Too frequently the people's violence is "greater than the tyranny of which they complain."[31] Where greater freedom might mean the loss of culture, the enlightened *philosophe* chooses peace, order, and civilization provided by the strong ruler.

It may be a sad conclusion, based on the recognition of realities, that "man is rarely worthy of governing himself,"[32] but Voltaire was deeply convinced that "reason consists in always seeing what things are."[33] As he grew older, he complained of the multitudinous reveries on government, the gullible faith in the ease of ruling by brochures, and the learned agricultural discourses propounded by Parisian fireplaces.[34] Power is a stubborn reality and no wishful dreaming will make it less so. Mankind's hope rests on the chance (proven by historical examples) that rulers conscious of our common needs, will employ power for our welfare. Good rulers may make the state a protector of culture and civilization. After all, though they cultivated their rocks in liberty,[35] what cultural contributions did the Swiss make? Yet, under Elizabeth private citizens built hospitals and schools; Louis XIV sponsored French art and literature; Peter I promoted the sciences; and the example of Vauban showed that good citizenship under absolutism is no idle dream.[36] Long before Voltaire, the Stoic Seneca had reconciled himself to the principate with the thought that, since the cosmos is ruled by a god, we live in a monarchy anyway. Voltaire, the wit, in a less reverent vein,

28. *Œuvres historiques*, p. 862 (*Louis XIV*); *Œuvres complètes*, XIII, 179 (*Essai...*), XIX, 33 (*Dict. phil.*), XXIII, 531 ff. (*Pensées sur le gouvernement*), XXVII, 322 (*L'A,B,C.*).
29. *Œuvres complètes*, XX, 544 (*Dict. phil.*).
30. *Œuvres historiques*, p. 720 (*Louis XIV*); *Œuvres complètes*, XIII, 120 (*Essai...*); and *Lettres choisies*, I, 401.
31. *Œuvres complètes*, XIII, 45 (*Essai...*).
32. *Ibid.*, XI, 529 (*Essai...*); XIX, 33, XX, 185 (*Dict. phil.*).
33. *Ibid.*, XVIII, 554, XIX, 395 (*Dict. phil.*); and *Romans et contes*, ed. R. Groos (Paris, 1954), p. 14 (*Zadig*).
34. *Lettres choisies*, II, 15 and 76; *Œuvres historiques*, p. 1292 (*Défense de Louis XIV contre l'auteur des* Ephémérides).
35. *Œuvres complètes*, XI, 526-29 (*Essai...*).
36. *Œuvres historiques*, p. 1212 (*Louis XIV*).

thought it natural that a barnyard be ruled by a rooster.[37]   In view of man's weaknesses, enlightened despotism might well be the best guarantor of our culture.

Voltaire's skepticism was not restricted to man's ability to govern himself, but extended also to his limitations as a creator of civilization. Culture requires leisure. The multitudes of this world always have had and always will have to work long and hard to make human life feasible. They will always be poor, although good rulers and officials can protect them against real misery.[38] If they have the good sense of the good gardener Karpos they will find a meaningful existence in being good husbands, good fathers, good subjects, and good gardeners. "I know not much more than what I am; I love God with all my heart and sell my vegetables at a reasonable price."[39]   Voltaire was impressed by hard work. He would not sneer at the honest workman from the heights of a leisurely semi-aristocratic existence. But he could not conceive of the 'man-in-the-street' as the mainstay of civilization. The bulk of mankind will not think, rarely read, work six days and spend the seventh in the tavern, never develop superior standards of taste but admire bombast and empty grandeur, finish a good meal with bad liqueur, want to be amused and deceived, and are always inclined to superstition. The elements and accouterments of culture are the creation of very few. The small circles of men who think, write, experiment, wisely administer, and originate projects for the common welfare form a nation's creative elite. They constitute an unpedigreed aristocracy of merit. Their thin front line is backed by larger battalions of the cultured who at least rethink the thoughts of the elite, who learn to share its sentiments and insights, and who implement its plans. Gentle ladies, intelligent and of refined taste, form the stabilizing link among the ranks of good society. And if a nation is fortunate, as was France under Louis XIV, then the good manners, the refined tastes and sentiments, the "sane philosophy" will seep down through all ranks of society and through all provinces.

37. *Œuvres complètes*, XIX, 619 (*Dict. phil.*).
38. "Il faut que ce grand nombre d'hommes soit pauvre, mais il ne faut pas qu'il soit misérable" (*Œuvres historiques*, pp. 996 [*Louis XIV*] and 1720 [notes to *Louis XIV*].
39. *Œuvres complètes*, XVIII, 87 (*Dict. phil.*).

Then true *politesse* can be found in every little shop.[40] The watchmakers of Ferney, employed by such an enlightened master as Voltaire, could acquire a limited measure of culture.

Although Voltaire desired equality before the law, a natural concomitant of man's sense of justice,[41] he rejected other claims for equality. He found that the pretensions of egalitarians too frequently resulted in social anarchy and mob tyranny.[42] With the usual sarcasm he reserved for the Savoyard vicar, he dismissed Rousseau's egalitarian schemes as "moral extravaganzas" and "impertinences worthy of an insane asylum."[43] Most notions of equality he considered to be the sort of wild fancy unworthy of a skeptic who understands this world. "Master Pangloss has always told me that all men are equal!"[44] but whenever Candide acts upon this advice, the perverse world hits him.

Every man has the right to believe in his heart that he is completely equal to other men; but it does not follow that the cardinal's cook may order his master to prepare a meal; still, the cook is free to say: I am like my master, like him I was born in tears; he will die like me in the same anguish and with the same ceremonies. We both perform the same animal functions. If the Turk takes Rome, and if I will then be cardinal and my master a cook, I will employ him.—This is a reasonable and just discourse; but while we wait for the Turk to take Rome, the cook must do his job, or human society will be subverted.[45]

Respectful of Voltaire's agile, flexible, and mercurial mind, one hesitates to say more than that it is unlikely that he would have thought the "cook's" time had come when the "Parisian Turks" made their revolution. Voltaire doubted that society might ever advance beyond mere equality before the law. He strongly believed in a measure of human progress. In one sense, the *Essai sur les mœurs* depicts the long climb of Western society. The *Siècle de Louis XIV* describes the astonishing advances made in French civilization during a brief period. The story of Peter the Great reveals how much ground one strong-willed individual can wrest from barbarism within a lifetime. Thus belief in

40. *Œuvres historiques*, p. 981 (*Louis XIV*).
41. *Ibid.*, p. 625 (*Louis XIV*).
42. *Ibid.*, p. 1041 (*Louis XIV*); *Œuvres complètes*, XII, 574, 576, XIII, 45, 68-69 (*Essai . . .*).
43. *Œuvres historiques*, pp. 1569-1570 (*Précis Louis XV*).
44. *Romans et contes*, p. 183 (*Candide*).
45. *Œuvres complètes*, XVIII, 476 (*Dict. phil.*).

progress was a part of Voltaire's historical viewpoint. But he hedged it with so many qualifications that it became a different idea of progress than that held by such *philosophes* as Turgot, Condorcet, and even Fontenelle.[46] He certainly did not adhere to the notion of man's indefinite perfectibility. Man can advance within the strict limits set by nature.[47] He can at best attain a certain plateau of cultured life. He can "perfect" himself and, above all, he can "perfect" parts of his civilization. Thus Voltaire spoke of the perfection of reason, the perfection of art, the perfection of manners. The attempt to perceive Voltaire's standards of such perfection leads to his appraisal of the culture in the *grand siècle*. "The age of Louis XIV comes closest to perfection."[48] There he could find the norms of judgment in the realm of the arts, the full measure of refined human intercourse, and the sane philosophies of a few thinkers and scientists (though some of these were English, they were for him part of the age). Against these norms he judged all other human endeavors in the realm of civilization. Man had been given a model which would be hard to equal or surpass.[49] Especially in the arts the spread of culture had not resulted in the preservation of the high standards of good taste. Although Voltaire approved of the greater diffusion of culture which had followed the age of genius, the last fifteen years of his life are filled with the complaints that his own age is a declining one.[50] Western man had seen four great creative ages, of which Louis XIV's age had surpassed all. "How could it happen that so many superior men in so many different genres flourished all in the same period? This wonder arrived three times in the history of the world and perhaps it will never reoccur."[51]

46. Cf. H. Linn Edsall, "The idea of history and progress in Fontenelle and Voltaire," in *Studies by Members of the French Department of Yale University; Decennial Volume* (New Haven, 1941), pp. 163-184; and J. Delvaille, *Essai sur l'histoire de l'idée de progrès* (Paris, 1910), pp. 210-223, 304-346, 388-423, and 605-738.

47. ."...il est perfectible...jusqu'au point où la nature a marqué les limites de sa perfection" (*Œuvres complètes*, XI, 20 [*Essai*...]).

48. *Œuvres historiques*, p. 617 (*Louis XIV*).

49. *Ibid.*, p. 1021 (*Louis XIV*).

50. *Ibid.*, pp. 1568-1571 (*Précis Louis XV*); and *Lettres choisies*, I, 123, 225, 261, 295, 342, II, 18, 24, 48, 51, 77, 81, 92, 102, 105, 136, 143, 179, 187, 193-195, 218-219, 227, 250-252, 262, 313.

51. *Œuvres historiques*, pp. 1285-1286 (*Défense de Louis XIV*...).

Voltaire was too skeptical of the human potential to believe in easy progress. We are insects of a summer's day; our energy is limited; and our weak reason—the greatest glory we possess— is forced to put its *non liquet* underneath some of our most troubling question. Nor did Voltaire trust the efficacy of those human tools whereby man tries to preserve and expand his little cultured garden. If unbridled, the intolerant ignorance of many may force Reason and her daughter Truth to return to their hiding place in the well.[52] Unpredictable nature could bury the products of man's labor within seconds. The consequences of our own actions cannot be fully foreseen. Constantine would be as amazed to see that he built his capital for Mohammed II as Romulus would be to see his city in the hands of the papacy. The study of history warrants no knowledge of the future; any historian who thinks otherwise is unworthy of his profession and an insane impostor.[53] Unlike Condorcet, Voltaire said little about education as a tool for the perfection of man. With all his respect for the written word, his trust in the influence of the *Encyclopédie* and the academies, he still had his misgivings about the efficacy of books.[54] He thought much more highly of the theater as a civilizing tool.[55] He spent his life in propagandizing a vision of a better life. And others, among them Condorcet, thought him the great fighter against all superstition which stands in the path of civilization. Yet, in spite of his occasional optimism over this struggle, how sure did he feel of man's chance to free himself? "We will always have passions and prejudices because it is our destiny to be subject to passions and prejudice."[56] The bulk of mankind will always be superstitious and unenlightened. At best, it can be saved from being plain *canaille* by the Herculean efforts of enlightened mandarins under whose guidance the realm of stupidity may be hemmed in so that the benefits of civilization may penetrate all ranks.[57] The fight of this small class to preserve

52. *Romans et contes*, p. 524 (*Éloge historique de la Raison*).
53. *Œuvres complètes*, XI, 256 and 394 (*Essai...*).
54. *Œuvres historiques*, pp. 1183 (*Louis XIV*) and 1295 (*Défense de Louis XIV...*).
55. *Lettres choisies*, I, 223, 274, 415-418, II, 235; *Romans et contes*, p. 273 (*L'Ingénu*); and *Œuvres historiques*, pp. 908 and 1016 (*Louis XIV*).
56. *Œuvres complètes*, XVIII, 349 (*Dict. phil.*).
57. *Ibid.*, XIII, 162-163 (*Essai ...*) and especially XX, 456 (*Dict. phil.*).

man's cultured garden is inevitably hard; and it is a miracle that man does not everywhere live *en Tartare*.[58] With such conceptions, where was there room for a "history of the common man"? One may indeed wonder why Condorcet restrained his criticism of Voltaire.

Condorcet could advocate the history of the common man because he did not share Voltaire's doubts about the common man. Against Voltaire's predilections for creative elites, capable of reaching the highest forms of culture, Condorcet placed his all-consuming desire for establishing true equality in all realms of life. He supplanted Voltaire's limited conception of progress by a theory of indefinite perfectibility. He did not share Voltaire's concerns for the dangerously delicate balance of cultural forces, but trusted instead in reason as the only necessary regulator of civilization. Distrustful of Voltaire's belief in absolute monarchy as a civilizing agent, Condorcet sought methods and institutions to further and to guarantee an egalitarian society.

It has been said that Condorcet had an "intellectual love" of the people.[59] In the justification of his life written during the Revolution (a book on which he worked in hiding until his wife urged him to write the justification of mankind instead, the *Esquisse*), Condorcet describes his continuous effort to secure the freedom and equality of every man and woman.[60] Twelve volumes of his collected works corroborate this modest self-appraisal. Rarely has mankind had a more dedicated advocate of the virtues of human equality. Condorcet went beyond the grand apostle of equality, Rousseau, who had glorified man's natural and social rights. As he pointed out while defending Voltaire against the charge of jealousy toward Rousseau, Jean-Jacques "had declared himself the enemy of all learning and philosophy."[61] Ignorant equality was no solution for Condorcet. The good so-

---

58. *Œuvres historiques*, p. 376 (*Pierre le grand*).
59. J. Salwyn Schapiro, *Condorcet and the Rise of Liberalism* (New York, 1934), p. 272. Among other books and treatises on Condorcet, see the following: Robinet, *Condorcet; sa vie, son œuvre 1743-1794* (Paris, n.d.); F. Alengry, *Condorcet: guide de la Révolution française; théoricien du droit constitutionnel et précurseur de la science sociale* (Paris, 1903); Gilles-Gaston Granger, *La Mathématique sociale du Marquis de Condorcet* (Paris, 1956); F. G. marquis de La Rochefoucauld, *Mémoires de Condorcet, sur la Révolution française, extraits de sa correspondance et de celles de ses amis* (2 vols.; Paris, 1824). The latter must be used with care.
60. Condorcet, *Œuvres*, I, 574-605 (*Fragment de justification*, July, 1793).
61. *Ibid.*, IV, 231 ("Avertissements...").

ciety could only be built on free and equal participation of all in a truly cultured life.

More than merely analyzing and advertising the glories of equality, Condorcet searched for the means and institutions which would implement and guarantee equality. He vigorously expressed his faith in a system of complete political liberty for all members of society through his actions as a councillor of Paris during the phase of the National Assembly, then as a prominent member of the Legislative Assembly, and finally as an independent in the strife-torn Convention. He responded to the events of the great Revolution with an uninterrupted flow of writings on the virtues of political equality. He enthusiastically supported the idea that a nation's political life henceforth was to be based upon the solemn proclamation of man's natural rights. He profoundly believed in the desirability of a written constitution and was instrumental in formulating many of those plans later tabled by the Convention. He fought tenaciously for a unicameral system of legislative representation and strongly defended the virtues of local assemblies. Inspired by the American example, he argued for a provision which should ensure periodic revision of the constitution. He wanted to grant the people the right to censure legislative action. He vigorously opposed the extension of power to any corporate entity within the state and society. He consistently resisted any real infringement of popular sovereignty.[62] He was among the first to acknowledge the failure of constitutional monarchy and pleaded for a republic. He criticized the property qualifications of the 1791 Constitution, the recognition of priests as state officials envisaged in the Civil Constitution of the Clergy, and the Convention's failure to respect the rights of the "common citizen," Louis Capet. His ardent plea for recognition of the political rights of women and his opposition to the seating of representatives who owned West Indies slaves contain the strongest evidence of his political egalitarianism.[63]

Few fellow revolutionaries were as convinced as Condorcet that

62. In these contexts, John Adams' criticism of Condorcet's political naïveté (especially on American matters) constitutes a nice corrective to the Frenchman's idealizations. See John Adams, *Works*, ed. Charles Francis Adams (Boston, 1854), III, 137, VI, 252, 299, IX, 623-624, X, 19, 145, 256-257.

63. *Œuvres*, IX, 469-485 (*Au corps électoral contre l'esclavage des noirs*), X, 119-130 (*Sur l'admission des femmes...*).

political rights and equality must be buttressed by measures assuring economic, social, and cultural equality. He warned that
the great Revolution must not be permitted to end in bourgeois
domination. With his ideal of a classless society he opposed the
attempts "to establish a bourgeois aristocracy, such as obtains in
some of the cantons of Switzerland, where the nobility has been
humiliated but where the people have become enslaved to the
bourgeois."[64] He fought against indirect taxation because he
considered it a means for establishing such a moneyed aristocracy.[65]
Condorcet believed in complete freedom of trade and yet wanted
laws to assure a measure of economic equality to the poorer segments of society. "Inequality of fortune is a great evil, but it is a
political evil, like all other evils . . . only just laws can remedy it."[66]
Of great interest are his speculations about the effects of an insurance system to ameliorate the condition of widows and older
people.[67] There are even hints that he believed a machine age
would improve the economic lot of the people.[68] He recognized
that the general welfare depended upon the size of the population,
but, unlike Malthus, he felt confident that an enlightened mankind would not proliferate beyond the limitations compatible with
human happiness.[69] The depth of his social and economic egalitarianism is most clearly revealed in his concern over the treatment
of women and slaves. In his last advice to his little daughter, he
admonished her to treat animals and all forms of life with genuine
compassion. As a young nobleman he had given up the pleasures
of the hunt for the same reasons. His fertile mind constantly explored how science and wise legislation might turn the *égalité
formelle* into an *égalité réelle*, "the final end of the social art."[70]

64. *Ibid.*, XI, 223 (*Réflexions sur le commerce des blés*).
65. *Ibid.*, X, 80 (*Adresse sur les conditions d'éligibilité*).
66. *Ibid.*, V, 178 (*Vie de Turgot*). See also: III, 553 (*Éloge de l'Hôpital*); V,
188 (*Vie de Turgot*); VI, 245-246, 248 (*Esquisse...*); X, 135-136 (*Sur le préjugé
qui suppose une contrariété d'intérêts entre Paris et les provinces*); XII, 625-636
(*Sur l'impôt progressif*). He also advanced the idea of treasury-financed public
defenders for the economically less privileged, cf. V, 191 (*Vie de Turgot*).
67. *Ibid.*, VI, 247-248 (*Esquisse...*); XI, 392-393 (*Sur les caisses d'accumulation*). Alexandre Koyré, "Condorcet," *Journal of the History of Ideas*, IX
(1948), 131-152, made a noble effort to remind us of the numerous suggestions in
which Condorcet anticipated modern policies and realities.
68. *Œuvres*, VI, 256 (*Esquisse...*); VIII, 459 (*Sur les assemblées provincales*).
69. *Ibid.*, VI, 256-258 (*Esquisse...*). For Malthus' interesting criticism see:
An Essay on Population (2 vols.; London, 1914), II, 1-10.
70. *Œuvres*, VI, 237 (*Esquisse...*).

Few apostles of Enlightenment can match Condorcet's absolute faith in rationality. He was as deeply convinced as any man can be that ignorance is the sole root of evil and that all goodness and virtue are based upon rational insight.[71] "The most simple reason suffices for being virtuous."[72] To us moderns who stand this side of Baudelaire, Nietzsche, and Freud nothing is perhaps so indicative of Condorcet's virtual enslavement to rationalism as his notion that art, if it wishes to be good, must submit to the demands of reason.[73] All truth, in his opinion, is based on man's nature as a sentient being who reasons about his sense experience.[74] Man's best knowledge comes through measurement. Condorcet's faith in science was boundless; his efforts to apply science to human problems were ceaseless. Probability calculus constantly appears as his tool for the solution of social issues. Absolute certainty may be unattainable, but probability calculus makes knowledge "almost" certain.[75] This calculus allows the statesman to figure out the best election system; insurance schemes are based on it; social statistics are the foundations of social science.[76] Man's ever-continuing progress in the future depends upon the never-ending growth of scientific knowledge. To his bitter end, during a turbulent period out of tune with scientific deliberations, Condorcet made life difficult for himself by submitting all suggested legislation to the rigorous test of reason. Robespierre sneered at him, the "great mathematician in the opinion of the literary men, and the great literary man in the opinion of the mathematicians, . . . a timid conspirator, despised by all parties."[77] As history willed it, such a man's distrust of intellectuals was fatal to Condorcet.

The events of the Revolution reinforced Condorcet's conviction that further progress demanded a continuing enlightenment.

71. *Ibid.*, III, 464 (*L'Hôpital*); IV, 177 (*Vie de Voltaire*); and VII, 253 (*Instruct. pub.*).

72. *Ibid.*, VII, 236 (*Instruct. pub.*).

73. *Ibid.*, IV, 43, 85-86 (*Vie de Voltaire*); VI, 215, 255 (*Esquisse* . . .); VII, 304, 406 (*Instruct. pub.*).

74. *Ibid.*, VI, 11-12, 88 (*Esquisse* . . .); X, 122 (*Sur l'admission des femmes* . . .).

75. *Ibid.*, III, 641 (*Éloge de Pascal*) a passage directed against Pascal's skepticism; VI, 86-87, 203-204, 254 (*Esquisse* . . .); IX, 293 (*Sur la forme des élections*).

76. *Ibid.*, VI, 220-222, 259-260 (*Esquisse* . . .); X, 71 (*À Monsieur* ***); and Schapiro, *op. cit.*, p. 117, who used a treatise on the application of calculus which is not included in the *Œuvres*.

77. *Moniteur*, May 8, 1794.

When admitted to the Académie Française in 1782 he exclaimed to his new colleagues on the achievements of the last decades: "Truth has conquered! And mankind has been saved!"[78] In later years he became more interested in the contention: "enlightenment increases when it spreads" and not when it is ever more plentifully concentrated in the heads of an elite.[79] The greatest task of the revolutionaries is "to make reason popular."[80] The enormous progress resulting from the successful political revolution must be fortified by a diffusion of knowledge through the entire society. The newly won equality before the law must not be impaired by inequalities of knowledge and moral refinement. The notion of man's indefinite perfectibility demands that every member of society participate to the fullest in the extension of human knowledge. Thus Condorcet's greatness is to a large degree found in his elaborate thought on education: in the *Esquisse*, which sums up his vision of mankind's gradual education, and in the memoirs *Sur l'instruction publique*, which contain his great scheme for universal education.

"Inequality of education is one of the chief sources of tyranny!"[81] It is vain to proclaim all sorts of equality if the common man is dependent upon the superior knowledge, the higher morality, and the better taste of those who have privileged access to mankind's most advanced thought. Therefore, "Generous friends of Equality and Liberty, unite to obtain from the public power a system of instruction which will render reason popular, or fear to lose all the fruits of your noble efforts shortly. Do not imagine that the best combinations of laws can make the ignorant the equal of the trained man or free him who is a slave of prejudices."[82] A society which conceives of life as "a voyage made in common by brothers,"[83] must educate all, men and women, poor and wealthy.[84] It must provide an education which accomplishes three things: making each one the proper judge of public affairs, giving each the necessary training for his livelihood, and mobilizing all social resources for the further promotion of human perfectibility.

78. *Œuvres*, I, 390 (*Discours de réception à l'Académie Française*).
79. *Ibid.*, VII, 477 and also 209 (*Instruct. pub.*).
80. *Ibid.*, VII, 226 (*Instruct. pub.*).   81. *Ibid.*, VII, 171 (*Instruct. pub.*).
82. *Ibid.*, VII, 226 (*Instruct. pub.*).   83. *Ibid.*, VII, 225 (*Instruct. pub.*).
84. *Ibid.*, VII, 169 ff., 215-216, 388-389 (*Instruct. pub.*); and VI, 264 (*Esquisse ...*).

In his elaborate scheme for public instruction, Condorcet wrestles with Voltaire's problem: is it reasonable to assume that men of unequal ability, tied forever to the necessity of earning a living, may become full-fledged members of the cultured classes? Condorcet's answer to this important question does not seem entirely straightforward. He admits differences in natural talent and expresses fears that absolute equality in all realms of human endeavor is a chimera.[85] Not only are division of labor and expertise of specialized professions features of advanced civilization, but they are also mandatory for continuing progress. To an important degree the advancement of knowledge rests on discoveries made by special talents. The diversity, and not the sameness, of individual abilities accounts for the richness of society.[86]

Apparently Condorcet hoped that by the use of the right educational system the inequalities of nature would not result in legal and social inequalities. To a high degree he looked upon talent and genius, knowledge and culture, as social and not as natural products. At one time he hoped that further progress might succeed in wiping out all undesirable features of cultural stratification within three generations after the Revolution.[87] It certainly remains the educator's and the legislator's task to eliminate the "fearful phalanx of error standing between the people and knowledge," and thus to open cultured life to all.[88] Condorcet envisaged a system of elementary education, free of any special point of view or doctrine,[89] which could prepare each member of society for intelligent and responsible citizenship. This civic training, assuring political independence, must be supported by intelligent judgment in all social and cultural matters. He therefore urged the suppression of all corporate bodies within society, and was especially concerned that no single profession should assume a privileged position by virtue of its necessary expertise.[90]

85. *Ibid.*, VII, 176, 195, 441 (*Instruct. pub.*); X, 146 (*Sur le préjugé qui suppose...*).

86. Very interesting in this connection is his essay *Sur le préjugé qui suppose une contrarieté d'intérêts entre Paris et les provinces*, in *Œuvres*, X, 131-163.

87. *Ibid.*, VII, 174, 182, 374 (*Instruct. pub.*).

88. *Ibid.*, VI, 165 (*Esquisse...*); and Schapiro, *op. cit.*, p. 137.

89. *Œuvres*, VII, 204, 208, 273 (*Instruct. pub.*). The state shall supervise and finance education, but shall not dictate any of its content. Condorcet criticized ancient education for inculcating a specific type of patriotism. See VII, 197-202 (*Instruct. pub.*).

90. *Ibid.*, III, 539 (*L'Hôpital*); VII, 175, 191, 205, 286 (*Instruct. pub.*).

Institutions, such as the vitally important academies, must not become revered oracles. The widest possible dissemination of knowledge must be assured through formal schooling, supplemented by lifelong education through journals, exhibits, museums, libraries, botanic gardens, public lectures, and so forth. He considered all of this feasible, because he was convinced that true knowledge is essentially simple. It remains to the learned to make simple what is not already so. Texts must be devised which condense knowledge in easily accessible form. He hoped that the "art of combinations and generalizations," using tables and charts, might provide genuine short cuts to learning.[91] In addition, there must be methods of instruction which train students in the use of tools of judgment and investigation, so that each can contribute new insights, according to his ability, to the further advancement of knowledge. Thus each member of society could be a free and responsible citizen and simultaneously aid in the never-ending process of perfecting mankind.[92]

Such ideas on human existence and its continuous progress directed Condorcet's historical interests to problems which had hardly existed for Voltaire. Condorcet, as the first among historians, envisaged a history of the common man. Voltaire had blocked the road to such a history by his skeptical view of human nature and of progress, by his ineradicable doubts about the fitness of most men to participate creatively in the cultural processes. Condorcet replaced such skepticism with an unshakable belief in our common human nature. Thus he fought ceaselessly for the ordinary human being as the beneficiary and even the carrier of civilization.

Voltaire had been deeply impressed by the complex fabric of cultural forces; he therefore could not single out one simple factor as the obstacle to human progress. Condorcet had a simpler view of the past. Since all human achievement rested, in his opinion, on the advance of reason, he reduced man's total development to a "history of the human mind." Man is chiefly characterized by the fact that he is a sentient being who observes his sensations, reasons about them, and reduces them to a rational

91. *Ibid.,* VI, 241, 251-253, 269 ff. *(Esquisse . . .)*; VII, 196, 352, 416 *(Instruct. pub.).*
92. *Ibid.,* VII, 433 *(Instruct. pub.).*

simplified system. Nature has not limited this capacity of the mind to expand the scope of human awareness.[93] Thus, the "truest" history is that of humanity's ever-expanding horizon. But there is a phase in mankind's development, a kind of "prehistory," when man struggles to eliminate the obstacles thrown in the path of the unrestricted growth of knowledge. One villain, unenlightened self-interest, becomes responsible for regressions and occasional lack of progress. The bulk of Condorcet's *Esquisse* is a nine-stage account of the gradual liberation of the human mind from the shackles imposed by the evil exploitation of prejudice. The first three stages are the history of all men, a speculative exercise in which Condorcet relied heavily on anthropological analogy. Voltaire, restricting history to what can actually be known from records, would have decried this venture into the foggy origins of man. The remaining six stages almost exclusively tell the story of Western man, a fact which allowed Condorcet a more simplified view of progress than Voltaire, who had also concerned himself with the history of China, India, Persia, and Islam. When Condorcet reached the Revolution, which had truly freed man of the fetters of the past, he announced the transition from prehistory to man's true history. He then added, as a remarkable feature of his work, a tenth stage of development in which he prognosticated the future. Would his friend Voltaire have countered with the two sentences from the *Essai sur les mœurs*: "the historians who believe they can thus predict the future are unworthy to write on what has happened" and "sane reason teaches that he who predicts the future is a knave and a fool"?[94]

The many-colored richness of Voltaire's histories, his descriptions of varied cultural phenomena, all this is missing from Condorcet's stark outline of the progress of the human mind. Unquestionably, this is in part attributable to the fact that Voltaire could work for decades on his histories, while Condorcet, driven by the imminence of the guillotine, in haste sought to render his sketch of man's climb to ever greater happiness. But even with more time, more leisure, and more books, Condorcet's history

93. *Ibid.*, VI, 251-253, 272; VII, 178-180, 183, 386, 523 (*Instruct. pub.*); X, 70 (*À Monsieur ***), among many possible references.
94. Voltaire, *Œuvres complètes*, XI, 256 and 394 (*Essai ...*).

would have been restricted by his conviction that the growth of civilization is synonymous with the unfolding of rationality. There are many fascinating details in the *Esquisse* on political, social, economic, and cultural matters. But they are always treated as factors which either retard or advance the realm of human reason. The analysis of primitive economic life is adduced to stress the importance of leisure, of capital accumulation, and of division of labor for the development of the mind. Condorcet used the discussion of political events (almost *ad nauseam*) to prove that inequality and the lack of freedom results in mental stagnation. Religion appears only as the great enemy of intellectual progress. The Reformation was simply a revolt against authority which did not go far enough in its liberation of the mind. The arts' only role is to support or to illustrate the advance of a rational understanding of the world. Considering that Condorcet wrote the *Esquisse* without benefit of library, he revealed an astounding knowledge about the history of philosophy and science. With his far superior scientific knowledge and understanding he benevolently looks down on Voltaire's limited insights into this most important realm of civilization.[95] He reveals that same mastery in presenting scientific thought which characterized the *Éloges* he wrote as secretary of the Academy of Science. Voltaire had once praised him for those sketches: "The public hopes that each week another academician might die so that you might have a chance to speak of him."[96] It is altogether regrettable that Condorcet did not seriously undertake a history of science before the hectic days of the Revolution steeped him in other concerns.

However, Condorcet's sketch of man's past in the *Esquisse* is only in small measure the history of certain great scientists and thinkers whose genius "moved" humanity to enlightenment. The attention to those developments and inventions which tended to safeguard and disseminate knowledge is its more prominent feature. Here the treatment of the advance of the mind parallels the discussion of the spread of wealth (or perhaps its "socializa-

95. Condorcet, *Œuvres*, IV, 42 (*Vie de Voltaire*), and 222, 267 ("Avertissements ...").
96. *Ibid.*, I, 30 (*Correspondance*...). Morley, *op. cit.*, II, 228, also is full of praise for the *Éloges* as historical sketches of scientific development.

tion"?) for the benefit of all. Condorcet tied his division of history into stages to those events which constituted breakthroughs in the diffusion of knowledge. One such dividing point appears when society separates into those who teach and those who learn.[97] Another is the advent of alphabetic writing and a mathematical sign language for easier storing and transmitting of learning.[98] The subdivision of knowledge and research into specialized sciences and the creation of storehouses like the Alexandrian Library constitute another stepping stone in man's advancement.[99] The invention of printing becomes the most momentous event in history for Condorcet because it prevents a relapse into that barbarism where an elite could manipulate human knowledge for its unenlightened purposes.[100] The intellectual revolution wrought by Descartes signifies to him the advent of freedom for all men from all forms of irrational authority.[101] He praises the *philosophes* especially for their popularization of enlightened thought.[102] In all his investigations of the past he remains faithful to his conviction that man's progress depends not only on the growing understanding of the few but rather on the free access to knowledge for every human being. "All men have an equal right to be informed."[103] Only as each becomes knowing, and can thus employ his special gifts for the further growth of understanding, can mankind achieve the happiness, the peace, the brotherhood destined by nature.

Strictly speaking, the study of the past becomes the history of the common man only at that moment when the common man assumes his rightful position, that is, during the tenth stage following the Revolution. But even in the earlier nine stages, Condorcet views the past already from the perspective of that neglected factor, the common man. "We shall endeavor, above all, to exhibit the influence of this progress on the opinions and welfare of the great mass of people, in the different nations, at the different stages of their political existence."[104] Special attention must be given to

97. Condorcet, *Œuvres*, VI, 30 (*Esquisse...*).
98. *Ibid.*, VI, 53-56 (*Esquisse...*).   99. *Ibid.*, VI, 60-78 (*Esquisse...*).
100. *Ibid.*, VI, 103, 107, 138-143 (*Esquisse...*). See also: III, 403 (*Éloge de Franklin*), 565 (*Éloge de l'Hôpital*), and XII, 229 (*De la république, ou un roi est-il nécessaire à la conservation de la liberté?*)
101. *Ibid.*, VI, 169, 202 (*Esquisse...*). and also III, 633 (*Éloge de Pascal*).
102. *Ibid.*, VI, 186-189 (*Esquisse...*).   103. *Ibid.*, VI, 178 (*Esquisse...*).
104. *Ibid.*, VI, 232 (*Esquisse...*).

the relation between public opinion and the most advanced knowl-edge of a time.[105]   The difference between the religion of the books and the religion of the people must be investigated; the relation between laws and the people's sense of justice must be studied with greater care.[106]   All necessary material and observations for the common man's history will have to be collected.

It is this most obscure and neglected chapter of the history of the human race for which we can gather so little material from records, that must occupy the foreground of our picture; and whether we are concerned with a discovery, an important theory, a new legal system, or a political revolution, we shall endeavor to determine its conse-quences for the majority in each society.   For it is there that one finds the true subject matter for philosophy, for all intermediate conse-quences may be ignored except in so far as they eventually influence the greater mass of the human race.[107]

Thus, all history must be viewed through the common man; thus history can become the true science of man.

In his program for a history of the common man Condorcet summed up a body of thought for revolutionaries. He, more than any other of his revolutionary colleagues, visualized the age of the common man which the Revolution initiated. He foresaw, in innumerable details, the forces and realities of a world domi-nated by the common man and dedicated to the welfare of the common man. He was the quietest and the most reasonable revo-lutionary, but by the nature of his thought he was the most radical one, for his vision of the civilization of the common man was the most far-reaching revolutionary program imaginable. Even if the French Revolution had never occurred, the gradual realiza-tion of Condorcet's program would have been the greatest revolu-tion in human affairs. Most of the program of the French Revo-lution could have been accomplished by men with Voltaire's outlook; for the vaster revolution, which put the world into the hands of the common man and his rising expectations, one had to follow Condorcet.

Can the difference between these two men which underlies this breakthrough to the history and the world of the common man really be explained by reference to a world which changed

105. *Ibid.*, VI, 175 (*Esquisse...*).   106. *Ibid.*, VI, 234 (*Esquisse...*).
107. *Ibid.*, VI, 234-235 (*Esquisse...*).

between 1770 and 1794? That it seemed so to Condorcet we have seen before. Voltaire's world had been that of benevolent despots like Louis XIV, Peter I, Frederick II, and Catherine II; it was a world in which the rise of science and enlightenment were still dampened by the horrors of the legal murder of Calas and the disaster at Lisbon; in that world a reformer like Turgot could be summarily dismissed; while the sales of the *Encyclopédie* increased, the younger generation lost its respect for the elegance of language and manners; the effects of a gradual revolution in technology, biology, and chemistry were hardly felt by Voltaire. On the other hand, Condorcet could take faith from the great experiment of the American Revolution, the reforms of the French Revolution, and the first fruits of a new scientific and technological revolution. All this may readily be admitted, and yet the real difference between these two *philosophes* seems one of human outlook, of personality, of temperament, and of interest. In their respective attitude to the feasibility of a history of the common man they illustrate two positions toward life which differ in more than the experience of a younger and an older contemporary. If Voltaire was "one-half poet, one-half philosopher,"[108] Condorcet was three-fourths scientist, one-fourth philosopher. With the interests of the poet, Voltaire fought for aesthetic beauty of language; as a scientist, Condorcet wanted to create a more precise and useful language. While Voltaire sought to persuade by plays and wondrous fables like *Candide*, the geometer used probability calculus and scientific schemes of education. Where Voltaire feared for the preservation of the most delicate flowering of the mind and good taste if it were to fall into the crude hands and minds of the many, Condorcet dreamed of tables, charts, and intellectual devices whereby the most advanced thought could become accessible to all. Whereas Voltaire paid respectful deference to the miraculous appearance of genius, Condorcet sought ways to raise as many as possible to the level of genius. Voltaire never lost his sense for the precariousness of all human achievement; he sensed the ever-lurking barbarian in man and the indifference— even the hostility—of the universe to the works of man. He hedged on all simple solutions, was averse to system-building, and

108. Voltaire, *Lettres choisies*, II, 305.

sought refuge instead in paradox and wit. He glorified reason, but never lost sight of its limitation. Good taste and skeptical resignation to not-knowing were at least as important to him. On the other hand, Condorcet, the desperately sober and earnest scientist, did not hesitate to lead ideas to their conclusion. He transported the systematic quality of science into the less rational world of man, and unhesitatingly put more trust in the dictates of a science of man than the skeptical observation of human realities. Although his knowledge of science, especially in its quantitative character, was far superior to Voltaire's, it served him less well in the understanding of man. He correctly prophesied many realities of a brave new world, but his science misled him in not foreseeing the limitations and even the horrors of the age of all too common men. Did Voltaire's resignation to an imperfect but passable life, the only one possible in view of the limited human potential, entail a less correct prophecy? Did the future really belong to the younger *philosophe* with the more "modern" experience, who based his hopes on a visionary dream he called social science? Or did it belong to the resigned skeptic and wit who made fun of men when they ran after fanciful dreams? Underneath the two approaches to history lay world views and temperaments which are not merely the product of time. Condorcet once exclaimed: "The only founded reproach one can make against Monsieur Voltaire is that he exaggerated the evils of humanity."[109] But then Voltaire took pride in being a realist.

109. Condorcet, *Œuvres*, IV, 223 ("Avertissements...").

A TEMPERATE CRUSADE: THE
PHILOSOPHE CAMPAIGN
FOR PROTESTANT
TOLERATION

Geoffrey Adams

In 1788, in one of the last significant decisions of his administration, Louis XVI signed an edict releasing the Calvinists of France from the limbo to which they had been relegated by Louis XIV's revocation of their civil rights in 1685. Because the decision of 1788 fell short of giving the Calvinists full civil liberty, and because it was so soon to be superseded by the more radical legislation of the revolutionary decade, there has been a tendency to overlook its significance and to deprecate its worth. A recent study of French Protestantism in this period describes the edict of 1788 as "one more example of the clumsiness of the old regime, and of the obstacles which that regime faced in any effort to save itself through reform."[1] In fact the passage of the edict constituted a signal triumph of the liberal spirit over the opposition of most of the upper clergy, much of the magistracy, and, in certain parts of France, the unthinking prejudice of the Catholic masses. This triumph, as we shall see, was above all else the product of the active intervention of the French *philosophes* in behalf of their afflicted Calvinist fellow citizens and of the ideal of religious toleration.

The early history of French Calvinism is one of anguish and uncertainty. From their first appearance in the 1520's until 1598, the Calvinists enjoyed but brief periods of public tolerance, interrupted by bouts of active repression and bitter civil strife. Then,

GEOFFREY ADAMS *is associate professor of history of Loyola College (Montreal).*
1. Burdette C. Poland, *French Protestantism and the French Revolution: A Study in Church and State, Thought and Religion, 1685-1815* (Princeton, 1957), p. 88.

in 1598, by his Edict of Nantes, the Calvinists' one-time champion Henry of Navarre, since become the Catholic king of France, awarded his former coreligionists full civil rights in the hope that this concession would cause them to rally round the *panache blanc* of his newly established dynastic authority. To assure even more fully their support of the new regime, Henry IV allowed the Calvinists to maintain themselves in scores of fortified strongholds throughout the nation and thus permitted them to become a kind of state within the state. This pseudo-sovereignty was withdrawn from the Calvinist community by Cardinal Richelieu in 1629 following Calvinist subversion of royal authority in Languedoc and at La Rochelle in the 1620's. The Calvinists, however, remained in full possession of their purely civil rights until 1660.

With the accession to power of the young Louis XIV, government policy toward the Calvinists changed decisively. Bit by bit the provisions of the Edict of Nantes guaranteeing the civil status of the Calvinists were modified, even annulled; meanwhile, an increasingly intensive campaign of proselytization sought to draw the main body of French Calvinists into the Roman communion. Then, in 1685, came the sudden dramatic decision of the Sun King to revoke altogether the Edict of Nantes and thus to make the French Calvinists virtual aliens in the land of their birth.[2]

Whatever the motives of the king, the provisions of the Edict of Revocation left the Calvinists in a most unenviable position. Calvinist churches were declared outside the protection of the laws; the sacraments according to the Calvinist rite might no longer be practiced; most crippling of all, the pastors of the Calvinist community were obliged to quit the kingdom at once. Yet the Protestant laity was forbidden to follow the pastors into exile. By the terms of the 1685 legislation, France's Calvinist population was obliged to remain within the kingdom where it was to be the object of forceful proselytizing. Pending its complete return to the Catholic fold, this lay population was permitted a specific form of "non-Catholic" marriage and burial. But, to assure the long-term success of the campaign of conversion,

2. W. J. Stankiewicz, *Politics and Religion in Seventeenth-Century France: A Study of Political Ideas from the Monarchomachs to Bayle, as Reflected in the Toleration Controversy* (Berkeley, 1960), p. 196.

children of Calvinist parents henceforth were to be baptized within the Catholic communion.

In 1715 a government *ordonnance* cavalierly declared the conversion of France's Calvinist population complete. All Frenchmen were now either Catholics or "New Converts"; therefore all Frenchmen were henceforth subject to canon as well as civil law. This new legislation effectively deprived those Calvinists who had remained in France after 1685 of all security of status. The marriage of Calvinists in the presence of their own pastors was now declared to be adulterous; children of such marriage were illegitimate and might not expect the support of the courts in asserting their right to inherit. Thus, a generation after the Revocation, even more terrible options faced the French Calvinists than those left open in 1685. The Calvinists might attempt an illegal and dangerous exodus to join the refugee streams which had coursed across the frontiers of France since the beginnings of discriminatory legislation in the 1660's; they might seek security through a hypocritical conformity to a religion not their own; or they might essay a hazardous underground existence by remaining in France as practicing Calvinists. The penalties for this last course were barbarous. To be caught at an illegal church service could mean for men life sentences as galley slaves in the king's Mediterranean fleet, for women imprisonment in the medieval fortress at Aigues-Mortes. For pastors caught officiating at these services, at least until after the case of François Rochette in whose behalf Voltaire made a vain appeal to the authorities, the penalty was death.

The grim pressures thus brought to bear on the Calvinists helped to effect a radical change in the social basis of their church. In its earliest manifestations in sixteenth-century France, Calvinism had attracted converts from all social classes, including restive grandees who frequently embraced the new faith as a shield for anti-royalist attitudes. With the triumph of Cardinal Richelieu's policy of centralization, many of these aristocrats whose centrifugal political outlook was thus checked returned to the Catholic church in exchange for advantages at court promised by the wily cardinal. The dominant role in the Calvinist community thus passed to the substantial middle classes. With the punitive legislation of 1685 to 1715 these bourgeois elements either fled from the kingdom or gave token loyalty to the Catholic church. French Calvinism became overnight and by default a faith of artisans and peasants.[3] This new social orientation of French Calvinism was especially marked in the south of France, in Languedoc and in the Cévennes hills. Guided by self-appointed and sometimes illiterate prophets, the rural masses of the south formed themselves into a "church of the desert," whose illicit outdoor assemblies began soon after the Revocation and lasted until the Revolution. This religious fervor was matched by a willingness to take up arms against the king, as Louis XIV's legions discovered in their long and bitter campaign against the Camisard rebels (1702-1710). In the 1760's, rumors of a revived insurrectionary spirit among the Calvinist rural masses of the south brought the well-to-do bourgeois elements in the Protestant community to reassert their authority in the councils of their church.[4]

The reappearance of these bourgeois elements undoubtedly encouraged sympathy and support for the Protestant cause among the *philosophes*. The *philosophes*, discovering the plight of the Calvinists in mid-century, welcomed the ammunition provided by the aggrieved Calvinist minority for their long-term campaign against persecution, intolerance, and clerical authority. Yet the coming together of *philosophe* protectors and Calvinist protégés in the eighteenth century was never to be altogether harmonious. The Calvinists tended to look askance at the deistic ideas they found in the manifestoes designed to promote their own emancipation. And, skeptics or devotees of rational religion, the *philosophes* encountered among the Calvinists much of that same dogmatic spirit they were at such pains to combat in the Roman communion. Pierre Bayle, the father of French *philosophie*, whose Calvinist background forced him out of France after 1685, had passed devastating judgment on his fellow-exile the Calvinist theologian Pierre Jurieu, attacking him for intellectual intransigence and narrowness of view. This mental and moral gulf separating the *philosophes* and their protégés narrowed noticeably

3. Poland, p. 17.
4. David D. Bien, "Religious Persecution in the French Enlightenment," *Church History*, XXX (1961), 333.

with the renewed presence in the councils of French Calvinism of bourgeois Calvinists who were more ready than their zealous ancestors to accept an attenuated, deistic version of the Christian faith not too far removed from the Voltairean credo.

The attitude of mutual reserve between Calvinists and *philosophes* is apparent in those cases in which Voltaire and Rousseau intervened to promote increasing toleration.   Rousseau's Calvinist origins led many French Protestants to suppose that he would espouse their cause.   And, indeed, in an open letter to Christophe de Beaumont, the archbishop of Paris, published in 1763, Rousseau urged that all religions which respected the national morality, professed the basic dogmas of Christianity, and were devoted to peace, be accorded recognition.   Such a guarantee could be safely extended to France's Calvinists, who had been excited to rebellion in the seventeenth century not by the teachings of their theologians but by discontented grandees.   But, in contemporary France, "What intrigues or cabals can merchants or peasants form?"[5]   When pressed by the Calvinists to commit himself to more concrete intervention, Rousseau replied brusquely that his letter to the archbishop constituted a definitive step.   Smarting from the cool reception recently given his deistic *Émile* in Calvinist circles in Switzerland, Rousseau went on rather testily that "the Protestants, gentle perhaps when they are feeble, are very violent as soon as they become the stronger party."[6]   They ought to be content with the "tacit toleration" already allowed.

Like Rousseau's *Émile*, Voltaire's *Traité sur la tolérance* (1763) evoked a mixed reaction from Calvinist readers.   The *Traité* was a propaganda piece in favor of religious freedom.   "We have Jews in Bordeaux, Metz and Alsace; we have Lutherans, Molinists and Jansenists; can we not suffer and contain Calvinists on roughly the same terms under which Catholics are tolerated in London?"[7]   However, Voltaire made it abundantly clear that he remained opposed to all fanaticism, Calvinist as well as Catholic, and urged that the Calvinists, while deserving toleration, should

5. Jean-Jacques Rousseau, *Jean-Jacques Rousseau, citoyen de Genève, à Christophe de Beaumont, archevêque de Paris, etc.* (Amsterdam, 1763), p. 85.

6. Rousseau to Pastor Petitpierre, May 26, 1764, *Bulletin de la Société de l'Histoire du Protestantisme français*, III (1854), 329 (hereafter cited as *Bulletin*).

7. F.-M. A. de Voltaire, *Traité sur la tolérance, à l'occasion de la mort de Jean Calas* (n.p., 1763), p. 42.

remain without all the privileges of public worship and without access to certain high offices of state. Two Swiss Calvinists who read the manuscript made a vain appeal to the sage of Ferney to modify its "philosophic" tone. One pastor feared lest the pious reader be confused and troubled by Voltaire's mixture of good with "poisonous" reasoning.[8] But, with all their mental reservations about Voltaire's spiritual outlook, the late eighteenth-century Calvinists were lucid enough to recognize his contribution to their increasing freedom. Paul Rabaut, dean of the southern pastors, observed in 1768: "If we are enjoying relative tranquillity in our part of the world, it is to that man that we should give thanks."[9]

During this debate concerning their toleration, in which the *philosophes* vigorously participated after 1760, one of the most persistent and damaging charges leveled against the Calvinists was that they were congenital political subversives, given to republican and even to regicide views. Their sixteenth-century apologists Francis Hotman and Theodore de Beza had in fact advanced radical political theories; and the ambiguous political behavior of the Protestants in the 1620's lent some justification to the charge of subversion in the early part of the seventeenth century. But with the political settlement promulgated by Richelieu in 1629 the Protestants' tendency to political radicalism abruptly ended. Owing their continued civil freedom exclusively to the absolute monarchy established by the cardinal-prime minister and deprived of aristocratic leaders won back to Catholicism, the Calvinists in the years 1629-1685 sang a chorus of adulation for the monarchy even more lusty and more sustained than that intoned by their Catholic fellow citizens. One present-day scholar has argued very persuasively that this zealous submissiveness to the principles of divine-right monarchy made it virtually impossible for the Calvinists to find solid foundations for resisting their own expulsion in 1685.[10]

Indeed, even after the Revocation, the Protestants did not easily resort to anti-monarchical or insurrectionary principles. Opinion among them was bitterly divided. Pierre Jurieu, it is

8. Pierre Encontre to Paul Rabaut, Feb. 3, 1763, Archives of the Nîmes Consistory, Papiers Rabaut, XII, 158.
9. Paul Rabaut to Paul Moultou, Feb. 29, 1768, *ibid.*, I, E, fol. 198.
10. Emile-G. Léonard, "Le Protestantisme français au XVIIe siècle," *Revue historique*, CC (1948), 171 ff.

true, turned from a passionate defense of the monarchical ideal to notions of popular sovereignty in church and state, but his one-time friend and colleague Pierre Bayle argued as cogently that the Calvinists could expect relief and a return from their exile only from the indulgence of a monarch who might be taught by reasonable appeals to turn away from the dark counsel of reactionary clerics and ambitious courtesans.[11] After the brief relapse during the Camisard guerrilla war, the Calvinists who remained in France after 1685 abandoned the political radicalism of Beza and Hotman and turned to the quietistic outlook of the New Testament Matthew and Paul (or, for that matter, of Calvin himself).[12] Not even the expected descent on the French Mediterranean coastline of foreign Protestant soldiers during the wars of the eighteenth century tempted the Calvinists again to open revolt.

After mid-century the administration began to recognize the innate royalism of the Protestant masses. But reactionary pamphleteers did not allow the memory of Beza and the Camisard rebellion to die; the accusation of subversion plagued champions of toleration to the end. The speculative generalizations advanced by such *philosophes* as Montesquieu that there were natural affinities and parallels between Protestantism and republicanism added to the discomfiture of the Calvinists, whose main aim in the latter part of the century was to persuade the regime of their political respectability.

The real test of Protestant loyalty to the monarchical idea came of course with the cataclysmic events of 1789. The post-revolutionary fabrication of reactionary pamphleteers such as Xavier de Maistre that there was a conscious plot against the monarchy in which the Calvinists eagerly participated along with Freemasons, Jansenists, and *parlementaires* bears no relation to historical fact. In fact, the Calvinists of France, like the Catholics and freethinkers, had no conscious collective designs on French society before the Revolution. When the drama came, there were Calvinists to be found in every political camp: Antoine-Pierre-Joseph-Marie Barnave and the Marquis de Jaucourt were Feuil-

11. Guy Howard Dodge, *The Political Theory of the Huguenots of the Dispersion, with Special Reference to the Thought and Influence of Pierre Jurieu* (New York, 1947), pp. 232-233.
12. Poland, p. 59.

lants; Jean-Paul Rabaut Saint-Etienne and Marc-David Alba La-
source were Girondins; Jean-Bon Saint-André and Jean Julien of
Toulouse, Jacobins; and, finally, François-Antoine Comte de Bois-
sy D'Anglas was an opportunist like so many others. If any general
political tendency can be detected among those Calvinists who remained in France after the Revocation it is that of abiding loyalty
to the monarchy, interrupted only by the desperate guerrilla
conflict of the first decade of the century.[13]

Much of the *philosophe* effort in behalf of the Calvinists took
the form of essays and pamphlets putting the general case for
toleration in terms borrowed largely from John Locke. But a
great deal of energy and effort was expended as well in concrete
interventions on behalf of *galériens,* prisoners at Aigues-Mortes,
pastors and laymen arrested at "desert" assemblies, alleged par-
ricides, and a host of men and women whose social status was
jeopardized by their illicit Calvinist marriages.

The case of the Languedoc hosier Jean Fabre was typical, except perhaps for its especially happy ending. Fabre had served
on the king's galleys since 1756 as a voluntary substitute for his
aged father, arrested at a "desert" assembly. When two Frankfort
businessmen learned of his situation, they used the influence of
their brother-in-law, a banker in the army of the Duke de Broglie,
to pen a memorandum to Broglie's secretary. The missive came
ultimately to the attention of Madame de Pompadour, who secured Fabre's release through an appeal to her friend the "philosophic" minister of the navy, the Duke de Choiseul, in May,
1762.

Fabre's story attracted the attention of the liberal writer
Fenouillot de Falbaire, who thought that it justified dramatiza-
tion. The result was the play *L'Hônnête criminel, ou l'amour
filial,* written in the rather sentimental style of the contemporary
drame bourgeois. The locale is Toulon, where the hero, the
pastor's son André, is serving a galley sentence in his father's stead,
his only consolation the kind words of a "philosophic" ship
captain. A change in André's fortune comes when his father ar-
rives aboard the galley determined to end his vicarious sacrifice:[14]

---

13. *Ibid.,* introduction.
14. Fenouillot de Falbaire, *L'Honnête criminel, ou l'amour filial,* cited in J.-F.
Marmontel, *Poétique française* (Paris, 1763), p. 70.

Je viens avec transport reprendre en ces moments
Des fers qu'il n'a pour moi portés que trop longtemps

The captain, deeply moved, pays tribute to André's heroism:[15]

Ah que vos coeurs sont grands, sont au-dessus des nôtres
Vous étiez à mes pieds, c'est à moi d'être aux vôtres!

Louis XV, through the agency of the captain, extends a protective hand over his erring but faithful subjects. Father and son, pledging their eternal loyalty to king and country, are released, and the curtain falls on an idyllic scene of reconciliation.

Voltaire was delighted with the play and planned to have it performed at Ferney. Fenouillot, in true *philosophe* fashion, observed: "It is of little import to me that I have or have not written a good play provided that, on the occasion of its production, good acts in favor of my hero are performed."[16] Good acts did in fact ensue. Fenouillot and others encouraged Fabre to petition the king for the full restitution of his name and property. Louis XV obliged by granting Fabre such rehabilitation on April 24, 1768.

The liberation of Fabre was followed by similar acts of grace from Choiseul and others in the ministry open to "philosophic" argument. The freeing of the cobbler Claude Chaumont condemned for attending a "desert" rally in 1751 was the work of Voltaire, who wrote Choiseul in the hope that someone might act at court, "where people do not even know that there are Huguenots on the galleys."[17] Yet the last *galérien* was not to be freed until September, 1775, during the first liberal ministry of Louis XVI.

Even less well known than the plight of the *galériens* was the anguishing situation of the women imprisoned at Aigues-Mortes. When the Languedoc commandant, the "philosophic" Prince de Beauvau, learned of their confinement in 1768 he appealed at once to the minister in charge of "New Convert" affairs, the Comte de St. Florentin, securing as a result the release of three or four of the most aged prisoners. His solicitude for the fourteen remaining caused him to visit the scene of their captivity. The

15. *Ibid.*, p. 83.   16. *Ibid.*, p. 10.
17. Voltaire to Jacques Necker, Jan. 2, 1764, in C. Dardier, *Paul Rabaut. Ses lettres à divers* (Paris, 1898), I, 369 n.

Chevalier de Boufflers who accompanied him, described his impressions:[18]

A picture at once hideous and moving. We saw a large round room without air or daylight; fourteen women languished there in misery and tears; the commandant had difficulty in restraining his emotion. . . . I can still see them, upon his sudden appearance, fall at once at his feet . . . then, emboldened by our consolations, recounting all together to us their common sorrows. . . . The youngest of these martyrs was more than fifty years old; she had been eight when they arrested her.

Beauvau wrote to the ministry at once, asking for the immediate release of the women. By December 15, 1768, there remained only five, two of whom were shortly to die, while the others left the prison before December 28, when the tower was forever shut to its dread purpose.

Execution of their pastors and terrible sentences handed down against the laity faithful to the "desert" church had afflicted the Calvinists intermittently since 1685. In the 1760's an excitable Catholic populace, especially *le petit peuple,* who in certain parts of the Midi resented the solid prosperity of their bourgeois Calvinist neighbors, threatened the Protestant community of the south with a very lively new terror. On two occasions, which have become almost legendary, Calvinist parents were charged with resorting to murder to prevent their children's conversion to Catholicism. Thus, what had seemed the dawn of a new age of tolerance was suddenly darkened.

The first of these dramas began on October 13, 1761, when Marc-Antoine, son of the well-to-do Toulouse merchant Jean Calas, was found dead of apparent strangulation in his home. Rumor among neighbors immediately had it that, to forestall his intended conversion to Catholicism, Marc-Antoine had been murdered by his father with the complicity of his mother, a brother, and, most shocking of all, a young Catholic visitor to the family. The local judge drew up a formal charge and ordered the immediate imprisonment of the family pending trial.

The Toulouse parlement came to its famous decision on March 9, 1762: Jean Calas, guilty of murder, was to be broken on the

18. Report of the Chevalier de Boufflers, cited in C.-A. Coquerel, *Histoire des églises du désert* (Paris, 1841), I, 524.

wheel. Voltaire, informed of the judgment, cried out against the "murder of Calas, committed in Toulouse with the sword of justice,"[19] remarking later "I am interested in the case as a man, even, a little, as a *philosophe*."[20]

Encouraged in his expressed desire to intervene by a committee of Geneva Calvinists, Voltaire felt from the start that the fight to redeem Calas's name depended on an appeal to the enlightened members of the ministry at Versailles and on the "public voice, by which I mean the voice of all honest men who reflect and, in time, carry an infallible judgment."[21] The full story of the *affaire Calas* was incorporated in the *Traité sur la tolérance* which Voltaire was currently writing and was circulated among liberals at court as soon as it was completed in May, 1762. Persuading eminent lawyers to join him, Voltaire organized an appeal to the ministry at Versailles for a revision. The ministry made known its decision on March 9, 1765: the memory of Jean Calas was cleansed of the dread stain of consanguine murder, and his widow, son, and the Catholic visitor were discharged of all guilt. Voltaire jubilantly acclaimed the judicial revision as "the greatest fifth act in any theater."[22]

Paralleling the Calas affair was the case of Pierre-Paul Sirven of Mazamet, whose daughter Elizabeth, a convert to Catholicism, had been found drowned in a well-pit on January 4, 1762. Influenced by rumors spread by local Catholic zealots that Elizabeth was, like the young Calas, the victim of parents outraged by her conversion, and persuaded by a preliminary medical report that her body had been tossed into the well after probable death by strangulation, the local judge concluded that death was the result of murder. In anticipation of the verdict which condemned him and his wife to be executed, Sirven escaped to Switzerland with his family, where they received moral comfort and financial aid from Voltaire.

A direct petition to the ministry at Versailles proving ineffectual, Voltaire urged upon his new protégé the only course left open—an appeal to the original court at Mazamet. Feeling that

19. Voltaire, *Traité sur la tolérance*, p. 1.
20. Voltaire to Pyot de La Marche, March 25, 1762, *Œuvres* (Paris, 1879), XLII, 71.
21. Voltaire, *La Méprise d'Arras*, 1771, *ibid*., XXVIII, 425-426.
22. Voltaire to De Cideville, March 20, 1765, *ibid*., XLIII, 497.

Sirven's presence might be invaluable in gaining a revision, Voltaire wrote his friend at Toulouse, the liberal Abbé Audra, asking him to guarantee Sirven protection should he undertake the trip. Despite these preparations, the appeal to the Mazamet court proved unavailing. Sirven, undaunted, went on to the immediate court of appeal, the Toulouse parlement, seeking full rehabilitation plus damages. The parlement handed down its verdict in June, 1771: rehabilitation for Sirven and his wife, since deceased, and restitution of their goods and properties.

When the Sirven family sat down over dinner to fête this triumph with Voltaire at Ferney, a special sauce was added to their banqueting by the news that the Toulouse parlement had also ordered Sirven's Mazamet judges to pay the expenses of the original trial. Voltaire, justifiably rejoicing in this signal victory, flattered himself that the settlement of some one hundred French Calvinist families at his Ferney estate might help to prevent the recurrence of such *affaires*.[23]

The reversal of judgment in the Calas and Sirven cases ended a grim stanza of the Calvinist *plainte* on a relatively serene note. The accession of Louis XVI to the throne in May, 1774, was hailed by the Calvinists and their *philosophe* protectors as the dawn of an age of genuine enlightenment and toleration. Voltaire encouraged the Calvinists to believe that "at the first opportunity there will be a regulation concerning marriages which will assure the status of children and the tranquillity of families."[24]

Real hope for change lay primarily in the disposition of some of the new sovereign's first ministers. The Calvinists urged Voltaire to use his influence with the most liberal of these.[25] One result of his intercession was the decision of the ministry not to renew a customary ban on the Calvinists' free disposal of their goods and properties. This economic relief brought a delighted response from those affected.[26] In 1779, the *philosophe*-adventurer Pierre Caron de Beaumarchais, asked by the ministry to draw up a report on the worsening economic situation, proposed that Calvinists be admitted to the chambers of commerce in the larger

23. Voltaire to Paul Ribotte, Oct. 25, 1771, *Bulletin*, IV (1855), 248.
24. Voltaire to Pastor Gal-Pomaret, Sept. 24, 1774, Archives of the Nîmes Consistory, LG, fol. 20.
25. Abbé de Véri, *Journal*, ed. Jehan de Witte (Paris, 1928), I, 253.
26. Rabaut to Etienne Chiron, April 5, 1775, in Dardier, II, 184.

French cities.[27] The proposal was ignored, although it made good economic sense in towns such as Bordeaux where Protestants had a large if not controlling interest in the vital shipbuilding industry.

The most active of the new ministers in behalf of toleration was Jacques Turgot, controller-general of finance from 1774 to 1776. Some years before, as a young seminary student, Turgot had defended toleration and attacked the Revocation:[28]

We have tolerant hearts; habit has made our minds fanatical. This way of thinking, which is too common in France, is perhaps the effect of the praise heaped upon the Revocation of the Edict of Nantes. Religion has been dishonored in order to flatter Louis XIV.

When a severe grain shortage threatened to develop into a crisis of national consequence in the spring of 1775, Turgot made bold to address letters to Calvinist pastors and to Catholic priests in Languedoc asking their aid in calming an excited populace. This was the first direct official contact between the administration and the Calvinist community since 1685 and constituted a kind of *de facto* recognition. Although Languedoc remained calm during the crisis, the pastors, seeing in Turgot's letter the promise of fuller recognition to come, resolved to preach a sermon on the obedience due the civil authority. In a letter to Turgot the pastors remarked that the unconditional royalism of their flocks was ample guarantee of civil peace while they waited patiently upon the king's grace to grant them toleration.[29]

As the day of Louis XVI's coronation approached, Turgot, backed by two ministers of state, Lamoignon de Malesherbes and the somewhat hesitant Comte de Maurepas, ventured to propose to his sovereign a change in the coronation oath. Might not the king replace the current vow to extirpate heresy with an older formula used by Louis XIV, which pledged that "all the churches of my kingdom should depend on my protection and justice."[30]

27. P. Caron de Beaumarchais, *Observation d'un citoyen, Œuvres* (Paris, 1809), IV, 481.
28. A.-J.-R. Turgot, *Deuxième lettre à un grand vicaire* (1754), *Œuvres* (Paris, 1913-1923), I, 425.
29. Gal-Pomaret, *Discours qui a été adressé par le pasteur protestant de Ganges en juin 1775*, Arch. Nîmes Cons., Papiers Gébelin, VI, fol. 83.
30. Turgot, *Formules de serment à substituer aux formules en usage, Œuvres* (Paris, 1809-1811), VII, 314.

In the end Maurepas's jealousy of the growing influence of Turgot at court and the strenuous efforts of the Catholic clergy persuaded the king not to accept the proposed modification in the oath. But Louis XVI's reply to Turgot praised the minister for acting as an *honnête homme* and for using forthright language.[31] Encouraged by the friendly tenor of this response, Turgot returned to the assault with a second *mémoire*, this time urging a frank policy of religious toleration.[32] The king again demurred. Turgot then proposed to bring back to France by a generous award of toleration the descendants of those Calvinists who had fled since 1685. Such toleration, as Frederick of Prussia was currently proving, would pay off economically. The arrival of these dedicated Christians in contemporary France would help to offset the losses to deism and irreligion which so upset pious patriots.[33] The liberal Abbé de Véri joined Turgot in stressing the considerable capital which the return of the French refugees would bring the state.[34] However, the ministry of Louis XVI was unwilling to act on Turgot's proposal. Meanwhile, Turgot's liberal colleague, Lamoignon de Malesherbes, lent a friendly ear to the briefs of a representative of the moderate northern Calvinists, Louis Dutens, asking for a civil form of marriage. Malesherbes sounded out the ministry as to the possibility of having parish priests officiate at Calvinist weddings purely as civil officials. The suggestion was rejected, but Malesherbes, acting on his own, wrote a letter to all intendants and bishops on May 11, 1776, denouncing the excessive zeal of priests who registered Calvinist children as *naturels* in the parish book. The priest in future should enter the child's name and status in strict accord with the statements made by his parents. Although Malesherbes's directive became formal law only in 1782, it constituted a great moral and psychological advance. Calvinist children henceforth enjoyed a secure status in society.

The fall of the ministry which had included Turgot and Malesherbes in May, 1776, dashed the newly aroused hopes of the

31. Louis XVI to Turgot, June 10, 1775, *ibid.*, IV, 554.
32. Turgot, *Projet de mémoire au roi, ibid.*, IV, 558-567.
33. Turgot, *Discours sur le rappel des Protestants prononcé en Conseil de France en 1775, Bulletin*, XXXVI (1887), 379-384.
34. Abbé de Véri, I, 383.

Calvinist community. Voltaire lamented that all reform "has been put very much aside and one must wait."[35] The appointment of the Swiss Calvinist Jacques Necker to high office in June, 1777, failed in the end to revive these hopes. Necker had resisted efforts by the Archbishop of Paris to convert him. In the face of the hostility of the Catholic clergy to his appointment he felt obliged to do his utmost to avoid further antagonizing clerical conservatives.[36]

It was from the *philosophe* camp that the Calvinists again received concrete support. The Marquis de Condorcet now entered the lists with a work "composed under the auspices of the parlement and distributed by enthusiasts who hope thus to enlighten the government."[37] Condorcet emphasized the modesty of the toleration asked for: "We do not ask that the Protestants may have public worship; we ask merely that they may have children."[38] There was surely no harm in opening the universities and certain public offices to Calvinists? He concluded his remarks with a warning: Should the Calvinists not soon find relief, America, that "vast land . . . where freedom of conscience and political liberty reign, where all men are equal,"[39] might prove irresistible.

In March, 1785, the young Marquis de Lafayette, fresh from America, leagued himself with Malesherbes, now a retired minister and private citizen, to work for Protestant relief. Encouraged by Malesherbes, Lafayette made a tour of Calvinist centers in the south, meeting many of the "desert" pastors. Meanwhile, Malesherbes wrote a *mémoire* in the spring of 1785 in which he submitted that the best solution to the Calvinist question was to rescind all the laws concerning so-called New Converts and leave the Protestants with the civil status allowed them by the terms of the Revocation itself.[40] This *mémoire* was circulated to members

35. Voltaire to Gal-Pomaret, April 18, 1776, *Bulletin*, VIII (1859), 486.
36. Baronne de Staël, *Considérations sur les principaux événements de la révolution française* (Paris, 1818), I, 82.
37. Louis Bachaumont, *Mémoires secrets pour servir à l'histoire de la république des lettres en France* (London, 1777-1789), XII, 235.
38. Marquis de Condorcet, *Réflexions d'un citoyen catholique sur les lois de France relatives aux Protestants* (n.p., 1778), p. 187.
39. *Ibid.*
40. C.-G. de Lamoignon de Malesherbes, *Mémoire sur le mariage des Protestants, en 1785* (n.p., 1787).

of the Paris parlement known to be sympathetic to the cause of toleration.[41]

In December, 1785, with the blessing of Lafayette and Malesherbes, Rabaut-Saint-Etienne, the son of the dean of Languedoc pastors, Paul Rabaut, came to Paris to act as liaison between the Protestants and their champions at court.[42] Like his father, Rabaut-Saint-Etienne was a pastor, but unlike the venerable leader of the Calvinist "desert" community, he was a half-convert to *philosophie*. He came to admire Malesherbes deeply: "He is a clever man who deflects the prejudices which he cannot destroy; a lawmaker who speaks in the phlegmatic and impassive tone of the law where a flood of rhetoric would destroy everything."[43] The gulf of misunderstanding which in an earlier generation had separated the *philosophes* and their protégés narrowed considerably with the meeting of these two minds. The ensuing mutual comprehension at last placed toleration within reach. By July, 1786, Malesherbes, Lafayette, Rabaut-Saint-Etienne, and two new recruits to the campaign, the liberal writer Pierre-Louis de Lacretelle and a Paris *parlementaire*, M. de Bretignères, were pondering the next step in the pleasant surroundings of Malesherbes's country estate.

Their cheery confidence was upset when they received an order from the Baron de Breteuil, the minister in charge of New Convert affairs, that Rabaut-Saint-Etienne be excluded from the discussions "because the policy of the ministry wills it thus."[44] But happily, Breteuil's conversion to the cause of toleration was soon to follow and to prove of great value. The conversion resulted from Breteuil's interest in the dilemma of the Marquise d'Anglure, daughter of a marriage between a rich Calvinist and a Catholic. The Bordeaux parlement in 1783, by declaring the marquise an illegitimate child, had disinherited her. Her appeal against this verdict reached the Conseil des Dépêches in 1786. Moved by her situation, Breteuil gathered evidence from all the country concerning

41. Anon., *Projet d'édit concernant les Protestants*, May, 1785 Archives Nationales, 01 605, fol. 18.
42. Marquis de Lafayette, *Mémoires, correspondance et manuscrits* (Brussels, 1837-1839), II, 205.
43. Rabaut-Saint-Etienne, letter-report to Bordeaux committee, Feb. 12, 1788, Arch. Nîmes Cons., Reg. B 33, fol. 4.
44. *Ibid.*, fol. 5.

the chaos and injustice occasioned by France's laws dealing with Calvinist and mixed marriages. In the end he himself penned a brief in which, echoing Malesherbes, he suggested the simplest of remedies—the reissuing of Louis XIV's 1685 legislation concerning the marriage of Calvinists. "It is in the very laws of Louis XIV . . . that we find the wisest means of restoring a civil status to the Protestants."[45] The liberal Bishop of Alais, consulted beforehand by Breteuil, agreed with the wisdom of the proposal.[46]

A promising occasion for presenting the views which Breteuil now shared with the Malesherbes group came with the convocation of the Assembly of Notables in February, 1787, to help cope with the government's growing financial problems. Lafayette, a member of the Assembly's Second Bureau, rose before his colleagues on May 23 to move that the king be petitioned to grant civil rights to the Calvinists.[47] Malesherbes's nephew, the Bishop of Langres, seconded the motion, paying generous tribute to its sponsor: "Lafayette, he said, had talked as a *philosophe*, but he himself, as a bishop, liked [Calvinist] temples better than [irregular prayer-] meeting houses and ministers better than pulpiteers."[48] The following evening, the Second Bureau voted to forward to the king a petition in favor of toleration by which, in their words, a large body of loyal Frenchmen "would be relieved from the oppression of a proscription contrary alike to the general intention of religion, to good order, to population, to national industry, and to all principles of morality and politics."[49] The petition elicited no response.

Again the campaign needed a new stimulus. It came this time with the publication in the early summer of 1787 of the *Consultation* in defense of the Marquise d'Anglure by the liberal lawyer G.-J.-B. Target, a masterful and persuasive treatise ranging over all aspects of the Protestant dilemma. Mixed marriages like the one at issue, Target argued, ought to be tolerated because

45. Baron de Breteuil, *Mémoire ou rapport général sur la situation des Calvinistes en France,* Oct. 1786, cited in C.-C. de Rulhières, *Eclaircissements historiques* etc. (n.p., 1788), II, 60.

46. Bishop of Alais, "Mémoire sur le mariage des Protestants," Arch. Natl., H 1639, manuscript note.

47. The account which follows of Lafayette's action in the Second Bureau is taken from L. Gottschalk, *Lafayette between the American and the French Revolution* (Chicago, 1950), pp. 315-317.

48. *Ibid.*   49. *Ibid.*

"when it comes to separating the couple, to disturbing the public peace, to destroying social status, and to throwing children into the nether world of illegitimacy, the conscience of the sovereign must be deeply troubled."[50]   The style of Target's brief was described as "less that of an advocate than of a *philosophe*."[51]   Malesherbes, after reading the manuscript, had urged its publication "because I foresee that it will be on the occasion of [the publication of] this brief that a motion will be made on behalf of the [Protestant] affair in general."[52]   Malesherbes appealed to Target on July 25 to "work on the drawing up of the law concerning the Protestants."[53] Target in turn got in touch with Rabaut-Saint-Etienne, who, frustrated at his long stay in Paris without results, had just published a pamphlet summing up Calvinist aspirations and arguing boldly for a toleration which would include public worship.[54]

Events abroad now conspired to aid those fighting for toleration within France.   Frederick William II of Prussia invaded the Netherlands in September, 1787, on the pretext that its pro-French Patriot party had insulted his sister, wife of the Prince of Orange.   Amsterdam fell to the aggressor as did France's traditional allies the Patriots, most of whom were Calvinist.   The French ambassador at The Hague, the Comte de Saint-Priest, urged his government to open its doors to these beleaguered allies and allow them freedom of conscience should they seek asylum.[55] Such a step might serve as "rather a fitting avenue of approach to the law which it is hoped will be obtained in this matter from the wisdom of the king and his council."[56]

Feeling that the moment was propitious, Malesherbes agreed to rejoin the ministry, this time without portfolio, in June, 1787. In hectic twice-weekly sessions he and Rabaut-Saint-Etienne "pleaded, argued, wrote and often groaned"[57] their way through

50. G.-J.-B. Target, *Consultation sur l'affaire de la dame Marquise d'Anglure, etc.* (Paris, 1787), p. 67.
51. Bachaumont, *op. cit.*, XXXV, 336.
52. Target, *Journal*, cited in *Bulletin*, XLIII (1894), 607.
53. *Ibid.*, p. 605.
54. Rabaut-Saint-Etienne, *Réflexions impartiales d'un philanthrope sur la situation présente des Protestants, et sur les moyens de la changer* (n.p., 1787).
55. Memorandum of Comte de St.-Priest to Comte de Montmorin, Autumn, 1787, Arch. Natl., H 1639, fol. 19.
56. *Ibid.*
57. Rabaut-Saint-Etienne, Report to Bordeaux committee, fol. 13.

the final preparation of an edict to be placed before the Paris parlement for approval. Confident that the edict concerning the Calvinists would find favor in the parlement, the ministry decided to link to it a much less palatable fiscal measure, which launched a subscription to a loan of 450,000,000 livres. The king appeared before a special royal session of his parlement on November 19, 1787, to request the acceptance of "a project which I resolved upon a long time ago," the provision of "natural rights and what the state of society permits" to France's non-Catholics.[58] The chancellor, Malesherbes's cousin Lamoignon, added that the government was espousing a "wise tolerance and not a culpable indifference to all forms of worship."[59] But the *parlementaires* resented the government's attempt to add the edict concerning the loan as a rider to the Protestant bill and balked. Fortunately, a more serene atmosphere returned when the parlement reconvened on December 7. The edict concerning non-Catholics was again submitted, this time with no strings attached. After preliminary discussion, the *parlementaires* submitted their comments and criticisms to the king on January 27, 1788. The king and Malesherbes agreed to some minor modifications; the parlement in turn considered these and registered the edict as law on January 29. The final vote in its favor was overwhelming: 96 to 17.

The preamble to the edict sums up succinctly both the extent and the limitations of the victory gained for the Protestants.[60]

The Catholic religion ... will alone enjoy in our realm the rights and honors of public worship; while our other, non-Catholic subjects, deprived of all influence upon the order established in our states, declared in advance and forever incapable of forming a single body within our realm ... will obtain from the law only what natural justice does not permit us to deny them, namely the authentication of their births, marriages and deaths.

Full satisfaction would have to await the Revolution; still the main battle for Protestant toleration had been won. For although the edict of 1788 fell short of granting full civil rights, it marked an irrevocable step in that direction. Public worship was denied

58. S.-N.-H. Linguet, *Annales politiques etc.* (London, 1777-1792), XIII, 100.
59. *Ibid.*
60. *Édit du roi concernant ceux qui ne font pas profession de la religion catholique, etc.* (Paris, 1788).

the Calvinists in law, but in practice it was now resumed with the winking complicity of the authorities in all but a few areas. The elder Rabaut expressed a view typical of the Calvinists who had graduated from the frenzy of the Camisard revolt to the sober realism of the later eighteenth century when he remarked: "Now that we have a civil existence, our respectful moderation will win for us all that this first benefit leaves us without."[61]   Much of the credit for this happy end to one of the bitterest chapters in French domestic history must be awarded the *philosophes* and their sympathizers within the government who had labored long to bring to France their ideal of religious toleration.

61. Rabaut to Charles de Végobre, April 11, 1788, Dardier, *op. cit.*, II, 368.

FRENCH ADMINISTRATORS AND FRENCH SCIENTISTS DURING THE OLD REGIME AND THE EARLY YEARS OF THE REVOLUTION*

Harold T. Parker

To contemporaries and to many partisan historians ever since, the French Revolution was "a violent break with the past, a miraculous and sudden explosion cursed by some, blessed by others, but all convinced that the France of 1789, 1793, [and 1814] had nothing in common with the France of Louis XIV or of Saint Louis."[1] As the Revolution and Napoleon receded into the past, however, the Orleanist historians, such as Guizot, and later the more profound analyst Tocqueville observed that in many respects the revolutionary period had continued fundamental tendencies of French society. Tocqueville, whose *Old Regime and the Revolution* was published more than a century ago, emphasized the tendencies in centuries of French history toward centralization of government and equality of condition, which the revolutionary period continued and accentuated. In the time of Tocqueville, when historical writing on the revolutionary period was less monographic than at present, such a generalized statement concerning the continuance and accentuation of the centralized administration was a profound contribution to historical thought. But now that historical investigation is more specialized and perhaps more subtle in its analysis of the processes of historical

HAROLD T. PARKER *is professor of history at Duke University.*
* In the preparation of this essay I am indebted to the staff of the Archives Nationales for the uniform courtesy with which they extended its privileges. Without their aid this article could not have been written. All manuscript references are to cartons or registers in the Archives Nationales.
1. Gustave Lanson, quoted in Alexis de Tocqueville, *Œuvres* (Paris, 1952), II (1), 348.

change, one wishes to know *in detail* which elements of the
central administration continued and which changed during
the revolutionary period. Did the administrative personnel continue or change? The administrative procedures? Policies?
Functions? One also wishes to learn *how* and *why* continuity and
change occurred and administrative institutions grew. Definite
answers to these questions will be attained only after the completion of archival studies of the many bureaus of the French administration of the Old Regime, the French Revolution, and
Napoleon. However, the questions can be explored and tentative
answers can be offered as segments of the history of the administration are investigated. With these questions in mind this article
proposes to examine such a segment—the developing and continuing use of French scientists during the Old Regime and early
revolutionary years in the process of making decisions concerning
the regulation and supervision of French industry. Along the way
the role of ideas in maintaining administrative continuity and in
initiating change will be noted.

Nothing was simple about the Old Regime in eighteenth-
century France. For centuries the French economy, society, and
government, as well as the ideas defending or attacking them, had
developed inextricably together, and no single words, except perhaps "intricacy" or "complication," can satisfactorily define any
one institution.

"Intricacy" and "complication" would have to be applied to
the relations of the royal administration and French industry.
Although legally the controller general had the supervision of
French commerce and manufacture, nearly every other government department (the ministries of War, Navy, and Foreign Affairs, and the Household of the King) made decisions which affected French industry. And among the multifarious offices and
associated agencies of the controller general there were several
(the intendancies of finance, the divisions of "Eaux et Forêts"
and of "Ponts et Chaussées," the Ferme Générale, and the Régie
of powder and saltpeter) whose activities had implications for
manufactures. Nevertheless, within the sprawling, loosely co-
ordinated French administration there was one ministry, that of
the controller general, and within that ministry one bureau, that

of Commerce, which might justifiably claim to be the center of administrative thought concerning French industrial problems.[2]

Consultative in theory, the Bureau of Commerce was composed of four intendants of commerce and of six to eight auxiliary deputies from the chief commercial and industrial towns. Each of the intendants came to be responsible for an industry and a group of généralités.[3] They conducted preliminary investigations of petitions from industrialists and inventors and made recommendations to an executive officer (a director of commerce or a controller general), who co-ordinated their activities. From 1781 to 1787, however, there was no director of commerce and the controllers general were either nonentities in the field of industrial policy or uninterested in its details. For six years, each intendant of commerce tended to go his own way. Though the "committee" of intendants still met and the full Bureau of intendants and deputies held sessions, each intendant conducted the preliminary investigations, prepared the influential first reports, and developed or failed to develop policies for his généralités and industries. To a degree anarchy prevailed. Some intendants believed in regulation, others were lukewarm to it; some kept abreast of the routine of affairs, others fell behind. Most important, there was no administrator to develop a coherent economic or industrial policy for the kingdom. To restore administrative efficiency and a unity of direction and of policy especially necessary during the industrial depression which followed the Eden Treaty (1786), the Chief of the Royal Council of Finances, Loménie de Brienne, abolished the posts of three intendants of commerce and appointed the fourth, Tolozan, to be, in effect, director of commerce and manufactures for the

2. The history of the changing structure of the Bureau of Commerce through the eighteenth century is outlined in an essay by Eugène Lelong, published by the Minister of Public Instruction. (See: Ministère de l'instruction publique et des beaux-arts. Archives nationales. Conseil de commerce et bureau de commerce, 1700-1791. *Inventaire analytique des procès-verbaux*, by Pierre Bonnassieux. *Introduction et table* by Eugène Lelong [Paris, 1900]. Hereafter referred to as Bonnassieux and Lelong.)

3. For example, one intendant of commerce, Tolozan, supervised (a) the fabrication of hosiery and other knitted goods throughout the kingdom and (b) all industries, except those specifically assigned to his colleagues, in the généralités or provinces of Rouen, Caen, Alençon, Brittany, Bourges, Orléans, and Moulins. ("Compte rendu par M. Tolozan des différents objets qui concernent son Département, Envoyé à M. de Villedeuil, Contrôleur Général des finances, le 13 Mai 1787," F12 657.)

kingdom.[4] Tolozan worked closely with the reorganized Bureau, but he retained supervision over the preliminary investigations, flow of correspondence, and preparation of first recommendations. Momentarily, he was able to restore a degree of efficiency and coherence to royal industrial policy.

In this administration years and years of discussion of particular cases and the steady thought of several directors of commerce had developed both a process of decision-making and a complicated network of considerations for members of the Bureau of Commerce to keep in mind when they were viewing matters such as a petition for government support of a factory employing an allegedly novel device. A petition would arrive at the office of the Bureau's secretary, who (from 1781 to 1787) would refer it to that intendant of commerce supervising the *généralité* or industry of its origin. The intendant would determine whether the question raised could be decided on his own knowledge or whether additional information should be sought. Such information could be obtained by asking for the previous documents on the case or by sending the petition to representatives of the Ferme Générale (How will a toll exemption affect the king's revenue and the conditions under which one signed a lease? What of this tariff proposal?), to officials of the division of "Eaux et Forêts" (Is sufficient wood available for fuel?), to a scientist (Is this process novel? Is it any good?), to the deputies of the commercial and industrial towns in the Bureau of Commerce (How will this proposal affect the general prosperity of the kingdom and, specifically, of your region?), or to the intendant of the *généralité* in which the petition originated (Tell me, in effect, about the petitioner, his circumstances, the validity of his proposal, and its relations to the local economy). After assembling these data, the intendant of commerce would prepare a report. On the balance of a number of considerations he would offer a recommendation, to be discussed and then accepted or modified in a meeting of all the intendants of commerce and forwarded to the controller general for approval. In reaching a decision many issues would be considered first by the responsible intendant of commerce, then by the committee of intendants, and occasionally by the controller general.

4. Bonnassieux et Lelong, p. xli.

These issues might concern (1) questions about the access of the factory to fuel, raw material, market, labor, and transportation; (2) principles governing the tests of new processes, the imposition of zoning rules, the regulation of methods of labor and of manufacturing methods, and the granting of such encouragements as permits to cut wood for fuel, exclusive privileges to manufacture, imposition of tariffs and tolls, and exemption from tariffs and tolls; (3) policies to be pursued for each region and each major industry; and (4) assumptions regarding the nature of the kingdom, the interrelations of agriculture, industry, and commerce, and the necessity of a favorable balance of trade. After a decision in a case had been reached, the accumulated papers were filed, by either industry or region, in the cartons of the supervising intendants of commerce.[5]

Through the seventeenth and eighteenth centuries French administrators had involved French scientists in this process of making decisions and developing policy considerations. The use of scientists was suggested by the conditions and problems of French industry and by the ideas and activities of the scientists themselves. Obviously, it would be imprudent, not to say unscholarly, to attempt here a description of French industry in the eighteenth century. One can describe, however, the French industrial world as it appeared in the administrative reports, and hence, in the minds of French administrators. The reports were peopled with artisans, inventors, promoters, and manufacturers of all types. Occasionally there was the honorable artisan, intelligent and skilled, who understood his craft and was devoted to its perfection.[6] He insisted on giving his product its last polish before exhibiting it for sale. He might test new products for the Bureau. He might be "Sieur Perret, Me Coutellier, rue de Tissanderie," whose published *Description of the Craft of the Cutler* was ap-

5. "Compte rendu par M. Tolozan des différents objets qui concernent son Département, Envoyé à M. de Villedeuil, Contrôleur Général des finances, le 13 Mai 1787," F12 657.

6. See, for example, "Observations faites par M. De Bacalon, Intendant du commerce dans son voyage en Picardie, Artois, Haynaut, et Flandre, l'an 1768," F12 650; Trudaine to Sage, Jan., 1777, F12 1330; report by Berthollet "Sur un acier fondu présenté par M. Tripier," Nov. 30, 1785, F12 656; folder entitled, "1787; 3 pièces: Le Sr. Bara, Serrurier méchanicien...", F12 1396; "Mémoire sur l'état actuel de la filature des cotons," considered at the Bureau of Commerce, May 2, 1790, F12 1341.

proved by the Academy of Sciences.[7]   Yet, partly because he was devoted to the perfection of a handicraft process, he was unconsciously falling behind his English competitors.

More frequently, however, there appears in the reports an artisan of the other extreme: ignorant, negligent, a creature of blind routine working somewhat in the dark, possessing perhaps a special family recipe or trick of manufacture, secretive, suspicious of royal authority, and sometimes irrational in his approach to technological problems.[8]   As late as 1784 an observer remarked that "the theory of glass-making had made great progress in France during the last three centuries," but its principles were ignored by nearly all glassmakers.   Very few of these examined their methods. "Each master glassworker has his way of operating, and this way is generally a routine.   The director often is only a simple workman who slavishly follows his predecessors."[9]   Roland de la Platière, inspector of manufactures at Amiens, remarked that before the publication in 1762 of the treatise on bleaching by the English chemist Home, French workmen bleached cloth gropingly, by practices at once minute and uncertain.   The artisans did not know precisely what they were doing or what was happening in their processes, and they made a mystery of both their ignorance and their knowledge.[10]   Turgot, as intendant of Limoges, wrote in 1767 to Trudaine de Montigny, of the Academy of Sciences:

You know better than anyone the state of the art of dyeing.   The most common procedures are not widely known.   The craft is different, so to speak, with each dyer; each one knows a certain number of procedures that he keeps carefully to himself and confides to no one; the

7. Report by Macquer on the "Acier fin présenté par M. Sanche...," July 26, 1783, F12 656.

8. "Mémoire sur divers moyens de perfectionner et d'accélérer le moulinage des soyes...par George Villard," circa 1765 à 1758, F12 1449; Esmangart to Trudaine, Bordeaux, Dec. 21, 1773, F12 1300; "Procès–Verbal dressé [par Grignon] à Rives en Dauphiné," Aug. 9, 1778, F12 1303; "Observations sommaires [de Grignon] sur les fabriques de fer et d'acier de la Province de Dauphiné," August 20, 1778, F12 1300; "Mémoire pour le Sieur Joseph Esnard, entrepreneur de la verrerie de Pierre Bénite," circa 1778, F12 1488B; Montaran to Brisson, January 5, 1780, F12 1327; Inspector Libour to De Montaran, Dec. 5, 1784, F12 1327; "Observations faites par M. De Bacalon, Intendant du commerce dans son voyage en Picardie, Artois, Haynaut, et Flandre, l'an 1786," F12 650; Report on "Manufacture Roialle d'horlogerie," circa Feb., 1788, F12 1325A; Roland de la Platière, Encyclopédie méthodique: Manufactures, arts et métiers (3 volumes and a supplement: Paris, 1785-1790), II, 237, 265-266; Journal des arts et manufactures, Prospectus.

9. Anonymous, "Mémoire sur les Verreries," 1784, F12 1486.

10. Roland de la Platière, I, Part 1, 59.

operatives who work with him are themselves ignorant of the trick on which success depends. It follows that the skill of each dyer is quite limited and that each one who succeeds a little better than the rest in one color enjoys a little monopoly of which he cannot be deprived and which he utilizes to exact a higher price of the manufacturer. Since a dyer is not able to succeed as well with other colors, the manufacturer is obliged, in order to fill out his range of patterns, to address himself to several dyers and sometimes even to transport his fabrics to distant places, all of which raises the price. New discoveries may remain the secret of a few for a century, and run the risk of being lost. The craft itself improves very little, because this mysterious veil which envelops all its operations does not permit educated physicists and chemists to learn what is already known. Before they can engage in researches for the advancement of the skill, they must lose time and money inventing those operations which simple artisans employ every day and obstinately persist in keeping secret. By their secretiveness the craftsmen who ply the trade most susceptible of being enlightened and perfected by the researches of physicists and chemists deny themselves the opportunity of acquiring knowledge infinitely more extensive than that which they possess. The craft remains condemned to a perpetual mediocrity.[11]

Amid the artisans and other members of French society, there were inventors and promoters of every description. Vaucanson, the inventor of silk-throwing machinery, was only one author to remark on the craze of many people to pass as "creators." "They were charmed to be able to say, I invented this machine; I perfected this craft; I made such a discovery."[12] Some of these were earnest students of a technological difficulty that was obstructing the progress of an entire industry; others were cranks. Both types were apt to be slightly mad in their devotion to a single project. Somehow French administrators, who wished to encourage inventors and invention, had to discriminate between the fanatic whose machine or procedural innovation was a valuable contribution to industrial progress and the crackpot whose device was of no great use or novelty. Then there were the promoters, offering to establish with government subsidy a factory whose product would equal or surpass that of England. Some of these projectors, such as John Holker, were imaginative, driving industrial capital-

11. Turgot to M. de Trudaine de Montigny, May 14, 1767, F12 1330. The observations of this passage are confirmed by Roland de la Platière in *Encyclopédie méthodique*, I, xxxi-xxxii.
12. "Une lettre de Vaucanson," Oct. 5, 1765, F12 1449.

ists; others were get-rich-quick schemers, eager to swindle the government out of a few thousand livres.

To deal with the artisans, inventors, and schemers, French administrators needed informed counsel. They needed the aid of educated men, such as the scientists, who were accustomed to analyzing materials and processes, to setting up tests, and to seeking a rational explanation for what had occurred. There was support in seventeenth-century theory and practice for using scientists in a practical way on behalf of industrial progress. Descartes had "published in 1631 a short treatise on the simple machines of his time,"[13] and later had suggested the establishment of an industrial museum for housing the most modern tools and machines. Professors of mathematics and physics, one to each industry, would explain to artisans the operation of each machine and the nature of new discoveries.[14] Colbert persuaded Louis XIV to charter in 1666 the Royal Academy of Sciences and later to have constructed a small museum of technology. The 1699 Règlement of the Academy of Sciences linked the Academy to the museum. Article XXXI of the Règlement provided that "The Academy will examine, on the King's order, all the machines for which a royal privilege is solicited. It will certify whether they are novel and useful, and the inventors of the approved machines will leave a model" for placement in Colbert's technological museum.[15] Later in the eighteenth century the local academies of sciences, belles-lettres, and arts of Lyons, Dijon, Rouen, Bordeaux, and Montpellier as well as the Royal Society of Medicine in Paris began to appraise inventions.[16] Meanwhile, in 1711 the Royal Academy of Sciences had charged the physicist and mineralogist Réaumur "to

13. Joseph Fayet, *La Révolution française et la science, 1789-1795* (Paris, 1960), p. 285.

14. *Ibid.*   15. *Ibid.*, p. 290.

16. "Extrait des Registres de la Société Royale de Médecine," Nov. 10, 1778, F12 1502; "Rapport de Messieurs les Commissaires nommés par la faculté de médecine de Paris sur les Casseroles du Sieur Doucet," Aug. 2, 1779, F12 1308; "Examen [par De Motigny] d'un instrument proposé . . . par le Sr Grenier," June 22, 1780, F12 1325A; folder entitled "1781; 10 pièces; Mémoires des Srs Orsel et Saulnier, négociants à Lyon . . . ," F12 1506; Morize to Tolozan, June 27, 1781, F12 1453A; Geraud de Fonmartin to Calonne, *circa* Dec., 1784, F12 1502; "Extrait des Registres de L'Académie des Sciences, Arts et Belles Lettres de Dijon," Dec. 16, 1784," F12 1489B; folder entitled "1785; 10 pièces; Mémoire de Sr Thomassy, Inventeur d'une machine pour retordre les soies et cotons . . . ," F12 1453B; Roland de la Platière, Supplement to Vol. II, p. 32; André Rémond, *John Holker, manufacturier et grand fonctionnaire en France au XVIIIe siècle, 1719-1786* (Paris, 1946), pp. 49, 98-99.

prepare an inventory of all the crafts and manufactures." The efforts of Réaumur and his associates eventuated in a technological encyclopedia whose successive volumes attempted to depict the best methods and processes of each craft.[17] At the same time individual scientists prepared treatises on the chemistry and practice of dyeing, glassmaking, and iron manufacture. All this activity on the part of the scientists—the steady appraisal of thousands of inventions, the encyclopedic description of industrial processes, the individual treatises—was sustained by the conviction that science should be immediately useful to industry.

The Bureau of Commerce, in response to its continuing problems and developing policies, extended the use of scientists. Believing in the idea of lending government aid to inventors, but not wishing to be "taken in," the Bureau requested members of the Academy of Sciences to test new products and processes, the first recorded request being in 1725.[18] It appointed scientists as permanent salaried consultants: Dufay, Hellot, Macquer, and Berthollet in the art of dyeing,[19] Desmarest in paper manufacture,[20] Molard in textile machinery,[21] and others. To them, too, new products were referred.[22] A typical letter of referral is that of Tolozan to Berthollet, March 18, 1786:

Widow Pallouis who has already petitioned the administration several times but has always been turned down for failure to reveal the secret and the process she pretends to possess for making silk braid is now ready to have both examined. With your usual sagacity will you thoroughly study the truth and usefulness of what she announces, have her perform those experiments that seem necessary, and send me your report and recommendation.[23]

Scientists were employed by the Bureau in other ways. In the first decades of the eighteenth century the Bureau spent most of its time discussing the issuance and revision of regulations of methods of production and quality of product, chiefly in the cloth industries. Regulation, it believed, would elevate the activity of ignorant, negligent artisans to the respectable level of the best

17. Rémond, p. 21.
18. Bonnassieux and Lelong, p. xxvii.
19. *Ibid.*, pp. xxvii-xxviii.
20. *Ibid.*
21. Molard's concluding report on some of his responsibilities was presented to Roland, minister of the interior, Nov. 22, 1792, F12 1343A.
22. See reports of Hellot, Macquer, and Berthollet listed in notes 46, 48, and 49.
23. Tolozan to Berthollet, March 18, 1786, F12 1448.

current processes.[24]   But how could the best processes be pried
from secretive workmen?   The Bureau in 1733 commissioned the
chemist Dufay to confer with expert dyers, to conduct his own
experiments for the improvement of dyeing, and then to correct
the regulations of 1669 with respect to the dyeing of woolens,
linens, and silks.[25]

Regulation could be viewed as a form of instruction, as an
attempt to educate illiterate, inefficient operatives who were difficult to move by persuasion.   Later, after mid-century, as the evils
of excessive rule-making began to become apparent and to be
decried, the Bureau tried other means of instruction.   In Paris
Louis XVI established in 1782 an industrial museum at the Hotel
de Mortagne.   A geometer, Vandermonde, was appointed curator
and instructed to "assemble all that was technologically interesting
in French and foreign factories; construct those machines of recent
invention which the government wishes to diffuse; gather rare and
expensive tools which the Paris workshops lack and loan them on
occasion."[26]   In the chief manufacturing towns, resident inspectors, who sometimes prided themselves upon their knowledge of
chemistry, physics, and mathematics, counseled manufacturers
about the latest technological improvements.   Itinerant inspectors
traveled through France teaching the best methods of manufacture.   Gabriel Jars, Duhamel de Monceau, Chevalier Grignon
did this for iron and steel; Desmarest, for paper.   Jars and Desmarest were members of the Academy of Sciences; Duhamel and
Grignon, its correspondents.[27]   All four were thoroughly grounded

24. Léon Biollay, *Études économiques sur le xviiie siècle. Le Pacte de famine,
l'administration du commerce* (Paris, 1885), p. 354.
25. Bonnassieux and Lelong, *op. cit.*, p. xxvii; F12* 78, Dec. 13, 1731; F12* 80,
Dec. 17, 1733. Scientists were later consulted concerning the possible regulation of
the employment of varech (Le Noir to De Montaran, fils, April 24, 1781, F12 1486)
and sometimes called upon to give expert opinion on alleged violations of dyeing
regulations (F12* 106, Feb. 5, 1788).
26. Quoted in Fayet, p. 296.
27. "Journal de voyage de Jars [1769]," F12 1300; folder entitled "1778; 3
pièces; Mémoires et observations sur les fers et aciers fabriqués... sous la direction
du Chevalier Grignon," F12 1300; Grignon, "Description des opérations et des
machines de la manufacture d'acier de Néronville," April 20, 1778, F12 1303;
"Procès-verbal dressé [par Grignon] à Rives en Dauphiné," Aug. 9, 1778, F12 1303;
"Observations sommaires [de Grignon] sur les fabriques de fer et d'acier de la
Province de Dauphiné," Aug. 20, 1778, F12 1300; Administrative summary concerning the petition of Duhamel de Monceau [1778-79], F12 1300; folder entitled
"1781; 2 pièces, L'Intendant de Grenoble rend compte des moyens d'encouragement
...," F12 1300; Franc Bacquié, *Un Siècle d'histoire de l'industrie. Les Inspecteurs*

in geometry, chemistry, and physics. In addition, Hellot prepared a treatise on the dyeing of wool, Macquer on the dyeing of silk. Under the auspices of the Bureau, Desmarest published a treatise on the fabrication of paper and Berthollet treatises on the theory of dyeing and the production of iron and steel. The more modest of the treatises tried simply to describe the best current practices; the more ambitious essayed to explain the manufacturing process in terms of scientific theories and to reduce it to a few simple steps.[28] However, in its attempts to bring together the workman and the scientist, the Bureau encountered the problem of establishing mutual respect and communication. Antagonism between the two groups was always latent. The scientist tended to regard the artisan with condescension as a merely practical man; the artisan tended to dismiss the scientist as a mere theorist.[29] Cautious artisans concealed treasured craft secrets. They hid from Hellot and Macquer, for example, crucial steps in the dyeing process. When a reader of the treatises of the two chemists attempted to repeat the methods outlined, he often found himself checked by ignorance "of a slight preparation, of a delicate manipulation, of a twist of the wrist which was the secret of the workmen and on which success depended."[30] At the same time, the best-intentioned scientist frequently found it difficult to translate theoretic understandings into practical precepts that an ignorant artisan could comprehend.[31] When an inspector of manufactures, Brisson, proposed to derive a practical manual from Home's general treatise on bleaching, Macquer warned him to keep the manual simple, to reduce theory to a minimum, and to avoid such terms as alkali, acid, analysis, and fermentation. Brisson complied, and the result was a practical guide which, on Macquer's

des manufactures sous l'ancien régime, 1669-1791; étude historique et anecdotique d'après des documents inédits (Toulouse, 1927), pp. 33-37, 43-44, 370-371, 372, 375; Biollay, p. 432.

28. Roland de la Platière, I, xxxi.

29. "Mémoire de George Villard ... concernant le perfectionnement et l'œconomie des filatures et moulinages des forges en France," F12 1449; "Mémoire, dressé par George Villard ... sur les propriétés et les effets de la nouvelle mécanique qu'il a inventée," Nov. 28, 1774, F12 1449.

30. Turgot to M. de Trudaine de Montigny, May 14, 1767, F12 1330.

31. Roland de la Platière, Supplement to Volume II, pp. ii-iii; Esmangart to Trudaine, Dec. 21, 1773, F12 1300; Anonymous, "Mémoire sur les Verreries," 1784, F12 1486.

endorsement, was distributed to all the bleaching houses and cloth manufactures of the kingdom.[32]

Ascertainment and description of the best current practice facilitated the improvement of each industry through deliberate invention. For nearly every major industry the Bureau developed in the eighteenth century a strategy of economic and technological improvement, and then attempted to recruit scientists and top-flight mechanics for its realization. The strategy for the silk industry was one of the earliest devised and is certainly the easiest to describe. By 1750 the weaving of silk had been domesticated in France, and Lyons was the European capital for the production of fine silks.[33] In the southeastern provinces of Languedoc, Provence, and Dauphiné, the government had encouraged, somewhat indiscriminately, the growing of mulberry trees, the raising of silkworms, and the local unwinding of silk thread from the cocoons by *tireurs de soie*. Multiple evils developed. Mulberry plantations usurped good land that might have been better devoted to wheat, and wheat prices rose (it was said) 25 per cent. Indiscriminate encouragement of silkworm growers and *tireurs de soie* created a swarm of greedy, small operators, often ignorant and usually avaricious, who produced silk thread of uneven quality. The competition of many *tireurs* for cocoons raised their price until French silk thread was the most expensive in Europe, to the disadvantage of French industry. At the same time, the Lyons silk weavers still had to import from Piedmont the finer grades of silk thread, to the tune of eighteen to twenty million livres a year. For multiple evils many remedies were suggested: the prohibition of the employment of good wheat land by mulberry plantations; the regulation of the quality of silk thread; the establishment in each province of a school for the *tireurs et tireuses de soie*; the erection in each silk-producing province of a *halle* for the sale of silk.[34]

32. Montaran to Brisson, Jan. 5, 1780, F12 1327.
33. For a concise introduction to inventions in silk spinning, see Shelby McCloy, *French Inventions of the Eighteenth Century* (Lexington, Ky., 1952), pp. 95-98.
34. Documents revealing conditions in the silk industry and proposed remedies are scattered through F12 1435, 1436, 1439, 1449, 1450, 1451, 1452, and 1453A. See especially, folder entitled "1732; 12 pièces; Manufacture de Velours et autres étoffes de soie du S. Maris, Negt à Perpignan, érigée par arret du 21. 8bre. 1732, en Manufacture Royale," F12 1449; "Mémoire des frères Jubié sur la nécessité de corriger les abus des tirages de soye dans la Province du Dauphiné," Feb., 1749, F12

It so happened, however, that the Bureau had as director of commerce from 1749 to 1769 an economic statesman, Daniel Trudaine. He was also supervisor of the Ferme Générale and head of the division of Ponts et Chaussées, and thus had many strands of the administrative situation in hand. As director of commerce, he was comprehensive and realistic in his understanding of the French economy, of its needs and resources, and of the means to improve it. He was almost unerring in his ability to perceive the essence of a basically simple problem and to prepare a single, practical solution. At the same time he was ingenious, intelligent, and flexible when it came to devising a complicated multiple policy to meet complicated multiple needs. Constant in work, firm in execution, and without any preconceived system of administration or management, he knew how to choose men, industrialists as well as administrators, and to enlist them in the execution of his policies.[35] For the improvement of the silk industry he focused on the fabrication of silk thread. In each silk-producing province he encouraged by government subsidy several large manufacturers of fine silk thread. The policy was shrewd. The large manufacturers could be easily educated in modern procedure and their product easily inspected. By varying their subsidy with the quality of their product, they could be stimulated to improve their thread. Their methods could serve as a model for other *tireurs de soie*. As they would purchase only the best co-

---

1435; "Mémoire" sur les filatures de Montauban, 1751, F12 1436; folder entitled "1751; 3 pièces; Mr le Garde des Sceaux à Mr. de la Tour, Intendant en Provence, sur un Mémoire du Sr. Castellet, gentilhomme provençale . . . ," F12 1450; folder entitled "1754; 5 pièces; Lettre du M. de la Porte sur le Mémoire du Sr. Chazalet . . . ," F12 1453A; folder entitled "1754; 4 pièces; tirage des soyes de la Manufre de Tours du Sr. Chastellier, de l'année 1754; encouragement accordé en conséquence de cet état," F12 1451; "Le Sieur Rodier, élève des manufactures pour les soyeries en Languedoc, envoye un mémoire concernant les manufactures de Lyon," Aug. 12, 1754, F12 1439; folder entitled "1758; 13 pièces; Mémoires et observations du Sr. Buffet sur le perfectionnement de la manipulation des soies et de la fabrication des étoffes," F12 1453A; folder entitled "1761; 2 pièces; Mémoires de Sr. Landry, sur les moyens de perfectionner le tirage des soyes," F12 1453A; folder entitled "1779; 4 pièces; Le Sr. Papion du Chateau, Entrepreneur de la manufacture Royale de Tours pour la soye, propose d'établir des pépinières de muriers dans toutes les généralités," F12 1452; "Observations [par Villard] sur le Mémoire et Projet de Règlement pour la filature des Soyes, proposé par le Sieur Payan, fils ainé, du lieu de La Coste en Provence, en 8bre. 1781," F12 1449.

35. Trudaine's personality, functions, policies, and strategies are revealed in his dispatches and marginal comments on administrative letters and reports. For contemporary comment, see Anonymous, "Mémoire" [to the National Assembly, approximate date, before March 15, 1790], F12 652; Rémond, p. 95.

coons and pay a premium price for them, the growers of silkworms would be incited to better their procedures. Meanwhile, French silk weavers would be supplied with fine thread from a French source, and the drain of gold to Piedmont would be diminished.[36] Not content with these measures, Trudaine invited an ingenious artisan-mechanic, Villard, to invent more economical and rapid machinery for the large manufacturers of silk thread.[37] He and his successors also backed Vaucanson, member of the Academy of Sciences, when he applied theories of mathematics and mechanics to the invention of similar machines.[38] A bitter controversy developed over the comparative merits of the machine sequences of Vaucanson and Villard. Partisans bitterly debated the larger issue: how can the process of conscious, deliberate invention best be undertaken—through the thoughtful application of scientific theory or through the ingenious combination of existing mechanical elements?[39] No one denied, however, that invention should be deliberately undertaken.

36. Policy and calculations with respect to the fabrication of silk thread are given in documents found in F12 1434, 1435, 1439, 1451, 1453A. See especially, "Propositions [des frères Jubié] sur l'établissement d'une manufacture de tirage de soyes à la croizade dans le Bourg de la Sône en Dauphiné," 1751, F12 1434; De La Porte to Trudaine (?), March 23, 1751, F12 1434; folder entitled, "1762; 4 pièces; Gratifications accordées au Sr. Deydier, possesseur des moulins d'Aubenas, pour encourager dans sa manufacture le tirage des soies; et diverses réponses à ce sujet," F12 1437; folder dealing with the spinning of silk at Tours, 1771, F12 1451; "Soumission pour l'établissement de deux manufactures Royales en Dauphiné," June 1, 1773, F12 1434; "Observations [par Villard] sur le Mémoire et Projet de Règlement pour la filature des Soyes, proposé par le Sieur Payan, fils ainé, du lieu de La Coste en Provence, en 8bre. 1781," F12 1449; folder entitled "1785; 17 pièces; Pièces relatives aux Srs. Jubié et Enfantin . . . ," F12 1435.

37. "Mémoire et Propositions de G. Villard, pour introduire la connaissance et l'usage de sa mécanique sur les soyes dans les filatures et moulinages du Royaume," F12 1449; "Mémoire de George Villard . . . concernant le perfectionnement et l'œconomie des filatures et moulinages des soyes en France," F12 1449; "Mémoire sur divers moyens de perfectionner et d'accélérer le moulinage des soyes . . . par George Villard," circa 1756 à 1758, F12 1449; "Mémoire dressé par George Villard . . . sur les propriétés et les effets de la nouvelle mécanique qu'il a inventée . . . ," November 28, 1774, F12 1449; anonymous defense of Villard, a letter which begins, "Paris 14 (?) février 1776, Mon cher Maître . . . ," F12 1449; "Extrait des Registres de l'Académie Royale des Sciences du 17e mars 1781" [Report of De Montigny, Beaumé, Lavoisier, Le Roy, Vandermonde on the inventions of Villard] and "Observations de G. Villard sur l'extrait de rapport ci-contre," F12 1449.

38. Folder entitled, "1752 à 1754; 96 pièces; Divers arrêts et dossiers sur les privilèges et primes accordés à divers particuliers en Languedoc pour l'établissement du tirage et moulinage des soyes en cette province," F12 1439; folder entitled "Machines Vaucanson, 1774-1777," F12 654.

39. "Mémoire de George Villiard, . . . concernant le perfectionnement et l'œconomie des filatures et moulinages des soyes en France," F12 1449; "Réflexions sur les découvertes du Sr. Villard . . . ," F12 1449; a letter of Vaucanson, Oct. 5, 1765, F12 1449; folder entitled "1782; 2 pièces; Le S. Villard sollicite la commission accordée au Sr. Vaucanson pour le travail des soyes," F12 1453B; Rémond, p. 73.

Similarly in other industries the Bureau devised strategies for improvement and, when appropriate, recruited scientists for their implementation. In the manufacture of woolen, cotton, and linen cloth, French manufacturers needed better dyes and dyeing processes, improved bleaching methods, and spinning machinery.[40] The Bureau, as we have seen, hired a succession of able chemists, Dufay, Hellot, Macquer, and Berthollet, to test and seek new dyeing methods.[41] Under the auspices of the Bureau, Berthollet invented the process of chemically bleaching cloth in a few hours with chlorine gas instead of by exposure for weeks on meadows.[42] English workmen, encouraged and sometimes supervised by the Bureau, constructed working models of Hargreaves's spinning jenny, Arkwright's roller frame, and Crompton's mule jenny.[43] The Bureau then appointed the physicist Molard to test and perfect the machines and to exhibit them at the Hotel de Mortagne.[44] In the chemical products industry, France depended on Spain for the import of several million pounds of natural soda. In the 1780's the Bureau sought to encourage research in laboratory processes for the manufacture of artificial soda.[45]

Through the eighteenth century the Bureau's use of scientists matured and became more sophisticated; so too did the tests and reports of the scientists. The reports to the Bureau of Hellot in the 1740's, 1750's, and 1760's, of Macquer in the 1770's, and of Berthollet in the 1780's on tests of new dyes and dyeing processes reflect the increasing sophistication. Generally, Hellot was content with a unilateral, empirical examination of the finished product. Confronted with a piece of cloth dyed in an allegedly novel way, he looked at it and touched it, before and after boiling,

40 "Compte rendu par M. Tolozan des différents objets qui concernent son Département, Envoyé à M. de Villedeuil, Contrôleur Général des finances, le 13 Mai 1787," F12 657.

41. Bonnassieux and Lelong, p. xxvii.

42. Berthollet's description of his perfected process is presented in "Description de l'art du blanchiment par l'acide muriatique oxigéné," *Journal des arts et manufactures*, I, 192-255.

43. The importation of the spinning jenny by John Holker is mentioned in Tolozan, "Mémoire sur l'état actuel de la filature des cotons," *circa* May 2, 1790, F12 1338; the agreement with Jacques Milne to introduce in France the Arkwright roller frame is in F12 1340; the negotiations with Sr. Pickfort for the introduction of Crompton's mule jenny are in F12 1341.

44. Tolozan, "Mémoire sur l'état actuel de la filature des cotons," *circa* May 2, 1790, F12 1338.

45. Charles Gillispie, "The Discovery of the Leblanc Process," *Isis* (1957), XLVIII, 155.

and commented commonsensically on its color, texture, and ability to sustain rough treatment. Rarely did he conduct comparative tests of the old and new. Seldom did he examine the process behind the product. Only on occasion did he proffer administrative advice concerning the possible nature and amount of government aid.[46] More often than Hellot, Macquer examined the process of manufacture as well as the product. Also, he insisted on comparative tests of old and new procedures and results, and set rigorous standards of care, skill, and integrity for their execution. He insisted that in comparative tests minutes be kept to facilitate a repetitive check and that all factors be kept constant, save the novelty being appraised. "In these two tests everything was held perfectly equal, and there was no difference save the quality of the two dyes being compared."[47] If the results of the test were favorable, Macquer would recommend what type of government aid should be given in the light of current Bureau policy and of the invention's importance for its industry.[48] From Macquer it was but a step to the more elaborate tests and reports of Berthollet.[49] He affirmed the developing Bureau traditions of

46. Reports of Hellot include: on varieties of madder, Dec. 3, 1747, Dec. 20, 1761, Aug. 11, 1763, F12 655A; on glass-making, Feb. 8, 1752, F12 1487; on a scarlet dye, Nov. 10, 1765, F12 1330; on blue vitriol, Aug. 1, 1757, F12 1506.

47. Report of Macquer on cochineal, May 12, 1779, F12 655A.

48. Reports of Macquer include: on varieties of madder, Aug. 13, 1779, Jan. 17, 1782, F12 655A; on cochineal, May 12, 1779, F12 655A; on bleaching of silk, Sept. 29, 1780, F12 1453B; on the production of vegetable oil, administrative summary of his views, June 18, 1782, F12 1505; on manufacture of steel by Sr. Mongenet de Renancourt, F12 1302; on woolen cloth, each side dyed with a different color, April 14, 1769, F12 1330; on manufacture of artificial soda, July 31, 1782, F12 1507; on lead and white lead, Sept. 7, 1779, F12 1507; on oil from thistle seeds, April 7, 1781, F12 1505; on manufacture of steel, March 1, 1782, July 26, 1783, F12 656; on manufacture of crystals and enamel, Dec. 7, 1783, F12 1489B; on a black dye, Sept. 5, 1782, F12 1330.

49. Reports of Berthollet include: on indigo, Sept. 6, 1789, F12 655A; on the bleaching of silk, April 10, 1786, F12 1453B and June 16, 1788, F12 1438; on the manufacture of iron and steel, March 30, 1784, Sept., 1784, June 15, 1784, Nov. 30, 1785, May 31, 1786, Sept. 16, 1786, July 7, 1788, F12 656, and June 30, 1785, F12 1305A, and March 8, 1788, F12 1303; on printed silk, July 29, 1786, F12 1453A; on the manufacture of white lead, Feb. 2, 1787, and July 14, 1786, F12 1507; on a black dye, "Précis [by Desmarest] des deux rapports qui ont été faits sur la méthode de teindre en noir proposé par M. Dino," Dec. 28, 1789, and also December 15, 1785, F12 1330; on the memoir concerning manufacture of iron wire, May 3, 1788, F12 656; on the bleaching of silk, April 10, 1786, F12 1453B; on the fastness of printed colors on cloth, July 15, 1786, F12 1507; on the dyes of Count Beust, 1786, summary in F12 1329; on the manufacture of lead and white lead, Berthollet to Le Tellier, March 13, 1786, F12 1507.

The report of Le Roy and Bechet concerning the Pickfort spinning machines (April 25, 1791, F12 1341) articulates a complete theory of comparative testing embodying the tradition that had been accumulating through the eighteenth

examination of processes as well as products, of exactitude in comparative tests, and of the recommendation by scientists of the type of government encouragement. More frequently than Macquer he employed rudimentary scientific theory in devising chemical tests of new processes and in searching for the causes of what was occurring. So enamored was he of his scientific views that he tended to reject a process even when its success in practice contradicted his theoretical prediction of failure. Educated by the administrative discussion around him, he began to make recommendations concerning the strategy the Bureau should follow in given industries. In this discussion he was joined by Desmarest and perhaps by Molard.[50]

Thus by 1787 scientists had been thoroughly incorporated in the administrative discussion of the Bureau concerning French industry. They were involved in processes of regulation, instruction, appraisal, and planning. These processes involved the habitual attitudes, ideas, and actions of many people: ignorant and skilful artisans, inventors, get-rich-quick promoters, large-scale capitalists, intendants of the *généralités,* inspectors of manufactures, intendants and deputies of commerce of the bureau, and scientists. Sustaining the scientists in their activity was the continuing idea that scientists should be useful to industry. They should contribute directly to industrial progress.

With the onset of the Revolution, the Bureau of Commerce and its agents ceased to be obeyed and the Bureau eventually was abolished in 1791. Its authority dissolved just as Tolozan, its director since 1787, was beginning to make some headway in the restoration of its efficiency. Next to Trudaine, Tolozan probably had the most comprehensive view of the French economy of all eighteenth-century French administrators. He had a steady grasp both of immediate realities and of their relationship to future strategic policy. He had strategies for each separate industry and

century among members of the Bureau and associated scientists. Tolozan himself discussed the nature of comparative testing as applied to spinning machinery (Tolozan to the Controller General, Nov. 1, 1790, and to Le Roy, Aug. 13, 1791, F^{12} 1340).

50. Bacquié, pp. 370-371; Desmarest and Abeille to Tolozan, Sept. 7, 1789, F^{12} 651; "Notes des affaires qui sont entre les mains de MM. les Inspecteurs généraux et sur lesquelles ils n'ont pas encore donné leur avis," F^{12} 651. Molard's position as perfecter of textile machinery might have brought him into the current of discussion.

for many separate provinces as well as grand strategies for
France.[51]   Upon becoming director, he cleared up affairs that had
languished for months and years in the Bureau's offices,[52] tried to
keep abreast of current business, organized a census of French
industries,[53] and initiated a thoroughgoing review of such longstanding Bureau policies as regulation, presumably with an eye
to revision.[54]

However, for all his strategic grasp, Tolozan could not be as
effective as Trudaine.   Tolozan could not always enlist the co-
operation of his associates.   Unlike Trudaine, Tolozan was only
director of commerce and not supervisor of the Ferme Générale
and head of the division of Ponts et Chaussées as well.   Tolozan,
moreover, had just been promoted to the directorship from a
group of rival colleagues.   Apparently his views prevailed within
the Bureau,[55] but the associated deputies of commerce and general

51. Tolozan's personality, policies, and strategies are indicated in his many
reports, instructions, and orders, especially in "Compte rendu par M. Tolozan des
differents objets qui concernent son Départment, Envoyé à M. Villedeuil Contrôleur
Général des finances le 13 Mai 1787," F12 657, and in "Notes des branches d'industrie, des mécaniques et des procédés qui ont été établis, ou qui se sont perfec-
tionnés pour raison des quels il a été accordé des secours ou récompenses dans le
Départment de M. Tolozan, Intendant du Commerce, depuis la nomination de M.
de Calonne à la place de Controleur Général des finances," F12 1559; *Mémoire sur
le commerce de la France et de ses colonies* (1789), a book which he prepared with
the assistance of a S. Béchet; his discussions as recorded in Henri Lévy Bruhl,
*Un Projet de Code de commerce à la veille de la Revolution: le projet Miromesnil
(1778-1789)* (Paris, 1932). For contemporary comments on his character see Biollay,
pp. 377-378; letter of J. Bte. De La Place to Necker, Paris, Dec. 5, 1780,
F12 1305A; letter of Garnet to the Controller General, Oct. 24, 1787, F12 1340;
Boyetet to M. Cliquot de Bervache, Paris, April 8, 1789, F12 657; Anonymous,
"Mémoire" [to the National Assembly, approximate date, before March 15, 1790], F12
652.

52. F12* 106, July 19, 26, Aug. 2, 9, 16, 23, 30, and Sept. 5, 1787, for some of the
affairs cleared.

53. For the industrial census, see Hubert and Georges Bourgin, *L'Industrie
sidérurgique en France au début de la Révolution* (Paris, 1920), p. v; Bacquié, pp.
213-215, 218-222; folder entitled "1789, 2 pièces; Lettre de M. de Tolozan aux
insp.eurs des Manuf.res qui ont des Rafineries de Sucre dans leur Dep't," F12 1502.

54. Apparently Tolozan initiated a review of regulations, of the grant of exclusive privileges to manufacture a given article within a given area for a stated
number of years, and of the administrative procedures for granting permission to
erect a glass factory.   See Desmarest and Abeille to Tolozan, Sept. 7, 1789, F12 651;
"Notes des affaires qui sont entre les mains de MM. les Inspecteurs généraux et
sur lesquelles ils n'ont pas encore donné leurs avis," F12 651; Tolozan's marginal
note, June 13, 1789, in folder entitled "1789; 5 pièces; arrêt qui permet au Sr. Gau,
d'établir à Toulouse, une verrerie à bouteille, à la charge d'en employer que du
charbon de terre," F12 1490; a hint of discussion in "Avis des députés de commerce
sur la demande du Marquis de Vogué relative à l'établissement de sa verrerie de
S.te Catherine située dans le Marquisat de la Noele en Nivernois," Oct. 1, 1788,
F12 724.

55. On occasion, to be sure, the Bureau did oppose him (Tolozan to M. Le
Président d'Albertas, July 10, 1788, F12 1488A).

inspectors of manufacturers were not always inclined to acknowl-edge his superiority and to co-operate and obey.[56]   Trudaine, furthermore, had had the good fortune to live in a period of com-mercial and industrial expansion and to possess adequate means to implement his policies.   He received credit for successes that may have been due as much to general conditions as to his own efforts.   Tolozan, on the other hand, struggled with the difficulties of an acute depression.   After 1787 the royal government was short of money, and Tolozan simply could not allot to businesses as many subsidies as his petitioners wished and his own strategic planning required.[57]   He was roundly cursed for circumstances often beyond his control.

With the revolutionary events of the spring, summer, and early autumn of 1789, Tolozan's authority began to disintegrate and the activity of the Bureau to diminish in quantity and sig-nificance.   The enforcement of regulations governing methods of manufacture and quality of product dissolved in the face of mass disobedience.   It was the practice, for example, for manufac-turers to bring their cloth to a local inspection office.   There *gardes-jurés*, fellow manufacturers selected for the purpose, stamped the cloth, either with the word *Réglée* if it met with the standards of the law or with an octagonal mark and name of the manufacturer if it did not.   The operation was supervised and recorded by a local government official known as the *préposé*. In June and July, the manufacturers in many localities chased out the *préposés* and had cloth that did not meet the requirements certified as *Réglée*.   To protests from *préposés* and inspectors of manufacturers, the Bureau could only reply that in the circum-stances there was nothing to be done.[58]   The Bureau relinquished

56. Folder entitled "Affaires soumises aux Inspecteurs généraux, 1788-89," F12 651.

57. In denying a request Tolozan would sometimes refer to circumstances and sometimes more directly to the emptiness of the treasury. See, for example, Tolozan to Jubié, April 14, 1788, F12 1434; Tolozan to Crommelin, June 3, 1788, F12 1339; decision of Bureau of Commerce, July 10, 1788, with respect to the clock and watch factory of S^r. Bralle, F12 1325; "Mémoire relatif aux demandes de S^r. Valentino, chimiste pensionné à Lille . . . ," *circa* Sept. 24, 1788, F12 1507; Tolozan to Daly, Feb. (?), 1789, F12 1338; folder entitled, "1789; 5 pièces; deux Bons de M^r. le Controlleur G^{al} . . . en faveur de S^r. Dauffe," F12 1317; Tolozan to Valentino, July 9, 1790, F12 652; Tolozan to Aymat, July 31, 1790, F12 1338.

58. Vital to Committee of Agriculture and Commerce of the National Assembly, Feb. 19, 1790, F12 652; F12* 107-108, June 13, 1790. On Aug. 13, 1789, Tolozan wrote recalling one ambulant inspector from his tour: "Je crois que dans les cir-

review of regulations to the National Assembly, which eventually abolished them.[59]

Some inspectors of manufacturers in 1789 delayed submission of data that would have been useful for the industrial census. Tolozan appealed to the intendants of some of the *généralités* for the information and then abandoned the project.[60] On January 22, 1790, the Assembly suspended the payment of outstanding subsidies to inventors and manufacturers and decreed that each one must be revalidated before a Bureau of Liquidation.[61] The Assembly soon reserved to itself and to its Committee of Agriculture and Commerce the power of passing on new requests for subsidies and of fixing the amount.[62] Petitioners for government aid soon learned that the center of decision had moved from the executive bureau to a legislative committee and directed their requests to the committee.[63] Orally and in writing, Tolozan tried to counsel the committee in the strategies he was attempting to follow, but with little effect.[64] The sense of interventionist strate-

---

constances actuelles, il serait prudent de ne la pas continuer, et vous en revenir à Paris" (Tolozan to Lazowsky, Aug. 13, 1789, F[12] 1396). The current general codes of regulation were decreed in the "Lettres Patentes du Roi Concernant les Manufactures, Données à Marli le 5 Mai 1779" and in "Lettres Patentes du Roi Portant établissement de Bureaux de visite et de marque sur les différens ouvrages des Manufactures de Laine, Toile, Toilerie, Soierie et Bonneterie, et qui fixent les règles de la manutention desdits Bureaux, données à Versailles le premier Juin 1780," F[12] 1441. Abuses in the election of the *gardes jurés* appear in "Observations sur la conduite de Plusieurs fabricans d'Oloron qui influe considérablement aux abus dont vient d'être parlé, et cause des troubles à la fabrique," F[12] 654.

59. Biollay, p. 506.

60. Folder entitled "An 2; 15 pièces; Lettres, rapport, projets, etc. relatifs au manque d'écorces pour faire du tan et aux moyens à prendre pour s'en procurer," F[12] 1465; folder entitled "1789; 2 pièces; Circulaire de M[r]. le Controlleur G[al] à M[rs] les Intendants de Lorraine, Franche Comté, Flandre et Roussillon, pour connaître l'état actuel de la Bonneterie...," F[12] 1396 (it is a question whether Tolozan was here seeking routine information or information for the census; however, the circular and the accompanying draft letter reveal the recalcitrance of the inspectors of manufactures and the turn to the intendants).

61. Folder entitled "1792; 2 pièces; les entrepreneurs de la manufacture de ratine et autres étoffes de laine, établie à Andely," F[12] 1389-90.

62. A decree of the National Assembly (Aug. 3, 1790) allotted an annual sum of 2 million francs for encouragements, gifts, and gratifications, of which 400,000 was later reserved for the useful crafts.

63. As examples, see petition of Laisant (?), Bouquet, and Phillippot to the National Assembly, Oct. 25, 1789, F[12] 652; Meynier to Lambert, Jan. 25, 1790, F[12] 1389-1390; folder entitled "20 May 1791; 9 pièces; Le S[r]. Gorillot, Serrurier, Réclame une indemnité...," F[12] 1317; memoir of Jean Vaupopelen to the National Assembly, F[12] 652; "Mémoire soumis à l'Assemblée nationale par le S[r]. Valentino, natif de Rome et professeur en chymie et habitant de la ville de Lille," F[12] 652.

64. Tolozan to Meynier, president of the Committee of Agriculture and Commerce, Oct. 9 and 15, 1790, F[12] 1338; "Observations faites par M. Tolozan dans le Comité d'Agriculture et Commerce, le 21 mars 1791," F[12] 1509-10A.

gy dissolved in the shift of responsibility from a single executive director to a legislative committee, in the press of immediate problems, and in the drift toward laissez-faire.[65]

The Bureau, with less to do, met less frequently: fourteen times from January through April, 1789; eleven times from May through December, 1789; five times from January through April, 1790; and only eight times the remainder of 1790 before finally assembling for the last session on February 27, 1791.[66] The employees of the Bureau were not paid; as late as September, 1790, they were waiting for their salaries of 1789. In April, 1791, the functions of the controller general were divided between the two ministries of Interior and of Public Contributions and Revenues.[67] The dwindling functions of the Bureau of Commerce passed in April, 1791, to the sixth division of the Ministry of the Interior,[68] and the Bureau itself was formally abolished in September.

These changes did not leave undisturbed the relations of the French government to French scientists. Scientists were no longer associated in over-all planning, since no planning was going forward. The contract with Berthollet to publish his instructional *Theory of Dyeing* was honored, but no new instructional booklets were authorized.[69] With regulation in disrepute in some circles and regulations unenforced,[70] scientists were naturally not con-

65. For explicit declarations in favor of laissez-faire by ministers of the interior, see Roland to the president of the Committee of Commerce of the Legislative Assembly, June 12, 1792, and one of Roland's successors to the administration of the department of the Haute Garonne, June 18, 1792, F12* 178 (Mourgues was named minister of the interior on June 13, 1792 only to be replaced by Terrier-Monceil on June 18).

66. F12* 107-108, Jan., 1789, to Feb. 27, 1791, *passim.*

67. Jacques Godechot, *Les Institutions de la France sous la Révolution et l'Empire* (Paris, 1951), p. 81.

68. Report of the Minister of the Interior Cahier de Gerville on "Organisation du Départment de l'Intérieur," F1a 1.

69. F12* 107-108, Aug. 22, 1790.

70. Some manufacturers, especially established firms who derived a secure profit from selling a substantial quantity of goods of standard quality, preferred regulation. They were often supported by the local inspector of manufacturers, stand-pat theorists, and old-time members of the Bureau. Other manufacturers, who sought a mounting profit from selling a large quantity of goods of uncertain quality at a variable price to a wide market, preferred freedom. Such were the manufacturers of Nîmes, whose coarse cloth sold throughout South America. (The word "denims" comes from "de Nîmes.") The demands of such fabricators were coming to be supported by an increasing number of administrators and theorists. Tolozan, a middle-of-the-road pragmatist, seemed to believe that regulations should be retained but revised in the direction of liberty.

sulted in this area. However, there was some continuity in the area of scientific-administrative co-operation. The Depot of Machines at the Hotel de Mortagne was maintained and Vandermonde and Molard were retained as curators, the former to supervise the acquisition and the maintenance of the machines, and the latter to work at their perfection.[71] Government subsidies were still granted to inventors, and the practice of referring allegedly new processes and products to scientists for appraisal continued, at least until the end of our period (September, 1792).

In conclusion, the effect of the early years of the Revolution was thus to demobilize the over-all administrative-industrial policy of the Old Regime, while retaining two or three of its elements. If the historian is interested in continuity and change in administrative practices and attitudes, it might be useful to inquire why there was continuity of some elements and not of others. First, why was there continuity of the scientists' appraisal of new processes and products, for example? In part the reason seems to be that this practice was incorporated in many other continuities. There was the continuity of the industrial complex: artisans, skilful and ignorant, large-scale capitalists, get-rich-quick schemers and promoters, and inventors, all operating at a certain level of technology and all schooled in the expectation of government support if they invented a valid new process. The scientific complex continued: scientists, day after day, worked at the same scientific problems as under the Old Regime, met with their colleagues of the Academy of Sciences, examined new products at the Academy's request, and believed that scientists should be directly useful to industry. There were, despite changes, administrative continuities of personnel, structure, cases, documents, procedures, and ideas. Very early, in the autumn of 1789, the National Assembly's Committee of Agriculture and Commerce attached to itself as consultants two deputies of commerce, Rostagny of Marseilles and Tournachon of Lyons. They had participated in tests during the decade of the 1780's.[72] In 1791

71. F12* 107-108, Feb. 3 and Sept. 8, 1789; F12* 107-108, May 13, June 13, and Aug. 22, 1790; Roland to Vandermonde, Nov. 21, 1791, F12 1340; Minutes of the Central Committee of the Administration of Commerce, F12* 1131, Dec. 1, 15, 19, 1791, Feb. 13, March 8, 1792.

72. "Mémoire pour Monseigneur le Marquis de Brancas," F12 1502; "Extrait des Registres de l'Académie Royale des Sciences du 17e mars 1781" [Report of De

the Minister of Interior appointed within his sixth division a consultative Central Committee of Commerce.[73] It was conceived to be equivalent in structure and function to the old Bureau of Commerce.[74] Four of its seven members had been members of the old Bureau; three, Rostagny, Tournachon, and Rosselin, were former deputies of commerce, and the fourth, Blondel, the vice-president or director of the new Central Committee, was a former intendant of commerce. Blondel's chief clerk, Guillaume, became the chief clerk of the sixth division.[75] All these officials were aware of the testing routines. When the committees of agriculture and commerce of the National and Legislative assemblies, the Central Committee of Commerce, or the officials of the sixth division were approached by an old-time petitioner for government aid of an allegedly new process, they would ask in accord with time-honored practice for the documents on the case.[76] There they would read long descriptions of the tests of the old Bureau. When approached by new petitioners, members of the committee, faced with the continuing problem of distinguishing verity from fraud and believing verity should receive government aid, would naturally apply the old-time solution of requesting the scientists to serve as appraisers. The scientists,

Montigny, Beaumé, Lavoisier, Le Roy, Vandermonde on the inventions of Villard], F12 1449.

73. Report of the Minister of the Interior Cahier de Gerville on the "Organisation du Département de l'Intérieur," Fla 1.

74. Blondel to Tolozan, Feb. 20, 1792, F12 1341; Tolozan to Blondel, July 31, 1792, F12 1396. Also, see Biollay, p. 507.

75. Report of the Minister of the Interior Cahier de Gerville on the "Organisation de Département de l'Intérieur," Fla 1; "État des bureaux à la date de 8 mars 1792," Flb I* 531.

76. As examples, see "Rapport fait au comité d'agriculture et de commerce par M. Defontenay, Député de Rouen, à l'Assemblée nationale sur la demande du Sr. Reboul," F12 1339; folder entitled "1784 à 1792; 37 pièces; Le Sr. Frèdéric Hausser, fabriquan de rubans à St. Etienne...," F12 1430-31; folder entitled "1792; 53 pièces; Mr. Le Clerc, Entrepreneur de la Manufacture Royale de Brive La Gaillarde demande une indemnité 60,000...," F12 1343A; folder entitled "1792; 4 pièces; Le Cen Potot (?), Mre. cordonnier à Paris...," F12 1465; Cahier de Gerville to Tolozan, Jan. 7, 1792, F12 1465; Blondel to Tolozan, Jan. 16, 1792, F12 1330; Blondel to Tolozan, Jan. 18, 1792, and Tolozan's reply, Jan. 27, F12 1389-1390; Tolozan to Blondel, Jan. 27, 1792, F12 1454; Tolozan to Blondel, Feb. 3, 1792, F12 1454; Blondel to Tolozan, Feb. 4, 1792, F12 1454; Guillaume to Valioud, Feb. 21, 1792, F12 1446; Tolozan to Blondel, Feb. 22, 1792, F12 1454; Blondel to Tolozan, March 30, 1792, and Tolozan's reply, April 2, F12 1461; Blondel to Tolozan, April 27, 1792, F12 1340; Blondel to Tolozan, Aug. 9, 1792, and Tolozan's reply, Aug. 13, F12 1343A; Guillaume to Valioud, Sept. 22, 1792, and Valioud's reply, Sept. 23, F12 1340; Minutes of the Central Committee of the Administration of Commerce, F12* 1131, Nov. 7, 14, 17, Dec. 19, 1791, Jan. 12, 16, Feb. 9, 20, 1792.

believing they should be directly useful to industry, would accept and thus participate in the process of decision-making.[77]

In brief, there was continuity of the scientists' appraisal of processes because there were persons who had been performing steps in the procedure for many years and they kept on performing them. Under the Old Regime members of the Bureau of Commerce, interested in stimulating the industrial productivity of France, had encountered the problems of dealing with secretive and ignorant artisans and with inventors and promoters of every description. Facing these problems with ideas inherited from the seventeenth century, that scientists should co-operate in promoting industrial progress and the government should aid inventors, the Bureau devised various solutions. The solutions in the form of procedures and implementing ideas seemed to work and were repeated until they became habitual. Since the Revolution did not offer new problems in this area before the war, the old solutions continued to be used by the old personnel. No one was prompted to think of doing anything else. In the solution of continuing problems, ideas had directed the attention and the effort and then had helped to maintain the direction adopted. There were thus interlocking and sustaining continuities of people, resources, ma-

77. See, for example: report of Le Roy and Béchet on the Pickfort machines, April 25, 1791, F12 1341; Meynier to De Lessart, Sept. 20, 1791, F12 1340; folder entitled "1792; 7 pièces; Les Srs. Servan, Du Par et compe...," F12 1465; report of Hassenfratz and Lavoisier, March 4, 1792, F12 1465; Roland to president of the Bureau de Consultation des Arts et Métiers, Aug. 29, 1792, F12 1343A; Minister of Interior to Bureau de Consultation des Arts et Métiers, July 10 and 12, Aug. 29, 1792 in F12* 178, and July 12, 1792, in F12 1479; Minutes of the Central Committee of the Administration of Commerce, F12* 1131, Dec. 19, 1791, and Feb. 9, 1792; Minister of Interior to Mr. François, president of the Committee of Commerce of the Legislative Assembly, April 17, 1792, F12 1498A; Louis, president of the Bureau de Consultation des arts et métiers, to Minister of Interior, March 22, 1792, F12 1330. The National Assembly had formalized the procedure of appraisal by decreeing on September 12, 1791, the establishment of a "Bureau de consultation des arts et métiers," to test allegedly new processes and devices. Fifteen of the Bureau's thirty members were to be drawn from the Academy of Sciences and fifteen from the other learned societies.

It may be correctly remarked that this article demonstrates continuity of certain elements of administrative policy only until September, 1792, and not through the entire revolutionary period. On the other hand, it may be observed that in the realm of French governmental policy with respect to industry, the nadir of Old Regime interventionism and the zenith of laissez-faire was in the summer of 1792. Thereafter, rapid mobilization for war forced French administrators increasingly to return to interventionist practice. They often consciously revived or elaborated Old Regime interventionist procedures, including the use of scientists. If basic continuity of certain Old Regime policies has been demonstrated during the first three years of the Revolution, it has probably been demonstrated for the entire revolutionary period.

chines, problems, organization, documents, administrative practice, and ideas. These interlocking continuities formed "the force of tradition."

Why, then, did some of these same continuities fail to assure the survival of other administrative practices? Why, for example, did they not assure the survival of the regulation of manufacturing methods? The detailed answer to the last question would require another article, if not a book. Nevertheless, it can be indicated that the answer seems to lie in the realm of conditions and ideas. The expansive projects of many French entrepreneurs and the over-all growth of the French economy appeared to be hampered by regulation. The idea of regulation was no longer accepted by many people. In contrast, as has been indicated, underlying the continuing participation of the scientists in the process of reaching a decision was the continuity of the ideas that the government should aid inventors and that scientists should contribute to industrial progress, ideas that seemed to be demonstrating their usefulness in promoting the solution of certain problems of the time.

THE LEGEND OF VOLTAIRE AND THE CULT OF THE REV-OLUTION, 1791

Raymond O. Rockwood

Rowdy demonstrations by "patriots" and "aristocrats" erupted at the performances of Voltaire's *Brutus*, which was revived at the Comédie by popular insistence in November, 1790, and shown irregularly through 1791. Tribute was frequently paid to Voltaire: on the third night, November 22, the Marquis Charles de Villette, self-appointed manager of a campaign in the playwright's behalf, appeared on the stage to rouse support for a plan to vindicate the *philosophe's* memory. Voltaire's body, he urged, should be returned in triumph to Paris and honored by the Revolution by its burial in a pantheon the nation should establish for its heroes at the new Ste. Geneviève Church.[1]

Villette and his associates had futilely advocated various similar plans since October, 1789, in the columns of the *Chronique de Paris*, a mouthpiece of the moderate Société de 1789. Villette, a young cavalry officer of unsavory reputation, by rumor Voltaire's illegitimate son and sometimes mistakenly mentioned as his nephew, was introduced to the Ferney household through his mother's friendship for the sage. Here he married, without dowry but with fanfare, Voltaire's loyal *protégée*, Mademoiselle de Varicourt, whose undying admiration and benevolent spirit go far to explain her husband's activity in her patron's behalf. The couple purchased the Ferney estate after Voltaire's death and established a shrine for his heart there. Villette, a dissolute aristocrat and an amateur *littérateur*, possessed an enthusiasm

RAYMOND O. ROCKWOOD *is professor of history at Colgate University.*

1. *Chronique de Paris*, III, No. 329 (Nov. 25, 1790), 1314. For information on Villette and his wife, see "Villette," and "Villette, Marquise de," in *Biographie universelle* (2nd ed.; Paris, 1842-1845) and *Nouvelle biographie générale* (Paris, 1857-1866); see also Raymond O. Rockwood, "The Cult of Voltaire to 1791," unpublished Ph.D. dissertation, University of Chicago, 1935, pp. 146-149.

for philosophy, gracious manners, and conversational abilities which had ingratiated him with Voltaire in the first place. He embraced the Revolution and edited the *cahier* of the bailiwick of Senlis. But, for all his basking in Voltaire's glory, he was frustrated in his ambition to be elected either to the Estates General or the Legislative Assembly. Not till 1792 did he become a deputy to the Convention from the department of Oise. Death from natural causes in 1793 saved him from the fate of other Girondins. In the meantime he busied himself as a pamphleteer and correspondent for the *Chronique de Paris*, expressing rather advanced religious views.

Prior to Villette's *Comédie* appearance in November, 1790, the campaign for justice to Voltaire made little official headway. But in rhythm with the mounting religious controversy, the effort progressed thereafter, culminating in a magnificent Paris celebration on July 11, 1791, authorized by the National Constituent Assembly. Organized in the tense atmosphere following the king's flight to Varennes, the celebration stimulated considerable discussion about Voltaire's meaning to various groups of revolutionists and counterrevolutionists. It therefore offers an excellent opportunity for study of the Voltaire legend and for the role it played in the dynamic revolutionary situation of 1791.

Voltaire's triumph in 1791 was the zenith of a personal cult first fostered by his own achievements and perpetuated and crystallized after his death in 1778 by his loyal followers, many of whom were still active in the movement: Villette himself; Condorcet, his friend and biographer; Beaumarchais, publisher of his collected works, the famous Kehl edition; and De la Harpe, literary critic who had often sung his praises. The effort to exalt Voltaire was a calculated blow at the Catholic church, one designed to rectify the "injustices" resulting from the denial of Christian burial to him in Paris. Voltaire thus moved into the Revolution as the "persecuted" martyr of "bigotry" and "tyranny."[2]

2. For an extensive treatment of the rise and development of the legend of Voltaire, see "Cult of Voltaire"; also Gustave Desnoiresterres, *Voltaire et la société au XVIIIᵉ siècle* (2nd ed.; Paris, 1871-1876), VIII, Epilogue, chap. iv. For an effort to assess Voltaire's influence on the National Assembly, see Renée Waldinger, *Voltaire and Reform in the Light of the French Revolution* (Geneva and Paris, 1959), and Henri Peyre, "Influence of the 18th Century Ideas on the French Revolution," *Journal of the History of Ideas*, X (Jan., 1949), 63-87 *passim*.

In the public debate regarding his reputation, the main lines of the Voltaire legend, pro and con, had been set long before 1789.[3] For years Voltaire had been denounced by devoted Catholics as Antichrist and the *chef des incrédules*. Even before 1789 his most devoted disciples had hailed the "retreat" of "superstition" and the imminent downfall of *l'infâme*. Whereas before the Revolution enthusiasts claimed that Voltaire had wrought a revolution in thinking, they now regarded him as the Father of the Revolution itself, though, for some patriots, he shared the honors with other *philosophes* who were sometimes held in higher esteem.[4] After 1789 his name appeared frequently in the news sheets and pamphlet literature, his works were often cited, and his reputation was debated along traditional lines but with new insights and increased intensity. While the conservative and reactionary press was generally hostile, it was not averse, with a reverse twist of the pen and with tongue in cheek, to the citation of his writings, so subject to divers interpretations, against the Revolution.

Nevertheless, the relationship of the Voltaire legend to the new regime was initially somewhat ambiguous. There were good reasons why he was not entirely a propitious symbol of the new order. Representing an extreme anti-religious position, his myth did not fit the early tendency of the Revolution not to break with the Church, but to work with it. Moreover, for many "patriots," Voltaire's reputation—as a courtier, friend of aristocrats, upholder of enlightened despotism, and one who spoke contemptuously of the *canaille* and of representative assemblies—had much in it that needed explaining away.

The adoption of the Civil Constitution of the Clergy in the summer of 1790 and the resultant conflict between the orthodox and the constitutional churches changed the revolutionary situation radically. Villette's *Comédie* appeal of November, 1790, had come at an appropriate moment. Intensified anticlericalism[5] favored the growth and use of the Voltaire legend while the Voltaire legend, in turn, favored the development of political

3. "Cult of Voltaire," chaps. i-iv, on the Voltaire legend before 1789.
4. *Ibid.*, chaps. v-vi, on Voltaire's reputation, pro and con, in the period 1789-1791.
5. Albert Mathiez, *The French Revolution* (New York, 1928), pp. 117-118.

anticlericalism. The legend was fusing with an emerging cult of national patriotism which, until the end of 1790, had not necessarily been anti-Catholic.[6] Various festivals, organized at first to celebrate the ideals and achievements of the Revolution without hostility to the Church, were by 1791 being fostered by certain patriots as autonomous expressions of *civisme*.[7] Eternal principles, sacred days, consecrated documents, cherished martyrs, admired heroes, hated devils, sage French national prophets, all found concrete expression in elaborate symbolisms and rites. At first Voltaire was only one among many revolutionary saints. But by late spring, 1791, the Pope had anathematized the Revolution as a whole; anticlericalism, already associated with anti-privilege and anti-despotism in the revolutionary press, now had freer reign. What better method for expressing such patriotic conviction than to honor the Church's archenemy, Voltaire? His personal cult had not changed, but the revolutionary circumstance was now propitious.

Increased public consciousness of Voltaire's anticlerical image in 1791 was fostered not only in the pamphlets and journals, as we shall see, but also in the revolutionary theater. Following M. J. Chénier's lead,[8] the theater had become a school for national patriotism. Dramatists wrote plays featuring French historical situations, depicting civic virtues, condemning and ridiculing fanatical priests, attacking despotism and the aristocracy, and teaching the principles of liberty, equality, and justice.[9] Such were the themes of a number of plays concerning Voltaire, focused mainly on his role as the protector of the innocent victims of fanaticism.[10] Between December, 1790, and September, 1791,

6. Mathiez, *Les Origines des cultes révolutionnaires (1789-1792)* (Paris, 1904) traces the rise of the revolutionary cult; Raymond Rockwood, *Voltaire, a Revolutionary Deity, 1789–May 30, 1791* (Chicago, 1935); E. F. Henderson, *Symbol and Satire in the French Revolution* (New York, 1912); Cornwell B. Rogers, *The Spirit of Revolution in 1789* (Princeton, 1949).

7. Mathiez, *The Revolution*, p. 118.

8. Chénier, *De la Liberté du théâtre en France* (n.p., 1789), p. 15.

9. C. G. Etienne and A. Martainville in their *Histoire du théâtre, 1789-1799* (4 vols.; Paris, 1802), I, ii-iii, assert in their hostile account that the theater was not the least powerful weapon in the overthrow of the *ancien régime* and (II, 11) that the plays concerning Calas, LaBarre, and the Massacres of Cévennes and St. Bartholomew did more than all the orators of the Constituent Assembly to destroy the old order. See also Kenneth N. McKee, *The Role of the Priest on the Parisian Stage during the Revolution* (Baltimore, 1939).

10. "Cult of Voltaire," pp. 118-125.

five different dramatizations of the Calas incident and one concerning LaBarre were performed in Paris.[11] Voltaire was also featured in Chaussard's vigorously anticlerical *La France régénerée,* wherein the Sage of Ferney and Rousseau are eulogized by an enlightened priest.[12] Moreover, there was a dramatic upsurge in the number of performances of Voltaire's own plays in 1791—particularly *Nanine, L'Enfant prodigue, Mahomet, Adélaide, Mérope, Sémiramis,* and *Brutus*—partly attributable to the freedom of the theater.[13] The plays about Voltaire's fight against religious fanaticism, the revival of *Brutus,*[14] and the increased production of his plays all parallel the intensified religious strife and the more determined effort, begun in November, 1790, to secure honors for Voltaire.

Various plans were first proposed by Villette, Saint-Just, Anacharsis Cloots, and others in the *Chronique* after October, 1789: Voltaire's body should be brought back from the monastery of Scellières at Romilly (near Troyes) where it rested, and be given a magnificent funeral in Notre Dame or St. Sulpice or Ste. Geneviève.[15] Not everyone welcomed the idea. Villette complained of receiving anonymous letters whose "tone of fanaticism and of personal outrage" was the "style of 1589."[16] Moreover, the National Assembly refused to act and even ignored Palissot's request for the privilege of dedicating his edition of Voltaire's works to it.[17] Barère stated the issue clearly: Should or should not the legislature ally with the principles expounded in the books?[18] Hopes, centered on the twelfth anniversary of Voltaire's death, May 30, 1790, faded and the plan was postponed for a year. But,

11. Lemierre d'Argy, *Calas ou fanatisme,* Dec. 17, 1790, Théâtre du Palais Royal: Jean-Louis Laya, *Calas,* Dec. 18, 1790, Théâtre de la Nation; Willemain d'Abancourt, *La Bienfaisance de Voltaire,* May 30, 1791, Théâtre de la Nation; J. M. Chénier, *Jean Calas,* July 7, 1791, Théâtre français; and Jean-Baptiste Pujoulx, *La Veuve de Calas à Paris,* July 31, 1791, Théâtre italien. Also Marsolier des Vivètiere's *Le Chevalier de la Barre,* July 6, 1791, Théâtre italien; and d'Abancourt's *L'Arrivée de Voltaire à Romilly,* July 10, 1791, Théâtre Molière. For an admirable study of the Calas incident, David D. Bien, *The Calas Affair* (Princeton, 1960); see also the essay of Geoffrey Adams, above, pp. 74-75.
12. (Paris, 1791) Théâtre Molière, Sept. 14, 1791.
13. "Cult of Voltaire," pp. 114-116.
14. On *Brutus* in the period 1790-1791, see *ibid.,* pp. 104-113.
15. *Chronique de Paris,* I, No. 41 (Oct. 3, 1789), 163, and No. 119 (Dec. 21, 1789), 478.
16. *Ibid.,* II, No. 22 (Jan. 22, 1790), 86-87.
17. J. Mavidal, E. Laurent, *et al.* (eds.), *Archives parlementaires,* Series I (Paris, 1879 ff.), IX (Sept. 25, 1789), 182. Hereafter cited as *Archives parlementaires.*
18. *Le Point du jour,* III, No. 90 (Sept. 26, 1789), 108.

for the first time, Villette began to mention the possibility of transforming the Ste. Geneviève into a pantheon.[19] Early in November Villette's and Condorcet's joint appearances before the Jacobin Club[20] and the deputation of the Société de 1789[21] to Mayor Bailly brought no concrete action from the municipality. As Villette explained it, the National Assembly feared "the loud cries the priests would make."[22]

News of the impending sale of Scellières in February, 1791, which Villette called to the attention of Mayor Bailly on February 29,[23] evidently induced the municipality to appoint a two-man commission, Joseph Caron and Jacques Cousin, to make specific plans for a celebration that now seemed a foregone conclusion.[24] To honor Mirabeau, the Panthéon was established at the Ste. Geneviève on April 4 and future legislatures were empowered to accord recognition to the nation's heroes. The petition on which the decree was based specified Descartes, Voltaire, and Rousseau.[25] On his own authority Villette now changed the name of the Quai des Théâtins, where he lived in Voltaire's old apartment, to Quai Voltaire, and Palloy urged that Rue Platrière be named for Rousseau—actions confirmed early in May by the municipality.[26] At the end of April it was generally expected that the celebration would occur on May 30. But still no formal sanction by the National Assembly. A warning from the mayor of Romilly that the actual sale of Scellières would take place early in May and an ensuing quarrel between Romilly and Troyes for control of Voltaire's body, which threatened its division,[27] finally prompted the legislature on May 8 to order the

---

19. *Chronique de Paris,* II, No. 150 (May 30, 1790), 597-598; *Lettres choisies de Charles Villette sur les principaux événements de la Révolution* (Paris, 1792), pp. 62-68.

20. Dates vary according to a variety of authorities. See "Cult of Voltaire," p. 156 n. 1.

21. Sigismund Lacroix, *Actes de la Commune de Paris pendant la Révolution* (Paris, 1894-1898), Sér. II, I, 121, 209.

22. *Chronique de Paris,* III, No. 343 (Dec. 9, 1790), 1370.

23. *Ibid.,* IV, No. 74 (March 15, 1791), 294.

24. Lacroix, *Actes de la Commune,* Sér. II, III, 93.

25. *Archives parlementaires,* XXIV (April 3, 4, 1791), 537, 542-543.

26. *Chronique de Paris,* IV, No. 104 (April 14, 1791), 415 (on Villette's action); Bibliothèque nationale, MSS, nouv. acq. fr. 312, pp. 270-271 (on Palloy's action); *Feuille du jour,* No. 126 (May 6, 1791), p. 298 (on the municipal action of May 3, 1791).

27. *Chronique de Paris,* IV, No. 116 (April 26, 1791), 461; *Moniteur,* VIII, No. 142 (May 22, 1791), 454.

village to guard the coffin while the constitutional committee deliberated on the advisability of further action.[28] In urging prompt action, the mayor of Romilly had commented on the spread of Voltaire's writing into the most isolated country areas. "I myself am proof. Born to a poor daily worker who scarcely had enough to help me learn to read and assist at the mass, I have never read, in moral and political matters, anything but Voltaire's works."[29]

Early in May religious difficulties had reached an acute stage. News that the Pope had anathematized the Revolution had reached Paris. On May 7 the Assembly had tried to reduce religious strife between partisans of the two contending church factions by extending tolerance to the non-jurors. The desire not to aggravate the religious situation and the many more important matters at hand no doubt explain the Assembly's continued hesitation to vote national honors to the *chef des incrédules*. During the debate in the Assembly on May 8, a former Jesuit suggested that since Voltaire was considered a prophet, it would be more appropriate to send his relics to Palestine. Amid the ensuing laughter Jean Baptiste Treilhard, member of the ecclesiastical committee, tried to speak but only one word was audible, "fanatics."[30]

The friendly press hailed the decree of May 8 authorizing Romilly to guard Voltaire's body, but deplored the opposition.[31] Criticism could not be silenced. It was criminal negligence of duty, Linguet declared, for the Assembly to bother itself with the fate of a skeleton when it faced the task of completing the constitution.

Should hands full of the plunder from the clergy sign the law conferring divine honors on the most violent enemy which the clergy has had? Is it appropriate for those men whom people accuse of wishing to destroy religion—is it appropriate that they sanction the apotheosis of the one among all other men who has done the most damage to religion?[32]

28. *Archives parlementaires*, XXV (May 8, 1791), 661.
29. *Chronique de Paris*, IV, No. 116 (April 26, 1791), 461.
30. *L'Ami du roi* (Montjoye and Crapart), No. 129 (May 9, 1791), pp. 514-515.
31. *Chronique de Paris*, IV, Nos. 135, 140 (May 15 and 20, 1791), 537-538, 557-559; *Bouche de fer*, No. 55 (May 11, 1791), p. 262; *Courrier de Provence*, XVI, No. 270 (May 8-13, 1791), 41; *Les Bienfaits de Voltaire envers le bon peuple français* (n.d., n.p.), pp. 5, 15.
32. *Annales politiques*, XVII, No. 169 (May 26, 1791), 449-462.

The hope that the ceremony would take place on May 30, 1791, had to be abandoned. It would be held June 15, Villette then announced. "This should be the resurrection of Voltaire; May 30 is but the day of his death."[33] Simultaneously he appealed to the emigrés to return to France and let the fête be the occasion for reconciliation of the aristocracy to the Revolution.

On the thirteenth anniversary of Voltaire's death, the National Assembly, on petition of the Department of Paris and recommendation of Pierre-François Gossin, chairman of the constitutional committee, and with surprisingly little open expression of opposition, voted to place Voltaire's body in the Panthéon.[34] Gossin presented Voltaire as a man who had "prepared men for tolerance," striven to improve the lot of mankind, and earned the title of "liberator of thought." The Assembly, however, did not adopt Regnaud's further proposal that a statue of Voltaire be executed at public expense. Moreover, Rousseau, Montesquieu, and Mably were separately nominated for national recognition. The Assembly had gracefully accepted a bust of Rousseau and a copy of the Social Contract from Barère de Vieuzac[35] as early as June, 1790, and had ordered a statue of him on November 29, 1790. The decree of May 30 was thus a belated recognition of Voltaire.[36] Voltaireans nevertheless were elated.[37] How could any deputy have been "barbarous" enough to oppose the decree?[38] Most enthusiastic was the Chronique de Paris. The decree, it said, was the final blow to fanaticism whose ravages were still evident in the royalist journals. The elaborate pomp and ceremony envisioned would discharge the national debt to Voltaire and represent "a triumph of reason over errors and impostures."[39] The democratic Cercle Social's Bouche de fer predicted that the apotheosis would be "a certain mark of our regeneration."[40] Another democratic voice, Prudhomme, though sympathetic to Voltaire, warned against letting festivals distract attention from more important matters.[41] But counter-revolutionary opposition

33. Chronique de Paris, IV, No. 149 (May 29, 1791), 594-595.
34. Archives parlementaires, XXVI (May 30, 1791), 610.
35. Ibid., XVI, 414.   36. Ibid., XXI, 127.
37. Bouche de fer, IV, No. 62 (June 1, 1791), 16.
38. Révolutions de Paris, No. 100 (June 4-11, 1791), p. 446 n. 1.
39. IV, No. 152 (June 1, 1791), 605.   40. IV, No. 62 (June 1, 1791), 16.
41. Révolutions de Paris, No. 100 (June 4-11, 1791), p. 540.

grumbled at the "irreligious delirium" of the moment. The reactionary *Ami du roi* of Montjoye and Crapart acknowledged that honest people could admire Voltaire for some of his work, but all the same he was "one of the greatest corruptors of the simplicity of *mœurs* and of religion of our ancestors. ..."[42] Royou's *Ami du roi*, also reactionary in outlook, denounced Voltaire bitterly as an opportunist who in an age of fanaticism would have been a fanatic, but who had in his own day only pandered to the taste "of the great, the rich, the women, and all the libertines" to whom the yoke of religion "was very inconvenient." Voltaire is the real cause of the Revolution, the journal argued in a classic statement of the conservatives' case against the *philosophe*:

The Revolution never could have taken place if the French people had preserved even a glimmering of common sense. Long before the Estates General was convoked the pamphlets and the jests of Voltaire had spoiled the mind and corrupted the heart of the youth; spread in all the kingdom the venom of impiety; introduced egotism, pride and ignorance; deteriorated and degraded the moral character of the nation; founded a sect murderous and destructive of virtues, of the arts and of talents. In the eyes of all men of sense, of all impartial *philosophes*, Voltaire is the greatest scourge which has ever existed in Europe; he is the more formidable to society and to humanity since it has been demonstrated that religion and *mœurs* are the foundation of public prosperity. ... The Assembly which dares, before the nation, to consecrate, in the temple of the capital, the memory of a man whose very name alarms piety and decency, dishonors itself, dishonors the nation of which it is the interpreter, and proves to all Europe how incapable it is of legislating for a great empire, since it is ignorant of the contemptibility and criminality of the abuse of talents as well as of the nature of the influence of religion and *mœurs* on the government.[43]

All vestiges of clericalism were to be avoided at the fête. "I do not wish to see," Villette wrote, "either candles, or hangings of mourning, or sacerdotal decorations invented by imposture, adopted by interest."[44] Plans for the ceremony, published on June 4 and disseminated through journals and pamphlets,[45]

42. No. 151 (May 31, 1791), pp. 601-606.
43. June 1, 1791, pp. 1-2. Numbering of issues of *l'Ami du Roi* (Royou) stop with this one.
44. *Lettres choisies de Charles Villette*, p. 109.
45. Lacroix, *Actes de la Commune*, Sér. II, V, 123-125; *Moniteur*, VIII (June 20, 1791), 700; *Journal de Paris*, No. 171 (June 20, 1791), pp. 686-689; *Feuille du*

stimulated a war of the written word. The author of *Lettre apologétique* ridiculed various features of the fête,[46] while the so-called Jansenist *Pétition à l'Assemblée nationale*, by professed pro-revolutionaries (the second edition carried 160 names repre-senting 16 sections of Paris), heartily disapproved the secular as-pect lest the "aggregation of pagan ceremonies authorized by the department of Paris contribute to the formation of an entirely new type of fête."[47] But the petition merely fortified the original determination. Among responses to the Jansenist petition was one printed in the *Journal du Club des Cordeliers*, significant for its radical attitude toward the place of religion in the state.[48] While respecting freedom of thought, the writer condemned opinions "which are visibly contrary to common sense, reason, justice and gratitude. They dare say that religion does not allow one to render such great honors to a man who never had any. They fear that this ceremony might make a divinity of him and that the great saint might one day eclipse all the saints of paradise on the calendar." The writer was astonished that anyone could believe the "constitution is so tied to religion that one is in-separable from the other; as if only Catholics might live under a constitution which, without doubt, will bring happiness to all peoples, even to those who are not of our religion." Only secret enemies of the state and fanatics would oppose honors to Voltaire. The principles of the Revolution transcend those of any particular form of organized religion. Other similar defenses of the secular character of the fête could be cited.[49]

Always planned as a patriotic ceremony with strong anti-

jour, No. 172 (June 21, 1791), p. 699; *Translation de Voltaire à Paris. Ordre de la marche et du cortège.... Suivi du "Crédo" de Voltaire* (n.p., n.d.); *Détail exact et circonstancié de tous les objets relatifs à la fête de Voltaire. Extrait de la "Chronique de Paris"* (n.p., n.d.); *Ordre de la marche de la translation de Voltaire à Paris, le lundi 11 juillet, et sa profession de foi* (n.p., 1791).

46. *Lettre apologétique à Messieurs les administrateurs du Départment de Paris* (n.p., n.d.).

47. *Pétition à l'assemblée nationale relative au transport de Voltaire* (rev. ed.; n.p., July 4, 1791), reprinted in Jean F. E. Robinet, *Le Mouvement religieux à Paris pendant la Révolution, 1789-1801* (2 vols.; Paris, 1896-1898), I, 540-542; the first edition is entitled *Pétition à l'assemblée nationale* (n.p., n.d.).

48. No. 5 (n.d.), pp. 43-47.

49. [P. Ph. Gudin de la Brenéllerie], *Réponse d'un ami des grands hommes aux envieux de la gloire de Voltaire* (n.p., n.d.); *Journal de Paris*, No. 199 (July 18, 1791), p. 800; *Réponse à la pétition des 160 Jansenists* (n.p., n.d.)—signed: Marc-Antoine D.... T.

clerical implications, the demonstration took on added meaning
with the flight of the king (June 20-21)—a sense of urgency, a
determined feeling of rededication to the Revolution, and an
overtone of anti-royalist defiance. "How can our situation [re-
ferring to plans for the fêtes] be changed by the flight of one
man?" asked the *Chronique de Paris*.[50] The Cercle Social greeted
Villette's assertion that the "executive power" would witness the
fête in "majestic isolation" through a crack in the Pavillon de
Flore, where the king was under guard, with loud applause and
general laughter, leaving no doubt, the *Bouche de fer* reported,
as to the audience's profound contempt for "our fat fugitive."[51]
The Paris authorities seem to have agreed with Prudhomme that
"the national triumph of Voltaire should not be delayed except
by some great public calamity; the loss of a king and his deposition
is not one."[52] Delayed by the flight, Charon left for Romilly on
June 23, the day of the king's return, to supervise arrangements
for the transfer of Voltaire's body to Paris.[53]

Not till the evening of July 5, after considerable further delay
and a day of celebrating, did the procession start out from
Romilly.[54] A twenty-foot high chariot, drawn by four horses,
decorated with draperies, flowers, and the national colors, and
accompanied by units of the national guard, roused manifest
public interest as it moved slowly along the route to Paris via
Provins, Nanges, Guigne, Brie-Comte-Robert, and Créteuil. Using Voltaire's coffin as an altar of the Federation, municipal and
departmental officials at the different localities swore to defend the
constitution, to die for the law, and to prove their ceaseless fraternal attachment, according to Charon.[55] He had, in turn, assured all of Paris's loyalty to the constitution. Such ceremonies
illustrate how Voltaire's cult was merging with that of the Revolution; the flight of the king and not *l'infâme* was evidently
uppermost in the minds of the planners. Inscriptions on the
char read: "Si l'homme est né libre, il doit se gouverner," and

50. IV, No. 174 (June 22, 1791), 692.   51. No. 88 (July 10, 1791), pp. 2-3.
52. *Révolutions de Paris*, No. 105 (July 9-16, 1791), p. 3.
53. Lacroix, *Actes de la Commune*, Sér. II, V, 101.
54. Robinet, *Le Mouvement religieux*, I, 544; *Lettres choisies de Charles Villette*,
p. 177; "Cult of Voltaire," pp. 187-190. For the expenses of Charon's trip see AN,
F13 1136, *Église Sainte Geneviève, 1791-An IV* (June 24-July 14, 1791).
55. Charon's address at the barrier of Charenton, July 10: Lacroix, *Actes de la
Commune*, Sér. II, V, 336.

"Si l'homme a des tyrans, il doit les détroner."[56]   Once in Paris on the evening of July 10, the coffin was transported to the Place de la Bastille and elevated to a platform erected on a pyramid of stones from the demolished fortress, a reminder that Voltaire too had been a victim of despotism at that very spot.

As the cortège advanced from Romilly, preparations went ahead in Paris amid the tense political atmosphere complicated by economic unrest, religious strife, and fear of civil conflict and even of foreign attack.   Postponed several times because of the delays at Romilly, the fête was not definitely scheduled for July 11 until about July 8, when the organizers, working closely with Villette, made hasty last-minute arrangements.[57]   Palloy, patriotic architect and Bastille model builder who was responsible for soliciting support of various official and unofficial patriotic groups, emphasized in his invitations to them that the fête was not merely honoring an individual but was intended "to awaken in all heads and in posterity the hatred which despotism should inspire."[58]   A symbol of the victory of the new regime over the old,

the translation of the ashes of Voltaire into the walls of this city should be regarded as one of the most important results of our liberty, the honors rendered to his spirit will prove to all our neighbors that Frenchmen, become free, know also how to display their gratitude toward the great men who have taught them the road to true citizenship.[59]

Economic discontent and demonstrations of disaffected people clouded the situation.[60]   Aristocrats and clericals, it was said,[61] were inciting trouble and spreading rumors, broadcast by the Jansenist *Pétition*, among the unemployed and the poor to the effect that tremendous sums, some 500,000 to 600,000 francs, were being expended on a luxurious and useless festival at a time of misery and suffering.   The many reports of such grumbling[62]

56. *Révolutions de Paris*, No. 105 (July 9-16, 1791), pp. 3 ff.
57. Lacroix, *Actes de la Commune*, Sér. II, V, 283 f.
58. BN., MSS, nouv. acq. fr. 312, pp. 289, 295-304; for quote, see *ibid.*, 2673, p. 149.
59. *Ibid.*, 312, p. 300.
60. Mathiez, *The Revolution*, p. 123; George Rudé, *The Crowd in the French Revolution* (Oxford, 1959), pp. 82-84; *Nouvelles extraordinaires de divers endroits*, No. 57 (July 10, 1791), n.p. re the state of mind in Paris on July 11.
61. *Le Bulletin et journal des journaux*, No. 81 (July 8, 1791), p. 81.
62. *Ibid.*; *Le Spectateur national et modérateur*, II, Nos. 222 and 225 (July 10 and July 13, 1791), pp. 948, 959-960; *Le Babillard du Palais Royal ou l'écho de*

122 RAYMOND ROCKWOOD

and the efforts of the supporters of the celebration to counteract
the charges lend credence to the discontent. Villette assured the
public that most of the funds would come from private sources
and only 18,000 francs would be spent by Paris for an event that
should attract large crowds and considerable business to the city
(in fact the bill was ultimately pared down to 36,858 francs).[63]
The police had been on edge for some time as a consequence of
the religious strife which, Bailly contended, aristocrats were using
to stir up civil conflict.[64]   The night before the fête and that
morning violence was threatened at the Bastille in the St. Antoine
district.[65]   Scheduled to begin at 8 A.M. on July 11,[66] the celebration was postponed because of rain and then rescheduled for
noon that day; in response to rumored threats of violence and
the restlessness of participants and onlookers who had flocked
to Paris for the occasion (and the Federation of the 14th), the
procession finally started in mid-afternoon under special police
precautions.[67]   The Jansenist petition, posted throughout the
route overnight, had been torn down, defaced, or covered by
the department's proclamation of the order of the procession;
leaflets paying tribute to Voltaire were distributed to the crowd.[68]
The route of the cortège, as announced June 21, was to follow

l'opinion publique, No. 29 (July 12, 1791), pp. 7-8, and No. 30 (July 13, 1791), p. 2;
Gazette de Paris (July 12, 1791), p. 3; Journal général (Fontenai), No. 161 (July 11,
1791), p. 671, and No. 166 (July 16, 1791), pp. 691-692.
  63. Chronique de Paris, V, No. 191 (July 10, 1791), 769.   Accounts for the
fête are to be found in AN, Flc I, p. 84.
  64. Journal de Paris, No. 160 (June 9, 1791), pp. 642-644.
  65. Robinet, Le Mouvement réligieux, I. 545; Le Spectateur national et le
modérateur, II, No. 225 (July 13, 1791), 959-960.
  66. There are many descriptions of the procession, including Journal de Paris,
No. 194 (July 13, 1791), pp. 778-780; Révolutions de Paris (Prudhomme), No. 105
(July 9-16, 1791), p. 10; Moniteur, IX, No. 194 (July 13, 1791), 108; Feuille villageoise, No. 43 (July 21, 1791), p. 295; Feuille du jour, No. 193 (July 12, 1791), p.
91; Bouche de fer, IV, No. 90 (July 12, 1791), 1-6; Chronique de Paris, V, No. 193
(July 12, 1791), 781; Mercure de France, No. 31 (July 30, 1791), pp. 182-191;
Journal général de France, No. 194 (July 13, 1791), p. 780; Journal de la noblesse,
No. 29 (July 9-12, 1791), p. 299; L'Ami du roi (Montjoye and Crapart), No. 194
(July 13, 1791), pp. 775-776; Journal général (Fontenai), No. 166 (July 16, 1791),
pp. 691-692.   See also for further references, David L. Dowd, Pageant Master of the
Republic: Jacques-Louis David and the Revolution (Lincoln, Neb., 1948), p. 49 n. 18.
  67. For special police precautions taken, see letter of July 9, 1791, BN., MSS,
nouv. acq. fr. 2666, p. 350.
  68. Le Bulletin et journal des journaux, No. 83 (July 13, 1791), n.p.; Chronique
de Paris, No. 193 (July 12, 1791), p. 781; Correspondance nationale, No. 44 (July
16, 1791), pp. 138-142; Annales patriotiques, No. 647 (July 11, 1791), pp. 1654-1655;
Mercure universel (July 13, 1791), p. 199; Journal général (Fontenai), No. 166
(July 16, 1791), pp. 691-692.

the boulevards leading out from the Boulevard St. Antoine, up to the Place Louis XV, down the Quai des Tuileries, across the Pont Royal, along Quai Voltaire and the rues Dauphine, de la Comédie, du Théâtre Français and des Fossés M. le Prince, then onto Place St. Michel and up rue St. Hyacinthe and the Porte St. Jacques to the Place du Panthéon.[69] Further grumblings concerning the cost were overheard during the affair, but were easily silenced, we are assured, by the "reasonings of *gens sensées.*"[70]

The procession, some 100,000 strong says Villette,[71] was modeled on Greek apotheoses and Roman consecrations.[72] The classical pagan tone was set by the decorations, antique costumes, and specially constructed ancient musical instruments, and by a studious avoidance of traditional religious motifs.[73] Every detail was calculated to stimulate patriotic fervor. Banners carried by citizen groups and public officials again pointed to the serious political situation, upheld the ideals of the Revolution, and called for unyielding commitment to them. "Qui meurt pour sa patrie meurt toujours content."[74] A fraternal club from Les Halles denounced the hated devils and the sins repudiated by the new epoch (a reference to *fanatisme* or *despotisme?*):

Exterminez, grand Dieu, de la terre ou nous sommes
Quiconque avec plaisir repánd le sang des hommes.[75]

Another society, representing different classes of people, upheld the cardinal creed of the moment:

Les mortels sont égaux; ce n'est pas la naissance
C'est la seule vertu qui fait la différence.[76]

Still another device, carried aloft a pike, read: "De ce fer naquit la liberté."[77] On the paper bonnets of the printers of the

69. *Le Feuille du jour*, No. 172 (June 21, 1791), p. 703.
70. *Moniteur*, IX, No. 194 (July 13, 1791), 108.
71. *Lettres choisies de Charles Villette*, p. 188; *Feuille villageoise* (No. 43 [July 21, 1791], 295) uses the same figure.
72. *Lettres choisies de Charles Villette*, p. 190.
73. On the cult of antiquity in the Revolution, see Harold T. Parker, *The Cult of Antiquity and the French Revolutionaries* (Chicago, 1937). Jules Renouvier (*Histoire de l'art pendant la Révolution* [Paris, 1863]) refers to the apotheosis of Voltaire as "the first philosophical fête particularly dear to artists" (pp. 417-418) and places the classical costumes in the perspective of the movement begun by Talma in 1788 (pp. 468-469).
74. *Moniteur*, IX, No. 194 (July 13, 1791), 108.
75. *Feuille villageoise*, No. 43 (July 21, 1791), p. 295.
76. *Ibid.*
77. *Moniteur*, IX, No. 194 (July 13, 1791), 107 f.

Bouche de fer were the phrases: "Liberté de la presse" and "Vivre libre ou mourir."[78]

The cortège presented a panorama of official and unofficial revolutionary elements united in a dramatic show of civic devotion to the ideals of the Revolution expressed through their salute to the hero of the hour. The ingredients of a revolutionary cult were in evidence. Patriotic citizen worshipers marched with the new priests (civic officials) and lay brethren (leaders of unofficial groups) as an inspiration to the congregation (those who watched) and as a lesson to the sinners (the anti-revolutionaries). The procession comprised various military units (national guards, Gardes Françaises, cavalry to the front and rear); students, representatives of patriotic societies (it was noted, with some curiosity, that the Jacobins marched separately from other clubs[79]); the captors of the Bastille; an amazon who had stormed the Bastille; citizens from d'Assass, Varennes, and Nancy, the electors of 1789 and 1790; delegates from the theaters, academicians and men of letters; young artists; and deputations from the sections, the National Assembly, the department, the municipality of Paris and others in the department, and the various courts. Relics, sanctified by the Revolution, were borne in unwitting imitation of Catholic practices—the colors of the Bastille; a model of the fortress; bullets, cuirasses, and chains found there; minutes of the electors of 1789 and a history of the capture of the fortress by Dusseaux. In addition to patriotic slogans, patriotic leaders, dedicated citizen participants, sacred relics, and patriotic events, there were patriotic heroes: the captors of the Bastille, already mentioned; and a picture of the gallant Desilles, who had died rather than fire on French soldiers in the Nancy mutiny. Other precursors and "founders" of the Revolution (revolutionary saints) besides Voltaire were honored with portraits: Rousseau, Mirabeau, and Franklin. Even hymns of adoration and praise were not forgotten. At the Opera one composed by Gossec to Chénier's poetry was sung, reclaiming Voltaire for Paris after his "exile" by "tyranny," saluting his "sublime reason" for disarming "lying priests," calling on the "God of liberty" to permit France and its Revolution to prosper in peace, and praying for

78. *Bouche de fer,* IV, No. 90 (July 12, 1791), 1-6.
79. *Moniteur,* IX, No. 194 (July 13, 1791), 108 f.

civic virtues and *mœurs* "worthy of our laws."[80] Such acclaim, along with the slogans, sanctified revolutionary ideals and upheld the virtues of dedicated citizenship. Various choral groups accompanied the paraders chanting, we are assured, not the superstitious songs of orthodoxy, but new ones, written especially for the occasion. The peculiarly melodious sound of the ancient musical instruments along with the costumes of fair ladies dressed as muses and graces was intended to reproduce the atmosphere which had inspired patriots of antiquity to great deeds.

But Voltaire claimed the center of the attention. As one of the bibles of the Revolution, a "magnificent collection" of his works, the Kehl edition (donated with his usual flair for publicity by its publisher, Beaumarchais, to the Bibliothèque du roi as a gesture of his *civisme*)[81] was carried in a gilded chest. A cardboard replica of Houdon's famous statue of Voltaire smiling impishly and yet benevolently at the crowd (its head disintegrated at the end from the rain) was ported ahead of the sarcophagus, and pyramids were also borne with medallions attached on which were inscribed the titles of his major works.

Voltaire's body was carried by a magnificent triumphal chariot designed by the distinguished revolutionary artist, Louis David;[82] the chariot was "un vrai coup d'œil" even to a hostile witness,[83] though most unfriendly observers were not so generous. An Egyptian granite coffin, on which a reclining life-size figure of Voltaire draped in regal purple and being crowned by Immortality, towered forty feet above the ground. Drawn by twelve spirited light gray horses, four abreast, the *char* with its bronze colored wheels and incense burners on each corner added to the classical atmosphere of the occasion. None of the four inscriptions on it could be interpreted as anti-monarchical, but all,

80. Constant Pierre, *Les Hymnes et chansons de la Révolution* (Paris, 1904), pp. 205-208; M. J. Chénier, *Hymne sur la translation du corps de Voltaire* (Paris, 1791).

81. *Motion faite par Pierre-Augustin Caron Beaumarchais au comité des auteurs dramatiques pour aller au devant du convoi de Voltaire le 9 mai 1791* (n.p., n.d.).

82. For David's role in planning the procession as a whole, see Dowd's *Pageant-Master of the Republic*, pp. 45-54; Dowd's general account of the apotheosis, though based on his own review of the sources (including new materials), admittedly leans heavily upon the last chapter of the author's "Cult of Voltaire"; for another earlier account of the celebration, see Louise P. Kellogg, "Sur la translation des restes de Voltaire au Panthéon le 11 juillet 1791," *La Révolution française*, XXXVII (Sept., 1899), 271-277.

83. *L'Ami du roi* (Montjoye and Crapart), No. 194 (July 13, 1791), pp. 775-776.

again, attacked the devils and sins and upheld the virtues of the Revolution. One recorded the Assembly's decree of May 30 honoring Voltaire. Another was careful to defend Voltaire against the charge of atheism and to identify him with the ideals and reforms of the Revolution:

> Il combatit les Athées et les Fanatiques
> Il inspira la Tolérance.
> Il reclama les Droits de l'Homme,
> Contre la Servitude et la Féodalité.

A third acclaimed his genius as a founder of the Revolution:

> Poëte, Historien, Philosophe,
> Il agrandit l'Esprit humain,
> Et lui apprit qu'il devait être libre.

Finally, his humanitarian role was featured: "Il défendit Calas, Sirven, LaBarre, Montbailly."

The procession, a mirror of secular devotion to the ideals of the Revolution, prototype of a new patriotic faith, advanced through the wet streets, making several prearranged stops for special demonstrations, particularly at the Opera, on the Quai Voltaire in front of Villette's apartment, and at the Théâtre de la Nation. Each station was specially decorated. Most elaborate were preparations at the Quai Voltaire, where Madame Villette, in classical garb, and the daughters of Calas were featured in a touching scene of personal devotion. The columns of the *Comédie* were decorated with the titles of Voltaire's plays and actors appeared dressed as various characters in his dramas. The bedraggled marchers finally reached the Panthéon about 9:30 P.M. after darkness and heavy rain had dispersed much of the crowd. Villette's estimate of 600,000 onlookers is probably an exaggeration, but contemporaries agree that many people, including an influx attracted by the Federation, crowded the crossings and gardens and jammed the windows and roofs.[84]

Comments on the attitude of the crowd parallel those on the fête as a whole, ranging from ecstatic adulation to contemptuous ridicule, depending on the observer's perspective. The pro-revo-

---

84. *Lettres choisies de Charles Villette*, p. 188; *Feuille villageoise*, No. 43 (July (July 13, 1791), 107-108.
21, 1791), p. 295; *Mercure universel*, V (July 12, 1791), 182; *Moniteur*, IX, No. 194

lutionary press was generally enthusiastic and unrestrained, declaring the celebration a significant national festival. But the sneering, hostile journalists and other witnesses saw only a drab, disheveled, and disorderly *mélange* of modern and classical themes.[85] Madame de Genlis later declared it "the most foolish, abominable, and ridiculous absurdity that was ever seen in Paris prior to the festival given in honor of the Goddess of Reason, i.e. 1793."[86] The future Lord Palmerston, then on a visit to Paris, could only see "very shabby, ill-dressed people"; Gouverneur Morris, the United States minister, declared it "very poor"; and Earl Gower, the British ambassador, termed it "calculated to give entertainment to children."[87]

Enthusiasts interpreted the parade as a personal victory of Voltaire over his persecutors, an answer to the Paris clergy who had refused him Christian burial in 1778. But to most favorable commentators, it was not the man, with his pettiness, that was celebrated, but "saint Voltaire," apostle of liberty, the most prodigious man France had ever produced, the man who had written *Brutus*, fought superstition and fanaticism, acted as the benefactor and preceptor of humanity, prepared France for Revolution, and who, more than any one else, was responsible for the progress of the human mind. Thus, the apotheosis was hailed by Madame Roland as a triumph of reason over superstition, philosophy over theology, and of justice and tolerance over tyranny and fanaticism.[88] "It was necessary that expiring fanaticism see with impotent rage the triumph of its most mortal enemy and that unparalleled honors be discerned to this extraordinary genius," affirmed P. L. Ginguené, future founder of *La Décade philosophique*, mouthpiece of republican ideologues, in a long and laudatory post mortem.[89] Why should bigots now protest against

85. *Feuille du jour*, No. 193 (July 12, 1791), p. 92; *Journal général de France*, No. 194 (July 13, 1791), p. 780; *Journal général* (Fontenai), No. 166 (July 16, 1791), pp. 691-692; *L'Ami du roi* (Montjoye and Crapart), No. 194 (July 13, 1791), pp. 775-776; *La Rocambole des journaux*, No. 8 (July 13, 1791), p. 135; *Journal de la noblesse*, No. 29 (July 9-12, 1791), p. 299.

86. *Memoirs of the Countess de Genlis* (8 vols.; London, 1825), IV, 90.

87. Oscar Browning (ed.), *The Despatches of Earl Gower* (Cambridge, 1885), p. 105; "The Diary of Viscount Palmerston," *ibid.*, p. 289; *Diary and Letters of Gouverneur Morris* (2 vols.; New York, 1888), I, 430.

88. Claude Perroud (ed.), *Lettres de Madame Roland* (2 vols.; Paris, 1902), II, 327.

89. *Mercure de France*, No. 31 (July 30, 1791), pp. 182 f.

the secular character of the celebration since they denied Voltaire religious burial?[90] No mortal enemy of the human race, "king or queen, aristocrat or fanatical priests," was allowed to disturb the occasion.[91] The story was told of a woman who, on observing the *char*, cried out: "What beautiful wheels!" To which came the retort: "Yes, they are crushing fanaticism."[92] The death of fanaticism is imagined graphically by an anonymous contributor to the *Journal des clubs*:

All along the route I saw a long emaciated form, with protruding ears, its eyes bandaged, clutching in one hand a sword crossed by a dagger for its guard, in the other a bleeding heart being raised to its mouth. This form, that of fanaticism, was continually trying to stop the carriage, but at each attempt it fell prostrate on the ground and the four wheels passed over its body. It uttered frightful howls, got up again, always to repeat the process. I said to myself, this monster must have a tough life. In the square before the Sainte-Geneviève, the great quantity of rain which had fallen had made the ground very soggy; the form, thrown down once more and trampled on by the horses and the wheels of the chariot, was driven so deeply into the slough that it disappeared altogether and Voltaire entered the temple.[93]

The revelers at an unruly banquet, intended for the participating national guard units and held afterwards in the Salle des Papes of the Abbey Ste. Geneviève, left all of the pictures of the popes defaced by saber thrusts, we are told.[94]

To most favorable observers the event was acclaimed as a victory of the new order over the old, but there was also a note of republican anti-monarchical defiance and of consecrated Jacobin hostility to foes at home and abroad in many of the accounts. For the *Bouche de fer*, this "fête républicaine" revealed the "holy ecstasy and majesty of a grateful people," and demonstrated the "enormous difference which a free people makes between an imbecile king and the person who consecrates himself to useful deeds in the defense of the oppressed."[95] The image of

90. *Ibid.*
91. *Annales patriotiques*, No. 647 (July 11, 1791), pp. 1654-1655.
92. *Chronique de Paris*, V, No. 194 (July 13, 1791), 784.
93. III, No. 39 (Aug. 10, 1791), 674-675.
94. *L'Ami du roi* (Montjoye and Crapart), No. 198 (July 17, 1791), p. 792; the banquet is confirmed by the expense account, AN, F13 1136, *Mémoire du banquet ...à Ste. Geneviève* (July 11, 1791).
95. IV, No. 90 (July 12, 1791), 1-2.

Voltaire, already refurbished before the event with revolutionary polish, took on a special anti-monarchical hue after the fête in *Ami de la révolution ou philippique,* a paper with a left wing façade, supported by moderates to counteract the leftist press.

We make reparations in a single day for three centuries of injustice and barbarism. When the league of foreign and national tyrants begin their attack, it will be time enough for us to defend ourselves. Another subject now concerns our thoughts. We owe a great homage to him who first dared tell kings severe truths and to him who reduced the pride of parlements in exposing their turpitudes; who, while seeming to cuddle up to the nobility, subjected it to ridicule, by revealing from whence it sucked its sustenance and by delving into the ills which it caused the rest of humanity whom it insolently trampled under foot; we owe an acknowledgement equal to the offense involved, to him who long before the declaration of rights of man and of the citizen, said

> Les hommes sont égaux, ce n'est pas la naissance
> C'est la seule vertu qui fait leur différence. *(Mérope)*

Monarchs of Europe should pay obeisance at the tomb of one who taught us not to be dazzled "by the brilliance of the diadem" and incited "slaves to lack respect for their masters. He dethroned kings, unmasked priests. . . ."

Whereas the sage of Geneva set the foundation of the temple of liberty, the *philosophe* of Ferney amused himself at the expense of the Gods of the old regime. He gave us confidence [by revealing] their weaknesses, he gave the people the taste of thinking. He haunted the great to inform the little people of what went on there. He skilfully called attention to the swaddling clothes in which the nation was wrapped, as in its infancy; he gave it his hand [to enable it] to stand erect and to march in the path which others had prepared for it. Voltaire is truly the father of the revolution; he prepared it and foresaw it.

Now let us "hold ourselves ready to fight our enemies from without, and to keep in check our wayward brothers" lest we be "caught off guard."[96]

As the long paragraph just cited suggests, Rousseau was held in high veneration by many. Marat was particularly vehement in his criticism of Voltaire as a "plagiarist," "scandalous writer," "a

96. IV, No. 53 (July 10-13, 1791), 51-56.

perverter of the youth with lessons of false philosophy."[97] He favored "Montesquieu, the first apostle of liberty France produced, and Rousseau, the legislator of the nations." The *Ami des patriotes*, a paper in which the deputy, Regnaud, had an interest, concluded that Voltaire deserved the honors, although other *philosophes* may have been more worthy.[98] They were better friends of liberty, but Voltaire won more friends for it. For Palloy everything concerning Rousseau, "our Regenerator," held an "aura of the supernatural," a feeling no one else inspired except Voltaire.[99] The Revolution had transformed some foes of Voltaire into admirers. Such was the case of Fréron, the son of Voltaire's archenemy, editor of *Orateur du peuple* and critic of the moderate Lafayette, who confessed he no longer regarded the Sage of Ferney as "the irritable writer who spewed forth injuries and calumny" but as "the great man and benefactor of humanity."[100]

Although the *Ami du roi* had warned early that spring that with constitutional bishops one might expect anything, even the placing of the remains of the Voltaires and the Rousseaus on our "sacred altars,"[101] the constitutional clergy do not seem to have participated and some were among the signatories of the Jansenist *Pétition*. The festival, no doubt, further compromised the constitutional church in the minds of loyal Catholics and certainly alienated some of those who had considered themselves good revolutionaries. In fact, those who signed the *Pétition* claimed to have been supporters of the Revolution. On the other hand, if the fête alienated some moderates, it had the support of others. For example, Regnaud, who had advocated Voltaire's case in the National Assembly, voted for the reinstatement of the king,[102] and Pastoret, the *procureur général* of the Department of Paris, charged by the National Assembly with over-all responsibility for the fête, soon joined the ranks of the Feuillants.[103] Charon, the municipal officer delegated to organize the affair, who had been

97. *Ami du peuple*, No. 421 (April 6, 1791), p. 7.
98. *Ami des patriotes*, III, No. 35 (July 23, 1791), 12.
99. BN., MSS, nouv. acq. fr. 312, p. 721.
100. Cited in *Révolutions de France et de Brabant* (Desmoulins), VII, No. 85, 288.
101. (Montjoye and Crapart), No. 95 (April 5, 1791), pp. 378-379.
102. *Nouvelle biographie générale* (Didot) (Paris, 1866), XLI, 855-856.
103. Mathiez, *The Revolution*, p. 133.

active since March, was criticized early in June in the Jacobin Club as "the most aristocratic of the municipal officers."[104]   Although anti-monarchical and even republican implications could be read into the various slogans and comments on the ceremony, one must be more impressed by the relatively moderate tone of the festival, by Charon's care, when in the provinces, to pledge Paris' loyalty to the constitution and to exact a similar pledge from local authorities, by the elaborate police precautions, and by the lack of any untoward and prolonged demonstrations against the king as the cortège passed the palace.

Since the National Assembly refused to honor Voltaire before 1791, he was clearly an unacceptable official symbol of the Revolution till then.   That his legend dovetailed well with the revolutionary sentiment of that moment is also evident.   Renée Waldinger has tried to demonstrate that the Constitution of 1791 conformed in large measure to Voltaire's ideas (she does not claim he was the cause), but this question of fact, though relevant, does not concern us here.[105]   Given the diversity of pro-revolutionary groups in 1791 and the fact that both moderates and radicals responded favorably to Voltaire's legend (and some in both groups unfavorably), it is clear that for some the legend's association with the new order meant the Revolution had gone too far, for others it represented the Constitution of 1791, and for still others it symbolized a revolution yet to be achieved.   For reactionaries it helped explain the mess.   For revolutionaries like Marat, it was irrelevant.   For certain men on the street, on short rations or unemployed, it was a matter of indifference or a good reason to protest money that could have been better spent.   What is interesting to observe, however, is that a number of those who played leading roles in organizing and promoting the honors for Voltaire seem to have been men whose views already outstripped the settlement of 1791 and who, therefore, might be classified as individuals who were more or less in the vanguard of the Revolution.   Nicholas de Bonneville's *Bouche de fer,* Prudhomme's *Révolutions de Paris,* and Condorcet were backing

104. *Journal des débats de la Société des Amis de la Constitution,* No. 13 (June 10, 1791), p. 3; *Journal des clubs,* III, No. 39 (August 10, 1791), 673.
105. *Voltaire and Reform.*

the republican cause by mid-July, 1791.[106] It would be difficult to argue, therefore, that the legend of Voltaire was merely one that best fitted a more moderate (if it may be so termed) first stage of the Revolution, for it also seemed to burn in the breasts of many who were in 1791 poised to go ahead. Certainly, from the standpoint of the ultimate religious tendency of the Revolution, the spirit of Voltaire would find fulfilment in the atmosphere of 1793-1794.

The reactionary journalists ridiculed and denounced the honors accorded the *chef des incrédules* in ringing diatribes.[107] Beneath these outcries was the keen realization that many revolutionaries would no longer attempt to co-operate with orthodoxy in their solutions, that the Revolution, from the reactionaries', and even some moderates', view, had parted company with the orthodox faith. The National Assembly had deprived the Church of its newest and "most beautiful" building in Paris—Ste. Geneviève—and then had desecrated it by placing its bitterest enemy— "a precursor of Antichrist"—in it with honors. One embittered Christian exclaimed:

A few days after the pantheonization of Mirabeau (Oh my God, give me a fountain of tears), with an entirely pagan pomp, the odious remains and image of the chief of disbelievers was placed there in the church; this madman who, during his long life . . . found his principal pleasure in vomiting blasphemous sarcasm; who was the precursor of anti-Christ; who was the representative of the latter and is said to have dared declare, through an atrocious pride, that he was anti-Christ in person. . . . It is to this monster that the sacrilegious honors of an apotheosis have been awarded.[108]

The *Feuille du jour* found it necessary to answer an article published in an English paper charging that "atheism is the system dominating the French. They worship the relics of Voltaire, the father of unbelief."[109] The apotheosis had thus added to the complexity of the religious situation and made compromise be-

106. Mathiez, *The Revolution*, pp. 121, 129; George Lefebvre, *La Révolution française* (Paris, 1951), p. 219.
107. *Nouvelles ecclésiastiques*, Sept. 20, 1791, pp. 149-153; *Éloge véridique de M. de Voltaire* (Paris, 1791), pp. 11, 24, 31-34, 44, 49-51; Pierre de Vaissière, *Lettres d'"Aristocrates"* (Paris, 1907), pp. 297, 404; *Journal de la noblesse*, No. 9 (July 9-12, 1791), p. 299; *L'Ami du roi* (Royou), July 13, 1791, p. 3.
108. *Amende honorable à Dieu et à Sainte Geneviève* (n.p., n.d.), pp. 2-3.
109. No. 182 (July 1, 1791), p. 3.

tween the Revolution and orthodoxy more difficult. The constitutional clergy, now placed in a more embarrassing situation, had
to explain why they were allied with a National Assembly which
deified the *chef des incrédules*. It was the paganism and secularism of the fête that caused the greatest alarm, the portent of a
new civic religion with its own rites and symbols.[110]   Albert
Mathiez has pointed out that by 1791 symbolism representing
revolutionary heroes and ideals had already been developed.[111]
All that was lacking was a system of ceremonies constructed about
the new symbolism which would permit citizens to worship
periodically. A study of the apotheosis of Voltaire shows that
the nucleus of such a religious cult, in process since the beginning of the Revolution, had certainly been formulated by
July 11, 1791. Thus, Aulard seems incorrect in stating that the
first completely lay ceremony during the Revolution was held on
August 10, 1793.[112]

Neither a study in Voltaire's actual impact on legislation nor
a comprehensive analysis of Voltaire's place in public opinion
during the National Assembly period, the story of the pantheonization yet serves as a barometer of attitudes, an illustration of the
reciprocal reinforcement of ideas and events, and an example
of the emerging secular revolutionary cult of national patriotism.
It is obvious that friend and foe alike believed Voltaire had
played a major role in paving the way to Revolution—for better
or for worse—and that he was particularly to be blamed or praised
for the religious changes. His reputation had been well articulated before 1789, people were generally aware of its anti-clerical
implications from the start, and he shared credit for the Revolution, as a *philosophe* who had loved mankind, with other *philosophes*. As long as there was hope for the co-operation of the
clergy and the moral support of Catholicism, the National Assembly ignored efforts of energetic promoters of Voltaire's cause,
like Villette, to secure honors for their hero. But the Assembly's
desire to reorganize the Church produced an increasingly bitter
quarrel between the pious and the reformers, reduced the value
of the orthodox faith as a moral underpinning for the new order,

110. *L'Ami du roi* (Montjoye and Crapart), No. 194 (July 13, 1791), pp. 775-776.
111. Mathiez, *Origines*, pp. 38-39; and his *The Revolution*, p. 118.
112. *Le Christianisme et la Révolution française* (Paris, 1925), p. 94.

and opened the way for the development of a more secularized cult of national patriotism. Thus the plan of a few dedicated Voltaire partisans mushroomed into an appropriate and symbolic national event which favored an intensified revival of the anti-clerical Voltaire, who had fought superstition, fanaticism, and ecclesiastical tyranny. How far Voltaire's ideas actually had influenced this evolution of the thought and action of the National Assembly has not been an issue; what is clear is that the reformers identified their aims and ideals with certain anti-clerical reinterpretations of the Voltaire legend. The flight of the king then strengthened Voltaire's political image as a champion of equality and liberty. While events were thus reviving the memory of particular aspects of Voltaire's character and writings and absorbing them into the revolutionary cult, the memory, in turn, probably intensified by support or by contradiction the views men already held and sharpened the antagonism between factions.

ROBESPIERRE, ROUSSEAU, AND REPRESENTATION

Gordon H. McNeil

Early in the French Revolution there took place in Paris a dinner conversation, whose significance has been overlooked by historians.[1] The guests included Pétion and Robespierre, who still had time for such sociable diversions. In the course of the discussion Robespierre attacked the representative system, and Pétion offered objections to his arguments. One of the ladies present then asked Robespierre what system he would put in its place. On a previous occasion he had replied to this question, "that of Lycurgus"; but at that time the impossibility of following this precedent from ancient Sparta had been demonstrated. So this time he simply replied in a most revealing phrase, "I shall think about it."

Think about it he did, frequently. And this essay deals with his thoughts on representation as he struggled to reconcile theory —which was confusing at best—with the realities of political practice in a rapidly changing revolutionary setting.

It is a commonplace that Robespierre was a disciple of Jean-Jacques Rousseau. Qualification, however, is necessary once one goes beyond the "deceiving generalities," as the late Albert Schinz characterized the superficial conclusions of practically everything written about Rousseau's actual influence on the French Revolution.[2] Thus while Robespierre was a disciple of Rousseau, he also shared in the cult of antiquity which so influenced the revo-

GORDON H. McNEIL *is professor of history at the University of Arkansas.*

1. Alfred Stern, "Charles Engelbert Oelsner: notice biographique accompagnée de fragments de ses mémoires relatifs à l'histoire de la Révolution française," *Revue historique,* LXXII (Jan.-April, 1900), 322-323. No date is given for the dinner.

2. Albert Schinz, *État présent des travaux sur J.-J. Rousseau* (New York, 1941), p. 10. For the cult, see the present writer's article, "The Cult of Rousseau and the French Revolution," *Journal of the History of Ideas,* VI (1945), 197-212. For recent analyses of Robespierre's political thought, see Marc Bouloiseau, *Robespierre* (Paris, 1956), and Jean Massin, *Robespierre* (Paris, 1956).

lutionary generation.[3] His classical education and the cult of
antiquity had given him and many others, including Rousseau,
an exaggerated respect for the constitution-drafting role of Lycurgus as described by Plutarch and others, and as discussed by
Rousseau in the *Contrat social*.[4] According to Rousseau, the
Legislator, such as Lycurgus was for Sparta, is one who not only
establishes a constitution for a people but who, more profoundly,
institutes thereby a change in the very nature of each individual,
bestowing on each person his very life and being by virtue of the
social contract.[5] This fundamentally moral approach to government was also Robespierre's approach, and in his great speech
of 18 Floréal he was to pronounce the goals of the Revolution in
something very much like these Rousseauan terms.   But at the
time of the dinner-table discussions, he was more particularly concerned with the representative system as it was then being applied
in France, and with the manner in which this accorded with the
Rousseauan conception of the Legislator.

In the *Contrat social* Rousseau had devoted a chapter to the
Legislator, beginning with a utopian conception of the superior intelligence and authority required to create the laws for a society.
In short, he wrote: "It would take gods to give laws to men."[6]
He obviously did not literally mean "gods," for he discussed the
example of Lycurgus and other mortals. Yet for him the function
of law-giver was nevertheless unique, being quite distinct from the
performance of routine legislative duties.   The role of Lycurgus
had been familiar to Robespierre since his schoolboy reading of
Plutarch, and he no doubt was familiar with Rousseau's theory
and conclusions on this subject.   But he and his colleagues of the
Patriot party in the National Assembly occupied a decidedly
anomalous situation in the light of this theory.   For Robespierre,
Pétion, and probably others in attendance at the dinner party

3. Harold T. Parker, *The Cult of Antiquity and the French Revolutionaries*
(Chicago, 1937).
4. Book II, chap. vii.   The best critical and annotated edition of the *Contrat
social* is that by Maurice Halbwachs (Paris, 1943), which has been recently
reprinted.   Hereafter referred to as Halbwachs.
5. Halbwachs, p. 180.
6. *Ibid.*, pp. 179-180. This conception of the constitution-writing function, summarized in this aphorism, had been seized upon by the conservative critics of the
Revolution who were at the time citing Rousseau, not without reason, in their
pamphlets and newspapers.   See the present writer's article, "The Anti-revolu-
tionary Rousseau," *American Historical Review*, LVIII (1953), 818-820.

were engaged, not as gods but as mere men, in the Legislator's function of drafting a constitution for France. At the same time they were performing the routine legislative functions which Rousseau and Lycurgus (as Rousseau interpreted the historical record) had sharply distinguished from the Legislator's primary role of drafting a fundamental law or constitution. For Pétion such a dilemma must have been only theoretical; the precedent of Lycurgus was completely impractical. But Robespierre did continue to think about this dilemma, and he really never ceased to measure both his colleagues and himself against his classical ideal.

If the Rousseauan ideal of the godlike Legislator posed a problem for Robespierre, so too did the theory of the representative system as applied not to constitution drafting but to the routine legislative functions. This was a problem that had perplexed and would continue to perplex students of government.[7] Among them was Rousseau, whose ideas concerning representation were a unique mixture of pure theory and a practical understanding of political realities. But it was the theory as expressed in the *Contrat social* with which the revolutionary generation, as well as later generations, was familiar. It was axiomatic for Roussseau that sovereignty by its very nature could not be represented. In another ringing sentence he had written: "... the instant a people gives itself representatives, it is no longer free; it no longer exists." If, as the result of the inevitable decline of a society and an increase in its size, deputies of the people must be chosen to meet in their place, they do so not as representatives but as agents (*commissaires*), without power to make definitive decisions.[8]

Robespierre as a deputy of the Third Estate and then as member of the National Assembly found frequent occasion to reflect on these ideas, and both to apply these principles and to rise above them as the cynical cliché has it. For if he had to choose, theory gave way to tactical advantage.

The first opportunity for choice came very soon. When Sieyès proposed on June 16 that the Third Estate take for itself the title

7. A recent writer on the subject speaks of it as "one of those dilemmas which permit of no solution." Hannah Arendt, *On Revolution* (New York, 1963), p. 239.
8. Book III, chap. xv. Halbwachs, pp. 339-340, 342.

of National Assembly, Robespierre spoke in favor of this step, claiming later that he had insisted that approval of the royal ministers was unimportant. It was the will of the people which should be consulted, for "the power of the people is in itself; it is in the incorruptible integrity of its representatives."[9] Here of course he was identifying himself and his colleagues of the Third Estate with the sovereign people. The idea was not new; Sieyès had proclaimed it in his famous pamphlet early that year. Neither was it faithful to strict Rousseauan doctrine. But it was a skilful rationalization of what turned out to be a decisive step in the Revolution.

Prior to the convocation of the Estates General there had been much learned discussion concerning the powers of the members of the three Estates, with a pamphletary debate taking place in which one side argued that the members were restricted by their rigid instructions (*mandats impératifs*) to voting in accordance with their respective *cahiers*. Some who took this position cited Rousseau in support of this thesis. Robespierre, however, took the opposite position when the subject directly affected him and his powers. He represented Artois, a province that had enjoyed certain privileges and immunities by virtue of the terms of the treaty by which the French monarchy had acquired it in the preceding century. When the August decrees were proposed, wiping out such regional and personal privileges, he and his colleagues from Artois had approved them, despite their instructions to defend the privileges of their constituents. In a declaration to the voters of Artois they announced that they had done so in the interest of the general welfare of the nation.[10] Perhaps this was Rousseauan in its implication that the Artesian deputies saw more clearly than their constituents what the welfare of the nation and thus the general will required. But here Robespierre was far from being a mere agent without power to make important decisions, a position which Rousseau had prophesied for representatives in a large state.

As the National Assembly turned to the task of drafting a

9. Marc Bouloiseau, Georges Lefebvre, Albert Soboul (eds.), *Œuvres de Maximilien Robespierre*, VI, *Discours (1er Partie) 1789-1790* (Paris, 1950), 33. Hereafter cited as Robespierre, *Discours*.

10. *Ibid.*, pp. 52-53.

constitution for France, the question arose: what role in the law-making process should be played by the king? An acrimonious debate took place in September over the royal veto, with the final decision providing that the king would have a suspensive veto for the duration of two legislatures. Robespierre, not having the opportunity to present his opinion on this subject to the Assembly, published as a pamphlet the speech he had prepared. It is the first extant exposition of his political theory.[11] He began with the Rousseauan premise that the legislative power, which is inalienable, sovereign, and independent, was an attribute of the nation, meaning the entire society; thus the laws are simply the acts of the general will. A large nation cannot itself exercise its legislative power and therefore delegates it to representatives. At this point, however, he departed from Rousseau's conception of the representative as merely a subordinate agent, as he already had done in practice. He concluded that the will of these representatives ought to be respected just as the will of the nation, and that it should, as the will of the nation itself, have a sacred authority superior to any particular will. The particular will he had in mind was that of the king expressed through the royal veto, for the sovereign will of the people should prevail over the caprices of kings, who are merely the delegates of the people.[12]

Once it had been decided that the king would have a suspensive veto, there remained the constitutional issue of the power to declare war and make peace, posed by the Nootka Sound controversy. Robespierre in the Assembly supported a motion by Pétion which provided that legislative approval would be necessary before the king could declare war or undertake offensive action. As usual Robespierre began with first principles, disagreeing with previous speakers who had called the king the representative of the nation. He insisted that the king was the clerk (*commis*) or delegate of the nation for executing the national will, which of course was to be determined by the legislature. When called to order for this blunt statement, he responded with skill and finesse that he was certainly not lacking in respect

11. *Dire de M. de Robespierre député de la Province de Artois à l'Assemblée Nationale contre le veto royal, soit absolu, soit suspensif* (n.p., n.d.), in Robespierre, *Discours*, VI, 86-95.
12. *Ibid.*, VI, 87-88.

for his royal majesty, that by the word clerk he meant the "supreme function," the "sublime responsibility" of executing the general will. But only those who were especially charged with voicing the will of the nation could be called "representatives of the people."[13]

In this case Robespierre's doctrine was quite in accord with Rousseau's conception of monarchy, and he consistently maintained this thesis of the relative roles of monarch and legislature until the monarchy was abolished in 1792. It was otherwise with his theory of the relative role of the people themselves, of the nation as it was now defined, vis-à-vis the legislature. Here his position was by no means so consistent. For the Rousseauan premise that the sovereignty of the people could not be represented was compromised not only by the circumstances Rousseau had envisaged, but also by the particular circumstances of the Revolution and Robespierre's personal involvement in the course of events.

Thus he had insisted on the extended powers and authority of the National Assembly and its representative character on the several occasions just described, but on other issues he took the opposite position. He was unswervingly convinced that the problems of government were basically moral problems, and he was already beginning to question the motives, integrity, and loyalty to the Revolution not only of the king and his ministers but also of the majority in the Assembly. So the role of the people must remain both broad and unchecked. When an article concerning the touchy subject of taxes was proposed for the Declaration of the Rights of Man and of the Citizen, stating that each citizen had the right to ascertain the necessity of a tax and to consent to it freely, Robespierre insisted that the wording deprived the nation of the right itself to determine its taxes, leaving it with a mere veto power. He proposed a rewording which would give the nation alone (rather than a legislature) the right to levy taxes.[14] Although unsuccessful in this proposal, he was to persist in his attempts somehow to maintain the crucial legislative functions in the hands of the people.

There were times, he believed, when direct action by the

13. *Ibid.*, VI, 364-365.   14. *Ibid.*, VI, 64-67.

sovereign people must admit of no restraint. Thus in cold blood he could write to a friend, in reference to the lynching of Foulon in July, 1789, that "the people had sentenced him."[15]   In February, 1791, the constitutional committee, fearing further revolution and being anxious to repress the continued local disorders, had proposed a preamble decree as follows: "The entire nation, alone possessing sovereignty, which it exercises only by its representatives, and which can neither be alienated or divided, no department, no district, no commune, no section of the people participates in this sovereignty."[16]   The Declaration of the Rights of Man and of the Citizen adopted over a year before had prescribed not only that "The source of all sovereignty rests essentially in the nation" but also that "No body and no individual may exercise authority which does not emanate from the nation expressly."   At that time it was the king and his appointees whom the National Assembly had in mind.   Now it was a question of direct action by the people.

The committee's proposal was opposed by Robespierre, who argued that each section, each individual, was a member of the sovereign. Therefore the proposed decree was an attack on the basic principle of sovereignty.[17]   The subject came up again in August, 1791, during the conservative reaction against the violence of July, when the constitutional committee proposed the following articles:

Sovereignty is one, indivisible and appertains to the nation; no portion of the people may assume its exercise.

The nation, from which alone originates all powers, may exercise them only by delegation.   The French constitution is representative; the representatives are the legislative body and the king.

Robespierre spoke at length in the ensuing debate, and his marginal notes on the proposal have been preserved. As a good Rousseauist—the notes mention Rousseau—he saw a basic contradiction between the statement that sovereignty is inalienable and that no section of the people nor any individual may assume the exercise thereof, and the next sentence which provides that

15. Georges Michon (ed.), *Correspondance de Maximilien et Augustin Robespierre*, I (Paris, 1926), 50.
16. Robespierre, *Discours*, VII, 80-81.   17. *Ibid.*, pp. 81-84.

powers inherent in sovereignty may be exercised only by delegation. He paraphrased Rousseau, writing that one destroys sovereignty thus, for the legislative power may not be delegated, certainly not to the king.[18] He went on to point out that the proposed text made no constitutional provision for the nation to express its will concerning what its delegates had done in its name.
He cited Rousseau, reminding his listeners that they had decreed
a statue in honor of him, and emphasized Rousseau's thesis that
a nation which delegated its powers was no longer free, in fact no
longer existed. As for the prohibition against any section of the
people attributing to itself the exercise of the nation's sovereignty,
he objected to this absolute denial, insisting that one could not
say there existed a right (the powers appertaining to sovereignty)
which could not be used by the nation if it so wished. This kind
of absolute representative government, to which he said he preferred despotism, was painted by Rousseau in the odious colors it
deserved. When the spokesman for the constitutional committee
accused Robespierre of saying that the nation could not delegate
its powers, he insisted that he had simply said that the nation
could not delegate its powers in perpetuity, for this would be
an alienation. When all was said and done, Robespierre had his
way in part. The words inalienable and imprescriptible were
added to the text after the words "one, indivisible," but the injunction against the partial exercise of sovereignty was maintained.[19]

Robespierre's interpretation of the political realities of the
moment was that he, Robespierre, the Incorruptible, usually
found himself in opposition to the corrupt majority of the
National Assembly, and as the work of the Assembly neared its
end, he published his reflections on the situation in a pamphlet
addressed to the French people. In this statement he took a
first step in identifying himself with the people, who are neither
corrupt nor depraved, by claiming that it was not he whom the
opposing faction had attacked but the cause of the people.[20] In
his defense of himself against the attacks of the Girondins a year

18. S. Tardif (ed.), *Projet de la constitution française de 1791, notes manuscrites
et inédites de Robespierre* (Aix, 1894), pp. 8-10.
19. Robespierre, *Discours*, VII, 611-614.
20. *Adresse de Maximilien Robespierre aux Français* (Paris, 1791), pp. 1, 6.

later at the Jacobin Club, he testified that on the eve of the Revolution he had, as a member of the first assemblies, taken the lead in not only demanding but also exercising the rights of the sovereign people. At the beginning of the Revolution, he also testified, there had been awakened in him a *sentiment sublime et tendre* which linked him forever to the cause of the people. It was then that he had understood the great moral and political truth announced by Jean-Jacques, that men love sincerely only those who love them, that the people alone are good, just, and magnanimous, and that corruption and tyranny are the exclusive traits of those who disdain the people. And to the charge that he had flattered and led the people astray, Robespierre's answer was: "Je suis peuple moi-même!"[21]

If as one of the people he was good, then his opponents must be evil. He was sure that many of them served their own selfish "particular wills," conspiring with the ministry and the court against the general will. So definite limits must be placed on a representative body, which was at best a necessary evil and at worst just what the National Assembly had turned out to be.

To the argument that a royal veto was necessary to prevent legislative abuses, Robespierre had replied that the representatives should be elected for a very short term of office, after which they would return to their constituencies to undergo an impartial judgment.[22] In the debates he had supported an unsuccessful motion providing for a one-year term of office.[23] But the next spring when the Abbé Maury, speaking in opposition to a proposal to extend the life of the Assembly until the constitution was completed, cited Rousseau's dictum that representatives were only agents who could decide nothing definitively, Robespierre was silent.[24]

More consequential was his opposition to the constitutional

21. *Œuvres complètes de Robespierre*, IV, *Le Défenseur de la constitution*, ed. Gustave Laurent (Paris, 1939), No. 1, 32-34. Hereafter cited as *Le Défenseur de la constitution*. The statement concerning Rousseau's opinion of *le peuple* is difficult to explain, for Rousseau's ideas were significantly different from this. See, for example, his preference for the bourgeois citizenry of Geneva, and his blunt analysis of the lower classes in *Lettres de la montagne*, Letter IX, in C. E. Vaughan (ed.), *The Political Writings of Jean-Jacques Rousseau* (Oxford, 1962), II, 282-283. See also *Contrat social*, Book II, chap. xi, Halbwachs, pp. 218-219.
22. *Dire de M. de Robespierre* ... , p. 90.
23. Robespierre, *Discours*, VI, 77.
24. *Archives parlementaires de 1789 à 1860*, ed. J. Mavidal, E. Laurent, *et al.*, series I (Paris, 1879 ff.), XIII, 112. Hereafter cited as *Archives parlementaires*.

committee's recommendation that members of a preceding legislature could be re-elected to the next. Robespierre, perhaps with
the Lycurgus ideal in mind, argued that it would be preferable
for disinterested persons to debate this in the knowledge they soon
would retire to private life. So he proposed that members of the
existing Assembly could not be members of the next. The motion
was received with applause by both the minority right, which apparently hoped that a clean slate would produce a stronger representation for their views, and part of the left, which was now split
between Jacobins and moderates.[25]

Robespierre's defense of his proposal was one of the best
speeches of his career.[26] He began, significantly, with a reference
to the great legislators of antiquity who had returned to private
life after giving constitutions to their states. This was followed
by a personal affirmation, reminiscent of Rousseau, that this matter to him was one of principle, of integrity, of conscience. His
experience in the National Assembly had made him alert to the
danger that the general will all too often would be subordinated
to the particular interests of the members, who would tend to
combine with the ministry and the court against the people, thus
becoming themselves sovereign. This was the burden of his
argument, although he made other and perhaps more persuasive
points. Perhaps he relied on the practical, political considerations to win support. In any case the motion was adopted almost
unanimously.

Having decided the preliminary issue that members of the
constitution-drafting National Assembly would not be eligible
for membership in the next legislature, the members then turned
to the committee's further recommendation that, thereafter, members of any one legislature would be eligible for re-election to the
next. One of the speakers in favor of the proposal cited Rousseau
to support the argument that to forbid re-election would be a
denial of the people's freedom.[27] When Robespierre spoke at
length in the debate he made no mention of Rousseau, but he
emphasized his concern that in a representative system liberty be

25. Robespierre, *Discours*, VII, 377-380. The dinner party conversation described
at the beginning of this essay may have taken place at this time.
26. *Discours de Maximilien Robespierre à l'Assemblée Nationale sur la ré-
élection des membres de l'Assemblée Nationale,* in *ibid.*, VII, 383-394.
27. *Archives parlementaires*, XXVI, 152.

preserved by guaranteeing the purity of the representatives and by maintaining their identity with the people. History proved, he said, that prohibiting re-election was the surest way of preserving liberty and guaranteeing that legislators would be faithful interpreters of the general will. The very nature of their office required that they be recalled to the class of ordinary citizens, that they again become *peuple*.[28] Here is an adaptation and an accommodation of the rigorous Rousseauan injunction against the representative system, together with the familiar theme of the good, the pure people.

At the completion of the National Assembly's work there followed a year's interlude of the Legislative Assembly, when Robespierre, no longer a legislator by virtue of his own self-denying ordinance, nevertheless did not follow his own injunction to return as a simple citizen to his constituency. Instead he remained in Paris as a leader of the left faction of the Jacobin Club and soon established a journal, *Le Défenseur de la constitution*, as a sounding board for his ideas. Thus there was frequent occasion for him to apply both theory and tactics to the subject of representation, with priority as usual going to tactics.

The first occasion for the application of Rousseauan ideas was on the subject of war and peace. Robespierre, with his gloomy predictions concerning the results of a war, stood firm against any move which might lead France into conflict. At the Jacobin Club in December a member proposed that the people be consulted directly in their primary assemblies, thus forcing the government to take the offensive. Robespierre, knowing that the French electorate might very well be swept off its feet on the issue, vigorously opposed the proposal. He argued that such an appeal to the people was contrary to the constitution, that he was as devoted as anyone to the sovereignty of the people, but that it would be impossible for twenty-five million persons to express their opinion in such a manner. To him it would be absurd to decide the question of war and peace in any place other than the national legislature.[29] The next day a member who advocated war cited

28. *Second discours prononcé à l'Assemblée Nationale le 18 mai 1791 par Maximilien Robespierre député du département du Pas-de-Calais*, in Robespierre, *Discours*, VII, 404-405.
29. *Ibid.*, VIII, 37.

the authority of Rousseau, but Robespierre in a lengthy reply made no reference to the citation and confined his arguments to the pragmatic and practical considerations.[30]

Several weeks later he spoke again on this momentous subject and answered the critics who had accused him of having debased the people by opposing an appeal to them. Now once again his authority was Rousseau, who, because he loved the people more than anyone else, had given a more accurate idea of them than anyone: "The people always desire the good, but they do not always recognize it." Robespierre was not content to leave it at that, for if he could not trust the people to recognize sound policy, neither could he trust the legislature to agree with him. So he paraphrased Rousseau: "The representatives of the people recognize the good, but they do not always want it." And he suggested that one read Rousseau on the subject of representative government and then decide if the people should rest easy.[31]

He returned to this theme of the dangers of representative government in an editorial in his journal entitled "On the Respect due the Laws and the Constituted Authorities."[32] In Rousseauan terms he warned that the Legislator, even if this were the *peuple* themselves, was not infallible. The chances for error were even more likely if the people delegated legislative power to a small body, making it a fiction that the law then was the expression of the general will. Since it was only natural that representatives put their particular wills ahead of the general will, there was the crucial necessity of a free exchange of ideas, a free press, and an untrammeled public opinion. Without these freedoms, he wrote, even the shadow of sovereignty would disappear, and—again he returned to the familiar theme—it would be difficult to dispute the truth of Rousseau's anathema against absolute representative government.

The war which he had opposed was going badly by this time (the early summer of 1792), and before the summer was out, the laboriously drafted constitution and government had fallen in ruins in the face of military disaster, royal treason, and the bitter factional disputes in the Legislative Assembly. Robespierre as

30. *Ibid.*, pp. 39-43.   31. *Ibid.*, p. 90.
32. *Le Défenseur de la constitution*, No. 5, pp. 144-147.

both a participant in these events and as a commentator on them had abundant opportunity to continue to adapt Rousseau's doctrine on the subject of representation to the circumstances of the moment.

On the eve of the overthrow of the monarchy on August 10, he wrote in his journal that a despotic, intriguing legislature conspiring against the people was the key to the current crisis. Simply to oust the king would leave both executive and legislative power in the existing assembly, which would produce the worst of despotisms. So he hinted a double reform might be necessary: destitution of the king, and replacement of the Legislative Assembly by a national convention, chosen directly by universal suffrage in the primary assemblies. He returned to his self-denying proposal of the year before, recommending that no member of either of the two preceding legislatures be eligible for election. Here of course he was planning well ahead of events, but he claimed that the entire nation was already convinced that changes were necessary. Therefore he claimed, with more forensic skill than logic, that these changes could be considered as actual laws according to the constitution, which said that the law is the expression of the general will.[33]

Although the monarchy was overthrown on August 10, the Legislative Assembly remained, and Robespierre continued his criticism of that body, identifying himself with the revolutionary Commune and the sections of Paris, and serving as a spokesman for a delegation sent to the Assembly to protest the formation of a new departmental administration which he declared was destructive of the sovereignty of the people.[34] A week later, when the Legislative Assembly decreed the dissolution of the Commune and the replacement of its members, and the conflict between the two bodies had reached a climax on the eve of the September Massacres, Robespierre spoke in terms of *mandataires perfides* and the "will of the people clearly announced"—a euphemism for the insurrection of August 10 and the threat of violence against the Assembly.[35] Once the Legislative Assembly had bowed out and such elections as Robespierre had proposed for a Convention

33. *Ibid.*, No. 11, pp. 317-329.
34. Robespierre, *Discours*, VIII, 427-430.
35. *Ibid.*, pp. 445-446.

had been held, he could confidently write in an address to the citizenry that there had been a new revolution which had established the sovereignty of the people and the reign of the general will on the ruins of all the factions.[36]

The day after Robespierre had induced the Paris government to adopt officially a rather unusual election procedure in which the final balloting was by voice vote at the Jacobin Club,[37] he himself was the first to be elected a member of the Paris delegation to the Convention. Thus he found himself once again a legislator, but a much more influential one than when he had arrived at Versailles as an obscure provincial deputy.

In the first number of his new journal, the *Lettres à ses commettans*, published at the end of September, he explained at length his conception of the Convention's functions. In a decidedly rare burst of euphoria he wrote that, royalty now being abolished and political equality established, there was much less to be done than one might think to create the most auspicious of all governments. The "representative aristocracy" could be tempered by controlling corruption and guaranteeing the rights of the sovereign, all of which he was sure could be accomplished in several months.[38]

His concern over a "representative aristocracy" clearly reflected Rousseau's theory. It had been Rousseau's opinion in the *Contrat social* that an "elective aristocracy," consisting of those chosen because of their talents and virtue, was the best form of government—*if* one could be sure that they would govern in the interest of society and not in their own interest.[39] Robespierre confessed that to give a government sufficient power to make the general will prevail, while preventing the government from abusing that power, was the greatest problem for the legislator. The National Assembly had created what he characterized as a bizarre system of absolute representative government, without any

---

36. *Adresse des représentans de la Commune de Paris à leurs concitoyens* (Paris, n.d.), pp. 5, 12-13.

37. Robespierre, Président, Garnier l'Aulnay, secrétaire, Section des citoyens armés de la place Vendôme, *L'Assemblée générale de la section ... séance du 27 aout 1792, l'an quatrième de la liberté* (Paris, n.d.), in Robespierre, *Discours*, 443-444.

38. *Œuvres complètes de Robespierre*, V, *Lettres à ses commettans*, ed. Gustave Laurent (Gap, 1961), 1st series, No. 1, 16. Hereafter referred to as *Lettres à ses commettans*.

39. *Contrat social*, Book III, chap. v, Halbwachs, pp. 283-284.

counterweight in the sovereignty of the people. This arrangement was the most intolerable of tyrannies, and the next legislature had only made it worse. The Convention must do better, he
declared. Having thus paraphrased and adapted Rousseau, he
now quoted "the most eloquent of our philosophers" on the need
for gods to give laws to men.[40]

Godlike or not, as a leading Jacobin spokesman in the legislature Robespierre was directly concerned with the actual operations of the Convention and with the soon overriding problem
of the conflict between the Girondists and the Jacobins. The
Girondists, who had quickly undertaken an offensive against their
opponents, usually commanded a majority in the Convention.
But now they had against them not only the Jacobins and the
Jacobin-controlled Commune but also the sections of Paris and
the visitors' gallery.

In November the sections of Paris, continuing the tactics
which had worked so well at the time of the Convention balloting,
favored voice voting in the imminent municipal elections. The
proposal was opposed by the Girondists in the Convention, but
Robespierre, pointing out that such elections were acts of sovereignty, insisted therefore that they could not be subjected to any
other rules than those which the sovereign itself wished to apply.[41]
The next month, after a particularly tempestuous session of the
Convention in which Robespierre received a hearing only with
difficulty, he editorialized on his struggle in Rousseauan terms.
The majority, he pointed out in his journal, had no authority to
deprive a member of the right to speak which he holds from the
nation; otherwise the representative body would be substituting
its particular will for the general will, and factions and cabals
would prevail.[42] In this case his complaint was against his
Girondin colleagues, not the public galleries, for the latter were
serious and attentive when the people's interests were discussed
and showed irritation only when they saw their delegates de-
liberating with scandalous levity. Thus he regretted that the
physical setting of the Convention provided space for a gallery
of only several hundred. He suggested that the legislators meet

40. *Lettres à ses commettans*, 1st series, No. 1, pp. 18-21.
41. *Ibid.*, No. 5, pp. 67-68.   42. *Ibid.*, No. 9, pp. 127-128.

in the presence of ten thousand spectators, to his lights a simple and infallible means of guaranteeing that the *mandataires* of the people fulfil their obligations.[43]   In January he addressed an open letter to the Girondin leaders, reminding them that sovereignty belonged to the nation, that the *mandataires* of the people were the *commis,* the servants of the people, terms reminiscent of those he had applied to the king a year or two earlier.[44]

The issue that had aroused feelings to such a high pitch was the debate begun in November over the disposition of the deposed king.   Here again there was occasion to invoke and adapt the familiar theories of representation.   The burden of Robespierre's argument, presented in his journal in November, was of course political and pragmatic, but as usual it was written in a theoretical context.[45]   He began with Lockean rather than Rousseauan premises.   When a government has become tyrannical and the political pact is broken, he declared, society must return to its natural rights under natural law.   He insisted also that the sovereign people had the right to punish such a ruler by the laws of eternal justice, the inviolability clause of the Constitution of 1791 to the contrary notwithstanding.   Concerning the choice of tribunal to try Louis, he insisted that it should be the nation itself, if the entire nation could be assembled.   That being impossible, the court should be the body which presented the most perfect image of the national representation, in other words, the Convention.   This body could not delegate its authority, said Robespierre, for the representatives of the representatives would not be those of the nation.   Nor could the nation itself create an *ad hoc* tribunal, for, he asked, by what right could the Convention order the nation to create such a court when the nation had already assigned this task to the Convention?[46]

Two weeks later, however, Robespierre had changed his mind. He delivered to the Convention a carefully reasoned and bluntly phrased speech in which he concluded that since the nation had entered a state of nature vis-à-vis its former king, there need be no trial, which would only cause trouble by stirring up royalist sentiment.   The Convention need simply decree the execution of the deposed monarch.   But as always there was a theoretical

43. *Ibid.,* p. 128.
45. *Ibid.,* 1st series, No. 5, pp. 57-58.
44. *Ibid.,* 2nd series, No. 1, p. 191.
46. *Ibid.,* pp. 62-64.

context. This time it appeared in the familiar Rousseauan rather than Lockean terms. The people, he said, had decided that Louis should die, and he questioned whether the Convention had the right to have a will contrary to the general will of the people.[47]

Later that month, after a trial had been held, a debate took place on the Girondin proposal that the application of the penalty be referred to the people meeting in their primary assemblies. In reply to this, Robespierre repeated that the general will had spoken on the subject and that the will of the representatives must be in accord with it. For good measure, he added several practical arguments, pointing out the dangers of aroused emotions and demagogy, and the possibility that the sovereign people, once consulted, might assert the right to retry the case all over again.[48]

The issue was a crucial one on which the Girondin spokesmen had argued persuasively, and Robespierre returned to the subject in his journal early in January in his open letter to the Girondin leaders.[49] The Girondists had appealed to the sovereignty of the people and had argued that the people must make the final decision; otherwise the Convention's trial of the monarch would be a criminal usurpation of sovereignty. Robespierre answered that in this instance an appeal to the people was a parody of popular sovereignty, pushing it to the extreme of absolute democracy such as had never existed. It would be monstrous to combine the sovereign people and the representative body. One or the other must act. And he added a further caution, that once the people were assembled, the mandate of the representative body expired and the Convention would cease, with anarchy resulting. The concept is quite Rousseauan, as Robespierre's friend Desmoulins pointed out in the next issue of the journal.[50] But Robespierre himself was content to state the thesis without citing the authority of the *Contrat social*.

The next significant occasion for the application of Rousseauan ideas concerning representation came in the discussion of the new constitution to which the Convention had turned its attention shortly after the execution of the deposed king. The

47. Robespierre, *Discours*, IX, 123-130.   48. *Ibid.*, pp. 183-193.
49. *Lettres à ses commettans*, 2nd series, No. 1, pp. 189-204.
50. *Ibid.*, No. 2, p. 216.

Girondin draft, presented by Condorcet, had been attacked by the Jacobins, ironically because it gave too much power to the primary assemblies. It was not until April that the Convention took up its basic constitution-writing function in earnest. Robespierre, now a dominant figure, played a prominent role in the discussions. Several clauses in his draft of a Declaration of Rights reveal his maturing thoughts on the subject of representation. The people are of course sovereign and may at their pleasure change their government and dismiss their representatives, whose position in effect must be one of respectful subordination to the people. His draft provided, in a paraphrase of the Declaration of 1789, that no portion of the people may exercise the power of the people as a whole. He went on to add, however, that the opinion of a portion of those who must concur in forming the general will ought to be respected, and each section of the sovereign when assembled should enjoy the right of expressing its will with complete liberty.[51]

In early May, in the midst of rising tension both in the Convention and in the country, Robespierre read to the Convention a speech on the constitution itself, in which he revealed the adaptation he was making of Rousseauan ideas and terminology to the existing circumstances.[52] The speech began with a paraphrase of perhaps the most famous—and certainly the most misunderstood—of the many aphorisms of Rousseau: "Man is born for happiness and for liberty, and everywhere he is enslaved and unhappy. The purpose of society is the protection of his rights and the perfecting of his being; and everywhere society degrades and oppresses him." Not only society, but more specifically government; for Robespierre in this speech voiced repeatedly his familiar fear that the inevitable tendency of government was to violate the rights of its citizens, because those who govern have an individual will which is contrary to the general will. He proceeded to outline certain institutional arrangements designed to guarantee the preservation of liberty and the sovereignty of the people. These included an easy and immediate system of recall, and the arrangement whereby at the end of his term a legislator would be subject to the judg-

51. *Déclaration des droits de l'homme et du citoyen proposée par Maximilien Robespierre*, in Robespierre, *Discours*, IX, 463-469, articles XIV, XX.
52. *Ibid.*, pp. 495-510.

ment of his constituents. If he had lost their confidence, then he would be ineligible for any public office. Furthermore, he proposed this time that the legislature meet in a hall seating not ten thousand but twelve thousand spectators. Above all else, he insisted, the liberty of the sovereign people must be respected when it meets in its primary assemblies, for the size of the nation requires that it be divided in sections in order to exercise its sovereignty. No section of the sovereign should be placed under either the influence or the orders of any public body.

After the expulsion of the Girondists from the Convention at the month's end, the Jacobin leadership proceeded rapidly to draft a constitution in order to satisfy and reassure public opinion in the country. No longer was there the acute problem of a Girondist-dominated legislature repressing the Jacobin supporters among the Paris populace, whose political power in the primary assemblies therefore had to be protected. Rather it was now a problem of preserving the authority of a Jacobin-dominated Convention and revolutionary government against both the divisive influence of the popular societies and sections, and against the dissident localities stubbornly supporting the Girondists. The "outs" had become the "ins." So Robespierre now opposed, although unsuccessfully, an article allowing the primary assemblies to meet in special session with a bare majority present. This would be, he now argued, a threat to government itself which by an excess of democracy might overthrow the sovereignty of the nation. He had recently opposed restriction on the assemblies. Now he reasoned that if they were not restricted, they might deliberate on any subject and act against the established government and thus create a pure democracy rather than a democracy tempered by laws.[53]

Two days later, still thinking about Rousseauan theory, Robespierre returned to the knotty problem of the relationship of sovereign citizens and their representatives. It was the next to last statement he was to make on this obsessive subject. He repeated, without so identifying it, Rousseau's doctrine that the will of the people cannot be represented; while the legislature may make laws, they become laws only when formally accepted

53. *Ibid.*, p. 557.

by the people. But he immediately tempered the rigidity of this theory with the realistic qualification that this acceptance may be either expressed or tacit, in which case the sovereign will is not represented, it is presumed. A *mandataire* cannot be a representative, for this is a misuse of terms; and, he added, in France there had begun a return from this error.[54]

That may have been so, but just where France was now going in terms of Rousseauan theory was by no means clear. In the constitution as finally written some of Robespierre's ideas had been incorporated, some had not; and there was no more consistency or uniformity in the final draft than there had been in Robespierre's thinking over the period of months that had seen the shift from Girondin to Jacobin dominance in the Convention. For the practical solution to immediately pressing problems does not allow for the luxury of consistency. And the final inconsistency was the shelving of this constitution by the Convention, which in October declared the government to be revolutionary until the peace.

The Convention, and Robespierre, had turned from constitutional theory to the overwhelming problems facing the government, and there was little time or patience for divisive theories of representation, particularly if they implied any challenge to the power of the Convention or its agencies.[55] Thus when the Committee of Public Safety recommended that the Paris sections be allowed to meet only twice a week, and this affront to these agencies of direct democracy was protested in authentic Rousseauan terms, Robespierre, a member of the Committee, joined in the attack on the spokesman for the sections.[56] The following February, in his famous "Report on the Principles of Public Morality," which he delivered in the name of the Committee of Public Safety, he returned for the last time to the problem of representation, which he now envisioned in a thoroughly practical and pragmatic fashion. In defining democracy he insisted that this was not a system in which the people ruled on all public

54. *Ibid.*, pp. 568-569.
55. The role of Robespierre in this reversal of Jacobin policy toward the sections and the popular societies is summarized in Albert Soboul, "Robespierre und die Volksgesellschaften," in *Maximilien Robespierre 1758-1794, Beiträge zu seinem 200. Geburtstag,* ed. Walter Markov (Berlin, 1958), pp. 287-300.
56. *Archives parlementaires,* LXXIII, 601, and LXXIV, 310-313.

matters in continuous assembly. Still less was it a system in which a hundred thousand fractions of the people (read: primary assemblies and sections) by isolated, precipitate, and contradictory measures decide the destiny of the entire society. Democracy, instead, was a system in which, guided by the laws they have created, the sovereign people do by themselves everything they can do themselves, and do through their delegates everything they cannot do themselves.[57] The contrast with his earlier statements before his rise to power is striking—and to be expected.

This speech, primarily concerned with the Montesquieuan and Rousseauan conceptions of public virtue and political morality in a democracy, was based on a frequent theme in Robespierre's thought. And he must have felt as he read the familiar phrases concerning the public interest as distinguished from particular interest, the rules of political conduct, virtue, and the love of equality, that now at last all that was good and true in political theory would prevail. But the reader cannot fail to remark that the speech suddenly shifts from lofty and familiar sentiments of idealistic political theory to the even more familiar emphasis on the current crisis, the need to be harsh with traitors, the prevalence of intrigue. And these were his preoccupations during those last months—his next three speeches were on this subject—when, ironically and tragically, he had finally prevailed against the traitors who had opposed him and the Revolution, and when he might have developed and implemented his ideas on government and the representative system. But this was not to be.

Rousseau had written in the introduction to Book I of his *Contrat social* that if he were a prince or Legislator he would not waste his time saying what should be done. He would either do it or say nothing. His disciple Robespierre had discovered that being a legislator was by no means that simple, even though one were sure one knew just what should be done. If one could be a Lycurgus, yes; then one might establish the ideal system and retire from the scene with the applause of a grateful public ringing in one's ears. But being a member of a large legislative body

57. *Rapport sur les principes de morale politique qui doivent guider la Convention nationale dans l'administration intérieure de la République,* in Robespierre, *Discours,* X (in typescript). The author wishes to thank M. Marc Bouloiseau for giving him access to this manuscript of the last volume of the *Discours,* and for other courtesies and assistance.

was a different matter, even if one had the power Robespierre had acquired by the spring of 1794. One had to struggle against the corrupt individual wills of one's colleagues and the equally corrupt corporate will of the legislature itself, which was at best a necessary evil. Only the firmly held conviction that one was right, that one was *peuple* oneself, and that Revolution and the right would eventually prevail could have made the compromise with principles acceptable.

There was, as the above account has demonstrated, frequent compromise with principles. Robespierre had read and admired Rousseau, and Rousseau's ideas concerning representation were by and large congenial to his thinking and attitudes. That such ideas were impractical he had refused to admit at the dinner party described at the beginning of this essay, and he had insisted that he would continue to think about the problem. That he did so is a measure of both his intellectual stature and his sense of duty and conscience. That he tried to come to terms with the abstract doctrine of Rousseau on the knotty subject of representation is a measure of his discipleship, for "Follow me" is always the ultimate injunction to the disciple. But the overriding consideration for him was always the security and progress of the Revolution as he, Robespierre, conceived it. If, as at first, Rousseauan doctrine on representation usually accorded with his suspicions of the king and his opponents in the legislature, so much the better. But if, as came to be the case, Rousseauan doctrine stood in the way of Robespierrist policies designed to insure the success of the Revolution, then the doctrine inevitably had to give way. For while he was intellectually and apparently to a certain extent emotionally committed to Rousseau's doctrine on this as on other subjects, he was much more deeply and emotionally committed to the Revolution; which, like all revolutions had a way of devouring its children intellectually, as well as physically.

GOOD, EVIL, AND SPAIN'S
RISING AGAINST
NAPOLEON*

Richard Herr

Events of 1808 in Spain approach in intensity those in France during the Terror. When the year began, Napoleon's troops were pouring over the frontier, coming allegedly as allies to occupy Portugal and protect Spain's coasts against British attacks. On March 19 riots outside the palace at Aranjuez caused Carlos IV to abdicate in favor of his son Fernando. The personal influence of the French emperor brought Carlos, Fernando, and other members of the royal family to Bayonne, where early in May the two kings, father and son, ceded to Napoleon their rights to the throne of Spain. Napoleon named his brother Joseph Bonaparte king in their place and convoked an assembly of Spanish notables at Bayonne which accepted the new monarch and ratified a constitution for their country. Already, however, on May 2, the people of Madrid had risen against the occupying French troops, an event that became famous to later Spanish generations as the "Dos de Mayo." Although the French crushed this revolt, the unoccupied provinces took up arms to restore Fernando to the throne. Thus began one of the bitterest wars in history, which lasted for five years and brought fighting to all corners of Spain.

These events lend themselves to an analysis of the role of ideas in a revolutionary situation. If one takes the term "idea" broadly to mean the concepts present in the minds of Spaniards, different kinds of ideas existed that had originated in different ways and affected different aspects of the rising. One kind of idea consisted of the conflicting social, political, and religious phi-

RICHARD HERR *is professor of history at the University of California (Berkeley).*
  * The research for this paper was made possible by a fellowship from the John Simon Guggenheim Memorial Foundation and a grant from the Social Science Research Council in 1959-1960.

losophies that at first led some Spaniards to accept, and many more
to reject, the ideal represented by Joseph Bonaparte of enlightened monarchy limited by a written constitution, and later
inspired a good number of Fernando's champions to abolish the
Inquisition and establish the almost egalitarian Constitution of
1812 with a figurehead king, while others opposed these innovations in the name of monarchy and religion.   This is the kind
of idea that historians study most frequently.   Such philosophies,
however, could be grasped only by educated Spaniards.   If they
succeeded in spreading into wider circles, it could be only as gross
simplifications, catch phrases, and political battle cries.

A second type of "idea" was felt much deeper in society.
Historians know it by the name of nationalism, but it can be
looked on as one example of the common hostility of human
groups toward outsiders, as studied by anthropologists and sociologists.   This hostility has existed widely in Spain—and elsewhere among sedentary peoples—as rivalry between neighboring
towns.   The influx of cultural influences common to the whole
state through commerce, church, and government extends such
xenophobia into nationalism.[1]   This had occurred already in
Spain, and its rebellion against Napoleon was prima facie a movement directed against a foreign army and inspired by nationalism.

Hatred of the French was old in 1808.   As the most numerous
foreign colony in Spain in the eighteenth century, they had
aroused jealousy and antipathy.   Francophobia was particularly
prevalent among the clergy because they conceived of the France
of the Enlightenment as the enemy of religion and legitimate
government.   The French Revolution and the war waged by
Spain against the French Republic in 1793-1795 gave conservative
clerics a chance to impart their view of France to the common
people.   The war was inspired by the cry "For Religion, King,
and Country!"   After 1796 Carlos IV officially became France's
ally, but popular antipathy continued.[2]   When French troops

1. See for Spain in particular, J. A. Pitt-Rivers, *The People of the Sierra* (London, 1954), pp. 7-12, 29-30, 202-204; Julio Caro Baroja, "El Sociocentrismo de los
pueblos españoles," Universidad Nacional de Cuyo, *Homenaje a Fritz Krüger*
(Mendoza, 1954), II, 457-485.
2. Jean Sarrailh, *L'Espagne éclairée de la seconde moitié du XVIII siècle*
(Paris, 1954), pp. 329-335; Richard Herr, *The Eighteenth Century Revolution in
Spain* (Princeton, 1958), pp. 149, 213-231, 257.

entered Spain in 1801 to participate in an invasion of Portugal, Spaniards complained of their insolent, destructive behavior, and scuffles occurred in various towns.[3] The appearance of much larger French armies after October, 1807, brought on similar incidents that culminated in the Dos de Mayo.

The war that followed was fought once again for religion, country, and legitimate king, in response to a nationalism that contained both love of country and religious devotion. It was the first major example of the national rebellions in Europe that eventually destroyed Napoleon. Historians have stressed this aspect of the war, and this "idea" is thus the one commonly seen behind it.

Nevertheless, there was an even stronger, more immediate motive for the rebellion. It is a third kind of idea, one seldom studied by historians: a popular image, quasi-mythical in content, of the persons at the head of the state who were assumed to control the fate of the people. The image had taken shape in the previous decade and a half, during which time things had not gone well for Spain.

Since 1793 the country had suffered from almost continual war, at first against France and then in alliance with France against Britain. Each new treaty entailed loss of territory—Santo Domingo in 1795, Louisiana in 1800, Trinidad in 1802—but none of them brought lasting peace. The French invaded the country in 1794. The British did not in their war, but they blockaded the ports of Spain, capturing Spanish ships and cutting off trade with Europe and America. Catalan, Valencian, and Basque manufacturers, who had prospered before 1796, could not sell to their largest markets in the colonies and had to lay off many employees. The same industrial areas relied on imported wheat for much of their food and now had to forego this supply.[4] British commanders permitted the export of wool, wine, and crude iron to England, but Napoleon put an end to even this trade by forcing Spain's recognition of the Continental Blockade in February, 1807.[5]

3. André Fugier, *Napoléon et l'Espagne (1799-1808)* (Paris, 1930), I, 151-164.
4. Dispatch of Duhesme, Barcelona, Feb. 19, 1808, Archives historiques du Ministère de la Guerre, Vincennes, Armée d'Espagne, Correspondance (hereafter cited as "AHMG, Esp. Corr."), C84. See Herr, p. 132.
5. Fugier, II, 166, 246-247.

Nature had added its blows. In 1800 yellow fever broke out in Cadiz and rapidly swept through southern Spain, spreading death and fear. Panic seized Madrid. Carlos IV took Draconian measures to isolate Andalusia lest the contagion spread to all Spain, indeed to all Europe.[6] After two summers the epidemic subsided, but it broke out again in Málaga in 1803 and for two more years a cordon of troops cut off communication between Castile and Andalusia.[7] On both occasions France and other countries suspended maritime trade with the affected areas.[8]

During the second epidemic, earthquakes shook the afflicted region. On January 13, 1804, the Mediterranean coastal cities from Motril to Málaga and as far inland as Granada and the province of Seville suffered strong shocks, and many houses collapsed. The tremors continued at irregular intervals for more than a month. On February 16 another earthquake hit towns stretching from New Castile to Navarre, and the next day southern Spain experienced a sustained tremor. The official *Gazeta de Madrid* carried moving reports of these disasters and of the efforts of the crown to feed and shelter the homeless.[9]

Famine also hovered over the country in these dismal years. Heavy rains spoiled the harvests of 1803 and 1804. By September, 1803, Madrid was short of food. Fearing that the shortage would spread to the countryside, peasants, landowners, and town councils began to hoard their harvests, while Carlos IV appealed to Bonaparte to permit the export of French grain to Spain.[10] During 1804 bands of peasants attacked muleteers carrying supplies to Madrid, and hungry, jobless farm laborers wandered about rural Spain threatening the peace, despite attempts of the government to create work for them.[11]

6. *Real orden*, Sept. 16, 1800, and *circular*, Nov. 11, 1800, Archivo Histórico Nacional, Madrid, Consejos Suprimidos, Sala de Alcaldes de Casa y Corte (hereafter cited as "AHN, Consj., SACC"), Libro de Gobierno, 1800, fols. 1016-1018, 1624-1625; Urquijo to Berthier, Oct. 4, 1800, Archives des Affaires Etrangères, Paris, Correspondance diplomatique, Espagne (hereafter cited as "AAE, Esp."), Vol. 660, fols. 30-31.
7. *Real orden*, Nov. 25, 1803, Archivo Histórico, Nacional Hacienda, Colección de Ordenes generales de Rentas (hereafter cited as "AHN, Hacienda, Ordenes"); *circular*, July 5, 1805, AHN, Colección de Reales Cédulas (hereafter "AHN, Cédulas").
8. Archives Nationales, Paris (hereafter cited as "AN"), F78735.
9. *Gazeta de Madrid*, Jan. 27, Feb. 3, 21, 28, March 2, 9, 20, 1804.
10. *Circulares*, Feb. 10 and 24, 1804, AHN, Hacienda, Ordenes; Fugier, I, 320.
11. *Circulares*, March 23 and Sept. 17, 1804, AHN, Consj., SACC, Libro de Gobierno, 1804, fols. 1756, 1785.

In September, 1805, the supply of bread was again adequate in Madrid. By then the yellow fever had abated, and Spaniards might take hope that nature had relented in its treatment of their country. But the war had begun again, and so their afflictions were not over. A month later the *Gazeta* told them of wrecked ships struggling into Cadiz and corpses washed up on the nearby coasts. As the entire story unfolded, Spaniards learned that their navy—ships, crews, and officers—had perished off Trafalgar.[12] Within a year news came that the British had captured Buenos Aires.[13] Their rulers seemed helpless in the face of these defeats.

Financial hardship inevitably accompanied such calamities. The royal government could not receive its normal income from taxes in America, and the product of duties levied on exports to Europe and the colonies declined sharply. At the same time, the war, the famine, and other disasters added heavy burdens to the budget. The ministers devised new taxes, but these could not raise sufficient revenue from a depressed economy. So the ministers turned to foreign and domestic loans.

The foreign loans had no immediate impact on the Spanish people, but the domestic ones did because the main form they took involved the alienation of lands in control of the Church. In 1798 Carlos IV declared that all real property belonging to charitable institutions, confraternities, and certain religious endowments was to be sold at auction. The crown was to take the proceeds and pay the institutions 3 per cent yearly on the amounts received. Under this act a large amount of land changed hands in thousands of towns located in all the provinces of Spain.[14]

Although purchasers had reason to be satisfied, many persons were made unhappy. To the clergy the king's promises hardly seemed as good a guarantee of continued income as did the real estate they had lost. Some clergymen did not hesitate to denounce the sales as royal usurpation of God's belongings.[15]

12. *Gazeta*, Nov. 5, 1805, and following issues.
13. Buenos Aires fell June 27, 1806; Madrid learned the news Sept. 30 (Fugier, II, 119).
14. About one billion reales worth of land was sold, mostly in small lots (see AN, AF^{IV} 1680^B, plaq. 2^I pièce 8). I am currently making a study of the sales.
15. *Ibid.*, pièce 30; Juan Gabriel del Moral, "Memorias de la Guerra de la Independencia...," *Revista de archivos, bibliotecas y museos*, 3ª época, XVIII (1908), 421-422; Manuel Godoy, *Memorias*, ed. Carlos Seco Serrano ("Biblioteca de autores españoles," Vols. LXXXVIII-LXXXIX; Madrid, 1956), II, 233-237.

Furthermore, most of the lands and buildings put on the market were occupied by tenants. If the purchaser was not the tenant— and because the sales were at auction, tenant farmers were at a disadvantage in the face of well-to-do merchants and landlords —a decree of 1803 permitted the purchaser to raise the rent on the land.[16] (To check inflation the king had frozen rents in 1785. The new decree was the first official breach in the control.) The aim of this decree was to encourage sales, but its effect was to cast the burden of royal penury on the shoulders of the tenant farmers. Even those peasants who were not directly involved in the sales would be upset, for they were witnessing transfers of property that changed the immemorial patterns of local social status. Later in the century similar alienation of Church and municipal lands to private individuals was to induce strikes, terrorism, and armed risings among the peasantry of Andalusia.

All the royal financial measures—and the sale of Church lands was only the most extensive and revolutionary—failed to produce enough income. By 1808 the crown's accounts were many months in arrears. The salaries of its officials, widows' pensions, the bills of suppliers of the army and navy, and the interest on its debts (including that to the Church for its lands) were all unpaid. The inability of the king to meet his obligations, together with the war and natural calamities, produced acute disorder in the economy.

Contemporary Spaniards did not seek to analyze the causes of their ills in so complicated a way. If things were going wrong, was it not the fault of their rulers, who were responsible for the country's welfare? Was it not the particular fault of the royal favorite who had dominated the government for the past fifteen years, the Prince of the Peace?

This man's career had been truly astounding. Shortly after the fall of the French monarchy in 1792, Carlos IV replaced his aged and respected first secretary of state, the Count of Aranda, by a twenty-five-year-old officer of the guards, Manuel Godoy. A few months earlier the king had made Godoy a grandee, with the title of the Duke of the Alcudia. The sun did not cease to shine

---

16. *Real cédula*, Sept. 15, 1803, AHN, Hacienda, Ordenes.

on the handsome young man. Upon the conclusion of peace with France, Carlos made him Prince of the Peace, and henceforth he was referred to commonly as "the Prince." Soon he received a niece of the king in marriage. In 1798 he resigned his position as first secretary and for a few years remained outside the government. The war against Portugal in 1801 saw his full glory restored. Carlos invested him with the rank of generalissimo and gave him command of the Spanish armies. From now on, although he held no ministry, he was the unchallenged royal favorite and made his influence felt throughout the government. The city of Madrid gave him a splendid palace surrounded by extensive gardens, at the head of the fashionable Paseo del Prado. Honors never stopped coming. In 1807 he became admiral general, with authority over the navy and merchant marine.[17] Yet he had not been to sea, any more than he had ever fought a battle on land!

If his honors multiplied, so did his unpopularity. His sudden rise in 1792 stung many aristocrats, who felt themselves passed over in favor of this upstart. In 1794, when the war against France was going badly, manuscripts attacking him circulated in Madrid, and dissatisfied persons inside and outside the royal bureaucracy hatched plots against him.[18] The hard years after 1800 led to more manifestations of public hatred. One day he received a loaf of bread cut into four pieces, with a warning that the same fate awaited him. During the famine he dared not go out in public for days at a time.[19]

A historian setting out to study Godoy's role in history would normally try to pierce the contemporary popular image of him to discover the truth behind it. The historian would seek sources, both private and official, that the public of his day never saw. But if the historian is studying the career of the Prince of the Peace for the effect of ideas current in a society, he must eschew the "real" man and try to ascertain his appearance. Even though

17. Herr, pp. 316-318, 335-336, 398-400, 433-434; Fugier, I, 4, II, 187-188; Seco Serrano, "Estudio preliminar," in Godoy, Memorias, I, xl (his marriage); Enciclopedia universal ilustrada hispano-americana ("Espasa-Calpe"), s.v. "Madrid, Monumentos arquitectónicos, Ministerio de la Guerra" (his palace).

18. Herr, pp. 323-327.

19. Dispatch of Beurnonville, Madrid, 28 fructidor XI (Sept. 15, 1803), AAE, Esp., Vol. 664, fol. 464; Fugier, I, 300-301.

appearance was a gross distortion of "reality," the relation between the two will not concern the historian at this point.

   The figure of the Prince of the Peace decked out in all his official titles and honors was amazing enough, but the public saw it
transformed into something far more grotesque by stories that
came from unofficial sources.   Already before his assumption of
power, people in Madrid heard that Queen María Luisa had accepted him as her lover.   (Certain aristocratic circles spread the
story, and they attributed his sudden rise to her favor.[20])   He
never lived down the reputation of owing his position to his ability to give horns to his king, but this was only the first of the vices
imputed to him.   Though married to a royal princess, he lived
openly with a mistress.   Or was she a second wife?   A man who
made love to the queen would hardly be above bigamy.[21]
Through his influence, unqualified men rose in the army, became
intendants, and obtained choice offices in America.   For many of
them, the way to his favor had been to send their wives or
daughters to plead their cases while submitting to his pleasure.
His antechambers were filled day after day with hundreds of
these attractive women, who were admitted to his bureau one at
a time and came out flushed and rumpled.[22]   In his palace he
amassed piles of gold, which he hid in the cellars or buried in
the gardens.[23]   Such were the stories that spread through Spain.
Piecing them together, the historian can conceive in rough lines
what Godoy looked like to his contemporaries.   The sharpest
features of his popular image were deadly sins that everyone
could understand: lust and greed.   Fascinated and horrified by
what they saw, the Spanish people did not question the credibility
of the image, any more than their ancestors had questioned the
existence of the monstrous creatures represented in stone over the
doorways and naves of their churches.

   To add to Godoy's sins, in the public eye his policies were
disastrous.   The alliance with Revolutionary France, the un-

   20. Herr, pp. 317-322.
   21. José María Quiepo de Llano, conde de Toreno, *Historia del levantamiento,
guerra y revolución de España* ("Biblioteca de autores españoles," Vol. LXIV;
Madrid, 1872), p. 23.
   22. Dispatch of Alquier, 8 frimaire IX (Nov. 29, 1800), AAE, Esp., Vol. 660,
fols. 227-235; Antonio Alcalá Galiano, *Recuerdos de un anciano* (Madrid, 1913),
pp. 57-58.
   23. Fugier, II, 423 n. 2.

fortunate war with England, and the fiscal mess were all his work. By the end of 1807 the people were in rags, business was depressed, the Church despoiled, the army ill-equipped, the navy lost, all because of the incompetence, the immorality, the evil of "the Prince."

It seemed as though Spain had become a stage on which the rulers were acting out a kind of morality play before the eyes of their people. Godoy played the role of Evil, bent on ruining the country to satiate his ambition. The queen was his accomplice and the king his complaisant dupe. The outcome was not settled, however, for Good was also on the stage, represented by the young and virtuous heir to the throne, Fernando, Prince of Asturias.

Spain's gaze first fastened on Fernando shortly after Godoy's return to power in 1801. The following year Fernando, then eighteen, was married to Maria Antonia of Naples, and Carlos IV used the occasion to display his heir to his people. Carlos, María Luisa, Fernando, and Godoy journeyed to Barcelona to welcome the bride and celebrate the wedding with elaborate pomp. On the return trip the royal family made a roundabout and expensive progress through Catalonia, Valencia, and Murcia.[24]

A conflict between Godoy and Fernando had been implicit since Godoy became Prince of the Peace, for only in rare instances had any Spaniard borne the title of prince except the direct heir to the throne, the Prince of Asturias. After Fernando's marriage the political life of Spain came to consist in the public mind of an open struggle between the two princes, legitimate heir and scheming rival. When war resumed in 1804 Naples sided with England, and María Antonia was rumored to oppose the French alliance and hate Godoy, while Fernando adopted his wife's views.[25] In the public imagination, Godoy and the shameless queen, unnatural mother that she was, came to fear Fernando and María Antonia. They plotted to insure themselves of continued dominance in the eventuality of Fernando's accession, which was perhaps not very distant since Carlos IV had recently suffered

24. Camille Pitollet, "Notes sur la première femme de Ferdinand VII, Marie-Antoinette-Thérèse de Naples," *Revista de archivos, bibliotecas y museos,* 3ª época, XXXI (1914), 178-190.

25. *Ibid.,* XXXII (1915), 56-57, 265; Fugier, I, 367-368.

serious illness.[26]   In 1806 María Antonia died in mysterious circumstances. Godoy and María Luisa wanted her out of the way.
Would they have stopped at poisoning? How strange that the
official *Gazeta* should carry a lengthy analysis of her illness (tu-
berculosis, it said, which had been developing for years), as if
there were something to hide.[27]   A few months later rumors
circulated that Godoy was trying to marry Fernando to his own
wife's sister and to have himself and María Luisa named regents
in case of Carlos' death, although Fernando was well of age to
rule in his own right.[28]   Carlos' decree naming Godoy admiral
general at this point stipulated that he should be addressed as
"Highness" (*Alteza*), just as was the Prince of Asturias, and the
honors due him were those of an Infante. Perhaps Godoy and the
queen were plotting to eliminate Fernando entirely.   (These
rumors were not entirely spontaneous. Fernando's former tutor
and a group of high aristocrats who had ingratiated themselves
with the prince were actively spreading stories of the diabolical
plots of Godoy and the queen.[29])

The spectators witnessed the unfolding of the plot with growing apprehension. Good had not been utterly driven from the
stage, but more and more was at the mercy of Evil. Then suddenly the play came to a climax. From his autumn residence
in the austere granite monastery of the Escorial, on October 30,
1807, Carlos IV issued an extraordinary proclamation. God, he
said, had just preserved him from catastrophe. He was living
peacefully in the love of his subjects and the quiet of his family

when an unknown hand revealed and exposed to me the most outrageous, most unheard of plan drawn up in my palace against my
person. My life, which has so often been in danger, had become a
burden for my successor. Disturbed, obsessed, and alienated from all
the Christian principles that my paternal care and love had taught
him, he adopted a plan to dethrone me.

26. Fugier, I, 301.
27. *Gazeta*, May 27, 1806; on rumors of poisoning, Pitollet, *loc. cit.*, XXXI (1914),
309.
28. Bulletin, Madrid, Feb. 19, 1807, AAE, Esp., Vol. 671, fols. 121-123; Ch. A.
Geoffroy de Grandmaison, *L'Espagne et Napoléon, 1804-1809* (Paris, 1908-1931),
I, 81; Modesto Lafuente, *Historia general de España* (Barcelona, 1922), XVI,
162-163.
29. Fugier, II, 269-270, 286; H. Castro Bonel, "Manejos de Fernando VII contra
sus padres y contra Godoy," *Boletín de la Universidad de Madrid*, II (1930), 397-
408, 493-503, III (1931), 93-102.

Carlos had investigated in person, the proclamation continued, and, surprising Fernando in his room, had caught him with the plans in his possession. The prince was now a prisoner in his quarters and his accomplices were under arrest.[30] Four days later the king ordered all cities and towns to hold religious services of thanksgiving for the discovery of the plot.[31] A further announcement followed almost immediately that Fernando had written letters to his father and mother admitting his guilt and begging pardon and that Carlos had granted his plea.[32]

Although Carlos used both Church and government to inform Spain of his son's crime, he did not tell his people, because he feared the implications for his relations with Napoleon, that Fernando's real transgression had been to conduct secret negotiations with the French ambassador for the hand of a Bonaparte princess.[33] Without this key, the king's announcements were ambiguous and mysterious. Far from allaying public fears, they strengthened the conviction that mischief was afoot. Carlos' subjects refused to believe Fernando guilty of treason and concluded that the "unknown hand" in the royal proclamation was Godoy's, who had fabricated the whole affair to ruin the young prince.[34] These suspicions were confirmed two months later when the judges chosen from the Council of Castile to try Fernando's accomplices declared them innocent. Carlos, however, banished the accused men from his court and thus provided further proof of Godoy's hand in the affair.[35]

Tension mounted in the audience. Shut up with his treacherous mother and hoodwinked father, Fernando was at the mercy of his worst enemy. But help might be on the way. In October, 1806, Godoy had issued an enigmatic call to the Spanish people to arm for warfare on land. The intended enemy was unnamed but was generally taken to be France, for at the moment Napoleon

30. *Real decreto*, Oct. 30, and *circular*, Oct. 31, 1807, AHN, Cédulas.
31. *Circular*, Nov. 3, 1807, *ibid.*
32. *Real decreto*, Nov. 5 and *circular*, Nov. 6, 1807, *ibid.*
33. Fugier, II, 270-304.
34. Report of French agent, Barcelona, March 1, 1808, AAE, Esp., Vol. 673, fols. 274-277.
35. *Orden del consejo*, April 8, 1808, AHN, Cédulas; Fugier, II, 294-296; 359-361; Lafuente, XVI, 190-199. On the effect of the verdict, see Godoy, II, 255-256; and on Godoy's growing unpopularity, Geoffroy de Grandmaison, pp. 85, 110-111; Fugier, II, 360-361.

seemed doomed before the powers of eastern Europe. Napoleon, however, triumphed over his opponents at Jena, and Godoy took no further action; but since then he had been suspected of secretly favoring Britain, although publicly Spain continued as France's ally.[36] Ten days before the Escorial affair broke, two battalions of French troops entered Spain on their way to attack Portugal for its refusal to give up its British alliance. By the end of November the Portuguese regent and royal family had fled to Brazil and the war was over. Yet the *Gazeta* reported throughout the winter further arrival of French soldiers.[37] Why were they coming? Vague reports now circulated that Fernando had negotiated for a Bonaparte wife. Perhaps the French were coming to oust Godoy and protect Fernando.[38] Godoy himself seemed to suspect that the game was up. Heavy-laden mule trains were reported leaving his residence at night and proceeding to the ports. He was shipping his illicit wealth abroad in preparation for his own flight![39] In early March, 1808, there were rumors that Napoleon planned to call a meeting of the Cortes of Spain to accept the abdication of Carlos IV and place Fernando on the throne with a French queen.[40]

By this date Napoleon's armies controlled most of northern Spain. Suspicion and animosity were not entirely absent from the minds of Spaniards. Reports of heavy taxes levied on Portugal caused concern lest the same treatment await their country.[41] French troops seized the fortresses of Pamplona and Barcelona in February, and in several cities Spaniards reacted by assassinating French soldiers.[42] Nevertheless, the dislike of the French remained subordinate to the desire to see Fernando protected from Godoy.

36. Fugier, II, 129-147.   37. E.g., *Gazeta*, Jan. 29, Feb. 9, 1808.

38. Report of French agent, Nov. 7, 1807, and other evidence in Fugier, II, 366, 396-401; Manuel Izquierdo Hernández, "Informes sobre España ... del ... conde de Tournon ...," *Boletín de la Academia de la Historia*, CXXXVII (1955), 315-357; Bulletin, Valladolid, March 7, 1808, AHMG, Esp. Corr., C84; *Manifiesto de los procedimientos del Consejo Real* ... (Madrid, 1808) (in AHN, Cédulas), p. 1; Antonio Alcalá Galiano, *Memorias* ([Madrid], 1886), I, 138; A. L. A. Fée, *Souvenirs de la guerre d'Espagne* (Paris, 1856), p. 88.

39. Dispatches of Beauharnais, Madrid, Feb. 15, 16, 1808, AAE, Esp., Vol. 673, fols. 207, 221.

40. Report of French agent, Barcelona, March 1, 1808, *ibid.*, fols. 274-277.

41. Dispatch of Beauharnais, Madrid, Feb. 20, 1808, *ibid.*, fols. 237-238; dispatch of Darmagnac, Pamplona, Feb. 25, 1808, AHMG, Esp. Corr., C84.

42. AHMG, Armée d'Espagne, Inventaire analytique, 1er trimestre, 1808, No. 56 (Barceloneta, Feb. 23) and No. 60 (Valladolid, Feb. 24).

Mid-March brought matters to a head. French armies were approaching Madrid from the north, while the garrison of the city was ordered to proceed south to join the royal family at its winter residence in Aranjuez. To the public of Madrid it was clear that Godoy was planning to have the king imitate the Portuguese rulers by escaping to America, taking with him the queen, Fernando, and Godoy. People streamed out of Madrid behind the garrison, eager to witness the next scene. In this atmosphere of anxious expectation, a few accidental shots by Godoy's guard in the wee hours of March 18 set off riots at Aranjuez that lasted two days. The surging mobs frightened Carlos into dismissing his favorite and then abdicating in favor of his son. Only the intercession of Fernando kept the rioters from lynching Godoy.[43]

News of the unexpected accession of Fernando VII brought crowds swelling into the streets of Madrid. They sang and danced and then turned to sacking the houses of Godoy and his relatives, subsiding only when the new king refused to visit the city until order had been restored. When finally he did appear, on March 24, he received such a welcome that history could not recall its equal.[44] As the news spread to the ends of the country, scenes of joy repeated themselves in city after city.[45] A collective hysteria gripped the people, who suddenly felt their anxieties melt away in a happy ending.

Fernando's first acts added luster to his halo. He recalled from banishment his friends in the Escorial affair and other persons whose disfavor was attributed to Godoy's influence, like the former respected ministers Floridablanca and Jovellanos.[46] He

43. For the Aranjuez rising and aftermath, Lafuente, XVI, 220-235; José Gómez de Arteche, *Reinado de Carlos* IV (Madrid, [1890-1898?]), III, 287-306, 473-487.
44. Dispatches of Beauharnais, Madrid, March 18, 20, 25, 1808, AAE, Esp., Vol. 673, fols. 361-362, 386-387, 418-419; *bando*, March 20, 1808, AHN, Cédulas.
45. Dispatches of Tournon, Burgos, March 24, 1808, AN, AF^{IV} 1680, 9e dossier, pièce 9; Thouvenot, San Sebastián, March 25, 1808, AHMG, Inventiare, 1er trim. 1808, No. 97; Henry (Prussian ambassador), Madrid, March 28, AN, AF^{IV} 1691, 2e dos., pièce 89 (Badajoz); Duhesme, Barcelona, April 22, 1808, AHMG, Esp. Corr., C85; Archivo general del Palacio, Madrid, "Indice de los papeles reservados de Fernando VII," II, 239; Lafuente, XVI, 230 (Sanlucar de Barrameda); Manuel Gómez Imaz, *Sevilla en 1808* (Seville, 1908), pp. 172-173; José Palanco Romero, "La Junta Suprema de Gobierno de Granada," *Revista del Centro de Estudios Históricos de Granada y su Reino*, I (1911), 109.
46. AHN, Estado, legajo 1 P; Beauharnais to Junot, Madrid, March 22, 23, 1808, AAE, Correspondance diplomatique, Portugal, Vol. 127, fol. 65; dispatch of Henry, March 28, *loc. cit.*

ordered published the documents on the Escorial affair, which appeared to establish that his plot had consisted only of an attempt to make his father realize the excesses of Godoy.[47]   He commissioned the Council of Castile to try the latter for his crimes.[48] Best of all, he announced to his subjects that he was eager to relieve their suffering, and he asked them to tell him through their officials what measures would bring about their greater happiness.[49]

One of his first pronouncements said that the French Emperor was his ally and the French troops were friends.[50]   This was what the public had suspected all along.   Napoleon would soon visit Madrid, and Fernando made eager preparations.   On April 8 he announced his own departure to meet the Emperor and escort him to Madrid.   Ten days later he told his subjects that he was crossing into France to visit Napoleon in a country house near the frontier in order to cement the bonds of friendship that united the two rulers, and he urged them to ignore the predictions of dire events that ill-intentioned persons were spreading.[51]

Despite these assurances, Spaniards who read of his departure in the *Gazeta* or heard it announced by their local officials could hardly be indifferent as they saw their young idol vanishing beyond the Pyrenees.   For the French were behaving suspiciously. Neither their ambassador nor their commander, Joachim Murat, had recognized Fernando's accession.   Murat had protected Godoy's family and showed concern for Godoy's own safety.[52]   In April French officers began to say that Napoleon himself refused to recognize Carlos IV's abdication, and their statements were reported widely.[53]   On April 20 word leaked out in Madrid that Murat was having printed a proclamation restoring Carlos to the throne.   A mob gathered and forced the printer to stop.[54]   Two

47. *Real orden*, March 31, 1808, published April 8, AHN, Cédulas.
48. *Real orden*, April 3, 1808, quoted in *Manifiesto del Consejo Real*, pp. 5-6.
49. *Real decreto*, April 12, 1808, AHN, Cédulas.
50. *Real orden*, March 20, 1808, *ibid.*
51. *Real decreto*, April 8, *real orden*, April 18, 1808, *ibid.*
52. Dispatch of Beauharnais, Madrid, March 25, 1808, AAE, Esp., Vol. 673, fols. 418-419; dispatch of Henry, March 28, *loc. cit.*
53. Dispatch of Henry, Madrid, April 4, 1808, AN, AF[IV] 1691, 2e dos., pièce 66; dispatch of Duhesme, Barcelona, April 22, 1808, AHMG, Esp. Corr., C85; *Manifiesto del Consejo Real*, pp. 26-27.
54. *Manifiesto del Consejo Real*, pp. 22-23.

days later the *Gazeta* announced that Fernando, acceding to the wishes of Napoleon, was turning Godoy over to the French.

In spite of Fernando's pleas, attacks on French soldiers occurred in various cities of northern Spain as April wore on.[55] They reached a climax with the violent but unsuccessful insurrection of the Dos de Mayo in Madrid. Persons fleeing the capital carried reports of the French slaughter of civilians. A shudder of fury ran from town to town along the Lisbon highway all the way to the Portuguese border,[56] and crowds in Seville and Oviedo also demonstrated against the French.[57] The highest official bodies, however—from the Junta of Government established by Fernando to rule in his absence down through the Council of Castile and the Chancillerías and Audiencias—denounced the rising in Madrid as a violation of the wishes of Fernando.[58] The excitement died down. Spain's attitude toward the French armies had veered rapidly in the two months since Fernando's accession. The relief experienced at that time gave way to renewed anxiety as suspicion grew that the play had not ended after all. Nevertheless, so long as Fernando urged patience through his officials, no concerted opposition developed. Although Spanish historians have immortalized the Dos de Mayo, calling it the beginning of their War of Independence, it did not set off the explosion because the young king's name still conjured up hope of the ultimate victory of Good.

On May 8 the Council of Castile published a lengthy address to the people of Spain, which contained a series of documents. Two were statements of Carlos IV dated at Aranjuez on March 21 and the Escorial on April 17 declaring that his abdication was

55. AHMG, Inventaire, 2e trim. 1808, No. 3 (Burgos, April 6), No. 13 (Barcelona, April 10), No. 23 (Barcelona, April 19), No. 29 (Toledo, April 22); dispatch of Stroganoff (Russian ambassador), Madrid, April 23, AN, AFIV 1694, 2e dos., pièce 68 (Madrid, Aranda); Toreno, p. 56 (Gijón, April 29); *Manifiesto del Consejo Real*, pp. 37-38.

56. AHN, Estado, leg. 3, No. 74 (Trujillo); dispatch of Dupont, Toledo, May 5, AHMG, Esp. Corr., C86 (Torrijos); AHMG, Inventaire, 2e trim., No. 65 (Badajoz). See Toreno, pp. 45, 63-64, 68-69.

57. Toreno, pp. 56-57 (Oviedo), 63-64; Gómez Imaz, p. 175 (Seville).

58. *Manifiesto del Consejo Real*, pp. 28-30; proclamation of Chancillería de Valladolid, May 5, 1808, in Biblioteca Nacional, Madrid, Varios, Fernando VII, fol.; *Diario de Valencia*, May 7, 1808 (Valencia); José María Caparrós, "La Chancillería de Granada durante la dominación francesa," *Revista del Centro de Estudios Históricos de Granada y su Reino*, I (1911), 197-198; Toreno, p. 57 (Oviedo).

made under duress and was null and void. A third was an order signed by him at Bayonne on May 4 appointing Murat his delegate in Spain. The others were an undated letter of Napoleon to Fernando offering Godoy asylum in France and a royal order of Fernando dated at Bayonne on May 4 decrying recent attacks on French soldiers since, he said, only the friendship of "the Great Emperor of the French" could save Spain and bring it prosperity. Two days later the Council published a letter of Fernando to Napoleon abdicating the throne in favor of his father.[59] The *Gazeta* carried these documents in its issue of May 13. A week later the Council published a royal order of Carlos IV announcing that for the happiness of his subjects he was giving his rights to the throne of Spain to his friend the Emperor of the French. An accompanying letter of Fernando renounced his rights to the crown and urged Spaniards to accept these acts in order to avoid a useless blood bath and possible loss of the colonies.[60] The *Gazeta* printed these renunciations on May 20. This series of pronouncements brought home to Spaniards that their hero had unwittingly been abducted. At the same time Godoy and his royal masters had been spirited to safety in France. This realization set off a revolution.

The *Gazeta* of May 13 arrived in Valencia on May 20. People gathered in the main square, where copies of it could be rented. Excitement grew as a Franciscan friar harangued the crowd, but no action followed. Three days later the *Gazeta* of May 20 came with the news of the collective abdication of the Bourbons. This time the crowd cried "Viva Fernando VII!" and began rioting. Part of it marched off to demand that the captain general and Audiencia of Valencia take action. Its representatives placed the blame for events on Godoy and exculpated Fernando. The officials hesitated, warning that resistance to Napoleon would entail the ruin of Valencia; but finally, under threat, they issued a proclamation in the name of Fernando VII enlisting all men from sixteen to forty, although they did not state the purpose of the enlistment. Calm never returned. Two days later, still under pressure, the Audiencia approved the creation of a Central Junta of Government of the Kingdom (i.e., Valencia). The first act of

59. Both in AHN, Cédulas.
60. Published in Madrid, May 18, 1808, *ibid.*

this new body was to proclaim that Fernando's renunciation was not a free act and to call on all Valencia and Spain to join the city in defense of the legitimate rights of Fernando and the Patria.[61]

The news of Valencia's revolt traveled rapidly south and north along the coast, producing risings in support of Fernando VII. Even in Barcelona, which the French controlled, mobs screaming their hatred of the French and their own captain general tore down the notices of the abdication of the Spanish royal family. Many persons obtained arms and set off to Valencia to join the revolt.[62] During these same days and for almost identical reasons, independent rebellions occurred in Saragossa, Oviedo, and Seville.[63] Like Valencia, these cities then became foci for risings, which spread rapidly through Aragon, northwest Spain, and Andalusia. By early June the unoccupied provinces were in full revolt against Napoleon.

The religious and patriotic motives for Francophobia, blanketed temporarily but never extinguished by the even greater hatred of Godoy, now reappeared. Sermons of the clergy cried for a crusade against the foreign heretics.[64] In Valencia a brutal mob led by a demented priest murdered more than three hundred French residents who had sought safety in the fortress.[65]

There was plenty of fuel for a war against France, especially one begun by the occupation of Spain and kidnapping of the royal family. Nevertheless, the pattern of events preceding the rising reveals that even stronger than nationalism in igniting the explosion was the "idea" or vision that Spaniards had of their political world. It was a kind of Manichaean outlook, in which

61. Proclamations of May 23 and 25 in AHMG, Esp., Corr., C86; *Manifiesto del Consejo Real*, pp. 38-39; María de la Encarnación Soriano, "El P. Rico y el levantamiento de Valencia contra los Franceses (22-25 de mayo de 1808)," *Archivo ibero-americano*, 2ª época, XIII (1953), 257-327.

62. Dispatch of Stroganoff, Madrid, June 6, AN, AFIV 1694, 2e dos., pièce 132 (Murcia and Cartagena); dispatches of Duhesme, Barcelona, May 25, 27, June 1, AHMG, Esp., Corr. C86, C87.

63. Dispatch of Verdier, Vitoria, June 2, *ibid.*, C87; Toreno, p. 74 (Saragossa); Ismael García Rámila, "España ante la invasión francesa...," *Boletín de la Real Academia de la Historia*, XCIV (1929), 512; Toreno, pp. 57-58 (Oviedo); Gómez Imaz, pp. 85-114; Toreno, pp. 64-65 (Seville).

64. The collection of uncatalogued pamphlets of the Biblioteca Nacional has at least eleven published sermons and pastoral letters of 1808 supporting the war against France on religious grounds (Varios, Fern. VII, all 4º), and many other publications took this line.

65. Lafuente, XVI, 301-304.

their ills were attributed to the Evil One—Godoy—and their happiness was expected from the advent of the Good One—Fernando.
So long as the French armies were believed to be bringing help
to Fernando, they were tolerated. After Aranjuez, however, the
need for the French ended. Still, Fernando continued to call
them friends, and the Spanish people accepted his word. While
Fernando remained king, even the bloody massacre of Madrid
did not bring Spain to arms. The renunciations of Fernando and
Carlos meant that Evil had reappeared on the stage in a new
guise, a French uniform. Enflamed by the realization that not
only was the play not over but that it was to end in tragedy, the
spectators forgot that affairs of state were not the realm of the
people and rushed on the stage to save the hero.

Can the historian justify this explanation? Can he discover
what a whole people thought, or enough of a people to bring
about simultaneous risings in distant regions? Particularly can
he say that the obvious motive for the risings—hatred of foreign
domination—was not the compelling motive at the start of the
revolts, which consisted instead in a peculiar vision of their own
rulers? The course of events supports the latter explanation, but
one wants fuller evidence, and for this the historian, especially
when dealing with a society that did not have free political discussion, appears to lack the resources of a social scientist who
analyzes contemporary public opinion.

Common sense, and the experience of public opinion studies,
says that not all Spaniards held any single view on any subject,
including the relative merits of Godoy and Fernando. Godoy had
his partisans, or at least his sycophants. Many later became
afrancesados, supporters of Joseph Bonaparte. An even larger
number of Spaniards were undoubtedly apolitical, even as late
as the summer of 1808, in isolated towns and villages, where life
went on much the same one year as the next, where worry was not
about the royal court but about crops and the weather, local
rivalries, marriage, sickness, and inheritance.

Still, the misfortunes of the past two decades had been such as
to arouse concern for what went on outside the town limits. The
peasants would have been aware of the famine even if individual
villages may not have suffered hunger. In the south there had

been the plague, and every place had known of the sale of Church lands, if not within its town limits then through announcements of auctions taking place nearby. Institutions existed to provide contact with the larger world. Every separate town had its *justicia*, empowered to act as agent of the intendant and to enforce the king's law. As was customary, the royal orders and pronouncements of the winter and spring of 1807-1808 carried instructions that they should be sent to all *justicias* to impart to all the king's subjects. The clergy offered another channel of communication with the outside. Most parishes had full-time priests, and there were also many friars. The intendant might be a Godoyist, but the *justicia*, like other town officials, was chosen locally and owed nothing to Madrid, while the priest or friar probably hated Godoy for his anticlerical policies. At the local level to blame the upstart, corrupt, immoral Prince of the Peace for the suffering of the country was simple and convincing. The picture of the persecuted, innocent Fernando was equally easy to accept. People knew that things used to be better and imagined they could be again but for the royal favorite. And what can be argued for small towns holds a fortiori for larger towns and cities, where economic disorder, famine, and unemployment made themselves felt more acutely and close touch with the state existed through royal judges and bureaucrats, army officers, merchants, lawyers, ecclesiastical dignitaries, and the *Gazeta*. The revolts against the French began in such centers of population.

However much reason tells the historian all this, he still wants concrete evidence that hatred of Godoy and passion for Fernando lay behind the rising. There is evidence, of different kinds and reliability. Of great value is that which dates from the time of Godoy's favor. It is free from possible bias caused by knowledge of later developments that makes suspect memoirs written by eyewitnesses after the event. Because of the royal censorship it is scanty, yet enough exists to provide the foregoing account of the Spaniards' Manichaean view of their political world before March, 1808. What has been used here consists mostly of dispatches of Napoleon's diplomats, military commanders, and spies. During 1807 their reports of Godoy's unpopularity and Fernando's favor multiplied, particularly after the Escorial affair broke. For example, the Count of Tournon, a trusted agent whom Napoleon sent to Spain in November, 1807, informed his master:

On arriving in Madrid I found public opinion even more pronounced in favor of the Prince of Asturias and hatred of the Prince of the Peace even stronger than in the provinces. All classes detest him and accuse him of being the enemy of the country. The *grandes*, the nobility, the clergy, the merchants, the people, see in him only the shame of the nation.[66]

These agents reported increasing hatred of Godoy in the first months of 1808.

How much weight should their dispatches be given? As foreigners they could not have gained a wide knowledge of Spain in a few brief months. When they said that Spaniards were looking to the French armies to solve their domestic problems they might be reporting the words of Francophiles, with whom they would most likely be in contact. On the other hand, of all foreign rulers Napoleon had the greatest interest in obtaining accurate information on Spain, and his observers were by and large capable. The reports of Tournon reveal remarkable insight. When he told of Spain's joy at the accession of Fernando, he added the most sound advice Napoleon ever chose to ignore: The Emperor should give Fernando a wife of Bonaparte blood. This is what the Spanish wish. "By consolidating the changes that have taken place in Madrid in a way that is favorable to France, the Emperor will be more master of Spain than if His Majesty had there 300,000 of his best troops."[67] One may conclude that the French reports have definite value, particularly since the different agents independently describe the same phenomenon. They could perhaps be corroborated by dispatches from other countries' diplomats if the historian's resources were unlimited.[68]

Spanish observers were better endowed to know the opinion of their countrymen, but contemporaneous reports do not appear to have been preserved. Two later accounts are particularly noteworthy: Godoy's own memoirs and those of Antonio Alcalá

66. Dispatch of Tournon, Madrid, Dec. 20, 1807, AN, AF[IV] 1680, 8e dos., pièce 14.
67. Dispatch of Tournon, Burgos, March 24, 1808, *ibid.*, 9e dos., pièce 10.
68. Fugier's detailed account of Spain's relations with Napoleon supports the picture of growing public hatred of Godoy. Fugier worked in the diplomatic archives of Portugal and Britain as well as with the official records of France and Spain.

Galiano, an intelligent young man present in Madrid in 1807-1808. Both agree on the public hatred of Godoy and infatuation with Fernando. Alcalá Galiano recalled that Fernando had been not one but several myths, people of opposite opinions seeing in him all the qualities they desired in a future king.[69] Godoy, analyzing the causes of this hatred of himself, blamed it particularly on the clergy, furious over the loss of their property. They told the people that Fernando was a model of piety and that his first act would be to cut short the sale of Church lands. "What could be my fate when I had against me, with few exceptions, the majority, the great mass of monks and friars, in so many ways masters of consciences, masters of opinion, so powerful in the towns where so many people lived satisfied with their petty crusts of bread?"[70] But he also saw drawn up against him the partisans of reform, who believed that, since he was all powerful, it was his fault if Spain were not perfected overnight and that reform was only awaiting Fernando's advent.[71]

The accounts of both these men were written decades after the events and could be subject to false memory. Furthermore, both lived in the capital at the time. What was true of Madrid might not have been true of all Spain. Yet they agree remarkably with the French observers, and the existence of quasi-mythical images of Fernando and Godoy is supported by the events surrounding Carlos IV's abdication. Evidence of the period prior to the riots at Aranjuez, if it clarifies the motivation behind the riots, does not prove, however, that these images were vital to the revolt against the French. At least the anger over the abduction of Fernando could be expected to overshadow the recollection of Godoy. Here is where the most convincing evidence enters in, for it reveals, indirectly but clearly, that the revolt besides being anti-French was also anti-Godoy.

Many leaders of the rebellion were men whom Godoy had harmed, and victims of the mobs were as often his partisans. Two men whom Godoy had imprisoned led the revolt in Seville.[72] An admiral who detested him headed the Junta established in Léon.[73] The risings in Oviedo and La Coruña were directed

69. Alcalá Galiano, *Recuerdos*, p. 55, and *Memorias*, I, 138.
70. Godoy, II, 234.
71. *Ibid.*, p. 235.
72. Gómez Imaz, pp. 93-96, 159.
73. Garciá Ramila, *loc cit.*, p. 512.

against local officials who were hated for being his creatures.[74] In Badajoz a crowd lynched the governor, known as his protégé.[75] A relative of Godoy's mistress, the former governor of Málaga, was murdered in Granada.[76] Little wonder that Godoyists by and large became *afrancesados*.

More eloquent evidence, however, comes from the press. The insurrection brought a breakdown of censorship, both royal and inquisitorial, in the unoccupied provinces. In the next years proclamations and sermons appeared on all sides, offering a windfall to the historian. Primarily they called for war against France, but in making their appeals for public support they regularly excoriated the evils of the former reign and the vices of the royal favorite. Thus Spaniards who felt the need to justify their conduct during the first confused days of the rising cited in their defense their opposition to Godoy. The Council of Castile, discredited in the public eye by having published Fernando's renunciation, tried to regain favor with a manifesto that began by recalling how its members had flouted Godoy when they acquitted the accomplices of Fernando in the Escorial affair.[77] The Junta of Cuenca, accused of treacherous dealings with the French, replied, "No city in Spain had fewer relations than Cuenca with the abominable Godoy or the infamous agents of his evil acts."[78]

Godoy was to blame if Spain now had to fight France. Fernando had fallen into Napoleon's trap not because of his own credulity but because of the wiles of the Prince of the Peace. One sermon likened Carlos IV to Adam, María Luisa to Eve, and Godoy to the greedy serpent.[79] By contrast, Fernando, according to other preachers, was "a truly pious and clear sighted king, with straightforward intentions and pure morals," "a right virtuous Prince, another Moses, who is going to free our Spain of the oppression under which it groaned beneath the despotism of a criminal favorite, as tyrannous, as fierce, as inexorable as Pharaoh was for Israel."[80]

74. Toreno, pp. 57, 61.   75. *Ibid.*, pp. 68-69.
76. Palanco Romero, *loc. cit.*, p. 111.   77. *Manifiesto del Consejo Real*, p. 1.
78. *Manifiesto a España por la Ciudad de Cuenca* (Madrid, 1808), in AHN, Consj., leg. 50703, No. F 120.
79. *El Patriotismo catolico. Papel útil á toda clase de personas en las presentes circunstancias de nuestra España* (Mallorca, 1813), p. 5.
80. Ignacio de Michelena, *Reflexiones sobre la constitution de la monarquía*

If conservatives looked on Godoy as the ruin of morals and religion, liberals used his rule as evidence for the need of civil liberties and constitutional government. Had there been liberty of the press under Carlos IV, one of them argued, Godoy's despotism would have been impossible.[81] To prevent repetition of rule by a man "born without talent or merit except a modest ability to play the guitar," another urged election of royal ministers by the provinces.[82] The liberal Junta of Murcia expressed the thoughts of many like-minded Spaniards when it said, "We shall have achieved nothing if before the war is over we do not have a Constitution that will free us for ever from Tyrants and Favorites and restore dignity to the People."[83] Evidently the hatred of Godoy shared with ideas of political philosophy the drive that led to the Constitution of 1812. The fact that his religious and economic policies anticipated those of the Liberals who wrote the constitution did not mitigate the antipathy of the latter.

Still, one might expect that men of all shades who were fighting to restore Fernando should denounce Godoy. Less to be expected is that Spaniards who accepted Joseph Bonaparte did likewise. These men condemned the revolt because, they argued, the advent of the Bonaparte dynasty removed the need for it. The Spanish notables who went to Bayonne to recognize the new king addressed their countrymen:

It is true that we have reached a pitiful situation. But to whom do we owe it? Who reduced us to it but the vacillating, indolent, unjust government under which we have lived for twenty years? What is left for us but to submit peacefully and each in his own way contribute to the establishment of a new government based solidly on the sanctity of the liberty, rights, and properties of every person?[84]

española (Cadiz, 1809) (in Estado Mayor Central del Ejército, Servicio Histórico Militar, Colección documental del fraile, Vol. 35), pp. 48-49; Mariano Rosales, *Sermon ... en Sanlucar de Barrameda ... 14 de octubre de 1809* (Seville, n.d.) (in Varios, Fern. VII, fol.), p. 5.

81. *Memoria sobre la libertad política de la imprenta ...* (Seville, 1809) (in Colección del fraile, Vol. 61), pp. 27-28.

82. *Discurso sobre la necesidad de un gobierno que evite en lo sucesivo los males que sufre ahora la nacion española* (Valencia, 1808) (Colección del fraile, Vol. 27), p. 4.

83. Junta de Murcia to Junta Central, Nov. 29, 1809, AHN, Estado, leg. 2C, No. 36.

84. *Proclama* of June 8, 1808 in *Real orden* of June 13, AHN, Cédulas.

The address did not mention Godoy by name—had not Napoleon just saved his skin?—but who else was responsible for twenty years of bad government? The Bayonne Assembly hoped to calm the rebellion in Spain by identifying their new regime with opposition to the late favorite.

Those who fought Napoleon continued their denunciations of Godoy and panegyrics of Fernando through the war years. Whatever the writers or speakers might think about the two individuals in private, they acted on the assumption that their parties— conservative, moderate, or liberal—would gain popular support by identifying themselves as enemies of the former tyrant and champions of the absent king. These men came from all over Spain and were appealing to audiences both educated and illiterate, more often local than national. Their virtually unanimous judgment of the temper of Spanish minds gives the historian a reliable gauge of public opinion in a past age.

This convincing evidence that the images of Fernando and Godoy remained vivid in Spanish minds throughout the developments of 1808 confirms the tentative conclusion drawn previously from the course of events. Inspiring the insurrection was the vision of a duel between Good and Evil, as it has been called here for simplicity, embodied in these two men. Before 1808 Spaniards found the explanation of their fate in their image of the wicked Prince of the Peace and saw their hope in their image of the virtuous Prince of Asturias. The revolt was set off by the impulse to protect Fernando "el Deseado" ("the Desired"), as he came to be called, who, having at last destroyed his enemy, was being abducted. Nationalism remained a subordinate motivation until events equated the French armies with Evil in terms of the vision.

In other words, in May and June, 1808, the Manichaean vision of a duel between Good and Evil mediated between individual hardships and revolutionary action. Under Carlos IV Spaniards suffered physically, and social changes took place that upset them emotionally. Such "material" causes could bring about concerted violent action, however, only if Spaniards as a group felt that their ills had an obvious cause and a simple solution. "Reality" had little to do with the decisions they took in 1808. Fernando rapidly revealed after his restoration that he

was not the king they had imagined, and Godoy was not so poor
a statesman, though for a century no historian except Modesto
Lafuente dared challenge the unfavorable image of him; and
there are reasons to think that Spaniards would have benefited
from acceptance of Joseph Bonaparte. Yet the vision that Spaniards had, told them that the overthrow of Godoy and subsequent
revolt against Joseph to maintain Fernando on the throne was
the course that would provide Spain's salvation, and their actions
followed the dictates of this belief.

This is not the only example of a people seizing hold of a
simple, easily grasped belief in saviors and villains to explain a
frightening domestic or international situation whose complexities are too great for the average person to penetrate, and then
taking fateful actions inspired by these beliefs. The "Red" and
"Fascist" scares in modern Europe and America come to mind.
Political and war propaganda in democracies encourages such
oversimplifications. The case of Spain in 1808 indicates that
these visions and their effects existed before people obtained legal
responsibility for their fate. Despite the warnings of his agents
in Spain, Napoleon ignored the role of this kind of "idea." Historians should not.

THE LIBERALS AND MADAME
DE STAEL IN 1818

Ezio Cappadocia

In his interpretation of history the historian is constantly faced with the complex interplay of thought and action. He is faced with the task of tracing to what extent ideas are of influence in history. At the same time he is always working back from the ideas to the complex situation from which they spring. An examination of Madame de Staël's *Considérations sur les principaux événements de la Révolution française* (1818),[1] the first systematic liberal defense of the French Revolution, and of contemporary response to it by French Liberals may serve as a point of departure for the historian in his quest for the concrete realities that shape men's thoughts. Such a study may also throw light on Professor Stanley Mellon's thesis that we can learn of Restoration politics by examining the history then written. Because in the Restoration he found that history was "the language of politics," he turned to it "in order to understand politics."[2] We may test the truth of his thesis and his approach, and also test the truth of his application of the thesis to Madame de Staël and the Liberals. One may, at the same time, turn to the demands of politics in order to understand the histories and their contemporary reception.

During the Restoration, liberal defenders of the Revolution had to explain how it was possible for the principles of 1789—the distillation of the political ideas of the Enlightenment—to degenerate first into the Terror and then into the despotism of Napoleon. They had to reject the contention of the Ultra-Royalists that the period 1789-1814 had to be seen as a whole, with the

EZIO CAPPADOCIA *is associate professor of history at the Royal Military College of Canada.*
1. Anne Louise Germaine, Baronne de Staël-Holstein, *Considérations sur les principaux événements de la Révolution français* (3 vols.; London, 1818).
2. Stanley Mellon, *The Political Uses of History: A Study of the French Historians in the French Restoration* (Stanford, 1958), p. 4.

Terror the logical consequence of the principles of 1789 and Napoleon the necessary outcome of the chaos caused by the revolutionary upheaval. Restoration liberals had to justify the very existence of liberalism. On all these points the *Considérations* was a seminal study.

In the *Considérations* Madame de Staël was defending not only the liberal principles of 1789 and the early months of the Constituent Assembly, but also her own career and that of her father, Jacques Necker. Indeed, she had begun the work with the intention of examining only the actions and political writings of her parent. In writing, however, she was drawn to consider, on the one hand, the principal events of the French Revolution, and, on the other hand, the constitution of England, as a justification of the political opinions of her parent. By her own account, both she and her father believed in imprescriptible, invariable rights that could be claimed by civilized men under any circumstances. These rights included equality before the law, individual liberty, freedom of the press, religious freedom, careers open to talent, and taxation only with representation. For a large country such as England or France, they favored also a tempered hereditary monarchy in which legislative power was jointly exercised by a house of lords, a house of elected representatives, and a king who possessed the veto. In connection with a proposed house of lords she lauded the great nobles who had fought for liberty in England and might help preserve it in France. Her infatuation with the English nobility was quite evident throughout the work, as was her hope that the French nobility might emulate them. Again by her own account in the *Considérations*, Madame de Staël fought for her program during the Constituent Assembly, the Terror, and the despotism of Napoleon. In fact, during Napoleon's rule she suffered over a decade of enforced exile for her beliefs and won a reputation as "the conscience of Europe." In 1814 she was neither a Bonapartist nor a Bourbonist. When the defeat of Napoleon seemed inevitable, she had intrigued with the Tsar to have him replaced by Prince Bernadotte, the former marshal of the Empire who was then heir to the Swedish throne. However, she accepted Louis XVIII and the Charter, and during the Hundred Days she remained publicly aloof from

Bonapartism. From 1814 to her death in 1817 her salon in Paris became once again a center of political intrigue. These were also the years when she was writing the *Considérations*.

In her defense of the Revolution her theme was that in France liberty was ancient and despotism modern. She accepted Henri Boulainvilliers's thesis put forth in the eighteenth century that the Gauls were a free people when the Franks crushed their liberty. She estimated that out of twenty-four million Frenchmen only about a hundred thousand were descendants of the Franks. She defended the concept of liberty as the profound wish and messianic fulfilment of history and saw France's past as a constant struggle in which the nation strove to regain its liberties, the nobility (the hundred thousand) to retain its privileges, and the monarchy to assert its arbitrary powers. The effort of the monarchy to assert its authority had culminated in the reign of Louis XIV. The sources of the Revolution were to be found in the nation's longing for the liberties that had been destroyed by the monarchy in the process of becoming absolute. In the demand for representative government were contained the true principles of the Revolution, whose only object was to give "a regular form" to the legitimate historical demands of the nation. To her the Revolution was essentially a part of man's progress toward liberty and the establishment of representative government. The seventeenth-century revolutions in England and the 1789 Revolution in France were part of the same movement.

Madame de Staël saw the basis of the Revolution's disasters in the unwillingness of the Constituent Assembly to take the advice of her father, who wished to adapt to French circumstances the English constitution, and in the emigration of the nobility. The royalists of the *ancien régime* and the new constitutional royalists together might have formed a majority in the Constituent Assembly. They might have carried the country with them in the affirmation of a tempered, constitutional monarchy. Instead, they divided, the noble royalists of the *ancien régime* and several constitutional royalists emigrated, and the country drifted into the degradation of the monarchy, war, and Terror. France recovered somewhat under the Directory, only to fall into the hands of Bonaparte, an egoist of genius who by Machiavellian arts, great and small, reduced every Frenchman into dependence on him. His claim that he was the son of the Revolution was false.

In her concluding volume, written in 1816, Madame de Staël concerned herself with current politics and the future of liberalism in France. She was eager to expose as illegitimate the temporary association, whatever its motives, which Liberals had with Bonapartism during the Hundred Days. She characterized as a *niaiserie* the effort to disguise Napoleon as a constitutional monarch. Moreover, she was aware that Liberals, in order to capitalize on anti-Bourbon sentiment, might succumb to the temptation of adding Bonapartist overtones to their language. She would have feared the belief expressed by General Lamarque, who had been exiled for his role in the Hundred Days, when from Belgium he reminded the Liberals that the only way to speak "to the great majority of the nation" was to make constant references to the imperial army and its feats, because brilliant theories, reasoned arguments, and sophisticated epigrams are understood by only a few people.[3] Madame de Staël recapitulated her well-publicized opposition to Napoleon and warned Liberals, "the friends of liberty," to separate rigorously their cause from that of Bonapartists and admonished them "not to confuse the principles of the Revolution with those of the Imperial government." "Let us beware of calling those men Bonapartists who support the principles of liberty in France."[4]

She also evaluated the difficulties of establishing representative government under the Bourbons. She compared their return to France in 1814 to that of the Stuarts to England in 1660 and discussed the mistakes that had led to the Revolution of 1688 and to the establishment of contractual monarchy in England. Although the Restoration in France was "greatly similar" to that of England, she felt that the spirit of Louis XVIII recalled to mind Henry IV much more than Charles II. But in 1814 his ministers "ought to have taken as a model the conduct of the House of Hanover not that of the House of Stuart."[5] Although the dynasty had been re-established in 1814 by the machinations of foreign

3. Général Lamarque, *Mémoires et souvenirs du général Maximin Lamarque publiés par sa famille* (6 vols.; Paris, 1835-1836), II, 6-7.
4. Staël, III, 154-155.   5. *Ibid.*, p. 112.

powers and not by the will of the French people, she felt that what inspired aversion was not the dynasty but the Ultras, "the party that wishes to reign in its name" and which still believes in the Divine Right of Kings, "the absurd doctrine that ruined the Stuarts."[6] Frequenters of her salon quoted Madame de Staël as claiming that while Louis XVIII would die as king, his brother would meet "the fate of James II."[7]

The last pages of the *Considérations* were a panegyric to England, a country whose institutions were in harmony with the author's political sentiments, where "everything is stamped with a noble feeling" and morals and poetry were superior to any available. France had to copy, without deviating from it, every aspect of the English constitution: "We cannot believe that Providence has placed this fine monument of social order so near to France, merely to bother us with never being able to equal it." Madame de Staël went so far as to say that if one of the two nations, France and England, had to be annihilated, she would prefer to see France destroyed rather than England, which had "the most noble, the most brilliant and the most religious social order that exists in the world."[8]

The *Considérations* evoked an immediate response from both Right and Left. Neither group found it wholly satisfactory. While the reaction of the Ultras caused no surprise, that of the Liberals was unexpected and, at first sight, seems inexplicable. The *Considérations* has been accepted by recent historians as "the Bible of French liberals under the Restoration"[9] and as the "classic defence of the Revolution" that "lays down the line"[10] followed by other liberal historians. Why then did this study by a patron saint of liberalism receive an uncertain reception from Liberals, to the foundation of whose party "she contributed more than any one else"?[11]

A necessary distinction must be made between liberals and Liberals. One may be tempted to designate as Liberals all those

6. *Ibid.*, p. 10.
7. Comte Molé, *Le Comte Molé, 1781-1855, sa vie, ses mémoires* (6 vols.; Paris, 1923), II, 388.
8. Staël, II, 167.
9. J. Christopher Herold, *Mistress to an Age; A Life of Madame de Staël* (New York, 1958), p. 450.
10. Mellon, p. 19.
11. Paul Gautier, *Madame de Staël et Napoléon* (Paris, 1933), p. 280.

who defended the Revolution. Yet, until the murder of the Duc de Berri in February, 1820, such simplification of the liberal forces is unwarranted. The Liberals (those known in their own day by this name) represented the extreme Left and were also known to their opponents as Ultra-Liberals, Independents, Jacobins, Revolutionaries, and Bonapartists, as well as Liberals. The liberals, on the other hand, were the true conservatives of the Restoration. In the Chamber of Deputies they made up the Center, whose ideological spokesmen were the handful of Doctrinaires. Liberals and liberals made common cause in defending the Revolution and its achievements, but until 1820 they disagreed over the nature of future political developments. The extremism of the Liberals caused men such as the Duc de Broglie, Madame de Staël's son-in-law, to leave them and join the ranks of the moderate Center.

The disagreement between liberals and Liberals began with the return of the Bourbons in 1814. While the liberals had accepted the Restoration with enthusiasm, the future Liberals had done so with reluctance. The beginning of their type of liberalism can be seen in the futile effort of the Senate, Napoleon's appointed second chamber, to impose terms on the self-styled Louis XVIII. Unlike the liberals, who during the Hundred Days had remained studiously aloof from the Bonapartist venture and had welcomed the outcome of Waterloo, the Liberals had rallied to Napoleon and had even entertained the absurd hope of converting the Emperor into a constitutional monarch. After Waterloo they had opposed the second Restoration and were thereafter stigmatized as Bonapartists. The Liberal leaders were Lafayette, the standard bearer of the movement, Benjamin Constant, its theorist, General Foy and Jacques Manuel, its more effective orators, Jacques Lafitte and Casimir Périer, its bankers, and many others such as l'Abbé Grégoire, Voyer d'Argenson, and Dupont de l'Eure. In reviewing the *Considérations*, the Liberal viewpoint was represented by the *Journal du Commerce, La Minerve française, Les Lettres normandes,* and a brochure by a former Jacobin, Charles Bailleul.[12] The *Censeur* showed the attitude of the liberals.

12. J.-Charles Bailleul, *Examen critique des considérations de Mme. de Staël, sur*

The Liberals accepted Madame de Staël's book as a systematic glorification of the liberal phase (1789-1791) of the Revolution, and accepted, as liberals must, her contention that the only cure for the ills of liberty is more liberty. Yet they resented her praise of aristocracy and of England and her denunciation of Bonaparte. Bailleul's thesis was that Madame de Staël did not have the least understanding of what the Revolution was about. He disagreed with her views on the role of the monarchy in the *ancien régime*. Madame de Staël and other liberals condemned Louis XIV for his absolutism. Even many aristocrats accused him of emasculating the nobility. His defense, however, was not left, as has been suggested,[13] merely in the hands of a few Royalist Gallicans. The Liberal Left, too, took up his cause. Bailleul admired Louis XI, Cardinal Richelieu, and Louis XIV, all of whom Madame de Staël condemned, because they repressed the nobility which Bailleul saw as the curse of France. To him the Third Estate, the people, were never wrong; the majority was always right. As a former member of the Convention, he challenged Madame de Staël's views of the Terror and expounded the thesis later taken up by many defenders of the Revolution that circumstances and pressure from the outside and not doctrinaire belief had forced the Convention to adopt the Terror. To him 1794 was the necessary consequence of 1789. He emphasized that the war provoked by the émigrés—unlike Madame de Staël he made no distinction between the first (1789-1791) and second emigration (1792-1794)—had made the adoption of the Terror inevitable. Though he agreed with her praise of Lafayette and as a former Jacobin he shared her anti-Bonapartism, he felt that her main motivation was filial piety.

The *Constitutionnel*, also known as the *Journal du Commerce*, the name under which it reappeared when suppressed by the government for infraction of press laws, was the most successful Liberal daily, in fact the only one to be published uninterruptedly throughout the Restoration. The paper enjoyed the largest circulation in France, between 15,000 and 18,000 copies, and was

les *principaux événements de la Révolution française, avec des observations sur les dix ans d'exil, du même auteur, et sur Napoléon Bonaparte* (2 vols.; 2nd ed.; Paris, 1822).

13. Mellon, p. 66.

the most important reading matter in the Liberal cafés, both in Paris and in the provinces. As the self-styled interpreter of the opinions and interests emanating from the Revolution,[14] it waged a bitter and often hysterical campaign against all the symbols and remnants of the *ancien régime*. Though it professed loyalty to the Bourbons, it was the same kind of questionable loyalty which the Ultras espoused toward Louis XVIII's constitutional charter.

The paper understandably devoted considerable attention to Madame de Staël's *Considérations*. The book was examined six times,[15] and its reviewers found what she had to say both reassuring and disturbing. They praised the author's general interpretation of the revolutionary period, her liberalism, and her unquestioned devotion to liberty, "of which she was the support as well as the ornament," but reluctantly and regretfully they found it necessary to be uncomplimentary. The first reviewer attacked her "frankly avowed" indulgence toward the aristocracy—a sentiment that "seems to have become for her a dominating idea"—and pointed out that the nobility was merely a "privileged group born in violence of whom even the best are worthless."[16] Another review made the *Considérations* the point of departure for discussing the role of passion in politics. The writer felt that the author, "a lively and passionate woman," was too involved in father-worship; consequently all her views "revolve around and are subordinate to a eulogy of her father," and in the first months of the Revolution "she sees only her father and his friends." All her reactions were highly subjective. Because the Directory treated her well, she praised that regime, yet her passions so blinded her that she overlooked its weaknesses and the fact that no one regretted its fall. On the other hand, because Napoleon exiled her, "the enthusiasm he had first inspired in her turned to hatred, and this violent passion has dictated the final part of the book." She damns all who served Napoleon, yet in that class "were to be found her intimate friends, the Liberals and the Independents, whom she esteems the most." The writer accused her of believing that once she was exiled from France, the country "was plunged into darkness." He also heaped scorn on her un-

14. *Le Constitutionnel*, March 10, 1826.
15. *Journal du Commerce*, May 17, 23; June 4, 17, 20, 26, 1818.
16. *Ibid.*, May 23, 1818.

limited admiration for all things English and especially on her
contention that if forced to choose she would rather see France
destroyed than England. He concluded that while one often
finds "excellent principles" in the *Considérations*, one must read
it with distrust and with precaution against its many errors which
flow from her passionate feminine nature.[17]

If the *Constitutionnel* was the most steadfast voice of Restoration Liberalism, the *Minerve française* was its most erudite and
most brilliant one. A political and literary review designed to
appear at irregular intervals to evade the restrictions imposed on
the periodical press, it was founded in 1818 under the stimulating
editorship of Benjamin Constant and leading Liberal publicists.
They made the journal a lively organ and gave it an intellectual
content that was only rivaled by the traditionalists' *Conservateur*,
edited by Chateaubriand, which counted among its distinguished
contributors De Bonald, Lammenais, and De Maistre.

In the *Minerve*,[18] the *Considérations* was reviewed by Benjamin Constant, Madame de Staël's former protégé and lover,
whose appointment to the Tribunate by Napoleon in 1800 was
owing to her influence, as was also his dismissal soon after. He
shared Madame de Staël's exile, but those were years of turbulent
unrest for him as he strove to disengage himself from her overwhelming and debilitating presence. The self-conscious anguish
and despair of their relationship Constant later related in his
novel *Adolphe*.

Constant's political theories centered on the need to protect
private property, to restrict the franchise to the wealthy, and
above all to limit the power of the state. He was a key figure in
the Liberal opposition, whose parliamentary ranks he joined in
1819. Even more than in the case of the other contributors to
the *Minerve*, all of whom had served under the Empire, his role in
the Hundred Days left him open to the accusation of anti-Bour-
bonism which, in spite of their weak protestations to the contrary,
all Liberals deserved.

In 1814 he, like Madame de Staël, had attached himself to the
fortunes of Marshal Bernadotte. But when the Bourbons were
restored he, too, made his peace with them and seemed to be

17. *Ibid.*, June 17, 1818.
18. *La Minerve française*, II (1818), 105-110, 316-325, 601-610.

committed to their cause when news reached Paris that the Emperor was returning from Elba. On March 19, only two days before Napoleon entered Paris, Constant published in the pages of the *Journal des Débats* a tirade against him and vowed never to bend his knee before the tyrant. Yet, within a few days, in a remarkable but not unusual manifestation of inconstancy, Constant did bend the knee. He agreed to draft a new constitution for Napoleon, the "Additional Act to the Imperial Constitution," and cheerfully became a member of the *Conseil d'État*. Even Lafayette, that persistent enemy of Napoleon, now rallied to the Emperor in the vain hope of seeing him become a constitutional monarch, or, perhaps more accurately, he saw Napoleon as a lesser evil than Louis XVIII.

Benjamin Constant's treatment of the *Considérations* was woefully inadequate, though he devoted three articles to the book. Most of his comments were more concerned with his views of the many subjects discussed by Madame de Staël than they were with an analysis of her interpretation. Like all other commentators, he, too, praised the liberal principles of the author, but he concentrated on what Liberals considered the author's shortcomings —her admiration for England and her praise for the aristocracy. Constant even felt called upon to give assurances of her love for France, and he wondered whether the English constitution that Madame de Staël praised was that of post-Waterloo Britain or that of the eighteenth century. He was certain that a free constitution would have had even more beneficial effect on France than it had had on England. If liberty had made England famous, "it would bestow upon us the rank assigned to us by nature." He dismissed the author's preference for the power of the aristocracy over that of one man as no longer relevant, because in times of *commerce et lumières* (a favorite Liberal coupling) the power of a class is more nefarious than that of a single despot who cannot exist under modern circumstances. Now that pure despotism was impossible, the aristocracy remained the real threat.

Another aspect of the *Considérations* with which all Liberals could agree was Madame de Staël's praise for Lafayette as a "great and good citizen," one of the founders of constitutional liberty. Mindful of the criticism leveled at Lafayette for inept-

ness during the first months of the Revolution, she had stressed
that if in those days Washington had been the head of the
National Guards of Paris, he, too, perhaps could not have triumphed over circumstances. Constant joined in the glorification
of Lafayette and ridiculed the efforts made by his enemies to
calumniate him both in the election of 1817, when he was defeated in Paris, and in the forthcoming campaign in the Sarthe.
The reader is struck by the failure of Constant to deal with
Madame de Staël's comments on Bonapartism and with her insistence that Liberals must repudiate it. Charles de Rémusat,
then a young Doctrinaire, noticed this curious omission and
wondered whether it was possible to write articles with more "ill
humour and ire"[19] than there displayed.

Much more vigorous attacks on Madame de Staël were to be
found in the periodical Les Lettres normandes,[20] a vitriolic
enemy of the returned remnants of the ancien régime. Its anti-
Bourbonism was thinly veiled. It devoted most of its space to
praising the victories of Napoleon and to bemoaning the fate
that had befallen the retired warriors under the Restoration.
In it Léon Thiessé, a Liberal journalist-historian, paid Madame de
Staël the customary tribute of calling her a leading liberal endowed with a most distinguished talent. He wondered, however,
whether a book praised by all groups did not, in fact, mean one
devoid of all principles, since of necessity it had to contain the
most contradictory views. He could find no unity of principles
and, like all commentators, he, too, was saddened by her apology
for England. Her comments on post-1799 France he viewed
merely as a satire on that period. She was, he said, too much
under the influence of personal vicissitudes, too dominated by the
sensitivity of her unhappy memories, to write an impartial history
of those years. He tried to find reassurance in the fact that
Madame de Staël had not published the book herself.

Another writer in Les Lettres normandes took up the theme
that Madame de Staël was writing merely as Necker's daughter
and as Bonaparte's exile. He insisted that she was so obsessed with

19. Rémusat to his mother, May 4, 1818. Correspondance de M. de Rémusat
pendant les dernières années de la Restauration, publiés par Paul de Rémusat
(6 vols.; Paris, 1884), IV, 281.
20. Les Lettres normandes, May 29, 1818; II, 245-250; June 12, 1818, 295-330;
July 22, 1818, III, 92-100.

hatred of Napoleon that she heaped similar hatred on France, especially when she went so far as to say that under his reign "no kind of virtue was honored in France." The reviewer examined in detail Bailleul's answer to Madame de Staël and approved his interpretation of the Revolution whereby Louis XVI was presented as the victim of his predecessors and especially of the nobility. He felt that Madame de Staël could not see clearly the true events of the Revolution because she was torn between private affection for her father, her prejudice in favor of the nobility, and her passion for liberty, so that she succeeded in being simultaneously "an ultra-royalist and ministerialist, a liberal and a *philosophe* [a curious juxtaposition], impious and devout, English, French, and German." He also accused her of not understanding the need for the Convention, the Terror, or the Committee of Public Safety, all made necessary by external affairs and circumstances. He, too, ridiculed her justification of the Directory and her condemnation of Napoleon, decisions that stemmed, he said, not from a correct appraisal of the situation but from personal rancor. Because Napoleon was unwilling to follow the advice of women, "she has been unable to rise above a personal injury."

Unlike the Liberals, liberal-minded writers gave the *Considérations* a much more favorable reception along with sharp criticism of the Liberals' attitude. A long letter to the editor of the *Publiciste*,[21] a small journal that appeared at irregular intervals, praised the book and predicted that partisans either of Left or Right would not like it. The Liberals, said the writer, will pretend to like it but will kiss it "with clenched teeth and would willingly bite it, if they could do so without being observed." He felt that only Bonapartists could justifiably be angry at the author, though he, too, as a Frenchman, could level some reproaches. Another writer admitted that he did not like her cult of papa, but while he could forgive her filial piety he could not forgive her attacks on Louis XIV.[22] Still another reviewer hailed the *Considérations* as Madame de Staël's "last and best" volume.[23]

Madame de Staël also was defended in the *Modérateur*, another small liberal periodical, by a reviewer who, however, ex-

21. *Le Publiciste*, May 30, 1818, I, 786-796.
22. *Ibid.*, II, 117-130.   23. *Ibid.*, pp. 589-603.

pressed his surprise at the chapter "Les français sont-ils faits pour être libres?" Though her answer was in the affirmative, he had read the comments on England with "painful astonishment" and wondered how "so noble a heart" could even have thought of them.[24] In the *Journal général de France* the book was defended on three different occasions[25] as the work of a superior writer "de bonne foi," who belonged to the optimistic school of man's perfectibility.

The liberal position was most effectively expressed in the distinguished *Censeur*,[26] a journal founded in 1814 and edited by Charles Comte and Barthélemy Dunoyer, who had been punished by both Napoleon and the Restoration government for championing freedom of the press and opposing arbitrary government. The first review pondered the political hypocrisy of the age when secret admirers of Napoleon were boasting their loyalty to the Bourbons, when those who professed loyalty to the constitutional charter wanted to destroy it, and when many who invoked the name of the king and the Charter did so only as a form of precaution so as to express views otherwise considered dangerous. Given this political atmosphere, a volume such as the *Considérations* brought out all the hypocrisy of the times. Consequently, some accused the author of being anti-French, others attacked her as too aristocratic, still others claimed she was motivated by passions, each "while sharply criticizing what does not interest him, takes great care of keeping silent on those aspects that wound him." All reviewers had stressed the faults because too much in the book was only too true. Too many saw in it only their "unsatisfied pretensions or their wounded vanity." In fact, the only people pleased with the book were those not concerned with the fate of parties.

A lengthier sixty-two-page review[27] compared the *Considérations* with Bailleul's answer and discussed the two writers' attitudes toward various issues and events of the Revolution. The reviewer admitted that Madame de Staël's primary purpose in the book had been to vindicate her father's memory, but he insisted that the important thing in what she had to say was the fact that

24. *Le Modérateur*, May, 1818, I, 83-104.
25. *Journal général de France*, May 18, 20, 22, 1818.
26. *Le Censeur*, VIII, 384-386.   27. *Ibid.*, XI, 202-264.

it was inspired by the love for liberty and by her "enthusiasm for all institutions that according to her should produce it." He rejected the imputation that Madame de Staël was anti-French, and he stated that anyone would have to admit that on certain questions—i.e., philosophy, manufacture, agriculture—England had made "immense progress." It has had and still has some institutions that are worth more than all those that "we have along similar lines." He agreed that Madame de Staël's admiration did seem to him to be "too absolute," and he was convinced that, had she lived to revise the book, she would have changed the last part. Maintaining that her views on aristocracy were no longer practical in France, he still found the section on Napoleon impartial and thanked her for her picture of the Emperor. Bailleul's book was dismissed as a badly written personal apologia by a man who had misunderstood the *Considérations*.

The reception given the *Considérations* illustrates Professor Mellon's thesis that by studying the history written during the Restoration we can learn much about the politics of the period. At the same time, a study of the *Considérations* and of its reception enables us to refine and to correct his application of his thesis to liberal agitators and historians during the Restoration. In his exposition he tends to consider the liberal forces *en bloc*. In his first chapter he writes, "The first political task faced by the Liberals—that group which, in speaking of the Revolution, represented everyone from Doctrinaires to the Jacobin Left—was to sell the French Revolution."[28] Consequently, he tends to treat the development of the "Liberal" thesis about the French Revolution *en bloc*. While he indicates that different liberal writers advanced different subtheses concerning the Revolution, he does not relate these differences to divisions in liberal political opinion. However, to assume that all liberal-minded people who defended the Revolution made common cause in 1818 and 1819 is to engage in an unwarranted simplification of French politics and history. The varied reception of the *Considérations* shows that the liberal forces were not unanimous in their view of the recent past and suggests that the politics of the period were more complex than

28. Mellon, p. 3.

the reader might deduce from Mellon's admirable study of Restoration historiography.

In fact, a close study of the complexities of the politics of the Liberals (using the term narrowly) does account for their attitude toward Madame de Staël's interpretation of recent history. Some of their uneasiness about the book stemmed from the fact that it appeared at a time when they were preparing for the 1818 elections that were to renew one-fifth of the Chamber of Deputies. After four years of uncertainty they were experiencing a new self-confidence. In 1815, much to their dismay, they had witnessed not only the second Restoration but also, in the midst of the White Terror, the overwhelming electoral victory of the Ultras. Yet, the disaster they had anticipated had not materialized, because in September, 1816, Louis XVIII had dissolved the "Introuvable" Chamber of Deputies. For the next four years the moderate Center majority elected in 1816 sought to follow the king's policy of reconciliation between the new and the old France, and it was during those years that the Liberals became a significant factor in the political life of the country.

The Liberals' success was made possible by the Center's election law of 1817. Under the new law, one-fifth of the Chamber was renewed that year. The Independents, as the Liberals then called themselves to stress their separation from the Center ministry, elected only seven out of sixty-two deputies, but three of these came from Paris, where only a determined effort by the government prevented the Independents from capturing all seven seats. Special efforts had been made to defeat Liberal candidates, especially Lafayette, who were known for their antipathy toward the Bourbons. The Independent candidates had been attacked as "Bonapartist and Republican debris,"[29] names that recall "the Republic and the Hundred Days,"[30] the "scandalous names of the coryphaei of the Revolution and of the Hundred Days."[31] After the 1818 elections the Duc de Richelieu spoke of the need

29. Barante to Madame Arisson de Perron, Baron de Barante, *Souvenirs du baron de Barante* (8 vols.; Paris, 1890-1901), II, 294.

30. *Journal des débats*, Sept. 23, 1817.

31. Pozzo di Borgo to Nesselrode, Sept. 21, Oct. 3, 1817; Carlo Pozzo di Borgo, *Correspondance diplomatique du comte Pozzo di Borgo, ambassadeur de Russie en France, et du comte de Nesselrode, depuis la Restauration des Bourbons jusqu'au congrès d'Aix-la-Chapelle, 1814-1818* (2 vols.; Paris, 1890), p. 235.

to break the "monstrous alliance" between the Liberals and the Bonapartists.[32]

Madame de Staël's renewed attack on Bonapartism and her reiteration that liberalism had to eschew any understanding with it coincided with the infiltration of the Liberal ranks by retired officers of the imperial army. They made their first significant appearance in 1818 and were to become increasingly important for the election of the following year. The presence of these men—more concerned with memories of their military past than with the aspirations of liberalism—facilitated the Liberals' effort to capitalize on an anti-dynastic and pro-Bonapartist feeling that was widespread among anyone who had reasons to be dissatisfied with Bourbon rule. The Center government knew that the prevalent sentiment among Liberals was a determination to prevent it from succeeding in its attempt to royalize the nation and to nationalize the monarchy, as Decazes put it. The Liberals were so fearful lest the Center acquire a reputation of liberalism that they often opposed its liberal measures. In 1819 they were even reluctant to support the moderate Dessoles-Decazes ministry, in spite of its efforts to cater to some of their prejudices, because they were courting popularity in the country. They were so concerned lest their support be interpreted by their followers as surrender of political independence that they abdicated political responsibility. Much of the Liberals' aversion for the liberal ministry stemmed from its unwillingness to bow to their demands for the immediate return of all those exiled because of their Bonapartism during the Hundred Days.

The *Considérations* and the reception it received show that during the Restoration the interrelation between the demands of current politics and the writing of history was immediate and essential. Clearly, one way to recover the politics of the period is to study its histories, just as one way to understand its histories is to study its politics. In her *Considérations*, Madame de Staël, concerned with certain tendencies among Liberals, attempted to use history as a means to teach them not only how to think about the past but also how to behave in the present. The Liberals'

32. Cited in Ernest Daudet, *Louis XVIII et le duc Decazes, 1815-20, d'après des documents inédits* (Paris, 1899), p. 284.

views of the book were determined not by their general approval of her interpretation of the Revolution but by their anti-dynastic sentiments that made them willing to accept possible Bonapartist support.

Perhaps the differences that separated the new from the old France were too great to be bridged during the Restoration. But neither the Ultras nor the Liberals can be accused of being eager to make the effort at reconciliation a success. The partisan interpretation which Madame de Staël gave the revolutionary period of which she had been a participant or a passionate observer failed to satisfy her most fervent admirers. The Liberals no less than the Ultras were the prisoners of that history to which they appealed in justifying themselves.

THE HAUNTED HOUSE OF
JEREMY BENTHAM

Gertrude Himmelfarb

> Never does the current of my thoughts alight upon the Panopticon and its fate, but my heart sinks within me. (Bentham, *History of the War between Jeremy Bentham and George III*)[1]

> I do not like to look among Panopticon papers. It is like opening a drawer where devils are locked up—it is breaking into a haunted house. (Bentham, *Memoirs*)[2]

The Panopticon that so obsessed Jeremy Bentham was the plan of a model prison. He pursued it more energetically than any other project and mourned its failure more passionately. He complained of a conspiracy of persecution; today he might more legitimately complain of a conspiracy of silence. Historians and biographers, plodding through his vast tomes and mass of manuscripts, have ignored the readily available and far more readable material on the Panopticon. They have so resolutely closed their minds to the devils haunting Bentham that they can hardly credit the reality of his obsession, let alone the reality of the devils.

Thus, no one has adequately studied the actual plans of the Panopticon, its role in Bentham's private life, or its function in his philosophy and politics. His admirers invariably place it high among the credits earning him the title of the greatest reformer of modern times, without feeling the need to inquire into the exact nature of his proposed reform or the reasons for its rejection. His critics, preoccupied with his philosophical deficiencies, concede without argument the merits of this and other of

GERTRUDE HIMMELFARB *is author of* Lord Acton: A Study in Conscience and Politics *and* Darwin and the Darwinian Revolution.

1. Jeremy Bentham, *Works*, ed. John Bowring (11 vols.; London, 1843), XI, 103.
2. *Ibid.*, X, 250.

his practical reforms.   Even the smaller group of irreconcilables, who deride his facility for alternating between grand schemes of social reconstruction (constitutions, codes, and judiciaries created *de novo*) and what seem to be the crotchety schemes of a crank (Panopticon, Frigidarium, or Chrestomathia), are naturally more interested in the former than in the latter.   As a result, the documents on the Panopticon have gone largely unnoticed.   Not only historians and biographers but even legal and penal commentators seem to be unfamiliar with some of the most important features of Bentham's plan.

The structure of the Panopticon is sufficiently well known: a circular building with the cells at the circumference and the keeper in a tower in the center.   And the opening words of Bentham's book have been widely quoted: "Morals reformed, health preserved, industry invigorated, instruction diffused, public burthens lightened, Economy seated, as it were upon a rock, the gordian knot of the Poor-Laws not cut but untied—all by a simple idea in Architecture!"[3]   But even his admirers have not taken him seriously enough to find out how this "simple idea in Architecture" could have so revolutionary an effect.   Yet Bentham was nothing if not serious.   The title page of his book announced that the Panopticon was intended as a model not only for prisons but for "houses of industry, work-houses, poor-houses, manufactories, mad-houses, lazarettos, hospitals, and schools." And the second page elaborated upon its suitability for any establishment in which a number of people had to be kept under inspection, "no matter how different or even opposite the purpose: whether it be that of punishing the incorrigible, guarding the insane, reforming the vicious, confining the suspected, employing the idle, maintaining the helpless, curing the sick, instructing the willing in any branch of industry, or training the rising race in the path of education."[4]   Subsequent chapters of the book showed how the plan was uniquely fitted to serve each of these purposes.

Indeed, the Panopticon had not originally been conceived as a prison at all.   Bentham had borrowed the idea from his brother Samuel, who had constructed a workshop on this principle for

---

3. *Ibid.*, IV, 39.   The punctuation here, as elsewhere, has been slightly altered, mainly to eliminate the many dashes and commas.

4. *Ibid.*, p. 40.

the model community he tried to establish on Potemkin's estate in Russia. It was while visiting his brother in Russia in 1786 that Bentham thought of adapting the plan to other uses, particularly to that of a prison. He christened it Panopticon, from the Greek words meaning "all seeing." (Most of his inventions were subjected to this baptismal rite, as if Greek were a token of scientific grace.)

Certainly this was a fitting name for the "Inspection House," as the subtitle of his book described it. A remarkable quotation from the Psalms prefaced one of his sketches of the Panopticon—remarkable as much for its unlikely source (Bentham was little given to Scriptural citation) as for its perfect aptness:

> Thou art about my path, and about my bed: and spiest out
> all my ways.
> If I say, peradventure the darkness shall cover me, then shall
> my night be turned into day.
> Even there also shall thy hand lead me; and thy right hand
> shall hold me.[5]

Bentham did not believe in God, but he did believe in the qualities apotheosized in God. The Panopticon was a realization of the divine ideal, spying out the ways of the transgressor by means of an ingenious architectural scheme, turning night into day by means of artificial light and reflectors, holding men captive by means of an intricate system of inspection. Its purpose was not so much to provide a maximum amount of human control, as to transcend the human and give the illusion of the divine. The "inspection principle" was subtle and sophisticated:

It is obvious [Bentham wrote] that the more constantly the persons to be inspected are under the eyes of the persons who should inspect them, the more perfectly will the purpose of the establishment have been attained. Ideal perfection, if that were the object, would require that each person should actually be in that predicament, during every instant of time. This being impossible, the next thing to be wished for is that, at every instant, seeing reason to believe as much, and not being able to satisfy himself to the contrary, he should *conceive* himself to be so.[6]

This was the genius of Bentham's scheme. Aspiring to the "ideal perfection" of complete and constant inspection, he pre-

5. *Ibid.*, XI, 96.
6. *Ibid.*, IV, 40. All italics are in the original.

ferred to simulate this ideal rather than to compromise it. And this simulation was achieved by adopting another attribute of God—invisibility. As the inspector would be felt to have an "invisible eye,"[7] each inmate would "conceive" himself in a state of complete and constant inspection because he would never be able to "satisfy himself to the contrary." All the architectural details so elaborately worked out by Bentham—the exact arrangement of partitions, passages, floor levels, doors, and windows—were designed for this end: to combine "the *apparent omnipresence* of the inspector (if divines will allow me the expression), . . . with the extreme facility of his *real presence*."[8]

For schools, factories, and the like, the inspection principle was a necessary and sufficient condition. For the Panopticon as prison, however, it had to be supplemented by a second principle, the "law of solitude."[9] By treating the multitude as "solitary and sequestered individuals,"[10] Bentham hoped to improve upon the old adage: "Never less alone than when alone" was to become "Never more alone than in a crowd." This effect would be achieved by confining each prisoner to a private cell set off by walls and partitions in such a way as to block out the view of every other cell. Here the prisoner would sleep, eat, and work. He was even to have private toilet facilities so as to eliminate that occasion for gregariousness. To be sure, no ingenuities of architecture or plumbing could create an inviolable sound barrier, but that difficulty would be overcome by gagging the violators—a humane and painless deterrent, Bentham argued, compared with the irons used elsewhere to enforce solitude.

The Panopticon was also superior to other penitentiaries in not having to suspend the law of solitude even for Sunday morning religious worship. There was to be "no thronging nor jostling in the way between the scene of work and the scene destined to devotion; no quarrellings, nor confederatings, nor plottings to escape; nor yet any whips or fetters to prevent it."[11] Instead, the prisoners would enjoy the benefits of religious worship "without stirring from their cells," by the simple expedient of observing and hearing the services rather than actually attending them.

7. *Ibid.*, p. 79.   8. *Ibid.*, p. 45.
9. *Ibid.*, p. 47.   10. *Ibid.*
11. *Ibid.*

For this purpose, the chapel was located in the center of the structure just above the inspector's lodge, the chaplain himself (unlike the inspector) being visible to the inmates, and his voice made audible by means of the same system of speaking tubes used by the inspector to transmit his orders.

As Bentham was pleased, for reasons both of humanity and of economy, to dispense with the conventional chapel, so he was also pleased, for the same reasons, to do without the usual costly dungeon. In the Panopticon, he announced, "the man is in his dungeon already (the only sort of dungeon, at least, which I conceive any man need be in), very safe and quiet."[12] His mode of reasoning toward an extreme conclusion was familiar. If inspection was good, surely a maximum amount of inspection was best. If solitude was good, absolute solitude was best. And if safety and quiet were desirable, what could be safer, quieter, and better than a cell that was virtually a dungeon?

It could only be, he assumed, because "consistency is of all human qualities the most rare" that men might resist his plan. Thus most parents would agree that "children cannot be too much under the master's eye"; if parents were consistent, they "should be fonder of the principle the farther they saw it pursued." Instead, they provokingly drew back "when they saw that point screwed up at once to a pitch of perfection so much beyond whatever they could have been accustomed to conceive." They suddenly developed scruples and doubts:

Whether it would be advisable to apply such constant and unremitting pressure to the tender mind, and to give such herculean and ineludible strength to the gripe of power? Whether persons, of the cast of character and extent of ideas that may be expected to be found in the common run of schoolmasters, are likely to be fit receptacles for an authority so much exceeding anything that has been hitherto signified by *despotic*? . . . Whether the irretrievable check given to the free development of the intellectual part of his frame by this unintermitted pressure, may not be productive of an imbecility similar to that which would be produced by constant and long-continued *bandages* on the corporeal part? . . . Whether the liberal spirit and energy of a free citizen would not be exchanged for the mechanical discipline of a soldier, or the austerity of a monk? And whether the result of this

12. *Ibid.*, p. 54.

high-wrought contrivance might not be constructing a set of *machines* under the similitude of *men*?

But these liberal scruples, Bentham protested, were all beside the point. The only pertinent question was: "Would *happiness* be most likely to be increased or diminished by this discipline?" His answer was unequivocal, and if it was intended for school-boys, it applied *a fortiori* to prisoners: "Call them soldiers, call them monks, call them machines: so they were but happy ones, I should not care. Wars and storms are best to read of, but peace and calms are better to enjoy."[13]

"Safe and quiet," "peace and calms"—the Panopticon, like Hobbes's Leviathan, was born out of fear. Bentham was not the first prison reformer to discover the virtues of safety and quiet. But he was the first to make absolutes of these virtues, to take refuge in the dungeon as Hobbes had taken refuge in the absolute state. The Panopticon is so dramatic a scheme that less dramatic proposals tend to be ignored, or if not ignored then subtly denigrated, as Bentham himself denigrated whatever fell short of the absolute "pitch of perfection." In fact, the Panopticon was so far from being the only plan of prison reform current at the time that it was itself a response to an earlier plan that had actually been approved by Parliament.

The state of penal law and prisons had occupied reformers in and out of Parliament long before Bentham. A translation of Beccaria's *On Crimes and Punishments*, with a preface by Vol-taire, appeared in England in 1767, affirming the purpose of all law, and specifically penal law, to be "the greatest happiness of the greatest number."[14] It was followed in 1771 by William Eden's *Principles of Penal Law*, in which "public utility" was taken to be the practical measure of punishment.[15] Six years later, John Howard's exposure of *The State of the Prisons* led to new penal legislation. A bill of 1778, drafted by Eden and the eminent jurist William Blackstone, provided for the construction of "Houses of Hard Labour." These were to be administered by

13. *Ibid.*, pp. 63-64.
14. Cesare Beccaria, *On Crimes and Punishments* (London, 1767), p. 2.
15. Lord Auckland (William Eden), *Principles of Penal Law* (London, 1771), p. 6.

men appointed by and responsible to the government, and the prisoners were to be confined in moderate solitude and employed at varying degrees of hard labor.

This bill is interesting as an exhibit not only of the general tenor of penal reform at the time but also of Bentham's attitude toward the subject before he had seized upon the idea of the Panopticon. In spite of his attack on Blackstone only two years earlier, Bentham was so well disposed to this proposal that he published the bill together with a commentary by himself under the title *View of the Hard-Labour Bill.* In this pamphlet of 1778, he endorsed the bill's provision for moderate "solitary confinement"[16] (separate cells for sleeping and in special cases for work) and labor of the "hardest and most servile kind" for those physically capable of it.[17] Where the bill had provided for distinctive clothing to "humiliate the wearer" and prevent escape, Bentham proposed to supplement this with chemical washes applied to the forehead, cheek, or whole face, possibly spelling out the offender's name and jail.[18] He agreed that visits from family and friends should be prohibited, not only, as the authors of the bill thought, to prevent mischief, but also to shroud the prison in mystery and thus "enhance the terrors" of jail for "persons in such ranks in life" who were themselves potential criminals.[19] For the same reasons of security and terror, he approved of dungeons, although not unhealthy ones: fresh air, he pointed out hopefully, would not diminish the salutary terrors of isolation, silence, darkness, and strangeness; and if the presence of windows should occasion some small loss of terror, this could be made up for by additional deprivations of diet. For considerations of health, too, he recommended that prisoners be provided with sheets, bedsteads, and steam heating. And finally, "to inculcate the justice, to augment the terror, and to spread the notoriety" of the prison, he proposed the carving of suitable inscriptions and bas-reliefs over the entrance way. "Violence and knavery/ Are the roads to slavery" was one of his suggestions, accompanied by the picture of a wolf and fox yoked together to a cart and being whipped by the driver. "Let me not be accused

16. Bentham, *Works,* IV, 3.
17. *Ibid.,* p. 16.
18. *Ibid.,* p. 20.
19. *Ibid.,* p. 23.

of trifling," he concluded. "Those who know mankind, know to what a degree the imagination of the multitude is liable to be influenced by circumstances as trivial as these."[20]

The Penitentiary Act of 1779 adopted some of these recommendations (although not the poetic and artistic renditions over the gateway). But mainly because of the obstinacy of John Howard, who was one of the commissioners charged with putting it into effect, no site was decided upon and the act was left in abeyance. Seven years later, while visiting his brother in Russia, Bentham saw the means of implementing the act. Only instead of the penitentiary prescribed by Eden and Blackstone, he now put forward his plan of the Panopticon. In a sense, the Panopticon was the Penitentiary Act screwed up to that pitch of perfection of which only Bentham was capable. It is tempting to think of it as a fantasy, a mythical utopia, even a divine vision tainted by divine madness. Unlike Plato or More, however, Bentham regarded his creation not as an ideal against which reality might be measured, but as a practicable, potential reality. His friends in England had been assuring him that the time was ripe for reform: "Our ministers, as they have little to do abroad, seem to be full of schemes for domestic improvement."[21] The Penitentiary Act was a token of this mood of reform. And the Panopticon, he hoped, would become the new penitentiary.

There was one crucial difference between the Penitentiary Act and Bentham's scheme, apart from the differing degrees of seclusion and inspection. The act had meant to do away with the prevailing practice of confining prisoners to jail without work or farming them out to work for private contractors. It had been not uncommon for a contractor to take over an entire prison, hiring out workers as he chose, exacting fees from the inmates for their keep, selling them liquor and other amenities, and in general running it as a private and often exceedingly lucrative enterprise. The act proposed to change all this by making the prison what we understand it to be today—a public institution. A committee appointed by the government was charged with the general superintendence of the penitentiary and the selection of officers. Two members of this committee were to visit the prison

20. *Ibid.*, p. 32.
21. Trail to Bentham, Feb. 26, 1787, *ibid.*, X, 172.

fortnightly to investigate conditions, report abuses, deal with
breaches of discipline, and recommend commutation of sentences.
In addition, the prison was to be visited by justices of the peace
and, once a quarter, by a specially appointed inspector. At the
time, Bentham had entirely approved of these arrangements,
cautioning only against the delegation of too much power to the
governor of the prison: "Jealousy, not confidence," he had written,
"is the characteristic of wise laws."22

In drawing up the plan of the Panopticon, however, Bentham
reversed himself, as well as seeking to reverse the whole trend
of penal reform. In contrast to the penitentiary proposed in the
act, the Panopticon was to be run entirely by private contract
management. The contract system was so essential to his scheme
and so paramount in his mind that Bentham later denied having
ever favored anything else.23 Whatever his earlier views, his
book on the Panopticon minced no words: "To come to the
point at once, I would do the whole by *contract*. I would farm
out the profits, the no-profits, or if you please the losses, to him
who, being in other respects unexceptionable, offered the best
terms." The contractor would continue in possession of the contract on condition of his good behavior—"which," he added, "is
as much as to say, unless specific instances of misbehaviour,
flagrant enough to render his removal expedient, be proved on
him in a legal way, he shall have it for his *life*." And as in any other
private enterprise, the contractor would be given "all the *powers*
that his interest could prompt him to wish for, in order to enable
him to make the most of his bargain." There were, to be sure,
"some slight reservations" upon the exercise of these powers—
"very slight ones you will find they will be, that can be needful
or even serviceable in the view of preventing abuse." These reser-

22. *Ibid.*, p. 29.
23. In 1830 he claimed that his pamphlet of 1778 had criticized the public
management aspect of the bill and had thus been a "complete demonstration of its
inaptitude" (*ibid.*, XI, 98). Yet earlier, in the preface to the second edition of the
Fragment on Government, he had described the pamphlet more moderately: "The
tone, ... though free, and holding up to view numerous imperfections, was upon the
whole laudatory: for my delight at seeing symptoms of ever so little a disposition
to improvement, where none at all was to be expected, was sincere, and warmly
expressed" (*ibid.*, I, 255). Unfortunately, it is the 1830 statement that has been
generally credited by most historians. E.g., "The plan of the architecture and
management of a convict prison set forth in the bill was subjected to a severe
criticism" (Coleman Phillipson, *Three Criminal Reformers* [London, 1923], p. 120).

vations were: the publication of accounts, the obligation not to starve or maltreat the prisoners, and the promise to keep the establishment open for inspection at all times. Inspection, however, was to be not by an official visiting committee as was provided in the Penitentiary Act, but by "the great *open committee* of the tribunal of the world"—that is, private, casual observers without public status or authority.[24]

Even these slight reservations, Bentham reasoned, were largely supererogatory since the contract system, like the system of private enterprise from which it derived, was itself the best guarantee of the public welfare. The contractor, like any employer, had every incentive to keep his laborers well nourished and in good health, which is to say, in good working condition. An additional incentive was a novel insurance arrangement whereby the contractor would pay the government a fixed sum for the death of each prisoner—setting his contract, of course, at such a figure as would recompense him for the normal death rate. Such devices, Bentham hoped, would redeem prison contractors from the contempt in which they were commonly held. He himself professed greater trust in a contractor than in a magistrate, for the contractor in pursuing his own interest was also promoting the public good, whereas the magistrate, having no interest but "the exercise of his own power and the display of his own wisdom," was wilful and irresponsible.[25]

This plan of the Panopticon, based on the principles of inspection, solitude, and contract, was described in a series of letters written by Bentham while still in Russia in 1786. The letters, in a single packet, were sent to England in December with instructions to his friend, George Wilson, to have them published as a pamphlet.[26] Wilson, who was always urging Bentham on to bigger and better projects but was rarely happy with them when

24. Bentham, *Works*, IV, 46-48.   25. *Ibid.*, p. 51.

26. In the *Panopticon*, published in 1791, Bentham claimed that the letters had been written "without any immediate or very determinate view to general publication" (*ibid.*, p. 39). The correspondence, however, leaves no doubt that they were from the first intended for publication, the letter form being used only as a convention. When he sent them to Wilson, he described them as a "two-penny-halfpenny pamphlet, consisting, I suppose, from 150 to 200 pages," and he made specific suggestions as to publisher, printer, and format (*ibid.*, X, 165). His *Defence of Usury*, also carrying the dateline of Crecheff, 1787, was similarly cast in the form of letters.

they materialized, refused to see to their publication (as he also refused to do anything about Bentham's *Defence of Usury* that had been entrusted to him about the same time).

The letters were finally published in 1791. By that time, Bentham had had many afterthoughts and the pamphlet had grown into a considerable work (three small volumes in its first edition). The letters appeared substantially as they had been initially written (or so Bentham said), under the date line "Crecheff in White Russia, 1787"—1787 being the date of their originally projected publication. But they were now accompanied by a preface explaining the circumstances of their composition, and by a "Postscript" four times the length of the letters. In the preface Bentham explained that the postscript altered the original plan in many respects, but that he had permitted the letters to stand because he had not the time to recast the whole, because his "general principle" was equally well illustrated in either form, and because it would be amusing and instructive to exhibit the plan "in an historical and progressive point of view."[27] A more compelling reason, perhaps, which he did not mention, was that the government of Ireland, exploring the possibility of a "Poor Inspection House" to be constructed on the model of the Panopticon, had subsidized the printing of the letters.[28]

Panopticon: or the Inspection House, the title under which the work was published in 1791, included, then, both the original letters of 1786 and the lengthy postscript written five years later. Yet it has always been treated as a unified work, thus ignoring the gap of time separating the two parts and the substantial differences between them. In fact, the two parts are more distinctive than Bentham intimated. And looking at them from a "historical and progressive point of view," as he suggested, may be even more instructive than he thought.

The most obvious of the changes introduced in the postscript may seem at first to have been prompted by an accession of simple humanitarianism. This was the abandonment of absolute solitude. Instead of single cells, Bentham now proposed that each

27. *Ibid.,* IV, 39.
28. This also accounts for the fact that the part of the book consisting of the letters was printed in Dublin, whereas the postscript was first printed in London and then reprinted in Ireland.

cell be made to accommodate two, three, or four prisoners, the number to depend upon their character, their employment, and the fluctuating population of the prison as a whole. He hastened to say that the Panopticon system itself—the basic mode of architecture, inspection, and management—was unaffected by this change, being equally appropriate to this revised plan of "mitigated seclusion" as to the "absolute solitude" of the original plan. Under the original plan, as he now saw it, the Panopticon system "enables you to screw up the punishment to a degree of barbarous perfection never yet given to it in any English prison, and scarcely to be given to it by any other means." Under the revised plan, the Panopticon would have all the advantages of solitude without its "inconveniences." Absolute solitude, he now quoted Howard's earlier work, "is more than human nature can bear, without the hazard of distraction or despair." Its only proper use was "the breaking the spirit, as the phrase is, and subduing the contumacy of the intractable." But as such it could only be a temporary measure. "Why, then," he asked, "at an immense expense set up a perpetual establishment for the sake of so transitory a use?"[29]

"At an immense expense"—this, much more than the "barbarous perfection" of absolute solitude, appears to have been the main "inconvenience" of the original plan. By Bentham's own account, it was neither his belated attention to Howard nor his newly aroused sense of compassion that caused him to reconsider the merits of absolute solitude:

What startled me, and showed me the necessity of probing the subject to the bottom, was the being told by an architect, that the walls alone as expressed in Plate III might come to two or three thousand pounds. It was high time then to inquire what the advantages were that must be so dearly paid for.[30]

Nor was the cost of construction the only expense of solitude. Double, triple, or quadruple the occupants of the cells and the

29. *Ibid.*, pp. 71-72. Sir Samuel Bentham's wife claimed that it was her husband who persuaded Jeremy to give up the idea of solitary confinement (Maria Bentham, *Life of Brigadier-General Sir Samuel Bentham, K.S.G.* [London, 1862], p. 100). But her zeal to enhance her husband's reputation, particularly at the expense of her brother-in-law, makes much of this biography unreliable. If Samuel Bentham had indeed been opposed to solitary confinement, he would have been better able to exercise his influence at the time of the writing of the first plan, when they were in Russia together.

30. *Ibid.*, p. 138.

cost of heating, lighting, toilet facilities, and such are divided by two, three, or four. At the same time, the working opportunities are multiplied, not only by permitting trades requiring more room than is available in a single cell, but by permitting those requiring the co-operation of two or more workers. And the prisoners would be more productive, it being well known that "the state of the spirits" of the worker is reflected in his work, and that companionship is more conducive to a favorable state of the spirits than isolation.[31]

Bentham had earlier defended the Panopticon against the Penitentiary Act on the grounds that only absolute solitude could prevent the moral contamination of one prisoner by another and thus give the best hope of reformation. Now he was proposing considerably less solitude than that envisaged in the act (which provided for single cells) and claiming for his new plan all the moral superiority of the old. The system of inspection, he now decided, was sufficient in itself to forestall mischief; for while it could not actually prevent the communication of "pernicious instruction," it would make it impossible to act upon such instruction—at least "for many years to come."[32] He also discovered in mitigated seclusion the moral virtues of mitigated association, and was moved to a rare display of eloquence:

Sequestered society is favourable to friendship, the sister of the virtues. Should the comrades agree, a firm and innocent attachment will be the natural fruit of so intimate a society, and so long an union.

Each cell is an island: the inhabitants, shipwrecked mariners, cast ashore upon it by the adverse blasts of fortune: partners in affliction, indebted to each other for whatever share they are permitted to enjoy of society, the greatest of all comforts. . . .

A fund of society will thus be laid up for them against the happy period which is to restore them to the world. . . . Quitting the school of adversity, they will be to each other as old school-fellows, who had been through the school together, always in the same class.[33]

This paean to the old-school-tie did not survive the occasion that inspired it; certainly there is no reminiscence of it, as will be seen, in his provisions for released prisoners. And in general his newly aroused sensibility failed him when it was not sustained

31. *Ibid.*, p. 74.   32. *Ibid.*, p. 72.
33. *Ibid.*, pp. 74-75.

by economic advantage. He did not, for example, go so far in the mitigation of seclusion as to permit prisoners to attend chapel. Now, as before, they were to remain in their cells and worship from afar: "There they are in a state of continued safe custody; and there they are without any additional expense." To be sure, only half the prisoners could remain in the safe custody of their own cells; on his revised plan, only three tiers of cells enjoyed a view of the chapel, so that the occupants of the other three tiers had to be moved to the more fortunately located cells—this double complement of prisoners, he trusted, "awed to silence by an invisible eye."[34] Yet in spite of the obvious inconvenience of this make-shift arrangement—the very "thronging" and "jostling" his plan had been designed to avoid—he refused to consider a more conventional form of worship in a more conventional chapel.

Nor did he relent when he discovered, after the final architectural plans were drawn up, that there was a large unused space in the area of the chapel. For he then found a more profitable use for that space—as a visitors' gallery. He cited the examples of other sightseeing attractions: the Asylum (for the insane), the Magdalen (for retired prostitutes), and Lock Hospital (for the venereally diseased). Why should not the Panopticon be as popular as these? "The scene would be more picturesque; the occasion not less interesting and affecting." And the contributions that would be solicited from the visitors would encourage the contractor to "keep the establishment in a state of exemplary neatness and cleanliness, while the profit of them will pay him for the expense and trouble." The presence of visitors would also serve as a form of "gratuitous inspection," thus putting the contractor doubly on his mettle. Bentham did not seem to have considered the possibility that the contractor, so far from being inspired to greater exertions of neatness and cleanliness, might try to compete with the Asylum, Magdalen, or Lock Hospital in picturesque and exotic horrors. He did, however, take into account the criticism of one friend who suggested that this kind of "perpetual pillory" might have a corrupting effect upon the prisoners by hardening them into insensibility. To this objection

34. *Ibid.*, pp. 78-79.

he had several replies: that as the guilty were less numerous than the innocent, their serving as an example to others took priority over their personal reformation; that their offenses probably merited even more severe punishment than the pillory; that this form of pillorying was nothing to what they had been subjected at trial; and finally, if the objection persisted, that the prisoners might be provided with masks, thus sheathing the guilty while exposing the guilt.[35]

Behind each of these ingenious schemes and explanations was the overriding consideration of economy. The trinity of the earlier plan—inspection, solitude, and contract—gave way to a new trinity—lenity, severity, and economy. The "rule of lenity" prescribed that the conditions of imprisonment not be detrimental to health and life; the "rule of severity" that these conditions be no better than those of "the poorest class of subjects in a state of innocence and liberty"; and the "rule of economy" that "no public expense ought to be incurred, or profit or saving rejected, for the sake either of punishment or of indulgence."[36] The last was the primary rule: "Its absolute importance is great, its relative importance still greater."[37] Economy was both the measure of lenity (a malnourished or maltreated prisoner being an unprofitable worker) and the measure of severity: "for the ways in which any quantity of suffering may be inflicted, without any expense, are easy and innumerable," the best punishments involving "the imposing some coercion which shall produce profit, or the subtracting some enjoyment which would require expense."[38]

If the rule of economy was paramount in matters of punishment and management, it was more obviously so in matters of work. On this subject, the "historical and progressive point of view" that Bentham recommended may be particularly instructive, especially if the history of his opinions is traced back to the Hard-Labour Bill. In its first draft, the bill had provided for specified forms of servile labor (such as wheel-treading and hemp-beating), a six-day workweek, and a working day equivalent to the hours of daylight. Bentham had then approved of the principle of servile labor and of the specified occupations, adding only

35. *Ibid.*
37. *Ibid.*, p. 125.
36. *Ibid.*, p. 123.
38. *Ibid.*

that on the Sabbath the men ought to be allowed, if they wished, to work in their customary trades.[39] He did, however, object that the criterion of daylight would make for too long a working day in the summer and too short a one in the winter. The Penitentiary Act as finally passed fixed the hours of work at eight, nine, or ten, depending upon the season, but rejected Sabbath work of any nature.

In his first plan of the Panopticon, Bentham departed radically from both his pamphlet and the Penitentiary Act by opposing not only the specified occupations but the idea of any specification of occupation. As the contractor was to run his establishment with a view to profit, he had to be free to choose whatever occupations were most profitable, and as it happened, the servile forms of labor were the least suited to the Panopticon system. The authors of the act, he protested, had thought too much of punishment and too little of economy. He himself did not see "why labour should be the less reforming for being profitable."[40] The question of the hours of work he passed over in silence, unless it be assumed that he intended this matter, like the choice of trades, to be left entirely to the discretion of the contractor.

The revised plan of the Panopticon went much further in this direction. Bentham now explicitly repudiated the idea expressed in the name, "House of Hard Labour." The idea of hard labor, he now said, gave "a bad name to industry, the parent of wealth and population." "Industry is a blessing; why paint it as a curse?"[41] So much of a blessing, indeed, that there could hardly be enough of it. Neither the criterion of daylight of the original bill nor the eight to ten hours of the revised act now seemed adequate. Instead, he proposed that the working hours be "as many of the four and twenty as the demand for meals and sleep leave unengaged."[42] His program for the six working days specified one-and-a-half hours for meals, seven-and-a-half for sleep, one hour for exercise, and fourteen for work. "Are fourteen hours

39. In the *Panopticon* he wrote: "In my *View of the Hard-Labour Bill*, I ventured to throw out a hint upon the subject of putting the good hands to their own trades" (*ibid.*, p. 50)—the implication being that he had then spoken up against the idea of servile labor. But this suggestion had been made only in connection with voluntary work on the Sabbath and had not at all been intended to apply to the ordinary workweek.

40. *Ibid.*, p. 50.   41. *Ibid.*, p. 144.

42. *Ibid.*, p. 142.

out of twenty-four too many for even a sedentary trade? Not more than what I have seen gone through in health and cheerfulness in a workhouse by honest poor." Indeed the number could as well be fifteen "without the smallest hardship," for "let it not be forgotten, meal times are times of rest: feeding is recreation." And the only habit worse than over-sleep was lying in bed awake, which was a "waste of health and time, one may almost say of good morals." It was not often that Bentham was provoked to speak of "good morals" in this fashion; he did so now because he was outraged by the thought of "five, six, seven, precious hours, out of fifteen, thrown away as offal." "As soon would I turn Macbeth and murder sleep, as thus murder health by smothering it under a pillow."[43]

In the new and improved Panopticon, health, morals and industry all conspired to the same end—that of economy. Air and exercise, for example, were provided for in a minimum amount of space and in maximum seclusion by the device of having the prisoners "walk in a wheel," the speed and number of turns being determined in advance so that "a lazy prisoner cannot cheat you." This salubrious activity had the additional advantage of generating power "cheaper than you can employ even the powers of nature."[44] (Wheel-treading, rejected as a servile occupation, was thus reinstated as a mode of exercise.) Similarly the diet of the prisoners was such that both lenity and severity conduced to economy: lenity in allowing an unlimited quantity of food, thus satisfying the needs of the laborer; severity in making it of the cheapest, least palatable, and least varied type. (Bentham derided those reformers, like "the good Howard," who tried to control the quality of food and prescribed "butcher's meat for the lowest vulgar.")[45] And in the matter of beds and bedding, where he had earlier criticized the Hard-Labour Bill for neglecting to provide sheets and iron bedsteads, he now reverted to wooden bedsteads (in spite of the admitted likelihood of their becoming infested with bugs), or better yet hammocks which were cheaper still, and to sacks in place of sheets. It would be amusing as well as instructive to go into these and other details of his revised plan. But this

43. *Ibid.*, p. 163.   44. *Ibid.*, p. 159.
45. *Ibid.*, p. 154.

would mean transcribing a good part of the book, which would detract considerably from the amusement, if not from the instruction.

A point that deserves more than passing mention is the payment of the prisoner-worker. Bentham had earlier criticized the Hard-Labour Bill for not giving the prisoners any compensation for their labor, and he had worked out an elaborate formula for dividing one-sixth of the gross profit among them. His first plan of the Panopticon, however, spoke not of a distribution of profits but rather of piece-work wages set at a considerably lower level than that prevailing in industry generally: "The confinement, which is his [the prisoner's] punishment, preventing his carrying the work to another market, subjects him to a monopoly; which the contractor, his master, like any other monopolist, makes, of course, as much of as he can."[46] The revised plan, although more detailed in all other respects, was silent on the matter of wages, except for an oblique reference to "earnings" out of which the prisoner would supplement his diet; a footnote explained why this was desirable: "Reward must assume the shape of a present gratification, and that too of the sensual class, or, in the eyes of perhaps the major part of such a company, it can scarcely be expected to have any value; and if it take a sensual shape, it cannot take a more unexceptionable one."[47]

This deprecation of saving, combined with the exhortation to sensual gratification (even if only the gratification of the palate), comes oddly from one of Bentham's puritanical bent. It becomes intelligible, however, in the light of one of the most important innovations of his new plan: the provision for released prisoners. He had earlier praised the Hard-Labour Bill for its "foresight and humanity"[48] in allowing each prisoner a small sum of money upon his discharge, in addition to a certificate of good behavior if his prison record merited it. The first plan of the Panopticon made no mention of the certificate but strongly advised against the discharge allowance: "It might help to fit them out for trades; it might serve them to get drunk with; it might serve them to buy any house-breaking implements which they could not so well

46. *Ibid.*, p. 54.   47. *Ibid.*, p. 153.
48. *Ibid.*, p. 21.

come at to steal." The interests of the prisoners as well as of the contractor, Bentham vaguely suggested, would better be promoted by "continuing their manufacturing connection."[49]

In the revised plan of the Panopticon, the provisions for discharge were spelled out in great detail. Instead of the authorities granting the prisoner an allowance and a testimonial of good behavior, it was the prisoner who now had to provide the authorities with proof of his future financial security and future good behavior. According to this plan, the prisoner would be discharged only upon satisfying one of three conditions: enlistment in the army, enlistment in the navy, or the posting by a responsible householder of a £50 bond as a guarantee of good conduct. In the latter case, the bond was to be renewed annually, the failure of renewal to mean the return of the prisoner to the penitentiary —"though it should be for life." To induce a householder to post such a bond, the prisoner would have to contract his labor for a specified term (but as soon as the term was up, the householder would obviously refuse to renew the bond unless the contract was also renewed), with the understanding that the householder would have the same power as that "of a father over his child, or of a master over his apprentice."[50]

If the prisoner would not or could not meet these conditions, there remained only one recourse for him short of returning to prison. This was elaborated upon in a long footnote, as if in afterthought. "I take for granted," Bentham wrote, that "an establishment of some sort or other" would have to be set up to receive such prisoners. This "subsidiary establishment," he also took for granted, would be set up on the Panopticon principles. And obviously no one would be better fitted to run it than the contractor of the prison who would have "every facility for getting the most work done, and making the most of that work." Such an arrangement would be worth the contractor's while "because the convicts, having by the supposition no other course of life to betake themselves to, or none they liked so well, would serve on so much the cheaper terms." It would also be to the prisoner's advantage since the contractor is "a tried man in every respect, as well as a responsible one." Indeed, Bentham was so impressed

49. *Ibid.*, p. 55.   50. *Ibid.*, pp. 166-167.

by these mutual advantages that he thought the prisoner well advised to make an agreement with the contractor even before the expiration of his sentence: "I had rather the penitentiary governor should get the emancipated prisoners in this way, than any other undertaker, whom the view of profit, and not any particular connexion with, or friendship for the prisoner, might induce to bid for him." It was because he was partial to the contractor, he confessed, that he "viewed with satisfaction, rather than regret" the advantage enjoyed by the contractor in negotiations with the prisoner—although, he added, he would not entirely exclude other bidders since "such a monopoly would be a hardship on the prisoners, and that a needless one."[51]

"Needless" indeed. The contractor hardly had need of a formal monopoly in negotiating with a prisoner who was completely and exclusively under his control, not only for the duration of his sentence but potentially, as it now appeared, for the whole of his natural (or unnatural) life. It would almost seem that the whole matter of the text was really a pretext for the footnote, and that all the provisions for the "liberated prisoners,"[52] as Bentham euphemistically described them, were designed to benefit the contractor and promote his subsidiary establishment. It is hard otherwise to account for the many difficulties placed in the way of their release: setting the bond, for example, at so high a figure (£50 was a considerable sum at a time when the ordinary laborer received about ten shillings a week; for this sum the bondsman could engage a worker for two years without the expense of his upkeep); or making the contractor the judge of the bondsman's "responsibility";[53] or providing that those prisoners who chose the option of joining the army or navy be "stigmatized" and separated from other recruits for an unspecified probationary period until a ceremony reinstated them "in solemn form in the possession of lost character."[54] And not only the conditions of discharge but even the conditions of imprisonment seem to have been contrived for the same purpose. One can now understand Bentham's otherwise inexplicable encouragement of prisoners to spend their earnings on "present gratification."[55]

51. *Ibid.*, p. 166.
52. *Ibid.*, p. 165.
53. *Ibid.*, p. 167.
54. *Ibid.*, p. 166.
55. *Ibid.*, p. 153.   (See above, p. 216.)

One might even suspect that it was more than the rules of economy and severity that dictated the poor and unvaried diet prescribed by him, and that the "liberty" to purchase a "more palatable diet out of his share of earnings"[56] was intended to deplete the prisoner's savings and thus make him a more likely candidate for the subsidiary establishment.

Even in sheer size the subsidiary establishment looms large over the prison itself. There is no figure given in the book for the population of the prison at any one time, but elsewhere Bentham alternated between the figures of one and two thousand. These prisoners were serving sentences of varying length. (The Panopticon was not intended, as one might think, for long-term prisoners alone; on the contrary, its advantage, as Bentham saw it, was that it could accommodate all degrees of criminals without contamination.) Yet the conditions of discharge were the same for all prisoners, so that a man serving even a brief sentence was, literally, in bondage for life—hence a potential life-long inhabitant of the subsidiary establishment. How large, then, would this subsidiary establishment have to be to accommodate this turnover of "liberated" prisoners? Bentham did not say, and the mind quails at the thought.

"*Set a beggar a-horseback,* and the proverb tells you where he will *ride.* . . . The Penitentiary Act sets a whole regiment of such beggars on horseback, and it gives them no master to hold the reins." The question, Bentham concluded, was whether beggar or master was better qualified to hold the reins:

In the convict, you see a man in whose breast the passion of the day is accustomed to outweigh the interest of the morrow: in the contracting governor, you have a man who knows what his lasting interest is, and is in the habit of pursuing it. . . . This man, whom you know, is the man to deal with, and not the convict, of whom you know nothing but what is to his disadvantage.[57]

Bentham distrusted the "beggar on horseback." But he had complete faith in the contractor who would command not a regiment but an army of beggars.

The contractor was the key to Bentham's scheme, and in more than the sense that is by now all too obvious. As one proceeds in

56. *Ibid.*   57. *Ibid.,* p. 171.

this study of the Panopticon, what emerges is more and more a travesty of the model prison and the model reformer. But the travesty is not yet complete. The final turn of the screw, the final pitch of perfection, is the discovery that Bentham himself actually intended to be the contractor and the governor of the prison.

There is a poetic rightness about this identification of Bentham with the contractor, so that even if it were not the literal fact, one would have to assume it as a psychological fact. How else can one account for the extraordinary powers vested in one man, for the absolute confidence in his integrity, for the shaping of the whole scheme around him? Without some such conscious or unconscious identification, the Panopticon makes little sense.

In fact, the identification was not only conscious; it was also explicit and public. This introduces a subject that is as curious as the Panopticon itself: the strange, almost wilful inattentiveness of biographers and historians to the most striking feature of the plan and the decisive cause of its rejection. To them Bentham was a philanthropist who sacrificed years of his life and most of his fortune to the exemplary cause of penal reform and who was inexplicably, as one biographer put it, "not to be allowed to benefit his country."[58] Most books on Bentham and even some of the most respectable histories of penal reform do not so much as mention the contract system in connection with the Panopticon, let alone identify Bentham as the proposed contractor. Yet it was the contract system that distinguished the Panopticon from other plans for penal reform, and it was his personal stake in it that distinguished this scheme from most of his other projects of reform. His Chrestomathia (a model school) was quickly conceived and as quickly abandoned, while the Panopticon involved him personally and passionately for the better part of his life. And unlike the constitutions, codes, and legal reforms which he released to the world and which became, so to speak, part of the public domain, the Panopticon was reserved for his private use.

58. Charles Warren Everett, *The Education of Jeremy Bentham* (New York, 1931), p. 179. It is, perhaps, unfair to single out Mr. Everett's book for citation. The point could equally well have been made by quoting almost any biography of Bentham or history of Philosophical Radicalism. The subject of the gullibility and culpability of these biographers and historians is too vast to be documented here, but I shall deal with it at some length in my forthcoming book on Bentham.

THE HAUNTED HOUSE OF JEREMY BENTHAM 221

Bentham did not try to conceal his intentions. He could hardly do so while soliciting a contract that would commission him to build, manage, superintend, and virtually own the Panopticon. His official proposal to this effect was submitted to William Pitt in 1791. He there undertook to feed, clothe, lodge, employ, and otherwise minister to the physical and spiritual needs of the prisoners, "constantly living in the midst of them and incessantly keeping them in view." In return he was to receive "the produce of their labour" (minus an unspecified "share in the produce" to give them "an interest in their work"), in addition to a subsistence allowance from the government for each prisoner.[59]

When Burke was shown the plan of the Panopticon, he remarked: "There's the keeper, the spider in the web!" Recalling this years later, Bentham could only manage the feeble retort: "Always imagery."[60] But the image rankled because it expressed his own suspicion that there was something ignominious in the job. He tried to allay this suspicion by insisting, for example, that the inspector's lodge befit a "style of living, equal or approaching to that of a gentleman," since one of that status, "or not much below it," would be occupying it.[61] And in an earlier draft of his proposal to Pitt, he stipulated that the "station of gaoler" be elevated by "a mark of distinction, not pecuniary, such as may testify that I have incurred no ultimate loss of honour by the service, and afford me some compensation for the intervening risk"[62]—presumably a bid for a knighthood or peerage.

It was not only the position of jailer, the "spider in the web," that was felt to be ignominious, but also that of contractor. Thus, in his proposal to Pitt he slurred over the question of profit, alluding to it only in subordinate clauses, while carefully enumerating the obligations he was undertaking and the services he promised

59. Report of Parliamentary Committee of 1811, *Parliamentary Debates*, ed. Hansard, XX (1811), cxix-cxxi.
60. Bentham, *Works*, X, 564. According to a recent biographer, Burke made this remark in Bentham's presence at Bentham's own house (Mary Mack, *Jeremy Bentham* [New York, 1963], p. 204). But Bentham himself stated that he had met Burke only once, at Philip Metcalf's house (*Works*, X, 564).
61. *Ibid.*, IV, 76.
62. *Ibid.*, XI, 100. I have assumed that the proposal cited in Vol. XI of Bentham's *Works* was an early draft, in spite of his assurance that this was the proposal "in the terms in which it was sent in" (*ibid.*, p. 99). It seems reasonable to suppose that the official proposal was that cited in the Parliamentary Committee Report.

to perform. In the final paragraph he adopted the voice of the third person and the posture of the altruist:

The station of gaoler is not in common account a very elevated one; the addition of contractor has not much tendency to raise it. He little dreamt, when he first launched into the subject, that he was to become a suitor, and perhaps in vain, for such an office. But inventions unpractised might be in want of the inventor: and a situation thus clipped of emoluments, while it was loaded with obligations, might be in want of candidates. Penetrated therefore with the importance of the end, he would not suffer himself to see anything unpleasant or discreditable in the means.[63]

A situation "clipped of emoluments" and "loaded with obligations"—one would hardly recognize the estimable contractor described in his book, who "knows what his lasting interest is, and is in the habit of pursuing it."[64]

Bentham's profession of disinterestedness was less than candid in other respects. While he may not have thought of himself as a "suitor" when he "first launched into the subject," there is no doubt that he not only thought but declared himself as such long before the postscript, at any rate, was completed. As early as January, 1791, he was thanking Wilson for "the access you have got for me to the Contracts."[65] And on April 1 he reported to his brother: "I gave in a proposal to our Potemkin [Pitt] two months ago; but the Potemkins never give answers."[66] The proposal, therefore, must have been submitted early in February,[67] at which time only the original letters had been printed. The postscript came from the press in two installments, in May and July,[68] a delay that can only be accounted for by Bentham's delay in completing it. Thus the final plan of the Panopticon must have been written in full consciousness of his personal stake in it.

Nor was there anything of the diffident suitor in his importuning of friends, officials, politicians, even the king himself. To his brother he wrote:

Cast about with Carew all sorts of measures that appear to hold out a chance of bringing Panopticon to bear here;—the bribery plans, for

63. Hansard, XX (1811), cxxii.
64. Bentham, *Works*, IV, 171. (See above, p. 219.)
65. *Ibid.*, X, 247.   66. *Ibid.*, p. 249.
67. Not, as he later claimed, in March, 1792 (*ibid.*, XI, 99).
68. *Ibid.*, X, 261-262.

example, in the event of its not getting a hearing otherwise. This as from yourself: anything of that sort will come better from an intriguing Russian like you, than from a reformer like your betters.[69]

There is no reason to suppose that he was being facetious: bribery was certainly familiar enough at all levels of public life—as he himself testified in his *Introduction to the Principles of Morals and Legislation* published two years earlier, where he analyzed the different modes of passive and active bribery.[70]

He was equally tireless and ruthless in casting about for measures to improve upon his plan. Some of these he confided to a Scottish friend whom he was trying to persuade to apply for a contract for a Panopticon to be built in Scotland. The Panopticon, he assured his friend, was an even more profitable enterprise than he had ventured to suggest publicly:

With regard to economy, I will unbosom myself to you without reserve. Part of my expedients you will find in print. I was afraid of giving the whole of them, or placing them in the clearest point of view of which they were susceptible, for fear of being beat down, or seeing others reap the fruit of my labours. A man who begins with saving 50 per cent to the nation, may be allowed to think a little for himself.

Among the "expedients" he had not thought to mention either in his book or in his proposal to Pitt were economies of clothing (the elimination of stockings, shirts, and hats); diet (potatoes could be grown very cheaply on prison land: "I have been afraid to show how immense the saving may be, by the exclusive adoption of this article"—this at a time when potatoes were regarded even by the poorest as animal fodder); bedding (hammocks, straw sacks, and "coat, waistcoat and breeches" used for blanketing); and working hours ("I get sixteen and a half profitable hours, very near twice as many as our Penitentiary systems allow"). In return for these confidences, Bentham exacted a pledge of collusion: "But having thus unbosomed myself to you, I rely on your honour not to make the offer till you have communicated it to me, and till you hear from me that the terms of it will not prejudice my negotiation."[71]

All these ingenuities and machinations seemed to be in vain.

69. July, 1791, *ibid.*, p. 263.   70. *Ibid.*, I, 113.
71. *Ibid.*, X, 256-257.

The government was too preoccupied with more urgent matters to consider Bentham's proposal. The country was no longer in the happy state described by his friend four years earlier, when ministers, having "little to do abroad,"[72] could indulge themselves in domestic reform. Now there was all too much to do abroad. While Bentham was impatiently awaiting a reply from Pitt, Pitt himself was pursuing a foreign policy that threatened to overthrow his government and to precipitate a war with Russia. The crisis came to a head on April 1, the very day Bentham wrote to his brother complaining that "the Potemkins never give answers."[73] That Bentham could have been so oblivious of this crisis is particularly ironic, since only two years earlier he had himself publicly protested against the foreign policy that was now proving so disastrous, and he was later to attribute the failure of the Panopticon to his part in this controversy. At this time, however, he was too absorbed in the Panopticon to attend to anything else, while Pitt was too absorbed in affairs of state to attend to the Panopticon.

Despairing for the moment of Pitt, Bentham decided to offer his plan, and his person, to France. France was in the market for new codes, constitutions, institutions; he himself had already favored her with a manual of parliamentary procedures. Why not a prison as well? The Panopticon, he wrote Brissot, was "a project of improvement for which there is but too much room in every country, and I am afraid, not least in France: it is a mill for grinding rogues honest, and idle men industrious."[74] About the same time he suggested to his brother that they invite a French architect "to join us in fighting up Panopticon—his profit being on the building, ours on the management."[75] Later that year he made another appeal to the chairman of the Committee of Legislation of the National Assembly:

Allow me to construct a prison on this model—I will be the gaoler. You will see by the memoir that the gaoler will have no salary—will cost nothing to the nation. The more I reflect, the more it appears to me that the execution of the project should be in the hands of the inventor.[76]

72. *Ibid.*, p. 172.   (See above, p. 206.)   73. *Ibid.*, p. 249.   (See above, p. 222.)
74. *Ibid.*, p. 226. Bentham's editor erroneously attributed this letter to 1790.
75. *Ibid.*, p. 264.   76. *Ibid.*, p. 269.

He neglected to explain that the jailer, although receiving no salary, would receive the profits of the enterprise. Perhaps this omission accounts for the effusive reply of the National Assembly, which commended his "ardent love of humanity" and thanked him for his offer to serve "gratuitously" as jailer.[77] While his offer was not as altruistic as was supposed, he did give the French government an option he never extended to the English—that of adopting his plan without contracting for his services.

Bentham was more lenient in his offer to France because he had less at stake there. The English Panopticon was important not only for its own sake but for the success of another enterprise in which he and his brother had invested a good deal of capital and hope. This was a planing machine that Samuel Bentham had invented in Russia and that was the main reason for his return to England. Patents were taken out for the machine, and a full-scale model was erected in an outhouse in Jeremy Bentham's garden at Queen Square Place. Originally Samuel had planned to work the machine with steam, but its construction proved difficult and costly enough without assuming the additional difficulties and cost of a steam engine. The Panopticon providently took the place of the engine. As Bentham later explained: "Human labour, to be extracted from a class of person, on whose part neither dexterity nor good will were to be reckoned upon, was now substituted to the steam-engine, and the system of contrivance underwent a correspondent change."[78] Only the Panopticon could have provided a sufficiently large, cheap, and steady supply of manpower. "Now," Bentham told a friend who inquired about the progress of the wood-works, "is the season for experiment; for till it can be done in Panopticon, it will be hardly worth while to open shop."[79]

There is no mistaking the intimate connection between the Panopticon and this enterprise. In May, 1793, Pitt and his Home Secretary, Henry Dundas (later Lord Melville), came personally to Queen Square Place to view what Bentham called his "raree show,"[80] of which the chief exhibit was not the small table-model of the Panopticon but the planing machine in operation. The

77. *Ibid.*, p. 270.
79. *Ibid.*, X, 296.
78. *Ibid.*, XI, 167.
80. *Ibid.*, p. 291.

following year Dundas, recommending Bentham's proposal to the House of Commons, explained that he had been converted from the principle of transporting convicts to that of employing them by the spectacle of "a machine that gave the power of sight without eyes, and touching without hands."[81]

Bentham had assumed that the Panopticon would come under the Penitentiary Act of 1779, and that it would be necessary only to negotiate a contract with the Exchequer. After the visit of Pitt and Dundas, a contract was drawn up. It was not, however, signed, the government having decided that a new act of Parliament was required to authorize the plan. In October, 1793, Bentham reported that he was busy drafting a bill, "at the recommendation of authority," to be introduced in the next session of Parliament.[82]   The bill was speedily approved by both houses, in spite of the fact that it completely reversed the earlier act. Instead of the system of public management provided for in 1779, the Penitentiary Act of 1794 lodged entire responsibility for the "care, management, superintendence and control" of the prison in the hands of a single contractor-governor.[83] The act was tailor-made to Bentham's specifications—as it might well be, since it was he himself who tailored it.

The contract naming Bentham as the contractor-governor of the new prison was equally well disposed to him. Some of his more ingenious economies, to be sure, were abandoned. He promised to feed the prisoners "wholesome sustenance, composed of bread and meat, and other articles commonly used for human food" (this probably ruled out potatoes); to provide them with shirts as well as suits; to furnish sheets and blankets. In other respects, however, he was given far more latitude than might have been expected. Neither the wood-works nor the Panopticon itself was so much as mentioned. Thus, he was not bound even by his own plans and models. Instead the contract reserved to him the sole right to decide upon the structure of the building, the number of prisoners in each cell, the nature, hours, and conditions of labor, the mode of discipline, exercise, and all the other details of prison life. He was also given complete authority

81. *The Senator*, X (1794), 1162.   82. *Works*, X, 295.
83. Hansard, XX (1811), c.

over his staff as well as over the prisoners: "Every officer and
servant connected with the establishment is to be placed there
by his appointment and removable at his pleasure."[84]

Although his original proposal had stated that the government would not be asked to provide any capital, the contract
called for an advance of £19,000, which was Bentham's estimate
of the total cost of construction. In addition, the government
agreed to pay an anual per capita allowance of £12 for a guaranteed minimum of one thousand prisoners, even if the actual
number should fall below that. Three-quarters of the profits
were to be kept by Bentham, the remainder to be distributed
among the prisoners as earnings or annuities. The contract was
to be Bentham's for life, afterward passing to his brother, and
dissolved only after the death of both when their heirs would be
recompensed for the value of the buildings, stock, and other
assets, minus the funds initially advanced by the government for
construction. Provision was also made for the subsidiary establishment to house and employ not only released prisoners but also,
as one member of Parliament put it, "all those persons of blasted
character who, though acquitted for want of legal proof, were
thought to be guilty."[85]

The contract was to have been ratified upon the acquisition
of a suitable plot of land. Here Bentham encountered unexpected
difficulties. When he did finally get the necessary deeds, the
Treasury refused to ratify the original contract. For ten years
he tried first to have the decision reversed and then to be financially compensated.[86] Finally in 1811, a parliamentary committee
reviewed the plan and rejected it, at the same time conceding
Bentham's claim for compensation. For Bentham personally, "a

84. *Ibid.*, p. civ. These quotations are from the summary given in the report
of the Parliamentary Committee of 1811.
85. *Parliamentary Debates*, ed. Cobbett, XXX (1793), 959.
86. A curious episode occurred in 1798, when Bentham proposed that, as an
interim arrangement, he be assigned the contract for the Hulks—the moored
vessels that were being used as prisons and that were even more infamous than
the Bridewells of the time. Having been so long deprived of the "benefits" from
the new plan, he argued, why should he not at least reap the benefits from the
old? He granted that the Hulks were "too effectually vicious to admit of much
improvement"; yet he might be able to do something, and in any case he could
surely do no worse than the present incumbent (*Works*, XI, 117). This proposal
was not the impulse of the moment. Bentham submitted it to the Treasury twice
at an interval of several months, and it was twice if not actually rejected, at least
politely ignored.

gentleman of great respectability," the members of the committee professed the highest regard. This, indeed, they found to be the main flaw of his plan—that it depended rather upon the personal character of the contractor than upon principles of sound administration. They compared it unfavorably with earlier reform measures which prohibited the governor, for example, from profiting by the sale of articles in the prison, whereas Bentham's contract left it entirely up to him to sell what he chose (except for alcoholic drinks) at whatever price he pleased. They also compared it unfavorably with the penitentiaries recently established at Gloucester and Southwell, which were publicly managed and which provided for individual cells, moderate seclusion, and hard labor. The physical and moral welfare of the prisoners, they concluded, could be better secured by such a system of public management than by Bentham's, where there was no "channel of complaint" or "higher authorities to censure or control the keeper," and where every measure was "formed and directed by a person whose interest it must be that the prisoners committed to his charge should do as much work as they were competent to execute and that their labour should be exercised in the manner by which most profit would be produced."[87]

Bentham's testimony before the committee did nothing to allay these fears. He declined to be bound by anything but the literal sense of the contract. And since the contract gave him complete latitude to determine living and working conditions, he "reserved to himself all those advantages,"[88] including the right to assign the prisoners to night work if that proved economical, to lodge six or eight in one cell, and to use hammocks in place of beds. He refused to make provision, as the act of 1779 had done, for the commuting of sentences, and it was obvious that any such commutation would be a violation of contract since it would deprive him of the labor that was rightfully his. He also insisted upon the insurance scheme in place of the usual medical supervision, and upon the visitors' gallery in place of official inspectors. George Holford, the chairman of the committee and one of the great prison reformers of the century, was appalled

87. Hansard, XX (1811), ci-cviii.
88. George Holford, *An Account of the General Penitentiary at Millbank* (London, 1828), p. 14.

to hear Bentham speak of the "promiscuous assemblage of unknown and therefore unpaid, ungarbled and incorruptible inspectors," who would be attracted to the prison by such worthy motives as "curiosity and the love of amusement," and who would offer the best "security against abuse and imperfection in every shape." "For such inventions," Holford commented, "was it gravely proposed to us in the nineteenth century to abandon the ordinary principles of prison management."[89]

In a private letter to a member of the committee, Bentham denied the superiority of public management with its "channel of complaint" and appeal to "higher authorities." Everyone knew, he said, that in such cases real power always devolves upon some one individual, the only effect of an ostensible division of power being to divide responsibility, "and by dividing and dissipating the responsibility, to increase that power which in demonstration they are employed to reduce." The committee had made out the choice to lie between "a company of guardian angels" representing the public and "one tyrant devil" of a contractor. In fact, he protested, it was between officials appointed by the ministry and "rendering no account but to their assured protectors," and himself:

An unseated, unofficed, unconnected, insulated individual whose blameless life, known to have been for little less than half a century devoted to a course of unpaid, yet unremitted, howsoever fruitless, toil, in the service of mankind, has not been able to preserve his rights from being an object of neglect, and himself an object of silent oppression to every Administration for these last eighteen years.[90]

Thus, the image of the contractor in his book as a man consciously and entirely devoted to his own interest was replaced by the self-image of a dedicated, disinterested, persecuted toiler in the service of mankind. Disingenuously Bentham even proposed now to assume management of the prison "without a farthing's worth of pecuniary profit."[91] But coming at this late date, after the final rejection of his plan, and even then only in a private letter rather than in his official reply, the proposal was little more than an embellishment of his self-portrait.

89. *Ibid.*, pp. 14-16.   90. *Works*, XI, 160-161.
91. *Ibid.*, p. 160.

For twenty-five years Bentham fought for the Panopticon; for another twenty he grieved over its defeat. He never faltered in his devotion, at one point urging it upon the government of India (properly adapted for the segregation of castes and religions), at another composing edifying songs for the prisoners, and always fulminating against the "perfidy, waste, peculation and incapacity"[92] of his opponents. He had been thirty-eight at its conception; he was eighty-three when he memorialized it under the title, *History of the War between Jeremy Bentham and George the Third* (by "One of the Belligerents").[93] Brooding over the affair, he had come to see it as an elaborate plot by the king to exact vengeance for a letter written by Bentham as long ago as 1789, taking issue with the government's anti-Russian policy. (The letter had appeared in a daily newspaper under a pseudonym, but he was now convinced that George had penetrated his disguise.)[94] While he congratulated himself that his letter had been responsible for the government's abandoning of its warlike policy, he was also certain that it had brought down upon him the merciless wrath of the king:

> I paralysed his hand. I saved the two countries, perhaps others likewise, from this calamity [of war]. He vowed revenge; and to effect it he wounded me through the sides of this his country, not to speak of so many others.[95]
> Imagine how he hated me. Millions wasted were among the results of his vengeance. . . . After keeping me in hot water more years than the siege of Troy lasted, he broke the faith of Parliament to me. But for him all the paupers in the country, as well as all the prisoners in the country, would have been in my hands.[96]

It is tempting to dismiss this idea of a royal plot as paranoia aggravated by senility. Yet Bentham was so far from his dotage

92. Box CXX, *Catalogue of the Manuscripts of Jeremy Bentham in the Library of University College, London,* ed. A. Taylor Milne (London, 1937), p. 43.

93. Selections from this work have been published as part of the final volume of Bentham's *Works*.

94. Bentham's letter, signed "Anti-Machiavel," had been followed by a reply by "Partizan," whom Lord Lansdowne identified as the king. At the time and for many years (indeed as late as 1809), Bentham refused to credit this identification, supposing it to be another ruse on Lansdowne's part to provoke him to a more Whiggish and anti-royalist position. (See a note by Bentham quoted by Mack, p. 401.) It was not until 1821, when he first committed to writing the theory of the royal plot, that he assumed as a matter of course that Lansdowne had been telling the truth (*Works*, IV, 171-172).

95. *Works*, XI, 97.   96. *Ibid.,* X, 212.

that these last decades of his life were among his most productive periods. It was then that he developed the doctrine that is his unique contribution to philosophy and politics. The most comprehensive statement of Philosophical Radicalism is his *Constitutional Code*, written at this time and completed in the very years that he was working on his *History of the War between Jeremy Bentham and George the Third*. Whatever infirmities may be found in the *Code*, they are not those of mental incapacity.

The conjunction of the *History* and the *Code* dispels not only the suspicion of senility but also the notion that the Panopticon was a quirk of mind, a passing eccentricity having no bearing upon the rest of Bentham's life and thought. It is true that the Panopticon was first conceived at a time when he was pluming himself on his good fortune in living "in the age of Catharine, of Joseph, of Frederick, of Gustavus, and of Leopold";[97] when he was confident that in Russia "I could bring more of my ideas to bear . . . in a month than here [in England] in my whole life";[98] and when even his personal experience of the fiasco of Potemkin's model village did not diminish his enthusiasm for Russia: "I have learnt what the human powers are capable of, when unfettered by the arbitrary regulations of an unenlightened age."[99] This was the time, too, when he was most contemptuous of English liberalism, opposing every effort of Fox and of his own patron, Lord Lansdowne, to broaden the suffrage, abolish rotten boroughs, and otherwise "subjugate the well informed to the ill informed classes of mankind."[100] It is of no little significance that the Panopticon was born out of this amalgam of Toryism and enlightened despotism. But it is equally significant that Bentham did not abandon the Panopticon when he abandoned this ideology, that it survived intact his conversion to radicalism and democracy, and that he could write his *History* and his *Code* simultaneously, without any sense of incongruity.

Indeed, the Panopticon was more than a passive survivor of his conversion to Philosophical Radicalism. It played an active, perhaps a decisive, part in his conversion. William Wilberforce,

97. Élie Halévy, *La Formation du Radicalisme Philosophique* (3 vols.; Paris, 1901-1904), I, 367.
98. Mack, p. 64.   99. *Works*, IV, 52.
100. Halévy, II, 316. Mack's claim that Bentham was a "full-fledged radical democrat" by 1790 (*Jeremy Bentham*, p. 17) is refuted by this and similar evidence.

who witnessed Bentham's travails throughout the affair, was
certain that he turned to radicalism out of vexation and resent-
ment over the failure of the Panopticon: "He was quite soured
by it; and I have no doubt that many of his harsh opinions afterwards were the fruit of this ill-treatment."[101]   The chronology of
his conversion would seem to confirm this.   In 1808, with the
Panopticon obviously a lost cause and feeling thoroughly unap-
preciated in England, he tried to emigrate to South America; and
when this emigration scheme failed, he made his first overtures to
the radicals.   What is striking about this transitional period
(which coincided with the final death throes of the Panopticon)
was Bentham's disdain for most of the radicals with whom he
associated and his personal commitment to radicalism long before
he had worked out an appropriate ideology for it.   He evidently
sought refuge in radicalism as he had sought it in South America.
Later, explaining his early Toryism and belated radicalism, he
said: "I was . . . a great reformist; but never suspected that the
people in power were against reform.   I supposed they only
wanted to know what was good in order to embrace it."[102]   Disaffected with the "people in power" as a result of the Panopticon
affair, he turned to the radicals whom he had so recently and
heartily despised.

The Panopticon is interesting not only as it helps explain
Bentham's political and philosophical development, but also as
it helps elucidate his political and philosophical doctrine.   For
it was more than a catalytic agent, more than the innocent cause
and archaic survivor of his conversion.   It endured as much out
of conviction and principle as out of nostalgia, loyalty, self-interest, self-vindication, obsession, or any other personal and path-
ological motives that undoubtedly entered into it.   However
disenchanted Bentham became with the old people in power,
he never became disenchanted with the Panopticon in its various
manifestations, the most interesting of which was his Panopticon-
poorhouse. *Pauper Management Improved*, originally written in
1797 and reissued in 1812, applied the Panopticon principle to
the problem of the poor.   A "joint-stock subscription company,"

101. R. I. and S. Wilberforce, *Life of William Wilberforce* (5 vols.; London,
1838), II, 172.
102. *Works*, X, 66.

on the model of the East India Company, was to serve as a kind of holding company for 250 "Industry Houses," each to accommodate two thousand paupers under the "absolute" authority of a contractor-governor and under a regimen of life and labor similar to that of the Panopticon-prison.[103]

The two Panopticons were closely linked in Bentham's mind, as is evident from his grievance against King George: "But for him all the paupers in the country, as well as all the prisoners in the country, would have been in my hands."[104]   Bentham saw nothing unseemly in this complaint, just as he saw no irony, on another occasion, in concluding his diatribe against George with the warning: "While nations consent to put into any hands an uncontrollable power of mischief, they may expect to be thus served."[105]   Neither the self-righteousness nor the apparent incongruity of these remarks should be permitted to obscure their real import.   For their juxtaposition, like that of the *History* and the *Constitutional Code*, suggests that the Panopticon was nothing less than the existential realization of Philosophical Radicalism.

There was no real contradiction between Bentham's objection to the uncontrollable power of the king and his objection to being himself deprived of power over all the paupers and prisoners of the country.   For in neither case was he objecting to power, even absolute power, as such.   He never deviated from the position he had taken in his youthful polemic against Blackstone: that there could be no such thing as a "mixed" constitution or a "balance" of powers because power itself was illimitable.   His

103. *Ibid.*, VIII, 369-439.   This plan is perhaps even more unsettling to the conventional view of Bentham than the Panopticon-prison. The effect would have been to reduce the poor almost to the status of criminals. Not only was the company, for example, to have "coercive powers" to apprehend anyone "having neither visible livelihood or assignable property, nor honest and sufficient means of livelihood" (p. 370), but even the ordinary citizen would be allowed—indeed encouraged—to apprehend and convey any beggar to the nearest Industry-House. And the scale of operations was vast even by the standards of our time, let alone of that time. The Industry-Houses were to take care not only of the 500,000 poor but also of their children, who, after the discharge of their parents, were "to continue bound to the company in quality of apprentices," boys to the age of twenty-one or twenty-three, girls to twenty-one or nineteen, both regardless of marriage (p. 369). These apprentices would require an additional 250 houses, bringing the total population of the Industry-Houses to one million. (The entire population of England at the time was about nine million.)
104. *Ibid.*, X, 212. See also X, 591; XI, 96-97.
105. *Ibid.*, IV, 172.

conversion to radicalism required only a relocation of power. The old "people in power" were to be replaced by the populace empowered—the "democratic ascendancy"[106] represented by an "omnicompetent legislature."[107]   The object, he now insisted, was not to limit power but rather to reduce confidence in the trustees of power so as to increase the power of the people: "While confidence is minimized, let not power be withheld."[108]

The Tory Bentham and the Radical Bentham agreed upon the principle of the greatest happiness of the greatest number. The innovation of the Radical was to make the greatest happiness of the greatest number dependent upon the greatest power of the greatest number.   In his *Constitutional Code*, Bentham explained that the legislature had to be omnicompetent because "any limitation is in contradiction to the greatest happiness principle."[109] But as the greatest happiness of the greatest number meant nothing more than the greater happiness of the greater number, so the omnicompetence of the legislature meant in effect the omnicompetence of the majority.   One of Bentham's disciples was asked whether the greatest number always had the right to indulge its greatest happiness, whether the twenty-nine out of thirty people who decided to feast upon the thirtieth had the right and the power to do so—to which the disciple, with the impeccable logic of his master, coolly replied, "Yes."[110]

To Bentham, prisoners and paupers were in the unhappy position of this thirtieth citizen. If it was in the interest of society to confine them in Panopticons, to subject them to an absolute master, to exploit their labor, to attach conditions to their discharge, it was necessary and proper that all this be done. The traditional motive of reformers had been, as it still is, the relief of the unfortunate, those suffering special disabilities or deprivations, the afflicted minorities: Howard wanted to improve the conditions of prisoners, Wilberforce to prevent the enslavement of Negroes, Whitbread to give sustenance to the needy, Bell and Lancaster to educate the children of the poor.   If Bentham concerned himself with the same problems and even,

---

106. Bentham, *Plan of Parliamentary Reform* (London, 1817), p. xxxvi.
107. *Works*, IX (*Constitutional Code*), 119.
108. *Ibid.*, p. 62.   109. *Ibid.*, p. 119.
110. *Halévy*, III, 436.

in some cases, advocated similar solutions, it was not out of compassion for these minorities, but rather in the interests of society at large. There was no question of the "rights" of prisoners and paupers, for there was no such thing as rights at all. There were only interests, and the interests of the majority had to prevail. The greatest happiness of the greatest number might thus require the greatest misery of the few.

The principle of the greatest happiness of the greatest number was as inimical to the idea of liberty as to the idea of rights. Just as Bentham attacked those parents whose scruples about liberty made them apprehensive of a Panopticon-school, so he attacked those who expressed the same scruples and apprehensions in matters of government. "Liberty," "liberal," and "liberalism," he wrote toward the end of his life, were among the "most mischievous" words in the language, because they obscured the real issues, which were happiness, security, and good government. The common notion of liberty as "the right to do anything that the laws do not forbid" was nonsense: "For if the laws are *bad*, what becomes of liberty? And if the laws are good, where is its value?"[111]

There is obviously no room here for an adequate discussion of Philosophical Radicalism. These few reflections are introduced only to suggest that the Panopticon was not the anomaly it may first seem, and that for the later Bentham as for the earlier it was neither an aberration of thought nor a weakness of character. It survived his conversion to radicalism as so much else of his philosophy and program survived. Indeed there was little that did not survive, except his faith in enlightened rulers. His conception of law as positive and statutory continued to imply, as it always had, a rejection of common law, of judge-made law, and of a fundamental constitutional law to which all other laws had to yield. His conception of sovereignty as total and illimitable prohibited checks and balances in the democratic state as it prohibited channels of complaint or higher authorities in the Panopticon. His conception of self-interest became, if anything, more rigorous; where once he had thought it possible for a ruler to find his satisfaction and therefore his interest in promoting

111. *Ibid.*, p. 435.

the interests of his subjects, he now denied that there had ever existed or could ever exist "a human being in whose instance any public interest he can have had, will not, insofar as it depends upon himself, have been sacrificed to his own personal interest."[112]   (The very idea of disinterestedness appeared to him "as absurd in supposition as it would be disastrous in reality," for it belied the calculations of rewards and punishments upon which all rational behavior and thus all legislation were based.)[113]   His economic doctrines remained what they had always been—a peculiar combination of laissez-faireism that sometimes carried him beyond Adam Smith (as in his *Defence of Usury*), and an older variety of private, monopolistic enterprise (as in the Panopticon prison and poorhouses).   And finally, his philosophical method was unchanged: the rationality, universality, simplicity, and consistency that he prided himself on in the Panopticon continued to be the virtues he esteemed most highly—and not only as qualities of mind but as the criteria of valid reforms and of a valid political order.

The affinity between the Panopticon and the mode of thought represented by Philosophical Radicalism is further suggested by the attitude of the Radicals themselves.   His admirers today, one might say, are acquiescent out of ignorance, having not read the details of the plan or appreciated what they have read.   His associates, however, could not plead ignorance.   Yet not one of them criticized it or belittled it as a private, let alone disreputable, idiosyncrasy.   The only one to express any hint of misgivings was Samuel Romilly, who had the unenviable task of defending it in committee; but even he, while conceding the need for changes and personally absenting himself from most of the committee meetings to avoid embarrassment, professed to approve and support it.   (His equivocations were not lost on Bentham; perhaps they were the first signs of a deviation that finally led Bentham to read him out of the party.)   The other Radicals felt no need for even this degree of equivocation.   John Stuart Mill did not criticize the Panopticon even when he was most critical of Bentham.   But above all it was James Mill who publicly endorsed it

112. Bentham, *The Handbook of Political Fallacies,* ed. Harold A. Larrabee (New York, 1962), p. 230.
    113. Halévy, III, 472.

with the party stamp—and this long after its rejection by Parliament, when the Radicals, if they had been so minded, could have allowed it to lapse quietly into oblivion.

The occasion of its resurrection was an article on "Prisons and Prison Discipline," written by James Mill in 1822 or 1823 and published in the supplement to the *Encyclopaedia Britannica*. Bentham's plan, Mill wrote, was "so perfectly expounded and proved that they who proceed in this road, with the principle of utility before them, can do little else than travel in his steps."[114] And Mill did just this, reviewing and recommending every feature of the Panopticon: the architecture, the principles of inspection, labor, and economy, the contract system, the chapel and visitors' gallery, the insurance scheme, even the subsidiary establishment for released prisoners. Nor did he falter at the critical points: he was equally enthusiastic about the contractor's right to trade freely with the prisoners, to provide hammocks in place of beds, and to put two or four prisoners—"seldom more"—in one cell. (This was the figure in Bentham's book; later it had been increased to six or more.) And he concluded as he had started, abjuring any originality on his own part and praising the Panopticon for being superior to anything that "the imperfection of the human powers" generally allows.[115]

Mill's eulogy was so excessive as to be almost suspicious, particularly at this period of his life, when he was jealous of his reputation and wary of playing the part of the slavish disciple. One might be tempted to interpret his disclaimer of originality as a disclaimer of responsibility, a polite act of dissociation, were it not for a private letter by Mill to the editor of the *Encyclopaedia* explaining that he could do no more than recapitulate the details of the Panopticon "which appear to me to approach perfection."[116] Moreover, Mill was not alone in his enthusiasm. An article in the *Edinburgh Review* in 1813 had been similarly unstinting in praise. It is curious that this article should have been written by the then radical Henry Brougham; and that it was the no longer radical Brougham, many years later, who was one

114. *Encyclopaedia Britannica*, supplement 4th ed. (Edinburgh, 1824), VI, 385.
115. *Ibid.*, p. 395.
116. Alexander Bain, *James Mill* (London, 1882), p. 201.

of the few to expose the Panopticon as "a scheme absolutely and perfectly vicious in principle."[117]

If upon re-examination the Panopticon seems more worthy of the judgment of the later Brougham than of the earlier, it may be necessary to re-examine the conventional image of Bentham as the father of reform and of Philosophical Radicalism as the fount of reform. It may then emerge that the actual history of reform, and the particular reforms we value most highly, were brought about by other men under the impulse of other ideas— by Peel, for one, who was hardly a Benthamite. Similarly, the image of Bentham as the father of democracy and of Philosophical Radicalism as the genesis and prototype of our own democracy may also prove faulty. Benthamism may turn out to have as little in common with our democracy or democratic ideals as the Panopticon has with our actual, let alone model, prisons.

The devils that obsessed Bentham, it is now apparent, were all too real and far more mischievous than he suspected. The Panopticon was evidently not the only haunted chamber in his house. Those who have solemnly carried out his final instructions for the creation of an "auto-icon"—his skeleton attired in his own clothes, with a waxen likeness of his head and his favorite walk-ing-stick in his hand—might make it a mark of respect to a man so solicitous of his after-life and so credulous, as he admitted, of ghosts, to exorcise those devils. And for our sakes if not for his, to exorcise them not only from the Panopticon but from the entire edifice of his thought, which is our heritage.

117. Henry Brougham, *Historical and Political Dissertations* (London, 1957), p. 254.

ISABEL II AND THE CAUSE
OF CONSTITUTIONAL
MONARCHY

John Edwin Fagg

Spanish attachment to monarchy as an institution, which even now is strong, has survived frequent and profound shocks. Three unfortunate Hapsburg kings of the seventeenth century, the divided loyalties of the War of the Spanish Succession, the scandals and disasters of the time of Carlos IV (1788-1808), and the periods of revolution and reaction under Fernando VII (1808-1833) left respect for kingship untouched except among a few republican souls, who were rare indeed. The troubled reign of Fernando's daughter Isabel II (1833-1868) revealed what role the monarchical ideal could still play in the nineteenth century.

Isabel's difficulties stemmed in part from the events of the reign of her father. When Napoleon substituted Joseph Bonaparte for the Bourbons on the Spanish throne in 1808, he inadvertently raised Fernando VII to the status of a demigod. During the French occupation free Spaniards assembled in the unrepresentative Cortes of Cádiz and sought to prepare for the future when Spain would recover her independence and advance along a constitutional path. If their product, the Constitution of 1812, outlawed royal absolutism, it assumed that hereditary monarchy was essential for liberal institutions. When Fernando returned as king in 1814 he was rapturously welcomed, and his restoration of the absolutist system was overwhelmingly approved.

Fernando VII, however, did not long profit from the legitimist sentiment fostered by the effort to overthrow Joseph Bonaparte. Failing to deal with the problems created by the Napoleonic intrusion and the American rebellions, he was compelled by the

JOHN EDWIN FAGG *is professor of history and chairman, Department of History, Washington Square College, New York University.*

army in 1820 to proclaim the Constitution of 1812 and to sum-
mon the Cortes, many of whose members were in prison or exile.
During the next three years the constitutionalists floundered sadly
and aggravated tensions within the country. Fernando VII was
frequently insulted and threatened;[1] he had reason to fear that
his fate might be that of Louis XVI.[2] When he was carried off
to the south of Spain in 1823 as the French army invaded, this
time in the name of the Holy Alliance, crowds in Madrid clam-
ored for the death of the entire royal family.[3] The nation as a
whole, however, welcomed the French and the end of the constitutional experiment.

From Fernando's liberation in 1823 until his death in 1833,
excesses by the ultra-absolutists caused much dissatisfaction and
apprehension about the future. It seemed likely that the king,
who was in bad health, would soon be succeeded by his brother,
Don Carlos, a reactionary so rigid that he antagonized many ordinary conservatives. Carlos anticipated his own reign aggressively
enough to alienate Fernando VII, who was moved to marry for
the fourth time in the hope of producing a son and thus preventing his brother's accession. The bride was his young niece,
the Neapolitan María Cristina. In 1830, news of her pregnancy
cheered the opponents of Don Carlos, though it was realized that
a princess could not become sovereign because of the Salic law

1. Sir Henry Wellesley to Viscount Castlereagh, Dec. 28, 1820, F.O. 72/237, No.
250; Wellesley to Castlereagh, March 1, 1821, F.O. 72/244, No. 244; Lionel Hervey
to Castlereagh, April 23, 1821, F.O. 72/246, No. 4; Hervey to Lord Londonderry
(Castlereagh), Nov. 8, 1821, F.O. 72/248, No. 113; Hervey to Londonderry, July 5,
1822, F.O. 72/257, No. 82. These and subsequent references to British diplomatic
correspondence concern the files of the Foreign Office now in the Public Record
Office in London. In the course of his investigations, the author has examined
Cortes speeches on the monarchical question, Spanish newspapers and pamphlets,
and other conventional Spanish sources. While this account follows the interpretations of most Spanish primary and secondary works, a disproportionate number of references are to British and United States diplomatic papers. It is believed
that fresh material is thereby presented. British ministers in Madrid were much
better informed on high-level Spanish politics and court gossip than Spaniards
who have made their information available to historians. The strong interest
of the British in the success of constitutional monarchy in Spain caused their
diplomats, who were usually very able, to pay close attention to its fortunes. Both
British and American comments on popular reaction to events tend to be more
objective than the censored Spanish press of the time or the recollections of
most Spanish partisans.
2. John Forsyth to John Quincy Adams, Nov. 12, 1820, Department of State
despatches, Spain, Vol. XVIII, No. 23. This and later references to American
diplomatic correspondence are to the files of the Department of State now in the
National Archives in Washington.
3. Sir William A' Court to George Canning, Feb. 20, 1823, F.O. 72/270, No. 48.

introduced in 1713. It developed, however, that Fernando had discovered a pragmatic sanction approved by Carlos IV and the Cortes of Castile in 1789 which repealed the prohibition against female succession. For mysterious reasons this law had never been promulgated and had been kept secret. In March, 1830, the king proclaimed the pragmatic sanction suddenly and without consulting Don Carlos.[4] His motive was charitably attributed to a statesmanlike desire to save the country from the extreme absolutists if the expected child proved to be a girl. Yet Fernando was not a man to be moved by ideological considerations. Probably he merely wanted to spite his brother Carlos. And, of course, he was egged on by his young wife, who relished the prospect of being regent.

In October, 1830, the queen gave birth to a daughter, the future Isabel II, and a year later, to another, the Infanta Luisa. On what was almost, but not quite, his deathbed, Fernando VII withdrew the pragmatic sanction, but later he changed his mind again, thus weakening the legitimacy of any action he took with respect to the succession. In June, 1833, he summoned the prelates, grandees, and Cortes deputies to Madrid, where these dignitaries went individually before Isabel and stated: "I swear allegiance to the princess."[5] Don Carlos, now in exile, refused to take the oath and proclaimed that he was the lawful heir of Fernando VII. He pointed out that he was born before 1789 and was therefore not affected by the pragmatic sanction. The British minister to Spain, after careful study, concluded that Isabel's claim to the inheritance was "practically and morally imperfect."[6] Apparently many Spaniards thought it was too. The ceremonies of June, 1833, were marked by extreme coldness on the part of the participants and the population. Fernando was angered and blamed the whole situation on his ambitious wife, as did many others.[7]

María Cristina became regent when Fernando died in September, 1833. Within the next few months a fateful division of Spanish politics crystallized. Don Carlos, as "Carlos V," contested the succession and initiated the Carlist war, in which his claims

4. H. V. Addington to the Earl of Aberdeen, April 4, 1830, F.O. 72/368, No. 31.
5. Addington to Viscount Palmerston, June 20, 1830, F.O. 72/409, No. 94; Addington to Palmerston, June 29, 1830, *ibid.*, No. 99.
6. Addington to Palmerston, June 25, 1830, *ibid.*, No. 96.
7. *Ibid.*

were supported by the absolutists, Basque and other mountain people, and almost the totality of the influential clergy. It is altogether possible that a large majority of the people regarded his rights as legitimate and thus placed Isabel II in the position of a usurper at the outset of her reign. The cause of Isabel II and María Cristina was at the mercy of the army, where constitutionalist and even radical sentiments had been strong for many years, the Catalan industrialists, and such public opinion as was liberal, the latter being but a small sector, mainly from the educated classes. The dilemma was opened with which Isabel and her mother were never to deal successfully. If the queens were to rule at all, they had to cater to liberals whom they distrusted and who were a minority, and they needed the support of France and Britain, nations the Spanish disliked. María Cristina accommodated herself to the situation by opening Spain to liberalism, which came into the country as a flash flood in 1833, and accepting important, perhaps decisive, French and British military aid.

The *isabelino* forces filled the country with effusions about "our innocent little queen" and her beleaguered mother, identifying their cause with liberalism and constitutionalism. Behind the scenes important changes in the structure of society were being made. The Church was stripped of much of its property, and convents were burned, clergymen massacred, and Carlists despoiled. A considerable redistribution of wealth occurred, strengthening the queen's supporters and also whetting their hunger for political power. Many were also deeply convinced of the virtues of constitutional government when it had a hereditary monarch at the head. They had seen it function during their exiles in England and even in France.

María Cristina and her ministers were inept at waging the war, even though Don Carlos was still less skilful. By 1836 the country seemed to be disintegrating.[8] In August a group of sergeants forced their way into the queen-regent's summer palace, La Granja, and compelled her to proclaim that panacea of liberals, the Constitution of 1812. An outburst of rejoicing in Madrid and the queen's army indicated that higher-ranking men had inspired the sergeants and had devised thorough plans. A liberal Cortes

8. George Villiers to Palmerston, July 31, 1836, F.O. 72/460, No. 188.

was now installed, and two parties, the Moderates and the Progressives, took shape. The constitution of 1837, slightly less advanced than the one of 1812, was promulgated. María Cristina received a hearty vote of confidence from the Cortes. But this action, as the American minister reported, reflected no true expression of sentiment. Rather, he said, the revolutionaries had made such a mess that they could afford to do nothing else, though they would "gladly give her the gate in a minute if they dared."[9] For by this time María Cristina had proved not only weak and tricky as a ruler, but it was known that she had a lover, probably a morganatic husband, in Fernando Muñoz, and that she was treating the national treasury as her private purse. Hope now centered in the child queen. The legend of Isabel as a symbol of liberalism and constitutionalism (and anticlericalism) was implanted only too well.

At length the Carlists lost the war and agreed to an armistice in 1839 with General Baldomero Espartero, a Progressive who emerged as the hero of the constitutionalists. That many Carlists changed their views about Isabel's right to the throne is doubtful. Two decades later Carlism was sometimes judged as the most deeply rooted conviction of the country, particularly among the lower classes and the rural population in general.[10] For several years after the armistice of 1839 Carlists planned for Isabel II to marry one of Don Carlos' sons and thus set things aright. She became a focus of hope not only for the liberals, but also for the absolutists.

María Cristina had won the war and the throne for her daughter, but she had lost the good will of the constitutionalists. Once the war was over floods of handbills and articles in Progressive newspapers advertised her romance with Fernando Muñoz and her supposed pilfering of the treasury. Offensive as they were, these stories were essentially true. The young widow, who had been married briefly to a sick and aging king who was also her uncle, had not mourned long—only a few weeks. If she was married to Muñoz, she forfeited her lawful right to the regency;

9. C. P. Van Ness to John Forsyth, Sept. 20, 1836, Vol. XXXII, No. 124.
10. Lord Howden to the Earl of Clarendon, Sept. 13, 1854, F.O. 72/846, No. 211; Howden to Clarendon, Dec. 13, 1854, F.O. 72/848, No. 349, in which the American minister to Spain, Pierre Soulé, is quoted as agreeing with Howden about the great strength of Carlism in 1854.

if not, she almost deserved the jokes and tales that made her such a contemptible figure.   Her alleged thievery, which included charges that she stripped the palaces and sold necessaries of the daughters of Fernando VII,[11] was never proved, but her subsequent activities indicated that she was no slave to integrity.   She may have been simply "an amicable woman . . . who would gladly make the country happy if she knew how to do it,"[12] but no statesman and not even a good politician.

In 1840 the queen-regent maladroitly antagonized the British by being subservient to France, the Progressives by favoring the Moderates, and the liberal idol, General Espartero, by sponsoring a centralizing law that violated his armistice terms and outraged the Progressives.   During the furor she went with her Bourbon daughters to Barcelona and saw Espartero.   Scenes in that city, then becoming a hotbed of Catalan nationalism and radicalism, revealed how far the prestige of royalty had declined,[13] for it was Espartero and not the regent who drew the cheers.   In Madrid a usurping junta was impudence itself to María Cristina.   Confidence in her had sunk "to the point that she could not return to the capital with pleasure or even safety to herself."[14]   She went on to Valencia, and after a halfhearted resistance, decided to fight the politicians no more, whereupon she resigned the regency and seemed relieved after she did.[15]   With Muñoz and her children by him she went abroad, leaving Isabel II and the Infanta Luisa in Valencia.

The plight of the two royal orphans, seemingly abandoned by a worthless mother, stirred much sympathy.   Isabel, a homely ten-year-old with a severe skin trouble popularly ascribed to the sins of Fernando VII, and the beautiful Luisa caught the imagination of the public.   Yet the monarchical ideal must have dimmed during these postwar years.   María Cristina's personal and political behavior had tarnished the idea that royalty was superior to the rest of the human race.   Republicanism now claimed a few journalists and literary figures, together with assorted dreamers, adventurers, and proletarian reformers.   Yet the Moderates and

11. Aaron Vail to Forsyth, Nov. 13, 1840, Vol. XXXIII, No. 3.
12. Van Ness to Forsyth, Jan. 18, 1836, Vol. XXXII, No. 119.
13. Arthur Middleton to Forsyth, Nov. 2, 1840, *ibid.*, No. 4.
14. *Ibid.*
15. Newton Scott to Palmerston, Oct. 19, 1840, F.O. 72/555, No. 122.

the Progressives still hoped that Spain, after thirty years of depression and strife, could be pulled together under a constitutional system with Isabel II as its moderator and symbol. Much depended on how she would play her part, and she was given dedicated and able teachers to train her. The education failed lamentably to take. Isabel was not at all intellectual, and a surly nature suggested grave personality defects.

Espartero succeeded María Cristina in the regency. Like all Spanish rulers between Carlos IV and Francisco Franco, he was unable to wield authority long. Carlists and republicans agitated the right and the left. Moderates and Progressives competed viciously in the center, and among the Progressives factionalism was rampant. The country's economic life refused to flourish. If conditions had been helped by getting rid of "the army of monks," as the American minister, Washington Irving, put it, the soldiers were monopolizing political life and public revenues. Massive transfers of landed property had benefited "rich capitalists" but had not created a strong, free peasantry.[16] By 1843 Irving was writing about Espartero's decline in fortune and personal force.[17] Betrayed by his fellow Progressives, the regent soon resigned and withdrew from public life.

Since it was too difficult to agree on another regent, the Cortes decided to declare Isabel II of age, though she was only thirteen. A similar step in the case of the adolescent Pedro II of Brazil in 1840 had calmed that country and shown how useful the monarchical symbol might be. With much emotion, the Cortes acclaimed Isabel as reigning queen in October, 1843, and popular rejoicing was genuine. For days Madrid was absorbed, Irving wrote, in games, dances, parades, spectacles, and wine. Yet he observed in the midst of the festivities dark knots of politicians muffled in their cloaks holding mysterious conversations. "An occurrence that might shake the throne to its foundations," a fatal blow at the popularity of the queen and the safety of her crown, was known to the politicians and would soon be public information.[18] Isabel II had accused her first prime minister, Salustiano Olózaga, a Progressive, of using physical force to com-

16. Irving to Daniel Webster, Aug. 27, 1842, Vol. XXXIV, No. 3.
17. Irving to Webster, Aug. 3, 1843, *ibid.,* No. 27.
18. Irving to A. P. Upshur, Dec. 8, 1843, *ibid.,* No. 33.

pel her to sign a decree. Olózaga fled, tempers raged, and tongues wagged. Before long nearly everyone came to believe that the girl had lied, probably under prompting by Moderates in the palace clique. In her first days as constitutional queen Isabel had revealed a treacherous and mendacious nature worthy of a daughter of Fernando VII. Despite efforts to put her in a good light and to discredit Olózaga, the incident was too significant to be forgotten. Olózaga devoted much of the next quarter-century to undermining Isabel II, and the Progressives began a fateful series of conspiracies.

Disenchantment settled over the country as Isabel continued as nominal sovereign. Allying with the Moderates instead of remaining circumspectly above all parties, she invited her mother, a pro-Moderate, to return. María Cristina soon became ascendant in the palace. Carlists had always detested her, and so did Progressives after 1840. Now she was a general scapegoat for all that was wrong in Spain. She shared some unpopularity with another figure who became a stock character of Isabel's reign, the Moderate general, Ramón María Narváez. This passionate and overbearing despot was named prime minister in 1844 and dominated the scene until 1851. His policies, embodied in the neo-absolutist constitution of 1845, were to maintain rigid order while favoring the army and the beneficiaries of the property redistribution of the 1830's. Those who remembered the idealistic slogans of the Carlist war about liberty and constitutionalism had reason to wonder what the fighting had been about.

Narváez's dictatorship was blamed more on María Cristina than on Isabel. As the queen grew to womanhood she attracted some favor. Irving thought her dignity was "impressive in one so young,"[19] that she had a fine bearing and a winning, "confiding" manner.[20] She had a pleasing voice and brilliant, intimidating eyes. Her complexion improved, though it was always to be oily and rough; she was thought to be in very delicate health and was inclined to be fat; and she was far from beautiful or even handsome. Her deportment in public was then, and would continue to be, regal and yet friendly. Royal tours in the provinces, like

19. Irving to John C. Calhoun, July 3, 1844, *ibid.*, No. 47.
20. Irving to James Buchanan, Aug. 23, 1845, *ibid.*, No. 71.

the visit to the Carlist Basque area in 1845, elicited an outpouring of devotion that was awesome. No matter what the politicians and journalists would say in later years, or how rudely the *madrileños* behaved, almost to the end of her reign the provincials would respond to Isabel's presence with adoration.

Marriage proved a ruinous blow to the queen's opportunity for personal happiness and success as a sovereign. The notorious "Spanish marriages" of October, 1846, involved the double wedding of Isabel with her cousin, the Infante Francisco de Asís, and of her sister Luisa with the Duc de Montpensier, son of the French king, Louis Philippe. A royal union that might have proved popular and fortunate, such as Isabel's marriage with a son of Don Carlos, or—since a liberal branch of the Bourbon dynasty was selected—with Don Enrique, the manly brother of Francisco, was somehow blocked. As it happened, the sixteen-year-old queen was sacrificed to a man widely believed to be impotent, perhaps a deviate or an androgyne, while the Infanta Luisa was simultaneously married to a prince of the nation that Spaniards hated most. Was this not a plot to insure that Isabel would have no children and that a Frenchman's heirs would come to the throne? People were soon saying this. The Spanish marriages brought into public life as king-consort an unfortunate man who drew derision of the cruelest sort upon the royal family, turned Isabel into a defiant and wild woman, and created the Montpensier problem which plagued the monarchy for a generation. Don Enrique went bad and spent a futile, troublesome life that ended with Montpensier killing him in a duel in 1870. And the sons of Don Carlos, who were no more absolutist or fanatical than Francisco proved to be, remained wasted assets to the nation and a threat to the throne. Who was to blame for this multiple tragedy, some of whose consequences could have been foreseen? "Everyone" attributed it to María Cristina, who was thought capable of any folly or infamy.

The queen's honeymoon was disastrous, and all Madrid, an idle and gossiping capital, soon knew why. Isabel and Francisco separated. Perhaps she planned an annulment. Sympathy for her predicament, however, soon turned into prurient amusement as it was learned that she had thrown herself at the handsome General Francisco Serrano, an ambitious Moderate who was twenty years her senior. After the affair had gone on for some months, the American representative wrote:

It was said, (and too truly), that at La Granja, Her Majesty had thrown aside even the semblance of reserve, that no care was taken to conceal her relations with Serrano from ordinary observation—that, in short, her passion for him had destroyed all regard for her own reputation, the dignity of her station, and the welfare of her people; and could charitably be attributed only to mental madness or physical disease.[21]

That a teen-aged girl, cheated in an outrageous marriage, should have behaved in this fashion is not altogether incomprehensible. But Isabel II neither at this stage of her life nor afterward showed common sense, taste, or discretion in her amours. Serrano was followed by a veritable regiment of lovers. Rightly or not, people spoke of any soldier, official, actor, politician, or diplomat as the queen's lover if he went to the palace. No male seemed safe from the insatiable Isabel. People high in official life talked, the social set talked, the coffee-house idlers in Madrid talked, and soon foreign newspapers were spreading the royal scandal. And all this at a time when Isabel II, a supposedly constitutional queen, was being compared not to Catherine the Great but Queen Victoria! By mid-1848 the British minister, Sir Henry Bulwer, thought the Spanish royal family in such disrepute that he could bring about a change of dynasty or "get up" a republic.[22] His successor said that the Spanish scandal was worse than in the days of María Luisa and Godoy.[23] But only the upper classes, the educated, and the madrileños thought themselves so well informed about the queen's private life, and they despised her.[24] Most of the provincials did not know about it or did not believe what they heard until the concentrated anti-Bourbon campaign of the late 1860's.

About a year after their wedding, Isabel and Francisco were persuaded to reside together as the court migrated seasonally from

21. T. C. Reynolds to Buchanan, Aug. 19, 1847, Vol. XXXV, No. 24.
22. Queen Victoria to Palmerston, May 23, 1848, *The Letters of Queen Victoria* (3 vols.; London, 1907), I, 207-208.
23. Otway to Clarendon, July 16, 1854, F.O. 72/844, No. 48.
24. [Frances Erskine Calderón de la Barca], *The Attaché in Madrid* (New York, 1856), p. 95.

palace to palace—the Escorial, El Pardo, Aranjuez, La Granja, and the great 2,800-room affair in Madrid—and to be seen together on drives and at public functions. The king, a mournful and timid person, abandoned the liberalism of his family and associated with other misfits reputed to be superstitious and absolutist. Occasionally he intrigued in politics, but he was invariably defeated. Yet he had to be humored enough to insure his appearance at Isabel's confinements and to exhibit the infants as his own, a tragi-comedy he was required to enact on nine occasions. Apparently he and Isabel hated each other. People told lewd stories about him and referred to him as "Paquita," giving his nickname the feminine form.

The young queen's personal preoccupations practically kept her out of public affairs during these years. Narváez ruled so firmly that Spain was one of the few countries in Europe not to be involved in the revolutions of 1848. The Carlists and the republicans effected a curious axis and organized armed bands that tried to raise the Pyrenees area, but they failed miserably. Of more importance was the formal organization in April, 1849, of the Democratic party, which brought together an assortment of republicans and Progressives who favored a bolder course against Narváez and the Bourbons. As it turned out, no triumphant career awaited this party, but it gave direction to various anti-dynastic currents.[25]

In January, 1851, Narváez was dismissed, his harshness to the nation having pierced the court and offended the queen mother. A civilian Moderate minister came into power. Isabel deserved and received little gratitude for the change, for the civilian Moderates were almost as tyrannical as Narváez. Besides, the queen had scant conception of her duties as constitutional monarch, and it was her mother who, or so it was believed, wielded the royal power.[26] Whoever wielded it, the monarchical preroga-

25. C. A. M. Hennessey, *The Federal Republic in Spain* (Oxford, 1961) and the author's unpublished doctoral dissertation at the University of Chicago, "The Republican Movement in Spain" (1942) offer detailed accounts of the growth of the Democratic party and the activities of republicans in mid-nineteenth-century Spain.

26. Horatio J. Perry to General Franklin Pierce, President-elect, Jan 10, 1853, Vol. XXXVIII, private and confidential; Otway to Clarendon, July 16, 1854, F.O. 72/844, No. 48. Perry was secretary of the American legation in Madrid during most of Isabel's reign. Married to a minor poet, Carolina Coronado, who agitated

tive was doing little to bring about effective government, a matter all the more serious now that Spain at last was beginning to experience a spotty prosperity. Railways were being built (with María Cristina supposedly well rewarded for favoring certain contractors),[27] factories were going up, and Madrid was enjoying a construction boom. It was exasperating that the government was so corrupt and inefficient. Further, the idea of liberty still had great appeal, and all over Spain there were men who craved office and power. Constitutional monarchy was supposed to provide such opportunities, or so many had been taught. Since Isabel II seemed so unpromising as a sovereign, there was talk of replacing her with her sister Luisa, but as Montpensier's wife she would be unacceptable to Napoleon III. In 1853 a beguiling prospect opened when the king-consort of Portugal, Ferdinand of Coburg, became a widower, and the Progressives, Democrats, and many Moderates talked openly of bringing this respected royal figure to Madrid as king.[28] Not only would he provide the monarchical power they thought essential, but his heirs might unite Spain and Portugal, a notion long popular (in Spain). Indeed, there was so much criticism of Isabel II as a nonentity or a disgrace that it seemed she would soon be replaced, and several assassination attempts ended an ancient tradition that Spanish sovereigns were never endangered by physical violence. Yet, as noted, the agitation was mainly limited to Madrid, the upper classes, and the educated.

In January, 1854, the queen lost a child soon after it was born. The populace was as indifferent "as if a market woman had been delivered or a street foundling had died."[29] Isabel spoke with indignation of the coldness of her subjects and talked of abdicating.[30] Lord Howden, the British minister, thought there was little respect for the throne as an institution and a total want

for the freedom of the slaves in Cuba, he enjoyed unusual social and business connections in Madrid and was often extremely well informed. Yet he had many unedifying quarrels with successive American ministers and apparently was a busybody. It was typical of him to presume to write Pierce. Four years later, on January 7, 1857, he addressed a public letter on Spanish affairs to President-elect Buchanan and got himself suspended from his post.

27. *Ibid.* (both references).
28. Howden to Sir Richard Pakenham, Dec. 12, 1853, F.O. 72/842, cipher.
29. Pierre Soulé to W. L. Marcy, Jan. 20, 1854, XXXIX, No. 4.
30. Howden to Clarendon, Jan. 18, 1854, F.O. 72/842, No. 18.

of affection for Isabel.[31] In April, María Cristina told the American minister, the egregious Pierre Soulé, of her awareness of the dangers in the situation.[32] A few weeks later a military revolt occurred, led by a liberal Moderate general, Leopoldo O'Donnell, who probably planned to declare the throne vacant. In July the Progressives and Democrats produced revolutions in Madrid and other cities and most of the army went over to O'Donnell. The British representative asked for instructions in case the throne fell.[33] Soulé busied himself trying to promote a republic with funds and promises in the hope of purchasing Cuba for the United States.[34] But even if crowds set fire to María Cristina's palace and sought to lynch her and her recent ministers, the revolution showed that Isabel II was not as unpopular as she had seemed.[35] Comparatively safe in her palace, she protected her mother and urgently asked General Espartero to take over. After lecturing Isabel sharply on her waywardness as a woman and queen,[36] the aging hero agreed to become prime minister. The other military leaders, aware of the latent strength of Carlism, the explosiveness of the radicals in the cities, and the ominous interest of Napoleon III in Spain, accepted the continuation of Isabel as queen with Espartero as her prime minister, on the understanding that the question of the throne would be left open for a constituent cortes to settle.

Many incidents during the confusing weeks of the revolution of 1854 had shown how precarious was the crown of Isabel II. In the wave of good humor that swept over the country after Espartero's arrival—for now it seemed that Spain might redeem the liberal promises of the Carlist war—Isabel became mildly popular. A proletarian delegation invited her to visit their barricade. She comported herself with dignity and showed affection toward her subjects, and though there may have been fearful fights in the palace,[37] she was often seen with the king. To the

31. Howden to Clarendon, Feb. 9, 1854, *ibid.*, No. 51.
32. Soulé to Marcy, April 7, 1854, XXXIX, No. 7.
33. Otway to Clarendon, July 21, 1854, F.O. 72/845, No. 59.
34. Soulé to Marcy, July 15, 1854, Vol. XXXIX, No. 27; Otway to Clarendon, July 23, 1854, F.O. 72/845, No. 62.
35. *The Times* (London), July 27, 1854.
36. Otway to Clarendon, July 25, 1854, F.O. 72/845, No. 66; Howden to Clarendon, Oct. 25, 1854, F.O. 72/847, No. 273.
37. Howden to Clarendon, Aug. 2, 1854, F.O. 72/845, No. 149.

new set of leaders she was charming, or more. Discreet but powerful British pressures in her behalf were not without effect.[38]
Feeling against her subsided. To be sure, the plight of a queen
in danger, a woman beleaguered, was not without its appeal to
the chivalry of the military and the masses.[39]   Isabel was only
twenty-four and had never really tried to reign. With her mother
out of the picture she might yet be a worthy sovereign, and her
private life might improve. Whatever they had said a few months
before, the "in" group definitely decided by late 1854 to let her
continue as queen, and nearly every sampling of provincial opinion indicated that this decision had the country's approval.

A violent flurry took place after it was known that Espartero
(with the encouragement of Lord Howden)[40] had let María Cristina escape late in August. The radicals had eagerly been planning to bring her to trial for peculation to the extent of £700,000,
and they had Espartero's word that she would not be allowed to
leave. Since it had been decided not to remove the dynasty, the
prime minister did not care to subject the royal family to further
ignominy. And quite possibly the queen mother had been guilty
of nothing more than using state information for private speculation, just as reputable magistrates in recent democracies have
done. The charges against her were never proved; a Cortes commission which investigated the matter found nothing incrimina-
ting,[41] though perhaps it did not look hard. Her escape, however,
angered the Democrats and other radicals, who, said to be inspired
by Pierre Soulé,[42] tried to revolutionize Madrid. They failed,
but their effort probably caused Espartero and the other generals to support Isabel all the more firmly. As for María Cristina,
she went to live in Paris, though she often came to Spain on long
visits.

38. Howden to Clarendon, Nov. 18, 1854, Nov. 27, 1854, Nov. 28, 1854, F.O.
72/846, No. 303, 324, 325, respectively.
39. Andrés Borrego, *España y la revolución* (Madrid, 1856), p. 262.
40. Howden to Clarendon, Aug. 5, 1854, F.O. 72/845, No. 155.
41. Howden to Clarendon, June 25, 1856, F.O. 72/894, No. 213; Otway to
Clarendon, Nov. 9, 1857, F.O. 72/920, No. 921, enclosing a 155-page booklet by
three Spanish lawyers denying the charges.
42. Soulé to Marcy, Aug. 30, 1854, XXXIX, No. 34, contains the minister's
emphatic denial that he had participated. Soulé's enemy, Perry, likewise refuted
the accusations in a letter to Marcy of Sept. 6, 1854, in the same despatch. The
Madrid press published the interferences of Soulé as established facts.

When the constituent Cortes met in November, 1854, Isabel opened the session with an unusually gracious speech in which she admitted that everyone had made mistakes. The rousing reception she was given showed that the deputies were far more monarchical-minded than had been expected, and of course the leaders had already privately decided to allow her to remain sovereign. They fulfilled their promise to the nation to pass on the question of the throne, the proposition being that the lawful base of the constitutional edifice was Doña Isabel II and her dynasty. The fact that the matter was debated and voted on represented damaging blows to the cause of sacrosanct monarchy, though only twenty-one deputies opposed the proposition. During the course of the debates the republicans publicized the misdeeds of the Bourbons and one referred to the queen as "a thing."[43] In all, however, Isabel emerged from the affair with heightened prestige.

With Espartero as prime minister and O'Donnell as a near partner, the liberals set about to make Spain function properly as a constitutional kingdom. A new constitution was prepared and many liberal laws enacted, the most controversial of which was one authorizing the resumption of the sale of ecclesiastical property. Isabel, who had been assured that her eternal salvation was imperiled if she signed this law, balked for some weeks, but in April, 1855, she finally gave way before extreme pressures.[44] She also had to capitulate to Espartero's demands that the royal household be regulated by the cabinet. For many months after that, she was strangely passive, even bored, and perhaps not well.[45] The king was dominant in court circles for a period of two years because of her lassitude, or, it was said on good authority, because he held some compromising letters.[46] Real power, of course, was being exercised by Espartero and O'Donnell. Lord Howden thought that Isabel might last indefinitely as queen if she re-

43. Speech of the Marquis of Albaida, Nov. 30, 1854, *Diario de sesiones de las cortes constituyentes.*

44. Howden to Clarendon, April 30, 1855, F.O. 72/866, No. 188.

45. Howden to Clarendon, June 1, 1855, F.O. 72/867, No. 229, reporting a long conversation with the Duc de Montpensier on the palace circle; Howden to Clarendon, June 30, 1856, F.O. 72/894, No. 232.

46. Otway to Clarendon, Oct. 17, 1856, F.O. 72/897, No. 138; Howden to Clarendon, Nov. 7, 1856, *ibid.*, No. 235. Isabel II had a well-known weakness for penning unrestrained love letters.

mained quiet, but he had little confidence that she would, for she was "indescribably indiscreet."[47]

Spain's capacity for self-government during the liberal biennial of 1854-1856 was not impressive. Espartero and O'Donnell suspected each other. Both were inept and inexperienced. Or was the country simply ungovernable? Whatever the explanation, the government steadily lost prestige and social conditions worsened, especially in the south, where land redistribution injured many peasants, and in Barcelona, where industrialization was creating the usual problems of capital and labor. Disgust—that typical Spanish attitude toward government—soon enveloped the country. By the time the constitution was completed, late in 1855, little of the enthusiasm of July, 1854, remained. Isabel began to regain her confidence. Lord Howden rather embarrassedly reported that she had stood very close to him and clicked her teeth with her fingernail in the manner of a vulgar woman of Madrid and said: "Understand, I am afraid of nothing, and of nobody, nobody, nobody!"[48]

During the early months of 1856 it became apparent that Espartero was losing both public and royal favor. A protracted intrigue brought about his resignation in July and his final retirement. O'Donnell now became prime minister. A dedicated *isabelino* by this time (gossips offered an explanation), he set aside the new constitution, annulled most of the liberal organic laws, and suppressed the militia, the stronghold of Progressives and Democrats. Wild agitation and a sputter of revolts did not deter him. Scarcely had O'Donnell liquidated the revolution when, in October, 1856, Isabel indicated at a ball that she preferred General Narváez as a dancing partner. In the tearful scenes that followed[49] (Isabel usually wept when she fired her ministers), O'Donnell resigned and Narváez became prime minister to a futile cacophany of protests, shots, and barricade noises. Spain had simply enacted the European revolutionary cycle of 1848-1850.

47. Howden to Clarendon, March 29, 1855, F.O. 72/865, No. 135.
48. Howden to Clarendon, Nov. 16, 1855, F.O. 72/870, No. 304.
49. Howden to Clarendon, Oct. 26, 1856, F.O. 72/897, unnumbered. In this private letter written in Paris, Howden was reporting a conversation with Napoleon III and later with General Serrano.

The queen's position was now very dangerous. Again she had cheated the hopes of the very forces who had won the throne for her in 1839 and saved it in 1854, this time without the excuse of childhood. And her *camarilla* were as absolutist and clerical as the Carlists. Madrid was particularly hostile to her, the people refusing to be courteous in public and jeering whenever the royal march was played in theaters.[50] General Serrano, her first lover (probably), said she would have to go if she continued as an absolutist,[51] and later that she would have to go, regardless.[52] O'Donnell thought that she had behaved in a perfidious manner toward him, as of course did Espartero. The British and American representatives wrote that republicanism was making very striking advances,[53] and Lord Howden told Napoleon III in October, 1856, that Isabel might not last another year.[54] There was scarcely a political figure of importance who did not feel that he had been deceived by Isabel II as a sovereign, and often as a woman. As Augustus Caesar Dodge, the American minister, reported, the queen was severely censured for the way she changed cabinets. She had dismissed men who had recently and under trying circumstances attested their fidelity to her at a time of great peril to her crown and life, "thus furnishing another evidence of the wisdom of the injunction that we should not place our trust in earthly Princes."[55]

Having asserted herself politically, the queen cast off the domination of her husband. Perhaps she encouraged attacks on him in the English press while buying off criticisms of her own private life.[56] But if she thought of divorce, it was too late. No one who married Isabel "would have the respect of the nation."[57] Another crisis over paternity exacerbated relations of the king and queen. Somehow Francisco was prevailed upon in November, 1857, to display the newly born prince, first of Isabel's sons to survive, the future Alfonso XII.

50. *The Times* (London), March 10, 1857.
51. Howden to Clarendon, Oct. 26, 1856, F.O. 72/897, unnumbered.
52. Howden to Clarendon, May 7, 1857, F.O. 72/916, No. 187.
53. Perry to Lewis Cass, Jan. 30, 1854, Vol. XLI, private and confidential; Otway to Clarendon, Aug. 7, 1856, F.O. 72/894, No. 48.
54. Howden to Clarendon, Oct. 26, 1856, F.O. 72/897, unnumbered.
55. Dodge to Marcy, Oct. 11, 1856, Vol. XL, No. 36.
56. Howden to Clarendon, March 7, 1857, F.O. 72/914, No. 88.
57. Howden to Clarendon, March 10, 1857, *ibid.*, No. 96.

Once Narváez had restored order and suppressed the liberals and radicals, Isabel replaced him, in October, 1857, probably because he was too tyrannical over her household.[58] He knew she resented his domineering ways and had once seen her in a mirror making faces at him.[59] Possibly the queen thought it wise to make the regime more mellow by dismissing Narváez, but whatever her reason, her action was regarded only as the caprice of a silly woman, not the statesmanship of a constitutional queen. General O'Donnell returned as prime minister, backed by a party made up of progressive Moderates and moderate Progressives known as the Liberal Union. It proved a fortunate combination, lasting for nearly five years, the sunniest period of Isabel's reign. The Progressives were out of power and in eclipse. The Democrats busied themselves in internecine strife, mainly over the issue of socialism. And the Carlist cause, which the wretched king had been promoting,[60] all but collapsed with the capture and renunciation of two sons of Don Carlos in 1860 and their deaths, presumably of natural causes, in Austria a year later. Furthermore, O'Donnell benefited from a mild economic boom and from popular military adventures abroad, in Cochin China, Morocco, Mexico, and Santo Domingo. These successes inspired memories of the first Isabel, and Isabel II had moments in which she aspired to be another great queen.[61] The Moroccan campaign of 1859-1860 was immensely popular. The monarch was included in cheers by great throngs about the royal palace on two occasions, when Tetuán fell and when the army returned in triumph.

Isabel's royal progresses to the Mediterranean coast and Asturias in 1858 and to the Balearic Islands in 1860 were gratifying experiences. Yet when she returned from the Balearics a huge crowd awaited her at the railway station in Madrid, only to remain silent and stare sullenly.[62] Someone tried to kill her. Sir

58. Narváez tried to keep the queen from being so indiscreet with her favorite, Puig Moltó, in public. Otway to Clarendon, Oct. 14, 1857, F.O. 72/920, No. 85.
59. Howden to Clarendon, April 5, 1857, F.O. 72/915, No. 137, recalling a conversation with Narváez.
60. According to the Duc de Montpensier and others who should have known. Howden to Clarendon, June 1, 1855, F.O. 72/867, No. 229; Howden to Clarendon, Sept. 7, 1857, F.O. 72/919, No. 53.
61. Sir Andrew Buchanan to the Earl of Malmesbury, Nov. 25, 1858, F.O. 72/941, No. 275.
62. R. W. Woolley to Cass, Oct. 17, 1860, Vol. XLII, No. 15; Buchanan to Malmesbury, Oct. 17, 1860, F.O. 72/985, No. 313.

Andrew Buchanan, the British minister, wrote that never had the queen been more unpopular with the Madrid masses.[63] A spectacular tour of the south again showed her hold on the provinces. In the autumn of 1862 Isabel with her family and O'Donnell visited the Montpensiers in Sevilla. Hordes of peasants came into the city to acclaim the queen with great affection. A voyage by river steamer to Cádiz brought thousands to the banks of the Guadalquivir, where they rapturously cheered Isabel. In Cádiz itself, a city long in decline and a radical center, the reception was superlatively gratifying. At Loja, where Isabel distributed pardons for a curious jacquerie with republican tones, she was greeted almost as a divinity. And at Granada, Málaga, and Cartagena, foreign reporters could not find adjectives to describe the fervor of the queen's reception. Throughout she was dignified and lovable, demonstrating somewhat poignantly how well she might have served as a national symbol.[64] After she returned to Madrid she opened the Cortes, an annual ordeal usually conspicuous for the cold scorn with which the monarch was received. In December, 1862, however, she was hailed with marked enthusiasm because of the successful royal tour.[65]

The serene times came to an end in February, 1863, when O'Donnell lost control of his cabinet and was unable to assemble another one. For eighteen months the queen demonstrated her incapacity to choose wisely among the various alternatives. More than ever under the influence of Sor Patrocinio, a nun, now beatified, who claimed to have stigmata, and Antonio Claret, archbishop of Santiago de Cuba who was elevated to sainthood in 1950, Isabel had only one firm conviction about policies: refusal to recognize the new kingdom of Italy. This stand had perhaps hastened O'Donnell's fall, and it surely prevented her selection of a Progressive prime minister. Quite likely she was unwise to spurn the Progressives. The party was vigorous and hungry for

63. Buchanan to Lord John Russell, Dec. 10, 1860, F.O. 72/986, No. 398.
64. Perry to William H. Seward, Sept. 17, 1862, Oct. 23, 1862, Oct. 25, 1862, Oct. 30, 1862, Vol. XLIV, unnumbered, No. 88, No. 89, and No. 90, respectively; Sir John Crampton to Russell, Sept. 25, 1862, Oct. 6, 1862, Oct. 14, 1862, Oct. 19, 1862, Nov. 1, 1862, F.O. 72/1036, No. 355, No. 356, No. 357, No. 363, and No. 366, respectively. Foreign newspaper accounts also gave a vivid picture of the tour's success.
65. Crampton to Russell, Dec. 1, 1862, F.O. 72/1038, No. 387.

office; it was not yet irretrievably committed to her downfall.[66] Espartero might have yielded to an offer, or even Olózaga. General Juan Prim, long recognized as a promising Progressive politician, had recently sworn to defend Isabel to the last drop of his blood.[67] Yet Isabel picked a series of weak Moderate ministers and finally, as if in exasperation, named Narváez prime minister in September, 1864. By that time the Progressives had gone into *retraimiento,* a term with ominous implications, signifying rebellion and withdrawal from lawful political activities. Narváez's appointment caused angry currents to run through the nation, which correctly expected another dictatorship. The king and queen were alarmed at the hostility of the *madrileños,* who were largely Progressive, and by talk that since the fall of the Neapolitan Bourbons, Spain had the last of that "effete and degenerate" family.[68]

A determined campaign against the royal family was now under way. Most of the Progressives favored a change of dynasty, most of the Democrats a republic. Press censorship prevented open newspaper attacks, but there were many ways to discredit the monarchy: by ignoring it, or by praising Queen Victoria's constitutionalism or the merits of King Luis of Portugal, or by treatises on the failings of Marie-Antoinette and other doomed royal figures. Propaganda in the provinces spread stories of Isabel's immoralities, incapacity, and subservience to "fanatics" and absolutists. The Progressives and Democrats managed to win control of most of the municipal and provincial administrative bodies. Significantly, the Progressives labored effectively to convert the ranks of the royal army, as they had done in 1836. There was much material with which to work, of course, apart from Narváez's dictatorship. Not one figure at the court commanded affection or respect. Its doings seemed a repetitious soap opera of stock characters, all odious: the fat, sensual, and capricious queen; the contemptible king, whom suffering had not ennobled; María Cristina and her frequent visits allegedly for unsavory business reasons; and a parade of favorites, of Sor Patrocinio and Arch-

66. Crampton to Russell, May 30, 1864, F.O. 72/1080, No. 140.
67. Buchanan to Russell, Jan. 25, 1861, F.O. 72/1003, No. 38.
68. Woolley to Cass, Oct. 17, 1860, Vol. XLII, No. 15.

bishop Claret. Even Don Enrique was active, trying to blackmail the royal couple for money and titles in return for conciliating the Progressives.[69]

Isabel's luck was also running low. Whatever her failings, she usually received credit for kindness of heart and generosity. In February, 1865, she suddenly offered to turn over to the state the whole of the hereditary property of the crown valued at about £8,000,000, half the annual budget, with reservation of the royal residences and 25 per cent of the revenues. As usual, the government hovered near bankruptcy, though loss of confidence and poor management were the causes, for the kingdom was comparatively prosperous.[70] In the Cortes, now composed of browbeaten Moderates and Liberal Unionists, there was genuine emotion for this "magnanimous gesture," and a unanimous vote by the deputies to go to the palace and thank the queen.[71] The sycophantic section of the press effusively praised her, and loyal expressions of gratitude came in from the provinces to be laid at the foot of the throne. Yet the Progressives and Democrats largely spoiled the effect of the queen's proposal by asserting— unfairly, it seemed—that she would actually receive more income from the 25 per cent reservation than she had before, since much of the property did not really belong to the crown and, in any case, would be better managed.

Particularly offensive was a young history professor at the central university in Madrid named Emilio Castelar, who was also editor of a republican newspaper. Castelar, as a professor, was a state employee and had violated the law by attacking the monarch. When called upon to dismiss him, the rector refused, whereupon both were removed from the university. Student protest demonstrations in April became far more energetic than spring madness could account for; it was apparent that the anti-dynastic parties were inspiring successive evenings of riots. On April 10, General Narváez suppressed the demonstrators with the fury for which he was feared. Far more rioters were killed or injured than

69. Crampton to Russell, Nov. 15, 1864, F.O. 72/1082, No. 261.
70. Crampton to Russell, Jan. 2, 1865, F.O. 72/1097, No. 1.
71. Crampton to Russell, Feb. 21, 1865, F.O. 72/1097, No. 24.

official sources admitted.[72] Castelar, however, was allowed to escape through the command of Isabel herself.[73]

Things were never quite the same afterward, even though the queen's gift was accepted by the Cortes. Middle-class youths and intellectuals became more fervently anti-Bourbon than ever. Progressives and Democrats now had another atrocity to exploit. The brutality of Narváez even offended many in the palace, where there had long been dissatisfaction with his blustering and tyranny over the queen's inner circle.[74] In June he was dismissed. General O'Donnell accepted a call to form a government provided Italy would be recognized, the suffrage extended, Church and entailed lands sold, and Sor Patrocinio sent away.[75]

If the queen intended to appease the revolutionary parties by appointing O'Donnell, she failed. His easing of the repression permitted an explosive press and popular campaign to bring the crown into disrepute. Isabel was dismayed at the venom of the personal attacks on her.[76] It was even more alarming that for the first time the provinces were joining the effort to depict her as a depraved and treacherous person. Yet she was no more sensible than before about concealing the sordid facts of her private life. Spells of remorse and piety and numerous acts of charity could not alter the popular image that was now so firmly established. Nor did she ever exhibit any true grasp of what the role of a constitutional monarch was supposed to be.

General Prim was by now the most dangerous foe of the throne. Having changed his mind about the last drop of his blood, this able and attractive figure was definitely committed to making Spain a liberal state under a constitutional monarch—an obsession that would lead Europe and himself to tragedy in 1870. In January, 1866, he attempted a *pronunciamiento* of army units near Madrid, but succeeded only in giving the regime a bad

72. Speeches of Posada Herrera, April 25, 1865, of Cánovas del Castillo, April 26, 1865, and of Rios Rosas, April 27, 1865, *Diario de sesiones de las cortes*; Crampton to Russell, April 9, 1865, April 11, 1865, April 12, 1865, and April 19, 1865, F.O. 72/1098, No. 49, No. 50, No. 51, and No. 56, respectively; Perry to Seward, April 11, 1865, XLVIII, No. 187.

73. Ricardo Muñiz, *Apuntes históricos sobre la revolución de 1868* (2 vols.; Madrid, 1884-1885), II, 5-6.

74. Crampton to Russell, July 6, 1865, F.O. 72/1100, No. 124.

75. Crampton to Russell, June 23, 1865, F.O. 72/1099, No. 119.

76. Sackville West to Clarendon, Nov. 20, 1865, F.O. 72/1101, No. 17

fright. On June 22 a far more formidable insurrection occurred near the royal palace in Madrid, when two regiments of artillery rose, shot their officers, and seized the cannon. Thousands of Progressives and Democrats emerged from the residential quarters to build barricades. Yet O'Donnell and loyal troops were able, after many hours of fighting, to overcome the rebels.[77] Prim, who had engineered the affair, profited from his failures and continued to conspire. The Progressives and Democrats went ahead with plans for a mass uprising, a spontaneous revolution of the type known in other countries in 1848.

During the insurrection of June, 1866, General Narváez had helped O'Donnell keep the troops loyal. As soon as it was over, the queen, with stunning ingratitude, dismissed O'Donnell and installed Narváez as prime minister. O'Donnell was very bitter.[78] Words attributed to him, such as "Never again!" "That woman is insupportable," or "You can't govern with that lady," became slogans among his Liberal Union followers. He went to France, where he abetted Isabel's enemies and died in November, 1867. At the end of 1866 several Liberal Union members of the Cortes who reminded the queen that she had not convoked that body were arrested for their presumption. General Serrano, a Liberal Union leader, went to the palace on December 31 to reason with Isabel. After a cordial visit he was amazed to be told that he must leave the kingdom.[79] Now the Liberal Union joined the Progressives and Democrats in opposition.

Meanwhile, Narváez's methods were those only too familiar to Spaniards: executions, jailings, exile, seizures, and censorship. The emigration numbered many thousands.[80] The repression also reached into the provinces, where Progressives, Democrats, and Liberal Unionists were persecuted. Spain resembled a military encampment, Narváez's conception of an ideal state. Business conditions were very bad; the population was sullen and brooding.[81] Extravagant hopes were placed in *La gorda* (the fat woman) as

77. John P. Hale to Seward, June 24, 1866, Vol. XLIX, No. 34; West to Russell, June 22, 1866, June 24, 1866, and June 26, 1866, F.O. 72/1125, No. 169, No. 171, and No. 173, respectively.
78. Crampton to Lord Stanley, Jan. 11, 1868, F.O. 72/1178, No. 6.
79. West to Stanley, Dec. 31, 1866, F.O. 72/1126, No. 298.
80. West to Stanley, Oct. 20, 1867, F.O. 72/1149, No. 16.
81. Hale to Seward, Aug. 24, 1868, Vol. LI, No. 144.

people called the revolution which they thought must come, un-gallantly named for the portly Isabel II who must go.[82]

In France, England, and Belgium the exiles lived as best they could, finding inspiration in the conviction that revolution was inevitable. Their leaders were unwontedly co-operative, agreeing to work together to oust Isabel and to leave the future for a constituent cortes to settle. Except for several republicans of long standing, the men who counted were still convinced that a con-stitutional, hereditary monarchy was essential. They knew that a republic would be unwelcome in the European community, but further, they held doggedly to the belief that the mystique of royalty was needed to hold a state together and to link the past and present. Furthermore, republicans were still regarded either as utopians or as barricade-mongers with leveling ideas. Prim repeatedly said there were no Spanish republicans, though he surely knew better.

Prim's quarrel, and that of his confederates, with Isabel II was that she had consistently failed to serve as the symbol of respectability and unity that Spain required. Moreover, she had robbed the groups who had made her queen of the fruits of victory by denying their ideals of liberty, secularism, and repre-sentative government. And she had handled the various political groups so ineptly or perfidiously that all but the forlorn Moder-ates were now outlaws. Pathetic as it seems in retrospect, many of the conspirators of 1866-1868 sincerely believed that a properly run constitutional monarchy would work the necessary magic to turn Spain into an enlightened and progressive nation. That Isabel II must be regarded as hopeless for this cause was also the opinion of the British legation in Madrid, which compiled a long treatise on her degradation of constitutional monarchy to be read by Queen Victoria,[83] who scarcely needed the lesson.

During 1867 the queen continued as usual to move with the seasons from palace to palace. Having been endangered so often —by kidnaping attempts when she was a child, several efforts at assassination, rebellions, and unceasing conspiracies—she had be-

82. José Echegaray, *Recuerdos* (2 vols.; Madrid, 1917), I, 304.
83. West to Stanley, Oct. 20, 1867, F.O. 72/1177, No. 16, with enclosure, "Politi-cal State of Spain: Memorandum on Constitutional Government of Country," for the Queen.

come fatalistic, possibly apathetic or skeptical about the perpetual threats of dethronement. She opened the Cortes for the last time in December, 1867. Narváez died after a short illness in April, 1868, leaving Isabel bereft of any defender with prestige. A civilian ministry continued the repressive policies, but rumors of extensive preparations for a military and popular uprising kept the government fearful. Also agricultural distress was acute in 1868, affecting almost all parts of the kingdom.[84] In an effort to head off the expected uprising the ministry made many arrests. In July the Montpensiers were told of the queen's pleasure that they reside temporarily out of Spain.[85] Their relations with Isabel had been strained for some years now, and there was reason to believe that the duke was advancing funds to the conspirators. Isabel went to San Sebastián for the hot weeks of August, where she received the usual cordial welcome from rustic subjects. She hoped to visit Napoleon III, then at Biarritz, and secure his pledge to aid her in case of an outbreak in Spain.

In September, 1868, the long-nurturing plans of the revolutionists came to a head with marvelous, un-Spanish precision. The *gloriosa*, as the September revolution was known for a few years, involved only one battle and was immediately successful nearly everywhere. It caught Isabel at San Sebastián. She ordered a train to Madrid, where her appearance might have complicated matters, but the line was said to be cut.[86] The king, who was relieved to escape from an unbearable situation he had had to bear for years,[87] urged the royal party to go to France. With her current lover, family, and Archbishop Claret, Isabel went by rail to Bayonne, where the French imperial family consoled them. While they were talking at the station a trainload of returning Spanish exiles passed through and shouted at Isabel the contempt and hatred they had felt for years.[88] "I thought I had more roots in this country," she is supposed to have said, as she left it for the first time in her thirty-eight years.

The dethroned monarch settled in Paris, where she and Don

84. Crampton to Stanley, Feb. 28, 1868, F.O. 72/1178, No. 54.
85. Crampton to Stanley, July 14, 1868, F.O. 72/1179, No. 155.
86. Hale to Seward, Sept. 27, 1868, Vol. LI, No. 147.
87. Rafael Olivar Bertrand, *Así cayó Isabel II* (Barcelona, 1955), p. 255.
88. Hale to Seward, Sept. 27, 1868, Vol. LI, No. 147 and Oct. 9, 1868, No. 148.

Francisco separated. During the crisis over the candidacy of Leopold of Hohenzollern-Sigmaringen for the Spanish throne in 1870, Isabel abdicated in favor of her son. While she visited Spain in later years and at least once, at the second wedding of Alfonso XII in 1879, received a rousing welcome, she resided in Paris until her death in 1904.

In literature and folklore Isabel II has been a figure of fun, preposterous rather than tragic or even pathetic. Historians may well conclude that her contemporaries were too harsh, at least in appraising her statecraft. The men who overthrew her and "the spurious race of Bourbons forever" had little success in reforming or ruling Spain. After more than six years of turmoil and bloodshed—and inadvertent setting off of the Franco-Prussian war —most of the surviving revolutionists were only too glad to welcome Alfonso XII in 1875. Their ideas had proved shallow and unsuitable. The fissures in Spanish society were so deep and ill-understood that no one between 1808 and 1939 was able to dominate the country for long.

The persistence of the monarchical ideal in Spain for a half-century after the fall of Isabel II is scarcely remarkable in view of the fact that most Europeans accepted constitutional monarchy as a normal and even desirable system until the end of World War I. Spaniards had further reasons for cherishing it because of the memory of the chaotic years between Isabel's overthrow and the accession of Alfonso XII, and because the monarchy often seemed a flattering distinction between Spain and her republican heirs across the Atlantic. Conservatives considered the monarchy an essential tie with religion and other spiritual values they cherished, such as nationalism, tradition, and family. Liberals usually accepted, at least until the 1920's, the idea that a member of a traditional reigning house might strengthen and dignify the government by serving as a symbol of nationhood and arbiter of contending factions. Alfonso XII (1875-1885) and his widow, María Cristina, who was regent from 1885 to 1904, filled the royal role with considerable success. So did Alfonso XIII, who was born a king in 1886 and began his reign in 1904, until after World War I. By that time, however, royalty had lost its enchantment for much of Europe, and the Spanish government was failing to meet the demands of a growing proletariat and of the intellectuals. A new generation tended to repudiate royalty along with other symbols of the old order. The reign of Isabel II is thus an example of an idea carrying an institution through a period of inadequacy and frustration. The ideal of monarchy still seemed fitted to solve the problems that appeared important at the time, and any failures were blamed on the personal shortcomings of the sovereign. Once new problems arose and an abler monarch proved unable to cope with them, respect for the ideal of the monarchy declined.

THE MYTH OF COUNTERREVO-
LUTION IN FRANCE,
1870-1914

Edward R. Tannenbaum

In the beginning there was chaos.
Then forty kings created and preserved the cosmos—France.
(One weak king had needed a little help from a saintly peasant
girl.) The period when they held sway was a golden age. Everyone who counted derived a comfortable income from his land;
everyone else knew his place. The Holy Church sanctified the
status quo on earth and held the keys to the Kingdom of Heaven.
His Most Christian Majesty managed to keep France the dominant power in Europe while at the same time allowing the nobles,
the provinces, and the parlements to run their own affairs.
French art and letters flourished and were the envy of the world.

But the forces of chaos reappeared in the "serpent" Voltaire
and the "dragon" Rousseau and in that most sinister of organizations, the Freemasons. These forces managed to destroy the cosmos in that dreadful year, 1789. For the next twenty-five years
France was in chaos. Then the cosmos was temporarily restored.
But after 1830 France reverted to chaos again.

All believers in the true France must now work to overthrow
the forces of chaos and restore the cosmos.

Such in the nineteenth and early twentieth centuries was the
myth of counterrevolution, a variation of the archetype Paradise
Lost. The purpose of this essay is to suggest its role in shaping
the thought and behavior of those Frenchmen who believed in
it and to distinguish the nature of its role from other factors.
But first of all some introductory remarks are necessary to clarify
the meaning of myth and to justify the use of this much-abused
word.

EDWARD R. TANNENBAUM *is associate professor of history at New York University.*

*   *   *

A myth is an interpretation of a given reality that makes this reality bearable. It originates in the historic experience of a community and—through distortions by language, by prelogical ways of thought, and by dreams, communal rites, and other special kinds of experience—it is given symbolic forms that make it memorable. Myth, then, is an objectification of men's social experience (just as art is an objectification of men's individual experiences). As such, it enables men to become an integral part of their community and to reduce the tensions between themselves and the physical and social milieu in which they are called upon to live. In short, it gives them their *raison d'être*. New myths appear only when men are confronted with a radically new situation, one in which the old myths no longer "work." But, old or new, a myth "embraces all the elements of a situation or action, providing at one and the same time an explanation and synthesis of them, an indication of their future and of their necessity."[1]

It is this all-embracing quality of myth that distinguishes it from ideology. Whereas myth originates in historic experience, ideology is moulded by social situations—institutions, class structure, etc. And whereas the social function of myth is to bind groups together as a whole, the social function of ideology is "to segregate and serve special interests within societies in the competition of debate."[2] An ideology is a program of ideas whose purpose is to promote a specific path of action—usually political action. Unlike the symbolic forms of myth, which are couched in the more mysterious and compelling language of creative imagination, these ideas are formulated in the language of discursive logic.[3] Their function is to provide rationalizations for the necessity of certain kinds of action. Consequently, they do not give man a satisfactory "global" image of himself and they do not engage his total capacity for belief.

Modern myths have replaced formal divinities with, as yet, unconscious deifications of Science and History. Men now believe

1. Jacques Ellul, "Modern Myths," *Diogenes*, No. 23 (Fall, 1958), p. 27.
2. Ben Halpern, " 'Myth' and 'Ideology' in Modern Usage," *History and Theory*, I, No 2 (1961), p. 137.
3. Ernst Cassirer, *Language and Myth* (New York, 1946), p. ix.

in the universal capacity of Science as they once believed in an all-powerful God; there is no limit to what we expect from it. And when Khrushchev declares that History will decide between the Soviet Union and the United States, he is making History an eternal judge. Science and History are the underlying myths of modern man. Like the elemental, unrepresentable forces of ancient myths, they provide the religious charge that gives certitude to those modern myths that are closer to the level of conscious representation.

For there are several levels of myth—and because the symbolic forms of myth are not logical, these levels interpenetrate each other. Above the religious bedrock of Science and History are the myths that impel modern man to action, the "global motivating images"[4] of technology, happiness, progress, and the nation. Each of these, in turn, reveals itself through more transitory, secondary myths—or "image-beliefs." For example, the "image-belief" in the possibility of successful political revolution gives actuality and passion to the major modern myth of progress, causing it to shine, lending it color, and giving it heroes and a "history." The external trappings of the secondary myths wear away rapidly and have to be renewed and refreshed with other legends and heroes and—in modern myths—with ideas and ideologies. But, aside from these external trappings, the myths at each level mentioned here are all truly myths and will be referred to as such throughout this paper.

In the late eighteenth and early nineteenth centuries the "prophets of Paris," dissatisfied with the Old Regime and its myths, created the modern myths of progress, happiness, technology, and the nation. The purpose of these new myths was to explain a new situation—one in which Science began to unleash the latent forces of nature by a sort of magic for the benefit of man and in which History placed perfection in the future instead of in the past. Meanwhile, a social experience occurred, which produced a new "image-belief"—the myth of the French Revolution—to give passion and actuality to all four of the global motivating images.

The role of the myth of the French Revolution must be men-

4. Ellul, p. 27.

tioned briefly here for several reasons. It provides a foil for its opposite, which is the subject of this essay. In addition, it shows how ideas and ideologies about it played the dual role of embellishing it and revealing the more basic myths beneath it. Finally, I hope that this summary analysis will justify my preference for the term myth, rather than the term idea or ideology of counterrevolution.

Alfred Cobban summarizes what he takes to be the myth of the French Revolution as follows:

There once was a social order called feudalism. This was a terrible ogre and lived in a castle; but for centuries a bourgeois Jack the Giant-Killer climbed the beanstalk of economic progress, until finally in the French Revolution he liquidated the old order and put in its place something called alternatively bourgeois society or capitalism.[5]

As a conscientious historian, Professor Cobban is, of course, concerned with the facts. These belie the myth, and Cobban is certainly not alone in saying so. But, as we all know, the most important thing about a myth is that it is *believed*, not that the facts support or fail to support it. Besides, Cobban's formulation is merely one of the transitory, lesser legends that vivified the myth of the French Revolution, which, in turn, expressed the more important myths of progress, happiness, technology, and the nation, through which, in turn, Science and History revealed themselves. For true believers the myth of the French Revolution existed at all these levels.

The basic modern myths, like the religious myths of antiquity, often find their most dramatic expression in a mythical version of a social experience, like the French Revolution. Such was the case in nineteenth-century France. Positivists saw the French Revolution as a manifestation of Science and History revealed through progress, technology, and happiness. Orleanist Liberals viewed the Principles of 1789—which they too saw as History revealing itself—as an idea to be preserved in a constitution. Radicals transformed the Jacobin version of the myth of the French Revolution into an ideology, a justification for universal suffrage, anticlericalism, and patriotism. Marx, in turn, made the French Revolution a part of his ideology of the revolution of the future —again in the name of Science and History. Finally the counter-

5. *The Myth of the French Revolution* (London, 1955), p. 8.

revolutionaries themselves eventually tried to expropriate one modern myth expressed in the French Revolution—the nation.

These few examples illustrate the compelling character of the French Revolution as a myth. Even people who did not believe in it tried to put certain aspects of it to their own uses. It lost some of its emotional force once it was considered as an idea permanently enshrined in a constitution, which was the way the Opportunists (Cobban's triumphant Giant-Killers?) viewed it in the 1880's. The Radicals too were ultimately to pay only lip-service to it after their ideological goals had been achieved. Yet the myth lived on in the minds of millions of ordinary Frenchmen and, at least according to Cobban, of some outstanding historians.

Like the myth of the French Revolution, the myth of counter-revolution found expression as an idea and as an ideology in the nineteenth and early twentieth centuries. But the ideas of De Bonald and De Maistre and the ideology of Maurras had no more influence on the thought and behavior of French counterrevolu-tionaries than the ideas of Guizot or the ideologies of Gambetta and Alain had on the defenders of the Revolution. In both cases the myth itself was more compelling.

*   *   *

The myth of counterrevolution acquired its permanent features between 1814 and 1830. God was to it what Science and History were to the myth of the Revolution. God's law was the supreme authority, to be taken on faith. It had revealed itself in the political, social, and religious order that had supposedly lasted intact from the time of Hugh Capet until Cardinal Riche-lieu and that had partially survived until 1789 despite the central-izing efforts of the monarchy and the skepticism of the times. After that this order began to resemble the traditional myth of Paradise Lost, whose "global motivating image" was reaction—a return to the good old days.

Like the myth of the Revolution, the myth of counterrevolu-tion taught that an event decisive for everyone had really oc-curred. But for the counterrevolutionaries this event took on the color of The Flood—with the Comte d'Artois as Noah. This biblical coloring gave the next decisive event, the Restoration, a providential character. The Ultras did not view 1814 as a mere return to the elegant skepticism of the eighteenth century. Louis XVIII, to be sure, had "learned nothing and forgotten nothing." But the Ultras cried "Vive le roi quand même!" and waited for his brother, the real restorer of the really good old days. For them Charles X's anointment at Reims symbolized the true restoration.

A renewed faith ("image-belief") in the public role of the Church enhanced the myth of counterrevolution throughout the Restoration period and continued to influence the thought and behavior of counterrevolutionaries thereafter. Here too Charles X embodied the image of an intimate and sincere interpenetration between the throne and the altar. Although this image had little factual basis after Louis IX, the mythmakers pushed it forward to the time of Henry IV. (After years on the "Ark" of exile many Ultras felt that Paris was "well worth a Mass" even more earnestly than Good King Henry had.) In any case, it pictured the king supporting the Church as a great eleemosynary institution, as the main guardian of public morals, and as the only legitimate educational authority. The Chevaliers de la Foi, a secret order of pious noblemen organized in 1810, championed the interests of the throne and the altar during the Restoration period. Later in the nineteenth century other groups took up the clerical aspect of the counterrevolutionary myth out of political opportunism or social conservatism. Nevertheless, the ideology of clericalism helped to reinforce the myth of counterrevolution well into the twentieth century.

Along with its devotion to the Christian monarchy, the myth of counterrevolution expressed itself through an "image-belief" in the social and political role of the aristocracy. The rank and file of the Ultras consisted of the lesser, backwoods aristocracy. These people wanted not only their privileges revived but also their ancient function of public service. According to this aspect of the myth, the king had no better servants than his "corps de noblesse." As in the good old days, the nobles alone should be his ministers, ambassadors, and generals. At home, in the provinces, they alone should run things; again the age of Henry IV provided the idealized image. Just as the king was everybody's *seigneur,* so each *notable* should be a *seigneur* in his own baili-wick. Like clericalism, this conception of a ruling class was adopted later in the nineteenth century by other groups for other purposes. Non-noble factory-owners called themselves *patrons* in-stead of *seigneurs.* And they viewed their *patronage* as a re-furbished version of the *noblesse oblige* of the former social order described by the myth of counterrevolution.

In early years of the Restoration period the Ultras also developed the enduring "image-belief" of the *pays réel.* Already in 1814 they saw visible proof that the people were with them in the elections that produced the *Chambre Introuvable.* When the electoral system of 1816 restricted the vote to a *pays légal* of 90,000 Frenchmen of high birth and great wealth, the Ultras, having lost their majority, contended that universal manhood suf-frage would show that the *pays réel* was still on their side. There-after, they and their successors continued to believe in the old-fashioned good sense of France's rural masses. "Providential" military disasters in 1870 and 1940 were momentarily to rally enough Frenchmen to the support of reactionary leaders to re-vivify this belief. But during the long intervening periods the social and religious aspects of the counterrevolutionary myth sustained its true believers more than the hope of a new restora-tion of the monarchy.

Thus the Ultras provided a mythology that was to serve various counterrevolutionary groups in the nineteenth and early twenti-eth centuries. Their direct successors, the Legitimists, retired from public life between 1830 and 1870 and cultivated the social and religious "image-beliefs" of the basic myth on their country estates and in their parishes. The Legitimists came out into the open again in 1871, but the Comte de Chambord thwarted their chance of restoring the true king by refusing to adopt the tricolor flag in 1873 and by dying childless ten years later. After that the lineal heirs of the Ultras were called intransigents or simply reactionary royalists. Their myth might have died by the end of the nineteenth century if other groups had not adopted parts of it—groups like the Integral Catholics, the Social Catholics, the nationalist leagues, and, finally, the Action Française. The re-mainder of this essay will deal with the continuing impact of the myth in its various transformations, embellishments, and combinations with other factors from 1870 to 1914.

*   *   *

In 1871 the Legitimists had been out of action for over forty years—and it showed. A "providential" military defeat had just cleared the way for a new regime, and a "miraculous" electoral victory in February produced a monarchist majority in the National Assembly at Bordeaux. Yet the Legitimists were unable to bring about the event they desired. Many things were against them, to be sure: the Orleanists' insistence on a constitutional monarchy, Thiers's success in crushing the Commune, and the convincing public image of the conservative republicans. But the Legitimists' own myth handicapped them most of all. It had made their lives as "internal émigrés" bearable; it had also nourished their illusions about the *pays réel* yearning for its true sovereign. The Comte de Chambord's thirty years of isolation in an Austrian castle had made him the living expression of the myth. He was obstinate, mystical, and utterly unaware of what was politically possible.

Miracles do not repeat themselves; one has to take full advantage of them when they happen. The election of February, 1871, had made possible the restoration of Comte de Chambord as King Henry V; even the Orleanists accepted him until late 1873. (He was aging and childless, and their own Pretender, the young and prolific Comte de Paris, was next in the line of succession.) Furthermore, the monarchist majority had been elected on a ticket that promised peace with Prussia and order at home. This combination of circumstances was obviously unique and could not last. By not exploiting it, the Legitimists missed their last real chance for counterrevolution. The Comte de Chambord remained on the Swiss border; the newly elected Legitimist deputies remained in their state of surprise. "We gathered, we shook hands with the sad joy of men who are reunited with their own after a shipwreck."[6] Noah would have got to work immediately. Unfortunately for the Legitimists, Henry V was no Noah.

It is difficult to say whether the myth or the personality of

6. Vicomte de Meaux, *Souvenirs politiques: 1871-1877* (Paris, 1905), p. 7.

the Comte de Chambord himself played the greater role in preventing a restoration of the monarchy in the early 1870's. Certainly his own intransigence about keeping his white flag was a major drawback. After waiting almost three years for God to call him to the throne he finally asked Marshal MacMahon to proclaim him king in late 1873. When the newly installed President of the Republic refused to play the role of General Monck, Chambord began waiting for God's call again. One could argue that a more flexible and realistic Pretender might have been more successful. But one could also argue that the myth of counter-revolution itself made Chambord what he was, just as it made his supporters, the *chevaux-légers,* what they were.

The Legitimists' biggest political mistake was their refusal to co-operate effectively with the Orleanists. These two factions had shown the kind of success such co-operation could achieve in unseating Thiers in May, 1873, and replacing him with Mac-Mahon. But the Legitimists could never forgive the Orleanist Pretender for being the great-grandson of a regicide. Here too emotion and the myth that nurtured it were almost inseparable. Even after the death of the Comte de Chambord, many counter-revolutionaries stood aloof from the Orleanist Pretender. So powerful was the role of the myth in their outlook that they went on hoping for *their* kind of restoration long after there were no French Bourbons left. (The Comte de Chambord had been known as "the child of the miracle" because he had been born eight months after his father—the Duc de Berri, supposedly the last direct heir of Charles X—had been assassinated. But after 1883 the only "miracle" that could be hoped for was that some Orleanist prince would deny his own heritage and become a Legitimist by proxy.)

Meanwhile, in the mid-1870's the republicans were reversing the electoral superiority of the monarchists. They had been less active than the Orleanists under the Second Empire. Yet they quickly managed to revivify the myth of the Revolution and to make its main "image-belief" the Republic. In 1871 Legitimist noblemen still had much influence in their own bailiwicks as mayors and *conseillers généraux.* They had used this influence to get two hundred of their group elected to the National Assembly

in February of that year. Many of their constituents had turned
to them as their traditional leaders in a crisis. Although Thiers
and his cohorts soon made the Republic look respectable at the
top, the real shift in allegiance took place at the grass-roots level
—in the *pays réel*. There the republicans took over one local
office after another in "a quiet village revolution." Whatever the
reasons for their success may have been, they used their new
positions to oust many of the older *notables* from the Chamber as
well. By 1879 they finally gained control of the Senate and forced
MacMahon to resign. The end of the reign of "Patrice I" was
the final blow to any immediate hope for a monarchical restoration. Republican political action played an even greater role than
the myth of counterrevolution in this outcome.

*   *   *

The advent of a permanent republican majority in parliament
did not end the struggle between "the two Frances"; it merely
shifted the field of combat to religion. Both sides agreed that
being a practicing Catholic entailed continuing hostility to the
existing regime. As a result, millions of Catholics who were not
monarchists found themselves on the side of the counterrevolutionaries on the question of the Church. Almost all the "best
people" seemed to express their "right-thinking" in this way. At
the same time, anticlericalism became a rallying cry for all republicans. There were certainly divisions on each side on many
issues, and political opportunism played as important a role as
adherence to principles in the behavior of many militants on
both sides. Nevertheless, the conflict between *bien-pensants* and
anticlericals in the late nineteenth century heightened the role
of each other's myths.

Both sides bolstered their myths with new ideologies—positivism for the anticlericals and integrism for the *bien-pensants*. Although the anticlerical republicans did not accept Comte's creed
in toto, they used parts of it to give new life to their myths of
science, progress, and revolution. Gambetta expressed their general view when he said: "What we propose to do is to apply
positivism to the political order." This policy aimed at driving
the Church out of public life altogether. In the 1870's its pro-

ponents managed to nullify clerical pressure on the government
for military intervention to "liberate" the Vatican from Italian
control. They also thwarted the efforts of conservative Catholics
to give MacMahon's "reign" a new religious orientation under
the name of the *Ordre Moral*. Defeated in these two areas and
faced with an assault in the field of education, many clericals
became convinced that only a complete rejection of modern civilization and an "integral" return to Catholic "fundamentals" would
make them safe from their enemies. Their new integrist ideology
came from Pope Pius IX himself, who had provided it in his
Syllabus of Errors in 1864.

The way the struggle was conducted also played a role in
determining people's responses to it. Each side had its organization. The Freemasons, hitherto tolerant and deistic, became
militantly anti-Catholic and agnostic. Their influence was particularly strong among local republican party officials, and almost
every Radical deputy was a Freemason by 1900. (It was this new
"posture" of Freemasonry that made the counterrevolutionaries
begin to emphasize its role in causing the Revolution of 1789.)
With the government in anticlerical hands, the clericals organized
their counter-campaign in the press and the pulpit. Louis Veuillot
reached a limited audience for his integrist views in his newspaper *L'Univers*. The Assumptionist Fathers had a much wider
influence. This new religious order organized mass pilgrimages
and founded the daily *La Croix* (1883), whose Parisian and provincial editions reached half a million readers. Finally, the bulk
of the French clergy at all levels was hostile to the positivist Republic and said so with the unqualified support of the Vatican
until 1890.

Many Frenchmen clung to myths that they were on the point
of forgetting when the clerical issue turned into a struggle for
the minds of their children. The Falloux Law (1850) had made
religious instruction compulsory in the public schools. In the
early 1880's the proponents of the Ferry Laws charged that the
brothers and nuns were teaching superstition and reaction. The
clericals charged that the new lay teachers would teach positivism
and materialism. Since their prophecy turned out to be true,
they continued to oppose the state schools, even though they could

continue to send their own children to Catholic schools. True believers in both camps extended their intolerance toward each other's schools to the whole moral and political orders these represented. In this way the school squabble helped to revivify the myth of counterrevolution.

Anticlericalism was a more basic issue in France than in Germany, England, and even Italy in the late nineteenth century. In these countries too it was encouraged by the increasing need for universal primary education in an industrial society. Yet only in France did the struggle between clericals and anticlericals bring the regime itself into question. This situation came about partly because extremists on both sides viewed the regime in mythical, not merely ideological, terms.

* * *

But how was the regime to be overthrown? The longer it lasted, the more the majority of Frenchmen tended to view it as normal. Yet the Bourbon, Orleanist, and Bonapartist regimes had also been viewed as normal in their day. Each of them had fallen as the result of a military defeat or a revolution, but, in the 1880's and 1890's, few Frenchmen were willing to pay so high a price for the overthrow of the Third Republic. Its counterrevolutionary opponents therefore turned to the less expensive tactics of uncompromising obstruction (*politique du pire*), boring from within (*ralliement*), and the bloodless military coup (*appel au soldat*).

General Boulanger gained political prominence at a time when several competing myths and ideologies needed new heroes and new "image-beliefs." In the late 1880's he replaced Gambetta for the Radical Republican heirs of the Jacobins and Napoleon III for the Bonapartists. For them he became the champion of *revanchard* nationalism. The royalists had hitherto shied away from any man on horseback. Now some of them grasped at the illusion that a "right-thinking" soldier might help restore the king to his rightful throne. (After all, there was always the precedent of Joan of Arc.) Thus, they poured money into his campaign chest and tried to use him for this purpose.

The failure of General Boulanger to lead a military coup did not destroy the hope that an *appel au soldat* might save the nation from the Republic. Indeed, Maurice Barrès made this hope his "image-belief" for the next twenty-five years. In 1899, ten years after Boulanger fled France in order to avoid arrest, Barrès helped to found the League of the French Fatherland. Its purpose was to counteract the Dreyfusard League of the Rights of Man. Far more than the Boulangists this new nationalist league rallied counterrevolutionaries of every description behind the army and the nation as bulwarks against the "enemy" at home. Though Barrès himself never became an avowed royalist, he was to work closely with the Action Française in its early years. Like many other former Bonapartists, he brought the "image-belief" of an *appel au soldat* into counterrevolutionary thinking, where it was to re-emerge in 1909 in Charles Maurras's pamphlet, *Si le coup de force est possible.*

Political opportunism played as great a role as mythical thinking in making the counterrevolutionaries champion the army and the nation by the time of the Dreyfus Affair. It seemed to be a case of "my enemy's enemies are my friends." Many anti-Dreyfusards had previously had nothing in common with the counterrevolutionaries. But what a large number of them there were! And how opportune it was to have so many potential allies in the assault on a regime that was willing to jeopardize the honor of the army and the national security in the name of the rights of one man! André Buffet, the Comte Boniface de Castellane, and other prominent agents of the exiled Pretender organized their own anti-Dreyfusard leagues and tried to buy the support of others. Unfortunately for the counterrevolutionaries, there was no suitable man on horseback to stage a coup before Dreyfus' retrial and pardon. Still, once having tasted popular sympathy, they continued to look for new ways of linking the army and the nation with the myth of counterrevolution in the early 1900's, as we shall see presently.

Although the Dreyfus Affair momentarily revived the hopes of some counterrevolutionaries for a restoration of the king, others had already abandoned their royalism by the early 1890's. The Boulanger fiasco and Pope Leo XIII's call for *ralliement* played major roles in making them take this new position. But their formal acceptance of the Republic did not lead them to abandon the myth of counterrevolution. The *ralliés* hoped to bring about the desired reaction by taking over the Republic from the inside. (The Revisionist Marxists hoped to bring about the socialist revolution in a similar way.) This new tactic was adopted by the Comte Albert de Mun and the Social Catholics, and it led a significant minority of Catholics to vote for *ralliés* candidates. Once elected these *ralliés* co-operated with the Moderate Republicans, who, in return, softened their anticlericalism.

Those counterrevolutionaries (the majority at first) who resisted the pope's appeal were henceforth called intransigents. In order to maintain their holier-than-thou attitude toward the *ralliés,* some of them believed the fantastic legend that Freemasons had kidnapped Pope Leo XIII, imprisoned him in the Vatican dungeons, and put up an imposter to urge the false doctrine of *ralliement* on the faithful. (The Radicals were also receptive to this kind of thinking concerning the *ralliement;* Clemenceau said it was a Vatican trick.) It was awkward for the intransigents to have a "renegade" pope on their hands. Their myth prevented them from practicing a *politique du pire* against *him.* Instead they avenged themselves against the minority of "renegades" in France.

Throughout the 1890's and into the early 1900's the intransigents practiced their *politique du pire* against the *ralliés* in the press, in local church affairs, and in electoral campaigns. In 1893 there were sixty-four intransigent deputies and thirty-seven *ralliés* deputies in the Chamber. Five years later there were only thirty-five and twenty-one, respectively. Certainly the ability of the Moderate Republicans to "contain" the new Socialist menace (fifty-three Socialists had been elected to the Chamber in 1893) helped to draw votes away from the monarchists and clericals. But divisions within the counterrevolutionary ranks also weakened their electoral strength. Intransigent and integrist candidates who retired before the second ballot urged their electors to vote for their Radical rather than their *ralliés* opponents in a number of constituencies. This was a classic example of "favoring the worst." In the Catholic sections of Brittany, *ralliés* and integrist clergymen preached sermons in favor of their respective candidates, urged seminarists to write to relatives, and, in at least one case, even threatened recalcitrant parishioners with the expulsion of their daughters from religious orders. The *politique du pire* was also practiced by intransigent newspaper editors like Father Bailly in *La Croix,* Édouard Drumont in *La Libre Parole,* and, after 1908, by Charles Maurras in *L'Action Française.* Though their political influence declined, many die-hard counterrevolutionaries still refused to compromise with the *ralliés* and the Republican Center. *Fidelité* to their myth came first.

*   *   *

While the basic myth remained unchanged, it acquired additional secondary traits at the turn of the century. The Revolution of 1789 was still the great catastrophe. But the Dreyfus Affair took on a mythical character of its own and provided the basic myth with new "image-beliefs." The obvious role of the Freemasons and the Jews in fostering the Dreyfusard cause allowed the counterrevolutionaries to project these current enemies into the mythical account of how the Revolution of 1789 had happened. This event now came to be viewed increasingly as a "Judeo-Masonic conspiracy." True believers also refused to accept the possibility of Dreyfus' innocence. After 1899 they made the belief in his guilt almost as important a sign of *Fidelité* to the basic myth as the rejection of the Revolution itself. According to the principle "my enemy's enemies are my friends," the counterrevolutionaries also "adopted" the "right-thinking" officer corps of the army into their own "family." Finally, they tried to monopolize the role of defenders of the national interest.

But the counterrevolutionaries failed in their effort to make their brand of nationalism the only acceptable one for all Frenchmen. There were too many competing versions of the nationalist ideology. The nationalism provoked by the Boulangist campaign had united intransigent monarchists, ex-Bonapartists, socialists, and many Radicals. It had been essentially an expression of protest against the government of the Opportunists, who were laissez-faire liberals with a strong anticlerical stamp. By the late 1890's the monarchists and Integral Catholics had lost to the syndicalists and socialists the possibility of turning the proletarian protest against the injustices of the existing order to their own advantage. As the nationalism of the anti-Dreyfusards turned into an attack on the institutions of the Republic, the Radicals and Socialists became the chief defenders of the regime between 1899 and 1905. And after that conservative republicans like Poincaré and Barthou took away the lead in sponsoring nationalism from men like Barrès and Maurras.

The nationalism of the counterrevolutionaries was not only anti-republican, it also had strong nativist overtones. Its proponents argued that true Frenchmen had to have deep roots in the nation's traditional way of life. According to this argument, Jews, Protestants, and naturalized aliens obviously had no such roots, and Freemasons had severed theirs. Indeed, any Frenchman who was no longer a practicing Catholic—perhaps half the population by 1900—seemed partially uprooted and hence suspect from a nativist point of view. (One is reminded of the kinds of Protestant Americans who insist on prayers in the public schools.) By excluding so many people, especially in the cities, from the real nation, the *pays réel,* the counterrevolutionaries had difficulty in severing the myth of the nation from *its* roots in the Revolution.

The Dreyfus Affair temporarily made nativist nationalism popular, but this was not the only reason the counterrevolutionaries adopted it. The transformation of the cultural pattern by industrialization played a major role in making them take on this new outlook. Brought up according to the standards of expectation of an earlier age, they felt alienated from industrial society and its new ways of doing things. Like their counterparts in other modern countries, these Frenchmen viewed the new cultural pattern—with its "Jewish" finance, "English" parliamentary government, "German" science—as foreign to their *pays réel.* They stressed, more than alienated reactionaries elsewhere, the need to change the political system. But more and more their real enemies became the forces symbolized by the other modern myths besides the revolution: science, progress, and technology. They viewed these as culturally foreign to the true France of their own myth.

Changes in French social, economic, and cultural life brought new converts to the counterrevolutionary cause, especially as a monarchical restoration ceased to be its immediate goal. The new *déracinés,* city dwellers, began to share the hostility of the traditional reactionaries toward urban industrial society. They might never have been royalists or clericals back home in the provinces. But their inability to adjust rapidly to the new social and economic structure in which they found themselves made some of them adopt parts of the counterrevolutionary myth in order to make this structure bearable. This kind of reaction was especially common among white-collar employees. Uprooting often makes one man's Paradise Lost look pretty much like another's.

Expressions of the counterrevolutionary myth appeared in many guises at the turn of the century. *Bien-pensant* homes were cluttered with pious pictures and bric-a-brac of all sorts. *Midinettes* coming up the stairs of the new Paris subway (next to the Eiffel Tower the most horrible symbol of the modern myths of progress and technology) were comforted by the sight of street vendors selling flowers to honor some saint's day. In the theater, *Cyrano de Bergerac* epitomized all the virtues of the backwoods aristocracy in its days of glory. Many of France's most widely-read novelists—Balzac, Barbey d'Aurevilly, Barrès, Bourget—were counterrevolutionaries to the core and colored their works with their myths. The "other side" had its popular writers too: Eugène Sue, Jules Verne, Zola. But in sheer volume of sales none of them came near the Comtesse de Ségur. Over ten million copies of her children's novels were sold between the 1860's and World War I. More than any single writer she perpetuated the counterrevolutionary faith in God, country, *noblesse oblige,* and rural bliss. According to Madame de Ségur, in the good old days honest Frenchmen did not have to put up with majority rule, pushy Jews, and foreigners in their midst.

The period 1890-1914 was also the heyday of the conflict between republican and counterrevolutionary intellectuals. Among historians the myth of the French Revolution had its champion in Alphonse Aulard; its opposite had Augustin Cochin. While the universities inculcated the modern myths of revolution and progress (though they still resisted science), the Académie Française became a bulwark of the counterrevolutionary myth. Under Charles Péguy's editorship the *Cahiers de la Quinzaine* became a haven for young Dreyfusard intellectuals, but the columns of the

Revue des Deux Mondes and of many literary journals were safely in counterrevolutionary hands. Historians, philosophers, and literary critics intellectualized their respective myths into ideologies and applied these even to their professional methodologies. (The Marxists, of course, did this more thoroughly than anyone else.)

In the 1890's and the early 1900's the new myth of a working-class utopia complicated the struggle between the opponents and the defenders of the French Revolution. Nurtured by half-forgotten traditions of *compagnonnage,* syndicalism became a "global motivating image" for the more militant members of the labor movement. It called for a general strike, the abolition of the bourgeois state, and the reorganization of society on a working-class basis. Distrustful of intellectuals and politicians, it thrived on the hope of social emancipation, on impatience for deliverance, and on a genuinely revolutionary spirit. Its main "image-belief" was working-class solidarity. Syndicalism frightened both the bourgeois liberals and the *bien-pensants.* Much as they hated each other, they had to face the possibility of making common cause against this threat.

The working-class threat posed a special problem for the counterrevolutionaries. Their myth had already defined the bourgeois Republic as the equivalent of chaos. Still, it was obviously preferable to the kind of chaos advocated by the anarcho-syndicalists. The myth of counterrevolution had no place for a proletariat. But there it was, and something had to be done about it. Some Catholic employers tried *patronage* in the late nineteenth century and company ("yellow") unions in the early 1900's. The Social Catholics tried to revive corporatism. But in the face of anarchist bombings and labor strikes most of the intransigent and *ralliés* deputies in parliament supported the repressive measures of the, after all, not so "anarchic" republican government.

Socialism created a more permanent problem of adjustment than anarcho-syndicalism for the counterrevolutionaries. For there was no denying that the Socialists wanted a new kind of order—collectivism. It took a while for some counterrevolutionaries to stop thinking of the Socialists as just another kind of anarchists. But by 1905 the SFIO impressed them by its surface unity in the struggle to gain control of the French state and economy and also by its solidarity with foreign Socialists. The Action Française practiced a *politique du pire* by siding with the Socialists against Briand's strike-breaking policy in 1910. Yet all except three of the intransigent deputies in the Chamber joined the *ralliés,* the Moderates, and the liberal republicans in supporting Briand's policy. For all their hostility to republican governments, they still were on the side of private property and social order. Then, in the immediate prewar years, the pacifism and anti-militarism of the Socialists also made the counterrevolutionaries give grudging support to the existing regime. It simply would no longer do to favor Jaurès over Poincaré in the face of the German meanace. Even the Action Française finally came around to this realization.

*   *   *

In view of its claim to be the "integral" embodiment of the counterrevolutionary myth, how did true believers regard the Action Française? This movement had been founded at the climax of the Dreyfus Affair and had tried unsuccessfully to make the new, anti-Dreyfusard aspects of the myth its *raison d'être* between 1899 and 1905. But many of the faithful had not yet heard of this small coterie of reactionary-nationalist intellectuals, and its "conversion" to monarchism in 1902 caused no significant stir among them. Only when it adopted a clerical "posture" during the controversy over the separation of Church and state was it able to attract the support of eminent traditional counterrevolutionaries like the Marquise de MacMahon and the Marquis de la Tour du Pin. After 1905 the Action Française grew rapidly into a nationwide organization of die-hard monarchists, Integral Catholics, and reactionary nationalists. Both the Pretender and the new "integrist" pope, Pius X, gave it their qualified blessing. But the majority of the *bien-pensants* was always wary of this new movement of the radical right. These people preferred the more respectable Action Libérale of Jacques Piou, with its Jeunesse Catholique auxiliary founded by Albert de Mun. They had come to believe that one could accept the Republic and still oppose the Revolution.

The Socialist threat, the German menace, and the rowdyism of the younger members of the Action Française—especially the Camelots du Roi (founded in 1908)—made most counterrevolutionaries abandon their hope of overthrowing the Republic in the prewar decade. Many noblemen retired into the closed worlds of the Faubourg Saint Germain and of their provincial estates and pretended that they were still living in the past—like a quietist religious sect preserving its purity in sinful surroundings. Integrist bishops and priests concentrated their counterrevolutionary activities on rooting out "modernism" from their own midst. Whatever their profession or social status, most people brought up on the myth of counterrevolution had ceased to view it as something that could be realized by ordinary means of political action. They looked askance at the Action Française, with its street demonstrations, its *politique du pire,* and its talk of a *coup de force.* For them only a miracle could make the myth a reality. This patient hoping for a miracle expressed the abiding influence of the myth on its believers.

The Action Française never convinced the majority of French counterrevolutionaries that it could bring about the longed-for miracle. It was too new and too brash to be associated in their minds with their traditional myth. Maurras lacked the qualities of a heroic leader; he was viewed as what he was, an upstart intellectual. The Camelots du Roi, for all their campaigns on behalf of Joan of Arc, were no substitute for the Chevaliers de la Foi or the Assumptionist Fathers. Both the pope and the Pretender, the real heroes of the myth, treated the Action Française as a somewhat suspicious ally, not as their own crusading legion. Most French counterrevolutionaries dealt with it in the same way. The Action Française tried too hard to be convincing. Besides its lack of harmony with the traditional myth, the fact that its leaders were mere intellectuals deglamorized it in the eyes of the faithful. Miracles and intellectuals just do not go together.

Maurras's main role was to give the myth of counterrevolution an ideological reinforcement—a program of rational ideas to promote a specific path of action—much as Marx's ideology did for the myths of progress and revolution. Marxism came closer than integral nationalism to resembling a true myth (though

Marx would turn over in his grave at such a thought). It claimed
to be a revelation of Science and History, whereas integral nationalism was supposedly the product of what Maurras called "organizing empiricism." Furthermore, Marxism managed to supersede
its rivals (the utopian socialists) to a greater extent than did
integral nationalism. Marx's successors certainly argued among
themselves about what the prophet had *meant,* but what he had
said had already become gospel. Maurras had to keep rephrasing
what he said in order to convince the traditional counterrevolutionaries that his brands of nationalism and anti-Semitism belonged in their myth. Despite these limitations, however, Maurras
was in effect the Marx of the Right in France.

The ideologies of Marx and Maurras both reinforced myths
that appealed to people who would otherwise have found the
temporal structure of their lives unbearable. Here Marxism had
the advantage of dealing with a more convincing "global motivating image," for no matter how much one idealizes the past,
it is never as open to perfection as the future. Besides, Marx
argued that the first step toward the socialist millennium had
already been taken with the French Revolution. Workers alienated from bourgeois society could find real solace in the conviction
that their role was to take part in the inevitable consummation
of this great event. But Maurras's ideological reinforcement of
the myth of counterrevolution had its advantages too. His idea
of the nation had a more convincing mythical counterpart than
the idea of the solidarity of the international proletariat—especially by 1914. And his nativist nationalism (like later examples
elsewhere) gave comfort to alienated reactionaries by assuring
them that they were the "true Frenchmen" and that the "Old
Republican Party" consisted of a pack of Jews and foreigners.

In the immediate prewar decade the Action Française appealed more to "converts" than to "old believers." Many of the
youths who joined the Camelots du Roi did so because it was the
only important nationalist organization at the time. For these
"converts" monarchism gave color and vitality to nationalism.
For the "old believers" it was the other way around. The exploits of the Camelots and the witty newspaper articles of Léon
Daudet revitalized the myth of counterrevolution more than the

ponderous pronouncements of Maurras. His *Enquête sur la monarchie* had as little influence on the thought and behavior of counterrevolutionaries as *Das Kapital* had on revolutionary socialists. And the Action Française offered nothing comparable in popular appeal to the *Communist Manifesto*. While the "converts" reveled in its attacks on the existing order, the "old believers" retired into a mythical past and showed little interest in the present or the future.

*   *   *

Thus, a hundred years after its inception, the myth of counterrevolution still colored the thought and behavior of many Frenchmen. Only a small number of them accepted all of it, and even fewer believed in a monarchical restoration as a practical possibility. But, while the intransigents declined in numbers, the Integral Catholics held their own, and the integral nationalists gained more followers. *Ralliés* and so-called Moderates often accepted the Republic halfheartedly and the Revolution with no heart at all. Finally, perhaps a quarter of the total population— including millions of children brought up on the Comtesse de Ségur—held on to the counterrevolutionary "image-beliefs" of a conservative God, the superiority of native Frenchmen, *noblesse oblige,* and the joys of living in a pre-industrial society. For the French Revolution had come to be viewed as the event that had caused *all* the modern evils these people hated: state schools, the Eiffel Tower, the traitor Dreyfus, socialism and unions, the separation of Church and state, the German menace. These anti-modern Frenchmen also knew that the myth of the Revolution expressed the more basic myths of science, progress, and technology, and that it revealed itself in the idea of brotherhood and the ideology of egalitarian democracy. Anyone who was against any of these modern abominations could find solace in some aspect of the myth of counterrevolution.

THE DISSOLUTION OF
GERMAN HISTORISM*

Georg G. Iggers

I

Until the recent advent of Marxism-Leninism in Russia and Eastern Europe, in no part of the world were historians as consciously guided in their practice by a philosophy of history as in nineteenth- and twentieth-century Germany. And this was true under circumstances in which, except for the Hitler years, historians were free of such intellectual regimentation as prevails in Communist countries.

With much more justification than in France, Britain, or the United States we may speak of one main tradition of German historiography. This tradition, broad and varied in its manifestations, was given a degree of unity by its common roots in the philosophy of German Idealism. One of its founding fathers was Leopold von Ranke, but he was by no means the only one. Perhaps another equally important in the translation of German Idealist philosophy for historical practice and of greater influence on German historians in the mid-nineteenth century was Wilhelm von Humboldt. What gave the tradition its distinguishing characteristics was not its critical analysis of documents which we have associated so closely with the name of Ranke. The critical method and the devotion to factual accuracy were not peculiar to Ranke or the nineteenth-century German historians. To an extent they were developed by an earlier generation of historians, philologists, classicists, and Bible scholars.[1] They were easily exported and adapted by historians in other countries writing under

GEORG G. IGGERS is associate professor of history at Roosevelt University.
* I gratefully acknowledge fellowships from the John Simon Guggenheim Memorial Foundation and the Fund for Studies in Legal and Political Philosophy of the Rockefeller Foundation which enabled me to do the research for this study in Germany.
1. Cf. Herbert Butterfield, *Man on His Past* (Cambridge, 1955) and Joachim Wach, *Das Verstehen* (Tübingen, 1926-33), 3 vols.

the impact of very different outlooks. The critical method became the common property of honest historical scholars everywhere. What distinguished the writings of the historians in the main tradition of German historiography was rather their basic philosophic assumptions regarding the nature of history and of reality. It is this historical faith which determined historical practice. It determined the problems historians posed, centering for the most part on the conflict of the great powers. It also determined the methods they employed—their heavy emphasis on the use of archives and diplomatic documents to the neglect of social and economic history and of sociological methods and statistics. This faith also gave the works of these historians a political orientation—not in the narrow sense of party partisanship, for within the broad tradition we find conservatives, liberals, democrats, and socialists of every description, but in the central role they assigned to the state and in their confidence in its beneficial effects. There were, to be sure, important thinkers who were not part of this tradition, historians such as Jacob Burckhardt, Julius von Ficker, Johann von Döllinger, Max Lehmann, and Franz Schnabel, and philosophers such as Arthur Schopenhauer and Friedrich Nietzsche. Other scholars like Ludwig von Stein and Karl Lamprecht stood at the margins of this tradition in their attempts to discover great social and economic forces operative in history. Nevertheless, the basic philosophic assumptions upon which the tradition rested were accepted not only by the majority of German historians but also by many linguists, philologists, economists, jurists, philosophers, sociologists, and theologians in nineteenth-century Germany.

Historism has too many meanings to be useful as a term without careful delimitation.[2] When we speak of historism or of the "German idea of history" in this paper, we are speaking of the main tradition of German historiography and historical thought that followed Wilhelm von Humboldt and Ranke and that emerged in the revolt against the Enlightenment doctrine of natural law. German historiography shared with other major forms of historism the belief that all socio-cultural phenomena as

2. For an attempt to define the many conflicting meanings of historicism, see Dwight E. Lee and Robert N. Beck, "The Meaning of 'Historicism,'" *American Historical Review*, LIX (1953-1954), 568-577.

well as all cognitions of such phenomena are historically determined; consequently, cognitions and value judgments are always relative to a historical situation. The major forms of historism[3] thus exclude the possibility of universally valid values by which human institutions and actions can be judged.

The historism of the German historians, however, involved more than the mere insistence on the historicity of all values. They tried to work out a new philosophy of value. Herder in his *Also a Philosophy of History* already had indicated the basic elements of such a new philosophy of value.[4] We cannot apply universally valid values in judging a historical deed, he held; we must judge every situation in terms of its own values. From this Herder and the classical German writers, Schiller, Goethe, and Wilhelm von Humboldt, attempted to find a new concept of humanity which took into consideration the diversity of men. Mankind was one but many. The individual achieved his fullest humanity in the fullest growth of his distinct individuality. This assumed, however, that there existed a basic harmony between individual growth and universal humanity.

The task which German Idealist philosophy from Kant to Hegel set itself was to bring the unique character of the individual into harmony with the rational character of human history. Three concepts elaborated in this philosophic discussion later occupied a central role in the German historical tradition: the concept of individuality, the idea of identity, and the conception of the primacy of the state in society. Humboldt developed these concepts eloquently in his essay on the "Tasks of the

3. Theories of historicism have agreed in emphasizing the uniqueness of historical events. A distinct contrast is Karl Popper's definition of historicism in *The Poverty of Historicism* (Boston, 1957), p. 3: "It will be enough if I say here that I mean by 'historicism' an approach to the social sciences which assumes that *historical prediction* [Popper's italics] is their principal aim, and which assumes that this aim is attainable by discovering the 'rhythms' or 'patterns,' the 'laws' or 'trends' that underlie the evolution of history." Karl Popper has been sharply criticized for this use of the term, e.g., by Hans Meyerhoff in *The Philosophy of History in Our Time* (New York, 1959), p. 299.

4. E.g., in his later *Ideen zur Philosophie der Geschichte der Menschheit* and the *Humanitätsbriefe*. Cf. G. A. Well's "Herder's Two Philosophies of History," *Journal of the History of Ideas*, XXI (1960), 527-537; Rudolf Stadelmann, *Der historische Sinn bei Herder* (Halle, 1928), and Friedrich Meinecke, *Die Entstehung des Historismus* (first published in 1936), in *Werke*, Vol. III (München, 1959). Both Stadelmann and Meinecke consider Herder's retreat from his radically historicist philosophy of values in *Auch eine Philosophie der Geschichte* a sign of Herder's declining sense for history.

Historian" of 1821;[5] Ranke dealt with them more than a decade later in his essays on "The Great Powers" and "Political Dialogue."[6] The first concept was that of individuality. Behind the observable phenomena which constituted the past, Humboldt saw a realm which eluded the senses, the realm of ideas. The historian could reconstruct the past truthfully only if he grasped intuitively (verstehen, ahnen) the hidden meaning, the idea, which stood behind every concrete individuality. "Every individuality," he wrote, "is an idea that takes on phenomenal form."[7] But such an idea, although eternal and indestructible, was not to be understood in the abstract. Rather it was inseparable from the concrete individuals through which it expressed itself. States and nations too were such individuals, each resting on a unique idea. Ranke spoke of this relationship as "real-and-spiritual (real-geistig)."[8] In the realm of ethics this meant that there were ethical norms unique to every individual. Every individual contained his idea, his purpose, his norms. These individual traits could not be imposed from without. It was the ethical task of each individual, whether person, state, or nation, to develop according to his own idea. The state was thus never the artificial product of a social contract to be guided in its actions by universal and abstract precepts of political justice. Rather it was a unique individual embodying a unique idea that prescribed its unique tasks. Humboldt gave no clear answer to the question of the relation of individual and collective individualities. He assumed a "profound and mysterious" harmony between the developing energies of individuals and those of the nation. But the idea of the primacy of foreign relations which Humboldt had accepted in 1813, and which was shared as an axiom of politics by the whole tradition, implied the supremacy of the state over the individual. Only in the state could the individual person fully develop his own individuality.

The second basic concept which the German historians in-

5. "Über die Aufgabe des Geschichtsschreibers" (first published in 1821), Werke in fünf Bänden, I (Stuttgart, 1960), 585-606.
6. Translated in Theodore H. Von Laue, Leopold Ranke: The Formative Years (Princeton, 1950).
7. "Über die Aufgabe des Geschichtsschreibers," op. cit., p. 603.
8. "Politisches Gespräch," in Die grossen Mächte. Politisches Gespräch (Göttingen, 1958), p. 57.

herited from the idealistic philosophers was the idea of identity. Although every individuality and its idea were radically unique, nevertheless, in a mysterious way which we cannot perceive directly but can grasp only intuitively, they formed part of a divine plan. Not that all individuals could be fitted nicely into an upward cosmic process, such as Hegel had conceived, in which they formed stages in the fulfilment of the Absolute Idea. Such a conception would clearly violate individual character. Every individuality existed for its own sake and was in Ranke's words, "immediate to God." It was not a stage toward an end external to it. Nevertheless, "world history," as Humboldt observed, "is incomprehensible without a cosmic plan governing it."[9]

In following his own idea and destiny, the individual also accomplished a higher purpose. The greatest value in history lay in the growth and development of the greatest number of rich "individualities." Such growth, of course, might lead to conflict among individuals and to war among states. But in a basic sense, no real evil could result from such conflict even if apparent evil—suffering and killing—might occur. For, as Ranke had Friedrich say in the *Political Dialogue:* "But seriously, you will be able to name few significant wars for which it could not be proved that genuine moral energy achieved the final victory."[10] In this way Humboldt and Ranke could not help being optimistic regarding the course of history. Power and ethics were basically in harmony. In a sense they were more radically optimistic regarding the course of history than even Hegel or the classical theorists of progress in the West. The ideal of progress always implied that man lived in a world which at least at this stage of its development was imperfect and immoral. For Ranke, the politics of the great powers, if guided by their real power interests, could not be immoral.

Still missing in the writings of Herder, Kant, Goethe, or the very young Humboldt was a third concept that emerged in the midst of revolutionary turmoil and the German Wars of Liberation—the idea of the primacy of the state. Hegel's conception of the state as the embodiment of morality seemed perhaps too

9. "Über die Aufgabe des Geschichtsschreibers," *op. cit.,* p. 600.
10. "Politisches Gespräch," *op. cit.,* p. 59.

radical to the historians. Nevertheless, the state for Ranke embodied an idea which was derived from God. It represented a natural family superior to the individuals that composed it. The purpose of the state was not the welfare of the individuals but the fulfilment of its inherent "spiritual tendencies," tendencies which he, like Hegel, thought required above all the expansion of the state's external power.[11] As Humboldt had written in 1813, "only a nation which is also externally strong can preserve the spirit from which all domestic blessings flow."[12] If suffering and injustices to individuals resulted from the state's striving for power, this did not establish the immorality of politics, for the end of individual existence was not the achievement of happiness but the fulfilment of an idea.[13] A real conflict between power and ethics seemed as remote to Ranke as it did to Hegel and Humboldt.

These philosophic notions of history were to dominate German historiography for more than a century. They had their roots in the classical *Humanitätsideal* of Herder, Goethe, and Kant. As we already have seen, they acquired a modified and sharpened form in the period of stress and strain of the Napoleonic invasions and became a part of the national heritage in the enthusiasm which accompanied the Wars of Liberation. They were integrated into the political faith of a generation that in the decades of the Restoration strove against the forces of absolutism for national unity and the establishment of liberal institutions, but of institutions cleansed of alien French ideas and loyal to German traditions. Among conservative historians these philosophic notions were reinforced by Ranke's activities as historian, publicist, and teacher. In the years immediately preceding 1848, a more liberal generation of young historians, skeptical of Ranke's conservative leanings and looking for Prussian leadership in German unification, turned back for inspiration to Humboldt, Fichte, and Hegel. The failure of the 1848 Revolution convinced the

11. *Ibid.*, pp. 58, 59, 60-61, 73-74.
12. "Denkschrift über die deutsche Verfassung," *Wilhelm von Humboldt, Eine Auswahl aus seinen politischen Schriften,* ed. Siegfried Kaehler (Berlin, 1922), p. 89.
13. See Humboldt's even earlier "Ideen zu einem Versuch die Grenzen des Staates zu bestimmen" of the early 1790's in *Werke in fünf Bänden,* I, 87. The anti-utilitarian argument that happiness was not the purpose of man's existence was common to German Idealistic and historicist thought from Kant's "Idea of a Universal History from a Cosmopolitan Point of View" to Ernst Troeltsch.

same historians even more of the primacy of state action and of the ethical rightness of political power. The year 1871 seemed to them to be the culmination and justification of historical development. German nationalism had become inextricably interwoven with the "German" idea of history, which in turn now became equally closely associated with the Bismarckian solution to the German question. Conservatives, liberals, democrats, and to an extent even socialists shared in the common religion of history. Germany's entry into the area of world politics found historians firmly convinced that Ranke's conception of the great power could be extended to the world scene. World War I once more united most historians from left to right in a fervent defense of the "German idea of history" against "Western natural law doctrine."[14]

Thus, German historians moved in a world of their own which remained remarkably unchanged in the midst of the great transformations of the nineteenth and early twentieth centuries. Their intellectual capital remained that of the glorious days of the Wars of Liberation. They remained remarkably inattentive to the great social and economic changes brought about by industrialization. History to them remained primarily the interplay of the great powers, and archives and documents continued to offer the prime sources for historical study. Where historians did acknowledge the emergence of the masses as a political factor, as Sybel did in his study of the French Revolution, they assumed that the principles of international politics and warfare had remained essentially unchanged since the emergence of the modern absolutist state. Sociology was viewed with suspicion. And even the great tradition of economic history which came into being with Schmoller subordinated economic to political and power-political factors. Similarly, the circle of social and political reformers around Friedrich Naumann at the turn of the twentieth century, which included eminent men like Max Weber, Ernst Troeltsch, and Friedrich Meinecke, saw the primary solution for the domestic social and economic problems of an industrial society in an ex-

14. Cf. Ludwig Dehio, "Ranke und der deutsche Imperialismus" in *Deutschland und die Weltpolitik im 20. Jahrhundert* (München, 1955); cf. K. Schwabe, "Zur politischen Haltung der deutschen Professoren im Ersten Weltkrieg," *Historische Zeitschrift,* CXCIII (1961), 601-634.

pansive foreign policy; they championed democratization of government primarily as a means of strengthening the nation in the international power struggle. Despite their rejection of the classical idea of progress, German historians and social thinkers still remained remarkably optimistic regarding the future of the modern world at a time when a cultural malaise had become apparent among liberal thinkers in the Western countries. Burckhardt's and Nietzsche's words of warning, whatever their impact on broad masses of young Germans, fell mostly on deaf ears among the leading German historians. In 1914 German historians and social philosophers with very few exceptions were unable to understand the completely changed character of warfare and international realities. They were prisoners of an idea. This idea, with its roots in the nineteenth century, influenced their judgment of the political realities of the twentieth century.

II

The dissolution of the "German idea of history" was slow. Even World War I did not decisively affect the political values and historical concepts of practicing historians. To be sure, Walter Goetz called for a thorough re-examination of the political presuppositions of German historiography. German historians "had been so attached to the monarchy and the cult of the Hohenzollern House" since the Wars of Liberation, he wrote in 1924, that their sense of objectivity had suffered.[15] However, a majority, including such well-established scholars as Georg von Below, Erich Brandenburg, Hans Delbrück, Dietrich Schäfer, Max Lenz, and Hermann Oncken, remained loyal to traditional philosophic and historiographic assumptions. Defeat and war-guilt theses seemed to give them new incentives to defend the Bismarckian solution and the rightness of German intellectual traditions.

15. "Die deutsche Geschichtsschreibung der Gegenwart" in *Historiker meiner Zeit* (Köln, 1957), p. 419. The book reviews of Meinecke's *Idee der Staatsräson* offer an interesting barometer of the political climate among German scholars in the 1920's. Even a historian who made his peace with the Weimar Republic, such as Hermann Oncken, in the *Deutsche Literaturzeitung*, NF III (1926), 1304-1315, bitterly rejected the idea that German thought or policy had in the past placed an undue value on power. Carl Schmitt in the *Archiv fur Sozialwissenschaft*, LVI (1926), 226-234, rejects Meinecke's dualism of ethics and power. More sympathetic is Gerhard Ritter's review in *Neue Jährbucher für Wissenschaft und Jugendbildung*, I (1925), 101-114.

Friedrich Meinecke, who himself was deeply committed to these traditions, remained relatively isolated among his colleagues when in 1924 in his study on *The Idea of Reason of State in Modern History* he suggested that the interests of the state were often in conflict with morality. There were divergent tendencies, Otto Hintze's concern with institutional history, Friedrich Meinecke's stress on the role of ideas—both of which antedated the war—and Franz Schnabel's broad social and intellectual approach in his study of early nineteenth-century Germany. Schnabel even argued that the idea of a German nation-state under Prussian leadership had no roots in the German past before 1840. Nevertheless, these reorientations represented a minority.

Among cultural scientists and philosophers, as well as among broad segments of educated German opinion, the war marked a more radical break. Shattered were both the faith in history as a key to all culture and the optimism regarding the course of modern history. Ernst Troeltsch now spoke of the "crisis of historism." Oswald Spengler, Eduard Spranger, Erich Rothacker, and Karl Mannheim, all in very different ways recognized the relativistic consequences inherent in historical study. Their theoretical works were tragic attempts to rescue their Idealistic faith in the meaningfulness of history in the face of their intellectual realization of its meaninglessness. A more radical group of thinkers such as the philosopher Martin Heidegger, the political scientist Carl Schmitt, the poet and writer Ernst Jünger, and from a very different standpoint the cultural critic and philosopher Theodor Lessing, denied the existence of meaning or of objective value in history and based morality on subjectivistic grounds. The sources of the new relativistic and pessimistic orientation, which in Heidegger, Schmitt, and Jünger's cases bordered on ethical nihilism, were found in the philosophic discussions of the optimistic age before the war. Since the philosophers and cultural scientists rather than the historians were primarily instrumental in re-examining and destroying the philosophic assumptions of German historism, this section of the paper will deal above all with them.

German thought had been relatively free of pessimism in the years before the outbreak of World War I, despite the warning voices of a Burckhardt or a Nietzsche. German Idealism had been basically an optimistic philosophy, and German cultural thought remained committed to it until the war. The increasing orientation to the natural sciences in the course of the nineteenth century was not essentially in contradiction to this. For basic to German Idealism was not the concept that reality was idea but that the world was a meaningful process. Feuerbach and Marx did not basically refute this but in a sense rather translated basic concepts of German Idealist philosophy into the language of a more scientifically oriented age. And thinkers like Feuerbach, Marx, and Büchner represented merely extremes of German thought. Positivism as a philosophic conception of history in the sense of Auguste Comte or Henry Buckle had no significant representatives among German professional historians (unless we consider Marx as one), even if certain positivistic concepts and terms were integrated into essentially idealistic frameworks of thought as in the writings of H. von Sybel[16] or Wilhelm Dilthey. Karl Lamprecht came closest to positivism in his search for laws of historical development through the use of comparative studies, but his approach was more reminiscent of Herder or Hegel or even Burckhardt than of French or English models.

The hold of German Idealism on German thought was not essentially shaken by the methodological debates at the turn of the century. Today we possibly see the relativistic implications in the writings of Dilthey and the neo-Kantians out of their real proportions. In their essential aspects, Dilthey's and Windelband's methodological writings preserved the Idealistic faith in history as a meaningful process and in the possibility of objective cognition. Dilthey's attempt to write a "critique of historical reason" represented in a sense the climax of a tradition of epistemological literature, which since Humboldt's days had sharply distinguished between the methods of the historical or cultural sciences (*Geisteswissenschaften*) concerned with the understanding of the unique and individual event and the natural sciences aiming at the reduction of phenomena under general laws.[17]

16. Cf. the discussion of Sybel in Heinz-Otto Sieburg, *Deutschland und Frankreich in der Geschichtsschreibung des 19. Jahrhunderts (1848-1871)* (Wiesbaden, 1958).

17. Cf. Joachim Wach's attempt to trace this tradition in *Das Verstehen*.

Dilthey continued Droysen's efforts to defend the historical sciences against the application of the methods of the natural sciences proposed by French or British positivists, such as Comte and Mill. To be sure, he gladly took from them their rejection of metaphysics. For him, as for Comte, the history of human scientific inquiry showed man's steady emancipation from theology and philosophical speculation. In the growth of a scientific approach to the natural sciences as well as the human sciences, Dilthey saw an element of continuous progress in Western thought. He differed from Mill and Comte in considering induction and deduction to be insufficient tools of reasoning in the human sciences. "Understanding (*Verstehen*)" required a degree of intuition. But although such intuition (*Anschauung*) introduced a strongly subjective element, it did not exclude the attainment of real knowledge. Fundamental philosophic questions could indeed not be solved. The whole history of philosophy merely reflected the recurrence of three basic types of *Weltanschauung*. Any attempt to reduce reality or history to a simple formula merely reflected man's own emotions.[18] However, within the individual social sciences, once they had freed themselves from metaphysical presuppositions and questions, real knowledge was possible.

In his rare pessimistic moments, Dilthey realized the nihilistic implications of his philosophical skepticism. On his seventieth birthday he wondered gloomily whether in tracing the historical and subjective nature of all religious and philosophic ideals or systems he had not prepared the way for an "anarchy of convictions."[19] Nevertheless, Dilthey remained convinced that there was a fundamental and unified reality, Life, and that the variety of philosophic and religious views represented merely the various aspects of the richness of Life. By reducing subject and object to a common substratum, Life, Dilthey believed he had solved the apparent contradiction between his belief in the possibility of objective knowledge and the subjective origin of all cognition. Understanding was possible in the *Geisteswissenschaften* because Life "objectivated" itself in such institutions as the family, civil society, state and law, art, religion, and philosophy. As products

18. *Einleitung in die Geisteswissenschaften* in *Gesammelte Schriften* (Leipzig, 1922-1936), I, 97.
19. "Rede zum 70. Geburtstag," *ibid.*, V, 9.

of life and spirit they could be understood by the subjective mind of the cultural scientist who was also part of the life process. This reconciliation of mind and object was a return to something resembling the philosophy of identity.[20] Dilthey could thus assign to the state a role very similar to that which Hegel and Droysen had given it as an objective force. Essential for culture, it was yet free in the pursuance of its tasks from the restrictions of personal morality.[21] Whatever the pessimistic note in his remarks on his seventieth birthday, Dilthey was as deeply convinced as any of his colleagues of the meaningfulness of the historical process, the possibility of obtaining real knowledge, the rightness of the Bismarckian solution, and the future of Germany.

Nor did Windelband's famous address in 1894 on "History and Natural Sciences,"[22] in which he sharply distinguished between the nomothetic (law-giving) method of the natural sciences and the idiographic (describing the separate, distinct, individual) method of the historical sciences, introduce a new relativistic note. From an American perspective, Dilthey's and Windelband's methodological writings seemed to mark a sharp break with the nineteenth century's confidence in the possibility of scientific objectivity in the social sciences; from a German point of view their writings appear as the continuation of a tradition of thought with its roots in the early nineteenth century and before. Windelband's lectures on *The Philosophy of History*,[23] written during World War I, still reflected his deep belief that behind the variety of opinions and beliefs there stood an objective spirit which harmonized them all and guaranteed meaningful growth in history.

From the beginning of his career Ernst Troeltsch had probably been much more deeply aware than Windelband of the dilemmas inherent in the historistic position. In his lecture on the "Absolute Character of Christianity and the History of Religion" (1902), he had observed that "history is no longer merely

20. Cf. "Die Typen der Weltanschauungen und ihre Ausbildung in den metaphysischen Systemen," *ibid.*, VIII, 78 and "Der Aufbau der geschichtlichen Welt in den Geisteswissenschaften," *ibid.*, VII, 150.
21. *Ibid.*, VII, 170.
22. "Geschichte und Naturwissenschaft. Strassburger Rektoratsrede, 1894," *Präludien. Aufsätze zur Philosophie und ihrer Geschichte* (5th ed.; Tubingen, 1915), II, 136-160.
23. *Geschichtsphilosophie. Eine Kriegsvorlesung. Fragment aus dem Nachlass,* ed. Wolfgang Windelband and Bruno Bauch (Berlin, 1916).

one way of looking at things . . . but the basis of all thought about values and norms."[24] He also had recognized that whatever is historical in character must also be relative. Christianity therefore could no longer be regarded as the absolute religion but merely as one historical religion among others. Nevertheless, the history of religion did not reflect an anarchy of values. Only a limited number of higher religions have emerged, Troeltsch observed. Thus, within the course of history, higher values appeared to win out. Troeltsch stressed that history was not merely a rich multiplicity of individual events and values, which the historians arranged subjectively, but that it presented a real "objective context and process."[25] To replace the philosophy of history by epistemology and logic, as his contemporary Rickert had proposed to do, was impossible. The writing of history required the metaphysical assumption that "all of historical, individual reality in motion rests on an ultimate unity."[26] The individual perspective of the historian did not exclude his objectivity, Troeltsch observed. Humboldt, Ranke, or Hegel would have maintained the same. Behind every uniquely individual event, Troeltsch agreed with German Idealist thought, there was hidden a timeless absolute which could be intuitively approached but never reduced to an abstract concept because it represented a living reality.

Heinrich Rickert possibly saw the relativistic implications of historism for ethics more strongly than did Troeltsch. But even he was unwilling to cut the bond with the German Idealist tradition and concluded that historical values did possess an objective validity which transcended the historical situation. In defending the Idealist tradition against Karl Lamprecht's generalizing approach to history, German historians at the turn of the century liked to point to Rickert's distinction between the methods of the cultural disciplines and those of the natural sciences. Nevertheless, Rickert was the first neo-Kantian writer to doubt that history was an objective process, a basic assumption of the German Idealist philosophy of history. In contrast to a line of

24. *Die Absolutheit des Christentums und die Religionsgeschichte* (Tübingen, 1902), pp. 3-4.
25. Cf. "Über den Begriff einer historischen Dialektik, Windelband-Rickert und Hegel," *Historische Zeitschrift,* CXIX (1919), 382-383.
26. "Über Masstäbe zur Beurteilung historischer Dinge. Rede zur Kaisersgeburtstagsfeier der Berliner Universität," *Historische Zeitschrift,* CXVI (1916), 32.

thought that extended from Ranke to Meinecke, Rickert stressed that the historian no more painted a picture of reality than did the natural scientist. Rather, like the natural scientist, he reduced to concepts the flux and diversity of historical phenomena. He imposed order on the apparent chaos of historical events, not by measuring the role which these events played in an objective process of history, as Ranke or Windelband had tried to do, but by relating these events to the values which formed the core of a culture. The historian or cultural scientist related persons and objects to values (*wertbeziehen*); he could not judge the validity of these values. Still, Rickert was unwilling to draw the full consequences of his position. He agreed with Kant that the norms of ethics were universally valid and timeless. But these norms, central among which was the categorical imperative, were purely formal. They were not applicable to reality. Norms were always valid (*gelten*), never real (*wirklich*). In history man was always confronted by concrete, individual values which were not generally applicable to mankind, and man could never escape history. The logical consequences of such a position, Rickert admitted, would be nihilism, and nihilism would render meaningless all of mankind's logical thought and ethical action. But the rational nature of man's consciousness required that values be real and not merely arbitrary. In his *Limits to the Formation of Concepts in the Natural Sciences,* Rickert concluded that science and ethics were possible only if man accepted the metaphysical "conviction that there is an objective cosmic force of good (*Weltmacht des Guten*) which can never be the object of our cognition" but which nevertheless guaranteed that logical thought would arrive at logical conclusions and that ethical action would result in ethical results.[27]

Only Max Weber drew the full consequences for ethical theory inherent in Rickert's position. Like Rickert, he believed that the social scientist must study culture phenomena in terms of their value-relatedness free from his own value judgments. He agreed that the cultural sciences, because of the unique and qualitative character of their subject matter, required methods of inquiry different from those of the natural sciences. Like Rickert he

27. *Die Grenzen der naturwissenschaftlichen Begriffsbildung. Eine logische Einleitung in die historischen Wissenschaften* (Freiburg, 1896), pp. 736-738.

recognized the need of concepts, theories, and generalizations in the historical sciences, and he went considerably further than Rickert in exploring and defining the character of such general concepts.

But the thin link which still existed for Rickert between ethics and reason was cut abruptly by Weber. Two radically different worlds confront each other in Weber's essays, the irrational world of values and the rational world of cognition. Values, Weber held with Dilthey, were "never products of the progress of the empirical sciences."[28] Instead they were *Weltanschauungen* with non-rational, non-cognitive foundations. Unlike Dilthey, he no longer saw a unified cosmic reality, Life, manifesting itself in the conflicting philosophies of life. The cultural scientist could discern no deeper meaning behind the "insoluble struggle" (*unlöslichen Kampf*) of the "systems of value."[29] Norms never had real value (*gültig*), he disagreed with Rickert; they merely "were" (*seiend*).[30] No one could seriously believe any longer that "the world has a meaning."[31] Man is confronted by the ethical irrationality of the world.[32] On the other hand, in the best neo-Kantian tradition, Weber was convinced that, within limits, rational and objective cognition was possible, and he devoted the major part of his writing to formulating methods for the scientific study of social phenomena. His great contribution to the social and historical sciences doubtless was not his insistence on a value-free approach to cultural phenomena but his attempt to "introduce conceptual rigor into a tradition where either intuition or a naïve concern for the 'facts' had hitherto ruled unchallenged."[33]

28. "Die 'Objektivität' sozialwissenschaftlicher und sozialpolitischer Erkenntnis (1904)" in *Gesammelte Aufsätze zur Wissenschaftslehre* (2nd ed.; Tübingen, 1951), p. 154; cf. "'Objectivity' in Social Science and Social Policy" in *The Methodology of the Social Sciences*, trans. and ed. Edward A. Shils and Henry A. Finch (Glencoe, Ill., 1949), p. 57.

29. "Wissenschaft als Beruf," *Ges. Aufs. zur Wissenschaftslehre*, p. 587; cf. "Science as a Vocation" in *From Max Weber: Essays in Sociology*, trans. and ed. H. H. Gerth and C. Wright Mills (New York, 1946), p. 147.

30. "Der Sinn der 'Wertfreiheit' der soziologischen und okonomischen Wissenschaften" in *Ges. Aufs. zur Wissenschaftslehre*, p. 517; cf. "The Meaning of 'Ethical Neutrality' in Sociology and Economics" in *The Methodology of the Social Sciences*, p. 39.

31. "Wissenschaft als Beruf," *op. cit.*, p. 581; cf. "Science as a Vocation," *op. cit.*, p. 147.

32. "Politik als Beruf" in *Gesammelte politische Schriften* (2nd ed.; Tübingen, 1958), p. 541; cf. "Politics as a Vocation" in *From Max Weber*, p. 122.

33. H. Stuart Hughes, *Consciousness and Society: The Reorientation of European Social Thought, 1890-1930* (New York, 1958), pp. 302-303.

Historism became a problem for German historical thought only in the course of World War I. In a mild form, the new pessimism expressed itself in Friedrich Meinecke's essays between 1917 and 1922 which led to his *The Idea of Reason of State*.[34] Still profoundly believing in the basic correctness of the individualizing approach of traditional historical method and of the Bismarckian state, Meinecke nevertheless now sensed a gulf between ethics and power. Ranke's firm belief in the "victory of reason" in history was no longer tenable. The idea of the reason of state had called forth demonic forces which man could no longer control. Meinecke now felt that German Idealist philosophy had helped to unleash these forces by its optimistic interpretation of power as an ethical force.[35] The new forces of militarism, nationalism, democracy, and capitalism had radically changed power politics and revolutionized the character of war. New dams had to be constructed against power to re-establish the relation of politics to morality that had been broken in the course of the nineteenth century. The bridges to the Western conception of natural law needed to be rebuilt, Meinecke realized. Nevertheless, natural-law doctrine, he added, had failed to conceive of any organic tie between ethical ideals and the realities of political life. The only solution was to be found in the "ideas of historical individuality," held traditionally by German historians but freed from the conception of "identity." The ideal for each state had to be discovered within its own history but was not identical with it. Constant tension existed between the state's idea of its better self—he later compared this better self with a Platonic idea[36]—and its historically existing actuality. The high point of historism for him was not to be found in the realization that all values were temporal and historical, but, as he pointed out in his later *Origins of Historicism* (1936),[37] in Goethe and Ranke's intuitive

34. *Die Idee der Staatsräson in der neueren Geschichte* in *Werke*, I (München, 1957); English translation, *Macchiavellism, The Doctrine of Raison d'État and Its Place in Modern History*, trans. Douglas Scott, introduction W. Stark (New Haven, 1957). See also Walther Hofer's Introduction to the 1957 German edition and Richard W. Sterling, *Ethics in a World of Power: The Political Ideas of Friedrich Meinecke* (Princeton, 1958).
35. *Die Idee der Staatsräson*, pp. 477, 481-599.
36. *Die Entstehung des Historismus* in *Werke*, III, 602.
37. *Ibid.*, pp. 446-602.

search for the eternal idea contained within every historical individuality.

Troeltsch in his writings after 1916 saw much more sharply the dilemmas posed by historism. There was no escape from history. Instead of giving man understanding, historical study had undermined "all stable norms and ideals of human nature."[38] The historical spirit not only had shattered all ethical systems, it had undermined its own scholarly method. For how was objectivity possible if all human cognition was historically and socially conditioned?

There was no logical solution to the problems of historism, Troeltsch admitted. Historism contained within itself an insoluble logical contradiction. Yet the dilemma was only apparent, he concluded in 1916 as well as in 1922. This dilemma arose from the mistaken identification of reason with abstract norms and from the failure to realize that the concrete values held by historical societies, too, had a kind of inner logic—that the apparently irrational and spontaneous could also be an expression of rationality. The only norms man could now know were those embedded in historical cultures. The pressing problem of the age was how to find, in the face of the destruction of traditional values, a new synthesis of contemporary values. Yet, since man's judgment always was conditioned by historical and subjective factors, it would seem that his judgment would be purely non-objective. This fear could be banished, Troeltsch believed, if man had faith that at every moment of history reason manifested itself. Then in analyzing the values of culture and effecting a critical selection, valid norms could be obtained. The fear of subjectivism was banned if it was assumed that the historian as well as the object of his study were part of a great divine process and that the great value systems of history were revelations of divine truth. "Timeless, eternal, universally valid and absolute values" may be unattainable, but not objective norms.[39]

These objective norms, Troeltsch thought, could be discovered through an analysis of European culture. Human history was

38. "Das neunzehnte Jahrhundert" in *Gesammelte Schriften* (Tübingen, 1912-1925), IV, 628.
39. Cf. "Über Masstäbe...," *op. cit.*, p. 27; *Der Historismus und seine Probleme. Erstes Buch: Das logische Problem der Geschichtsphilosophie* in *Gesammelte Schriften*, III, 166.

beyond human ken because mankind was not a unit. The most comprehensive unity of meaning being a culture, there could only be histories of individual cultures, such as that of Western civilization. Historical study had destroyed the traditional values of the past by showing their genetic character. Historical study, Troeltsch asserted confidently, could now restore belief by creating a "cultural synthesis" of the best in the European tradition.[40]

The step from Troeltsch to Spengler was not great. Many of the basic concepts of Spengler's *Decline of the West* occurred in Troeltsch: the conception of cultures as closed, integrated systems, the relatedness of all values to a culture, the inability of man to transcend the truths and values of his culture, the denial of the existence of one human history. But the spirit was radically different. With the loss of the German Idealist belief in a fundamental unity of all existence, historism had now become a form of radical relativism. For Troeltsch, Western civilization always had been more than merely one of many cultures. It reflected divine reason and in a sense represented the highest achievement of the human mind. In the end, the history of the European world was still as closely identical for Troeltsch with that of man as it had been for Ranke a hundred years before. For Spengler this history now became man's fate: a world to which man was irrevocably bound, which came into life and would expire like the countless stars in the Copernican universe, a natural event without an ultimate meaning. With God's death, the last common bonds of humanity were shattered. "Faustian" or European man was no more capable of understanding Hellenic or Sinic mathematics or science than he was their art or religion.

To Troeltsch, Spengler's book, in sacrificing the rational and scholarly ideals of the West, seemed an invitation to return to barbarism and was itself an "active contribution to the decline of the West."[41] Nevertheless, Troeltsch's cumbersome *Historism and Its Problems* was read by few; Spengler's *Decline of the West* became a bible and source of inspiration for tens of thousands of educated middle-class Germans in a period of bewilderment.

40. "Über Masstäbe . . . ," *op. cit.*, pp. 45-46; and chap. iv in *Der Historismus und seine Probleme.*
41. Troeltsch's review of Spengler's *Der Untergang des Abendlandes* in *Gesammelte Schriften*, IV, 684.

In a less extreme way, these rational and scholarly ideals of the West were now being sacrificed by a broad current of irrationalist literature. As Karl Heussi noted in 1932 in *The Crisis of Historism,*[42] the great change which had taken place in German historical thought after World War I had been the loss of faith in the possibility of an objective study of history. Even a man as deeply influenced by Marx as Karl Mannheim denied the possibility of an objective method for the social sciences. Weber had recognized the irrationality of values but was convinced that logic and scientific method were one and universal.[43] Mannheim now denied the universality of method. Thought itself did not proceed deductively but rather expressed "unreflected life," he agreed with the vitalists. The categories of reason themselves were not eternal but subject to change. What prevented Mannheim from despairing about the scientific enterprise was his firm belief, inherited from German Idealism, in the "mysterious (*geheime*) relationship of thought and reality and the essential (*wesenhafte*) identity of subject and object." Rejecting the reduction of living historical reality to logical relationships, Mannheim nevertheless also condemned the irrationalist insistence that nothing existed except isolated human epochs. For Mannheim, like Troeltsch, remained convinced that history was a meaningful process; hence, the subjective cognitions of the historian or social scientist contained objective, even if one-sided or perspectivistic, views of truth, because he himself was part of the great process.[44]

Mannheim, with his interest in the role played by social and economic factors in history, stood outside the main tradition of German historical thought. Much more decisive in forming scholarly opinion in the 1920's were men like Eduard Spranger[45] and especially Erich Rothacker, who applied the concepts of *Lebensphilosophie* to the social sciences. Rothacker in his *Introduction to the Geisteswissenschaften* (1920) and his *Logic and*

42. *Die Krisis des Historismus* (Tübingen, 1932).
43. "Die 'Objektivität'...," *op. cit.,* p. 155; cf. *The Methodology of the Social Sciences,* p. 58.
44. "Historismus," *Archiv für Sozialwissenschaft und Sozialpolitik,* LII (1924), 1-60.
45. "Kulturzyklentheorie und das Problem des Kulturzerfalls," *Geisteskultur,* XXXVIII (1929), 65-90.

Systematics in the Geisteswissenschaften (1927)[46] set out to "re-approach the problems" raised by Dilthey. Every methodological controversy, Rothacker asserted, was a philosophical one. Every methodological position was determined by a *weltanschauliche* position. Hence, opponents in a scientific controversy, at least in the social sciences, could no more convince each other than opponents in a philosophic quarrel. Social science had to restrict itself to classifying theories of sociological or of historical explanation in terms of the three basic types of *Weltanschauungen* suggested by Dilthey. Dilthey at one point or another also had implied that the choice of methods was determined by prior philosophic orientation, yet his primary concern had been with the methods of philosophical speculation, not of scientific inquiry. In a sense, Dilthey stood much closer to Auguste Comte and the positivists than Rothacker wished to admit. For Dilthey thought that once it was accepted that the answers to all metaphysical questions reflected the philosophy of life (*Weltanschauung*) of the speculative thinker rather than the demands of logic, the methods of the individual human social sciences could be formulated and these fields of study raised to a scientific level.

Dilthey still had assumed, as Ranke earlier and Troeltsch later, that the subject matter of history had real existence and structure. This faith now was shattered and with it the belief in real continuous development central to classical German historical thought. For Rothacker, in contrast to Dilthey, the philosophy of life which colored and shaped man's methodological position had little to do with cognition. Every philosophy of life, and hence every so-called scientific picture of human and social reality, was an act of will and of creation. History, Rothacker stressed in arguing against Spengler's fatalism, involved constant creativity by individuals. And these acts of creativity were not governed by a general logic but were concrete, specific, and individual.[47] The individual was obliged to choose whenever he acted, and every choice was subjective and one-sided. However, Rothacker and Mannheim were saved from despair about man's intellectual

46. *Einleitung in die Geisteswissenschaften* (Tübingen, 1920); *Logik und Systematik der Geisteswissenschaften* (München, 1926).
47. *Logik und Systematik der Geisteswissenschaften.*

enterprise by their continuing idealistic faith in the ultimate identity of subjectivity and world.

But the idea of freedom developed by Rothacker could be carried further, if one assumed that every individual, constantly confronted by choices in concrete historical situations, had neither abstract reason nor tradition to guide him. It was not surprising that a generation which never had had faith in the ultimate rationality of man or the universe should after the catastrophes of the age lose its faith in history and tradition as well. This loss of faith occurred among the writers of the 1920's such as the political scientist Carl Schmitt, the writer Ernst Jünger, and the philosopher Martin Heidegger, who in current German writings have been labeled "political Decisionists."[48] For Jünger and Schmitt nothing was left but life, and life knew nothing but movement and action. Morality and civilization were for Jünger merely ways in which spirit committed treason against life. The only value that remained was struggle. On the political scene, those healthy forces which still accepted struggle, the soldier and the revolutionary worker, needed to merge to preserve the vitality of life. Indeed, Prussianism and Bolshevism were kindred movements, Jünger held. They alone might still regenerate life.

Historism as a theory had now arrived at its logical conclusion. If all truths and value judgments were individual and historical, then no place was left for any fixed point in history, neither for forces of History in Rothacker's sense nor for Life in Dilthey's. All that remained was the subjective individual.

The concept of *Geschichtlichkeit* (historicity) which began to dominate German philosophic discussion after the appearance of Heidegger's *Being and Time*[49] marked the negation of classical historism. As a doctrine, *Geschichtlichkeit* assumed—as did historism—that man had no nature but only a history. But it rejected the idea that man existed in history as an objective process and rather saw history as an inseparable aspect of man. It would be difficult to recapitulate the basic arguments of this fundamental work of German *Existenzphilosophie,* which at many

48. Cf. Christian Graf von Krockow, *Die Entscheidung. Eine Untersuchung über Ernst Jünger, Carl Schmitt, Martin Heidegger* (Stuttgart, 1958).
49. *Sein und Zeit* (6th ed.; Tübingen, 1949), Part I. Part I was first published in 1927; a second part never appeared.

points are open to conflicting interpretations. Nevertheless, the hard world of real, objective Being seemed to have dissolved. Man for Heidegger had no essence but only an existence. This existence found him placed in a Being-Here (*Dasein*), in which he was constantly confronted by decisions. A characteristic of human existence was the reality of death. Conscious of the finitude of his existence that leads to death, man was filled by care (*Sorge*) and anguish (*Angst*), which forced him constantly to define himself. Yet there were no objective values to which man could orient. Man was radically free and in his freedom had to make decisions. These decisions always involved choice and creativity, a choice within the framework of the concrete possibilities of the situation (*Lage*). In this situation, man was confronted by a heritage which contained not one history but the "possibility of various histories." The individual created his history not on the basis of the objective happenings of the past but by his decisions directed toward the future. Historism now had reached the end of its road. The last eternal values and meanings had dissolved. All that was left was historical, temporal, and relative. Even God had died and History had yielded to Historicity (*Geschichtlichkeit*) and Temporality (*Zeitlichkeit*), the basic human condition of never being able to transcend time. Constant in the flow of time were only the conditions of human existence, and these no longer possessed any content (*Gehalt*), but merely a structure of form (*Gestalt*).

A process that had begun with the philosophic discussion of the neo-Kantians was now completed. Dilthey, Windelband, Rickert, Weber, and Troeltsch had all recognized the relativistic implications of German historism for ethics and epistemology. All of them except Weber had attempted to avoid the logical conclusions involved in their positions by clinging to the optimistic view of history implicit in the German Idealist doctrine of Identity. Even Weber, who courageously faced the ethical meaninglessness of the world, remained committed to the Bismarckian state and its power-political interests. The impact of World War I had shattered these illusions. Men like Troeltsch and Meinecke attempted to salvage whatever possible from the ruins of the historistic faith. For more radical thinkers like Speng-

ler, Heidegger, Jünger, and Schmitt, the historicity of men spelled
the anarchy of values. For them the break with the humanistic
values of Western civilization, from which the classical tradition
of German Idealism had never completely divorced itself, was now
complete.

III

The break with political and historiographical traditions was
much deeper and more real after 1945 than it had been after 1918.
Expressive of this reorientation is the role which the concern with
the "break" has played in the writings of contemporary German
historians. The historian of Rome Alfred Heuss entitled a recent
book sold as a paperback the *Loss of History*. History has remained as a scholarly discipline, he observed sadly; as a living
memory it has been lost.[50] As conservative a historian as Reinhard
Wittram admitted that "historiography (*Historie*) has taken the
place of tradition."[51] All philosophers, sociologists, and historians
who have attempted to assess the German present since 1945,
Wittram notes, have become convinced "that a turn has taken
place which can be compared only to the greatest upheavals
known in history."[52] Hermann Heimpel, the well-known medievalist and director of the Max Planck Institute for History in
Göttingen, confesses that Germans have become thoroughly alienated from their past. And this alienation has had its good sides,
he believes, in putting an end to naïve historism.[53] Theodor
Schieder, the present editor of the *Historische Zeitschrift,* speaks
also for other social historians such as Fritz Wagner at Marburg
or Werner Conze at Heidelberg when he stresses the role of discontinuity as a major aspect of all history. The nature of the
break was complex. To an extent Germany shared its loss of traditions and historical consciousness with the rest of Europe. Particularly the new school of social historians stressed the radical
rupture which had taken place in the Western world with the
emergence of a technological mass society. The abyss separating

50. *Verlust der Geschichte* (Göttingen, 1959).
51. *Das Interesse an der Geschichte* (Göttingen, 1959), p. 97.
52. *Ibid.,* p. 95.
53. "Gegenwartsaufgaben der Geschichtswissenschaft" in *Kapitulation vor der
Geschichte?* (Göttingen, 1956), pp. 54-55.

the present from the past, Schieder observes, has widened since Burckhardt and Tocqueville first observed it. The very structure of history has changed. In the contemporary world the "present has run away from the past." The historical consciousness of modern industrial society "builds on discontinuity."[54] But for Schieder, as for almost all historians who critically observed postwar German realities, the gulf was even deeper in Germany than in the West, in part because of the terrible aberrations of the period 1933 to 1945, in part because of the failure of German historiography and historical thought until 1945 to take into account the great socio-economic transformations of the nineteenth and twentieth centuries as broad currents of French, American, and British historiography and social philosophy had done.

This consciousness of a rupture introduced a re-examination of German intellectual, political, and historiographical traditions which had not been possible after 1918. The German national orientation, the emphasis on political history, and the German Idealist tradition all became questionable now to such an extent that Gerhard Ritter bitterly complained in a review of Fritz Fischer's recent book on German war aims in World War I that an "increasingly one-sided self-deprecation has replaced the former self-deification in German historical consciousness."[55]

Nevertheless the break with the older patterns of thought was by no means complete. Men like Theodor Litt, who had consistently opposed the Nazis, and Erich Rothacker, who had not, continued to defend the German Idealist conception of history. The events of the Nazi years and World War II seemed to have had little effect on their historical thought. Eduard Spranger's piece in the *Historische Zeitschrift* on "The Task of

54. "Grundfragen der neueren deutschen Geschichte," *Historische Zeitschrift,* CXII (1961), 4; cf. "Erneuerung des Geschichtsbewusstseins" in *Staat und Gesellschaft im Wandel unserer Zeit* (München, 1958), 188-207; cf. Werner Conze, "Die Strukturgeschichte des technisch-industriellen Zeitalters für Forschung und Unterricht" in *Arbeitsgemeinschaft für Forschung des Landes Nordrhein-Westfalen. Geisteswissenschaften, Heft 66* (Cologne, 1957); cf. Fritz Wagner, "Begegnung von Geschichte und Soziologie bei der Deutung der Gegenwart," *Historische Zeitschrift,* CXCII (1961), 607-624; also "Rankes Geschichtsbild und die moderne Universalhistorie," *Archiv für Kulturgeschichte,* XLIV (1962), 1-26, and *Moderne Geschichtsschreibung. Ausblick auf eine Philosophie der Geschichtswissenschaft* (Berlin, 1960). The last title acquaints Germans with trends in French, American, and British social history.

55. "Eine neue Kriegsschuldthese? Zu Fritz Fischers Buch *Griff nach der Weltmacht,*" *Historische Zeitschrift,* CXCIV (1962), 668.

the Historian" consciously borrowed the title of Humboldt's classical essay. Once more Spranger defined the tasks of the historians in terms reminiscent of Humboldt and Ranke. The historian was to grasp intuitively the meaning, the spirit, hidden behind the collective formations of events and institutions. Each institution, from the family upward, represented an idea, and although the historian always was limited in his perspective by his vantage point in history, he nevertheless could gather from the fragments which absorbed him something of the meaning of these supra-individual entities.[56] More aggressively, the aged Litt in a series of writings engaged the "opponents of historism" and called in the *Historische Zeitschrift* for the "reawakening of historical awareness." He once more defended the historicity of all values. History was not devoid of meaning. Within every "concrete situation" there were to be found the values which fitted the specific individual. The Ought was never universal but always unique. Historism had been accused of ignoring the search for the essence of human nature. But man had no stable nature; his nature was in constant growth and consisted in his historicity *(Geschichtlichkeit)*. "It is indeed exactly this, the fact that man's character is not shaped by nature, that distinguishes him from all sub-human nature."[57] Erich Rothacker once more in 1954 presented in systematic form his contention that all thought was related to *Weltanschauungen,* and that all *Weltanschauungen* were functions of life. Thought always required dogmatic expressions and since all truths and values outside the realms of strict logic or pure facts always involved a creative response to a life situation, there were as many truths and values as there were great styles of life. "The problems of historism are the simple result of the simple fact that there are distinct cultural systems with distinct dogmas explaining these systems."[58] What prevented

56. "Aufgaben des Geschichtsschreibers," *Historische Zeitschrift,* CLXXIV (1952), 251-268.

57. *Die Wiedererweckung des geschichtlichen Bewusstseins* (Heidelberg, 1956), p. 79; cf. *Wege und Irrwege des geschichtlichen Denkens* (München, 1948), *Die Frage nach dem Sinn der Geschichte* (München, 1948), *Geschichtswissenschaft und Geschichtsphilosophie* (München, 1950).

58. "Die dogmatische Denkform in den Geisteswissenschaften und das problem des Historismus," Akademie der Wissenschaften und der Literatur in Mainz, *Abhandlungen geistes- und sozial-wissenschaftlicher Klasse* (1954), No. 6 (Wiesbaden, 1954), p. 32; cf. his brief autobiography in *Philosophen-Lexikon* (Berlin, 1950), II, 375-382.

Spranger or Litt, or probably even Rothacker, from assuming that all values and cognitions were purely arbitrary and subjective was their belief that a radical distinction between the subject and the object of history did not exist—a point re-emphasized in the recent important work by Hans-Georg Gadamer on hermeneutics, *Truth and Method*.[59] The historian himself was a part of the historical process. This gave his observations, no matter how subjectivistic, an element of objectivity. There were no universal values. The only truth was that of the "absolute historicity of existence." Even more radical, of course, was Heidegger's position. Although many intellectuals believed that Heidegger had rendered valuable services to the Nazis—before 1933 by his subjectivistic approach to ethics and history, after the advent of Hitler in his capacity as rector of the University of Freiburg—Heidegger's concept of *Geschichtlichkeit* continued to dominate German philosophic thought on history.[60]

The stress on the relativity of all values and the role of *Weltanschauungen* in historiography was still strongly reflected in the writings of Walther Hofer, a young historian, born only in 1920, a Swiss who taught at the Free University of Berlin until his return to a chair in Switzerland in 1960. Hofer too is convinced of the "historicity of all human cognition." Nevertheless, Hofer no longer believes that values are found within history. Man always approaches history with his subjective values. This in a sense is Heidegger's position, with the exception that the values for which Hofer decides are those of the democratic, humanistic West. Objectivity in approach is possible, according to Hofer, but to attain it historians must take into account the role

59. *Wahrheit und Methode* (Tübingen, 1960); cf. "Hermeneutik und Historismus" in *Philosophische Rundschau*, IX (1961-62), 241-276; the article "Geschichtlichkeit" in *Religion in Geschichte und Gegenwart*, II (1958), 1497-1498. The *Historische Zeitschrift* contained a long review article by H. Kuhn on *Wahrheit und Methode*, see "Wahrheit und geschichtliches Verstehen. Bemerkungen zu H.G. Gadamers philosophischer Hermeneutik," CXCIII (1961), 376-389. Other discussions of the concept *Geschichtlichkeit* occurred in Gerhart Bauer, *"Geschichtlichkeit": Wege und Irrwege eines Begriffs* (Berlin, 1963); Hermann Noack, "Probleme der Geschichtlichkeit," *Studium Generale*, XV (1962), 373-389; August Brunner, *Geschichtlichkeit* (Bern, 1961) which questions the absolute historicity of values and truths and Walther Brühning, *Geschichtsphilosophie* (Stuttgart, 1961).

60. Heidegger himself apparently modified his earlier philosophic position. Some of his disciples began to speak of a "turn" (*Wende*) in his thought after World War II from his radically existentialist position in *Being and Time* to the recognition of the reality of an essence transcending the existing individual. Cf. Krockow, *op. cit.*, chap. iii.

played by their biases. Bias or subjective interest must never determine the results of the historian's inquiries; it always determines the formulation of the problems of inquiry. Despite his admiration for Meinecke, to whom he devoted his first important work, Hofer insists that the historian never gains meaning from the study of the subject matter of history but must always approach history with a previously formulated conception of history. And this is, indeed, what the great historians in the *Historismus* tradition did. Ranke and the historians who followed in his tradition were never opposed to philosophy, Hofer argues. They applied philosophic categories and political values to history. Without such concepts their historical writings would have remained chronicles. No longer does "the man who thinks want to know merely what really happened (*wie es eigentlich gewesen*)," Hofer decides, "but what is to become of him and of his history."[61] History always has sought "to throw light on our existence (*Existenzerhellung*)" and thus always has reflected the concerns of the present. Human knowledge is always limited and perspectivistic. But this very limitation, Hofer thinks, could be overcome to some extent if man did not restrict himself to national history but attempted to attain a degree of objectivity through broad studies of universal scope.[62]

Hofer still believed in the historicity of all values. However, historism had become untenable for him. It assumed that values could be discovered through historical study. The concept of *Geschichtlichkeit*, as understood by Heidegger and in a modified form by Hofer, implied that man carried his values to history, but that these subjective values were themselves won in historical situations. Now, however, for the first time since the Enlightenment, important German thinkers began to challenge the historistic position and attempted to go back to something resembling natural law, namely to the belief that there were certain perennial human values that derived from the nature of man.

61. *Geschichte zwischen Philosophie und Politik. Studien zur Problematik des modernen Geschichtsdenkens* (Basel, 1956), p. 10; cf. "Geschichte und Politik," *Historische Zeitschrift*, CLXXIV (1952), 287-306; *Geschichtsschreibung und Weltanschauung. Betrachtungen zum Werk Friedrich Meineckes* (München, 1950). In addition to his studies of historicism, Hofer had made important contributions to the study of Nazism and the origins of Second World War; cf. his *Die Entfesselung des 2. Weltkrieges* (Stuttgart, 1950).
62. Cf. "Geschichte und Politik," *op. cit.*

The philosopher Gerhard Krüger opened the attack on the historists as well as on Heidegger in two highly controversial essays written shortly after the collapse of the Third Reich. History, as the sphere of human freedom and creativity, reflects the anarchy of values and opinions, Krüger argued. But there have been perennial human traditions which have not been broken by the catastrophes or social transformations of our time, the appeal to "reason and common sense, patriotism and concern for the common good, loyalty, humaneness, freedom and truth." More important than the question of what was is the question of "what ought to be and what always is, the old Platonic question about goodness and justice and about the constant ideal form of things. . . . Lasting truth is more important than our changing fate." This for Krüger assumes an objective order of things, an objective physical as well as moral world. "This is to say that things are not as we view and judge them but as they are themselves (an sich selbst)."[63]

Karl Löwith argues along similar lines. He too stresses that history is an objective, "dynamic process, independent of all written history."[64] But within history we can discover no meaning. "History, too, is meaningful only by indicating some transcendent purpose beyond the actual facts," he wrote in Meaning in History, a book first published in English before his return from exile which later became a paperback best seller in Germany.[65] Like Krüger, Löwith believes that modern man can learn from the Greek conception of history. The Greeks viewed history as a sphere of the irrational, devoid of ultimate meaning. For meaning, one had to turn to nature. Jews and Christians basically misunderstood the character of history when they saw it primarily as the history of salvation. In a secularized form, this faith in the meaningfulness of history had survived in the idea of progress and in historism. Today man must free his "conception of world history from its theological origins and regain a natural concept of the world. This concept must be based not on the nature of the natural sciences, but directly on nature herself as the measure

63. "Die Geschichte im Denken der Gegenwart" in Wissenschaft und Gegenwart, No. 16 (Frankfurt, 1947); cf. Geschichte und Tradition (Stuttgart, 1948).
64. "Die Dynamik der Geschichte und der Historismus," Eranos-Jahrbuch, XXI (1952), 252.
65. Chicago, 1949, p. 5.

of all that is natural."[66] In a similar vein, Leo Strauss, a refugee
from Nazism who did not return to Germany from exile in the
United States but whose writings have attracted more attention
in their German translations than in the United States, defends
natural law against historism. "To the unbiased historian," he
argues in *Natural Right and History*, " 'the historical process'
revealed itself as the meaningless web spun by what men did, produced and thought by nothing more than unmitigated chance—a
tale told by an idiot."[67] What remained constant was nature and
human nature, truth and justice. Far from legitimizing the historicist inference that all values are bound by a historical situation, he holds that history "seems rather to prove that all human
thought, and certainly all philosophic thought, is concerned with
the same fundamental themes or the same fundamental problems,
and therefore that there exists an unchanged framework which
persists in all changes of human knowledge of both facts and
principles. . . . If the fundamental problems persist in all historical change, human thought is capable of transcending its historical
limitations or of grasping something transhistorical."[68]

   Although Krüger's, Löwith's, and Strauss's desire to return to
the Greek models of natural law may represent a somewhat extreme form of anti-historism, a broad group of historians and
social thinkers now appear to share in the belief that there are
basic characteristics common to all men and that from this common human nature there derives a common morality by which
historical institutions may be judged. Karl Ludwig Rintelen in
a recent article saw the great contribution of historism in its
recognition of individuality and development, its great error in
the identification of historical individuality with value. Since the
appearance of the great prophets in East and West more than
two thousand years ago, he agreed with Jaspers, mankind has been
in accord on certain norms such as "moderation, the desire for
peace, willingness to help one's neighbors, readiness to compromise, freedom, and humaneness." These norms have formed the
core of natural law as well as of Christian ethics. The historian
must keep his sense of individuality but combine it with judg-

66. "Die Dynamik der Geschichte . . . ," *op. cit.,* p. 247.
67. Chicago, 1953, p. 18.   68. *Ibid.,* pp. 23-24.

ment in terms of this common human morality. In their treatment of contemporary history (*Zeitgeschichte*), German historians have increasingly come to such a position, Rintelen thinks. Friedrich Meinecke, Hans Herzfeld, K. D. Bracher, Walther Hofer, Hans Rothfels, Theodor Eschenburg, and Ludwig Dehio are among the historians who in Rintelen's opinion have effected this synthesis between historism and natural law.[69] Most of these historians had contributed to the publications of the Institute for Contemporary History (*Zeitgeschichte*) and its quarterly, the *Vierteljahrshefte für Zeitgeschichte*, perhaps the most important journal for the study of the Nazi past. Robert Koehl, an American historian of contemporary Germany, in a recent article on the Institute, arrived at an assessment of those men which resembled Rintelen's. "Relativism and positivism, history as myth and history as propaganda, have all become so identified for Institute writers with the totalitarian *Weltanschauung*," Koehl wrote, "that they have sought in the roots of their traditions the basis for a sounder scholarship. They seem to have found a threefold foundation in (1) the Christian ethic of responsibility, (2) the classical universality of the *Aufklärung*, and (3) the critical empiricism of scientific history."[70]

Closely bound with the rediscovery of the universally human element in history is the re-emergence of the belief in one human history which was so unpopular in the period after World War I. "We proceed upon the assumption that there is a history of man or of mankind," Golo Mann writes in the *Propyläen World History*, and this history is not merely "the history of individual cultures which are completely separate from each other."[71] Not that Mann can accept the grandiose conception of human history as a unified process which Karl Jaspers portrayed in his postwar

69. "Historismus und Naturrecht," *Geschichte und Wissenschaft*, XII (1961), 353-381.
70. "Zeitgeschichte and the New German Conservatism," *Journal of Central European Affairs*, XX (1960), p. 156. Cf. Hans Mommsen, "Politische Wissenschaft und Geschichtswissenschaft," *Vierteljahrshefte für Zeitgeschichte*, X (1962), 341-372.
71. "Einleitung," *Propyläen-Weltgeschichte* (Frankfurt, 1960-), VIII, 14. In striking contrast to the historicist position that man has no nature but only a history stand the three lengthy introductory essays to the new ten-volume *Propyläen World History*. Man's "intrahuman structure" cannot be perceived from a history of evolution, Alfred Heuss observes in the introduction to the first volume (p. 19). Through more than fifty pages, the philosopher Helmuth Plessner searches for the "*Conditio Humana*," the specific, constant human element which appears in all historical change (*ibid.*, I, 33-86).

The Origin and Goal of History.[72]   The idea of progress is dead,
Mann emphasizes. History does not contain a simple, easily de-
finable direction.   But the fact that it is human history gives it
meaning. Nevertheless, there have been advances toward the attainment of "slightly more" individual liberty and prosperity.
But these gains have always been threatened by the destructive
aspects of unchangeable human nature. Mann quotes Kant that
man has become civilized much more rapidly than he has become
moralized. He must find a transcendent belief that will give logical urgency to his "belief in mankind and human decency." If
not, his civilizational and technical progress may well end in disaster.[73] That history has now become world history, few historians
will still doubt, although Theodor Schieder asks the pertinent
question whether this world history can be projected in the past,[74]
and Reinhold Wittram wonders "whether apart from pale generalities, there really can be found anything that Neanderthal
man had in common with Goethe."[75]

The concern with world history has led historians away from
the concern with the individual culture or state to comparative
studies and the search for the typical.   Max Weber and Otto
Hintze already had pointed in this direction before.   If once historians had emphasized the distinction between the "generalizing"
methods of the natural scientist and the "individualizing" approach of the historian, with few exceptions they now were convinced that generalizations played an essential role in historio-

---

72. *Vom Ursprung und Ziel der Geschichte* (Zürich, 1949); English translation
(New Haven, 1953).

73. "Schlussbetrachtungen," *Propyläen-Weltgeschichte*, X, 623-625.

74. "Grundfragen der neueren deutschen Geschichte," *Historische Zeitschrift*,
CXCII (1961), p. 3.

75. "Das Faktum und der Mensch," *Historische Zeitschrift*, CLXXXV (1958),
68. The interest in world history has found expression in the journal, *Saeculum.
Jahrbuch für Universalgeschichte*, founded in 1950, and edited by Oskar Köhler.
One of the co-editors, Joseph Vogt, professor of ancient history at Tübingen, recently published the paperback, *Wege zum historischen Universum: Von Ranke bis
Toynbee* (Stuttgart, 1961). Othmar Anderle, formerly at the Institute for European History in Mainz, has founded an Institute for Theoretical History at Salz-
burg. Strongly influenced by Spengler when he contributed to the *Zeitschrift für
Geopolitik* in the 1930's, Anderle became a disciple of Toynbee in the postwar
period. His institute and the International Society for the Comparative Study of
Civilizations is dedicated not merely to the comparative study of institutions but
to the propagation of the view that a morphology of history is possible, that
there are self-contained civilizations, and that Russia represents a civilization distinct
from the Christian West, a position which contains strong political undertones.
Pieter Geyl strongly criticized Anderle in "Othmar F. Anderle, Unreason as a Doctrine" in his *Encounters in History* (Cleveland, 1961), pp. 328-330.

graphy. Even Gerhard Ritter, himself a part of the classical German tradition, told the German historians in 1949 at their first national convention since the war that "after all, both the typical and the unique can be found in historical reality."[76] History is concerned not always with the individual but also with the typical, Hermann Heimpel writes. In studying what man *was*, the historian grapples with the problem of what man *is*.[77] No matter how we comprehend historical individuality, Theodor Schieder observes, we cannot dispense with generalizations. "Consciously or unconsciously the way we look at individualities is determined in part by our images of types."[78] Max Weber's concept of the "ideal type" is taken seriously by social historians as a means of bridging the gulf between the individualizing method of the historian and the generalizing approach of the scientist which Rickert had considered to be unbridgeable.[79]

The new concern with the typical and with social history all strengthen the revival of interest in Jakob Burckhardt. Burckhardt's words of warning increased this appeal. Meinecke in his now famous 1948 address before the German Academy of Sciences wondered "whether, in the end, Burckhardt will not have greater importance than Ranke for us as well as for later historians."[80] But for many social historians, Burckhardt's conception of cultural history already seems too narrow in the mass technological age of the mid-twentieth century. "If we confront Ranke and Burckhardt as Meinecke last attempted to do," Fritz Wagner writes in 1962, "we shall not get beyond a narrow—we might call it an aristocratic—conception of culture. . . . Men who, like Ranke and Burckhardt, moved in the higher spheres of creative individual achievements and belonged to the small groups of Europeans engaged in exemplary action could hardly be expected to join in the realm of the anonymous millions of the remaining population of the earth who, so to speak, formed the dregs of hierarchically

76. "Gegenwärtige Lage und Zukunftsaufgaben deutscher Geschichtsschreibung," *Historische Zeitschrift*, CLXX (1950), 9.
77. "Gegenwartsaufgaben der Geschichtswissenschaft," *op. cit.*, p. 63.
78. "Der Typus in der Geschichtswissenschaft" in *Staat und Gesellschaft im Wandel unserer Zeit* (München, 1958), p. 172.
79. Cf. Werner Conze, "Die Strukturgeschichte . . . ," *op. cit.*, p. 18.
80. "Ranke und Burckhardt," Deutsche Akademie der Wissenschaften zu Berlin, *Vorträge und Schriften*, Heft 27 (Berlin, 1948); English translation in *German History: Some New German Views*, ed. Hans Kohn (Boston, 1954), pp. 141-156.

arrayed world history."[81]   For Wagner and others, German historians too long had neglected social and economic history at the expense of political and intellectual history.

Turning to their own past, German historians began to reassess their own national history. They were in virtually unanimous agreement that something had gone wrong, although they differed widely on what it was and the extent to which traditional interpretations of German history needed to be revised. Interestingly enough, those least critical of German traditions were a group of eminent historians of the older generation, Gerhard Ritter, Hans Rothfels, Hans Herzfeld, and the venerable Friedrich Meinecke (d. 1954), who had all been opponents of Nazism and in Rothfels' and Herzfeld's cases had been victims of Nazi persecution. Meinecke had implied in the *German Catastrophe* that the rise of the Nazis in 1933 had been in large part the result of "something like chance" rather than of "pressing political or historical necessity."[82] The breakdown of German Idealism among the German middle classes had facilitated the rise of modern totalitarianism.[83] Gerhard Ritter agreed with Meinecke that Nazism was a European phenomenon of the twentieth century, not primarily an outcome of peculiarly German traditions. Its intellectual sources lay in the French Revolution; its forerunners were Robespierre and Napoleon III, not Frederick the Great and Bismarck.[84] Bismarck continued for these historians to be relatively free of blemish, a diplomat of the old school, a great European, the preserver of peace. Basically they did not question Bismarck's solution of the German question.   On the other hand, Ritter recognized that the idealistic liberalism peculiar to Germany before the 1848 Revolution in its recognition of "moral responsibility . . . and service to the community" represented a true conception of individual liberty.[85]   Also, he realized that something went radically wrong in German history.   His latest

81. "Rankes Geschichtsbild und die moderne Universalhistorie," *Archiv für Kulturgeschichte,* XLIV (1962), pp. 6-7.
82. Cf. Friedrich Meinecke, *Die deutsche Katastrophe. Betrachtungen und Erinnerungen* (Wiesbaden, 1946), p. 95; translated as *The German Catastrophe* (trans. Sidney B. Fay, Cambridge, 1950), p. 63.
83. Cf. *ibid.,* ch. ii.
84. Cf. "The Fault of Mass Democracy," in *The Nazi Revolution,* ed. John Snell (Boston, 1959), pp. 76-89; cf. Andreas Dorpalen, "Historiography as History: The Work of Gerhard Ritter," *Journal of Modern History,* XXXIV (1962), 1-18.
85. *Staatskunst und Kriegshandwerk* (München, 1954-); three volumes have appeared so far.

monumental work, *Statecraft and the Art of War: The Problem of "Militarism" in Germany*, is dedicated to the problem of why it was that the "German people, for centuries one of the western nations most disposed to peace, should have become the terror of Europe and the world, hailing as their leader an adventurer who will go down in history as the destroyer of the old European order." In no European country, Ritter admits, was the supremacy of the civilian government so undermined by the military as in Germany, a development which had some roots in the past but matured only after 1890.[86]

Much less charitable about the German past than Ritter is Ludwig Dehio, the first postwar editor of the *Historische Zeitschrift*, and like his contemporary Ritter a man who grew up in the old historiographical tradition. Germany's fate in the late nineteenth and the twentieth century was "typical" of all hegemonic powers driven to expansion and catastrophe by the demoniac character of power. But aside from this "typical" condition inherent in the nature of power rather than in the German character, there was also a "uniquely" German, or rather Prussian, element which contributed to the terror of the German threat. Dehio did not believe that Frederick the Great and Bismarck were the direct ancestors of Hitler, but he did think that there was a line of continuity, that "old Prussian" ways of thinking about power dominated German political thought in the twentieth century and merged with new German ambitions in a particularly explosive mixture.[87] More important perhaps than these striking interpretations is the great number of less ambitious studies of the German past and German traditions undertaken by a host of younger scholars. There is little unanimity to be found among these writings, which include those of apologists of the past such as Walter Hubatsch[88] and critics as bitter as Fritz Fischer.[89]

86. *Ibid.*, I, 23.
87. "Preussisch-deutsche Geschichte, 1640-1945. Dauer im Wechsel," *Das Parlament*, Beilage, Jan. 18, 1961, pp. 25-31; cf. "Deutschland und die Epoche der Weltkriege," *Historische Zeitschrift*, CLXXIII (1952), 77-94.
88. Cf., e.g., *Das Problem der Staatsräson bei Friedrich dem Grossen* (Göttingen, 1956); *"Weserübung;" die deutsche Besetzung von Dänemark und Norwegen* (Göttingen, 1960); *Germany and the Central Powers in the World War 1914-1918*, ed. Oswald P. Backus (Lawrence, 1962), translated from *Handbuch der deutschen Geschichte*, IV, Part II (Koblenz, 1955); *Hohenzollern in der Geschichte* (Frankfurt a/M, 1961).
89. *Griff nach der Weltmacht. Die Kriegszielpolitik des kaiserlichen Deutschlands* (Düsseldorf, 1961). Interesting is also the new interest shown in the history of German liberalism, either in the examination of what went wrong, as in F.

Nevertheless, these studies indicate that the German past has become highly problematic.

The re-examination of the German past also has led to a re-examination of traditions of historiography and of historical thought. In the face of the catastrophe, German historians asked, as Gerhard Ritter did in 1949, "how so much erudition could be combined with so much political primitivity."[90] Generally they agree on two serious shortcomings of traditional German historiography. The first is its moral theory. Even a man as deeply committed to the great tradition as Gerhard Ritter confesses that Ranke did not recognize "the deep demonic forces which act throughout history."[91] And although he rejects the natural law conception of freedom as utopian and dogmatic (as compared with the Christian conception which recognized the role of corruption as well as the aspiration for good within man and his need for authority), Ritter nevertheless admits that "there are moral principles which are valid always and everywhere and which must be applied in every society if that society is to deserve the name of a moral community."[92] The second is the failure of traditional historiography to take into account the deeper forces of a changing society. The two great weaknesses of German historians, in Ritter's opinion, are that they have been either the heralds of German political ambitions or ivory-tower scholars. From Ritter to Fritz Fischer there exists a consensus that historians must seriously, even if not exclusively, turn to the problems of the recent past or even the present. On the extent and scope of this concern there exists a great variety of opinion. Hofer, as we saw, stressed the primary task of history as a scholarly means for "illuminating" the present. Ritter warns constantly against the danger of viewing history from the standpoint of present interests or present biases. History must not become a function of life but a study of

---

Sell's *Die Tragödie des deutschen Liberalismus* (Stuttgart, 1953), W. Hock's book on the 1848 liberals, *Liberales Denken im Zeitalter der Paulskirche. Droysen und die Frankfurter Mitte* (Münster, 1957), in the attempt as in Alfred Heuss, *Theodor Mommsen und das neunzehnte Jahrhundert* (Kiel, 1956) or in Wolfgang Mommsen's recent analysis of Max Weber's political views in *Max Weber und die deutsche Politik, 1890-1920* (Tübingen, 1959).
    90. "Gegenwärtige Lage . . . ," *op. cit.*, p. 8.
    91. Cf. "Historie und Leben. Eine Auseinandersetzung mit Nietzsche und der modernen Lebensphilosophie," in *Vom sittlichen Problem der Macht* (2nd ed.; Bern, 1961), p. 101.
    92. "Die Menschenrechte und das Christentum," *ibid.*, p. 85.

an objective reality. The task of the historian continues to consist essentially, he agrees with Ranke, "in setting out clearly the unique, unrepeatable particularity of each historical phenomenon and in making it understandable as such." Only then can judgment come. The great contribution of the scientific historian to the moral situation of the present is the destruction of political myths of the past.[93]

But the most radical break with traditional historiographical practices was probably represented by the new school of *Strukturgeschichte*. Karl Lamprecht finally appeared to have triumphed. An important group of German historians, including Fritz Wagner in Marburg, Werner Conze in Heidelberg, Otto Brunner at Hamburg, and Theodor Schieder at Cologne, turned increasingly to the methods of the social sciences. Social history had not been new in Germany. Schmoller and Hintze had represented important predecessors. But until World War II the economic and institutional historians more or less had shared in the national historiographical tradition. They had emphasized the central role of the state and of the great individuals and the unique element in national institutions. The new social historians recognized the power of impersonal social forces. As Theodor Schieder pointed out, the "quest for typical processes (*Abläufe*) of historical change has begun to take the place occupied a hundred years ago by the principle of individuality."[94] They rejected Rickert's distinction between the methods of the two sciences. Weber's concept of the ideal type, which attempted to find regularity among individual social phenomena, seemed indispensable to the historian.[95] German social historians turned increasingly to Western models, to American social science, but above all to the French historians around the journal *Annales: économies, sociétés, civilisations*, who in the tradition of Lucien Febvre, Marc Bloch, and Fernand

93. "Historie und Leben . . . ," *op. cit.* and "Wissenschaftliche Historie, Zeitgeschichte und 'politische Wissenschaft,'" *Jahresheft der Heidelberger. Akademie der Wissenschaften* (1957/58), pp. 3-23, translated as "Scientific History, Contemporary History and Political Science," in *History and Theory*, I (1961), 261-297. Other historians, like Hofer, as we saw above, stressed the primary task of history as a scholarly means for "illuminating" the present.

94. "Der Typus in der Geschichtswissenschaft" in *Staat und Gesellschaft im Wandel unserer Zeit* (München, 1958).

95. Cf. *ibid.*, p. 177; cf. also Conze, "Die Strukturgeschichte . . . ," *op. cit.*, p. 18.

Braudel concentrated on the material life of the common man.[96]
To them classical German historiography belonged to a pre-industrial technological age. In a 1962 article on Ranke's image of
history, Fritz Wagner recited its faults, its blindness to the impact
of social forces on politics, and to the effect of science and technology on the transformation of warfare.[97] Radically new social
conditions required radically new historiographical methods.
Nevertheless, the new social historians recognized that the role
of political factors in changes of the social structure must not be
ignored, and that individuals like Lenin may play a decisive role
in creating new structures and giving them their personal imprint,
or like Hitler destroy them.[98] But political history and individual
initiative must never be isolated from a social context.

The advocates of *Strukturgeschichte* probably represent a
somewhat extreme position in German historiography. A great
deal of postwar historical writing has followed more traditional
lines of political or intellectual history. Nevertheless, the impact
of the social historians and the new concern with typical phenomena or structures is reflected in such sessions of the German Historical Congress in 1962 as "Technology and History," "The
Corporate System and Absolutism," and "Problems of the Presidential State," and in the turning away from the nation-oriented
history in the formulation of these problems on a supranational
scale.[99] The great variety of orientations among historians is proof
that the hold of the classical historic tradition which still dominated German historiography in the Weimar Republic is now
broken.

IV

We thus come to the end of our story. There is no longer a
"German idea of history." As in Western countries, we are confronted by a multiplicity of historical philosophies and orienta-

96. Cf Fritz Wagner, "Begegnung von Geschichte und Soziologie bei der Deutung
der Gegenwart," *Historische Zeitschrift*, CXCII (1961), 607-624.

97. "Rankes Geschichtsbild und die moderne Universalhistorie," *Archiv für
Kulturgeschichte*, XLIV (1962), 1-26.

98. Theodor Schieder, "Strukturen und Persönlichkeiten in der Geschichte,"
Historische Zeitschrift, CXCV (1962), 265-296.

99. Hans Rothfels, "Mittler zwischen Skepsis und Dogma. Gedanken zum
Duisburger Historikertag," *Die Zeit* (North American edition), Nov. 16, 1962, p. 4.

tions which cannot be brought under a common denominator. The picture is even further complicated by the increasing alienation of German historians from German academic philosophy. Nevertheless, there appear to be certain characteristics common to the historical thinking of many of the practicing historians and philosophers in Germany. The commitment to historical truth and to methodological correctness inherited from the classical historistic tradition remains unquestioned, but many basic historist philosophic positions are repudiated. German historians are widely agreed that although individual historical situations must be faithfully re-created and understood, they nevertheless must be judged by the moral standards of the historian. And although there are few adherents of classical natural-law doctrine, there is a broad agreement that certain common standards of human decency exist, and that to understand is not to forgive. Again, their respect for the individual historical situation has not prevented today's historians from seeking the typically human element in historical variety. German historians by no means have neglected political history nor the roles of individual personalities. The great interest in the political history of the recent past demonstrates this. But they have increasingly recognized, like historians elsewhere, the interaction and interdependence of politics and the social structure, of the national state and the total world situation. Finally, they have rejected early nineteenth-century metaphysical conceptions which had idealized the power strivings of the state.

The decline of German historism was no doubt the result in part of its inner logical contradictions. Historism asserts that there are no ultimate values nor any cognitions that are not bound by time. What kept Ranke, Droysen, Dilthey, or Troeltsch from ethical and epistemological nihilism was their firm belief that there was an Ultimate Reality—whether God, Reason, or Life— and that all insights into truths and values reflected aspects of this reality. Once this religious faith had been rendered questionable by growing secularization and scientism, the decisionism of a Jünger or a Heidegger was a foregone conclusion. Also decisive in the crisis of historism was the fundamental change in the social and political structure, the emergence of a technologi-

cal mass society. The subject matter of history—or as Schieder
put it, the "form of history"—had changed, rendering historism
obsolete. What nevertheless kept the historistic tradition alive
into the twentieth century was the Bismarckian state in which
political traditions of an older aristocratic and dynastic order survived in the midst of a radically changed social and economic
environment. For Jünger, Schmitt, and Heidegger, not to mention a host of other political and social thinkers and prophets
after the national humiliation of 1918, nationalism remained a
meaningful value, but the German Idealist philosophy had become meaningless. The anti-libertarian values of the past, the
admiration of state and power, now freed from ethical restraints,
merged into a nationalistic philosophy of violence. In contrast,
the historians, more closely committed to the national state in
its traditional form, remained for the most part relatively loyal
to the idealistic heritage until the collapse of the national state in
1945, although the intellectual and social foundations of this faith
hardly corresponded any longer to German or world realities.

This brings us back to the question of the role of ideas in
history. The "German idea of history" developed in the specific
German situation of the early nineteenth century. It certainly
reflected to a great extent political and social conditions of the
time as well as the intellectual and religious traditions, which
themselves probably reflected previous social and political realities. The character and relative significance of these interactions
between realities and traditions would be difficult to assess, and
it would be foolish to relate in this paper the alienation of German historical thought from the main pattern of Western Enlightenment thought to specific factors in the eighteenth century
or in the more distant past, e.g., to the Lutheran Reformation or
the failure of the national monarchy to arise in the Middle Ages.
Nevertheless, German historism, once formulated in its classical
form by Humboldt and Ranke, did seem to attain a degree of
independence from the social and political conditions of its origin.
To an extent, of course, the political realities which prevailed
at the time of the birth of historism survived into a later period,
for example in the Bismarckian state. Moreover, the sharp decline of the historistic tradition with the destruction of the Ger-

man national state in 1945 probably further demonstrated the
dependence of history as an intellectual tradition on social or at
least political factors. Nevertheless, it is difficult to escape the
feeling that German classical historism itself influenced not only
historiographical practice but also political decisions, and in this
way helped to transform political and social institutions or to
preserve them in the face of changing economic and social conditions. It seems questionable whether a sociological analysis would
satisfactorily explain, let us say, the history of German liberalism
in the critical period of 1848 to 1867. The option of German
liberals for national power at the expense of liberal principles
was perhaps less an expedient compromise with political realities
or classic interests than an expression of their German historistic
faith. From historistic philosophy German liberal historians like
Sybel, Droysen, or the young Treitschke inherited their faith in
the moral value of the state, its supremacy over the individual,
and the spiritual character of power as well as their "idealistic"
disdain for the utilitarian doctrine of the greatest welfare of the
greatest number. They also inherited a confidence in the outcome of history, in the ultimate triumph of a native German
liberty that would accompany the growth of German power.
Similarly, the German democratic movement in the early twentieth century was deeply affected by the historistic philosophy. Men
like Friedrich Naumann, Max Weber, Ernst Troeltsch, and Friedrich Meinecke—among the spiritual fathers of the Weimar Republic—favored some democratization and extension of parliamentary authority in Wilhelminian Germany as necessary to
strengthen the German state in the international power struggle.

Historism was never merely a theory of historical cognition
or development. From the beginning it involved certain definite
assumptions regarding the nature of political society. And although the main currents of German liberalism and democracy
developed within the historistic tradition, the political assumptions of German historism appeared in clear contradiction with
classical Western principles of liberalism. Both classical liberalism and classical historism liked to assign the individual a central
role in their theories. Historism, however, despite its supposed
individualism, was essentially a theory of collectivism. For its

individual was not the empirical private individual with his concrete needs and desires, but most often a collective entity, an institution. The basic assumption of historism was that these institutions represented not merely empirical organizations but possessed a metaphysical reality. Even the hero in history was interesting not as an empirical individual but as the expression of an idea. In the end, historistic thinkers always had to place the rights of the collectivity over those of the individual. As long as historism furnished the theoretical foundations of the social philosophy of German political thought, a libertarian-democratic theory in the Western sense was impossible. Undoubtedly the survival of historistic attitudes was an important factor in the unwillingness of Germans in the Weimar Republic to accept liberal democratic institutions.

In the last analysis, libertarian political philosophies must always contain a strong element of anti-historism. What all forms of libertarian thought have had in common—whether liberal in the classical sense of opposition to positive state action, demo-

Anti-libertarian forms of democracy and socialism are concern with the freedom and welfare of individuals.

Anti-libertarian forms of democracy and socialism are conceivable, of course. Nevertheless, in its libertarian form, democratic socialists indeed may rely upon the state to an extent which classical liberals consider dangerous, but democratic socialists will agree with classical liberals in regarding the state not as an end but as an instrument in the service of the empirical individuals that make up society. In its classical anti-state form, as well as in its democratic and socialist form, libertarian theory can never free itself from a moralistic element. It possesses a conception of a free and just society which inevitably is in conflict to a greater or lesser extent with empirical reality. Thus, despite the optimism regarding the efficacy of reform among certain liberals, liberal or libertarian thinkers must always be somewhat pessimistic regarding the past and present course of history and skeptical of political power. This degree of pessimism was lacking in historism. Its disdain of the idea of progress notwithstanding, historism doubtless represented until World War I the most radical expression of historical optimism known in Western thought. It assumed that all that occurred in history was essentially valuable, that power, freedom, and morality were ultimately in balance within the divine economy. Once the absurdity of this optimism was demonstrated by the catastrophic events of the early twentieth century, historistic thought became pessimistic and nihilistic. Gone was the confidence in a divine economy; left was the will to power. After the nightmares of Nazism and World War II, the rejection of historistic premises by contemporary German historians is not surprising. Insofar as post-1945 Germans have come to accept Western-type liberal democratic institutions not as a mere expedient but as a desirable form of government, it would appear that they have also had to accept certain of the ideological traditions of liberal democracy. The stability of political institutions certainly requires that to an extent these institutions be regarded as right by those who are governed by them. It is difficult to conceive of any theory of liberal democracy which does not assume the dignity of the individual as a moral criterion by which historical deeds and institutions may be measured.

ERRATUM: Line 19 on page 328 should read:

cratic, democratically socialist, or anarchistic—is a primary con-

NATURAL RIGHTS: THE SOVIET
AND THE 'BOURGEOIS'
DIDEROT

George Barr Carson, Jr.

For more than a generation American historians have accepted as axiomatic that the blinders of Marxism restrict the horizon of Soviet historians, at least those who publish. Whatever Marxism may be—and the term is all too often an epithet substituted for the common words "prejudice" or "radical"—the implication is plain that Soviet historians are not objective and scientific in the sense that American historians are. Soviet historical interpretation has a teleological inspiration, as did Bossuet's universal history, with the doctrine of Marx substituted for the hand of God in explaining the course of human affairs. With the doctrine of Marx the Soviet society became the beacon for all mankind, lighting the way to salvation while the Soviet Union served as a nucleus for the rest of the world to join or be forcibly annexed to. We American historians, or to use the Soviet terminology and broaden the base from narrow nationalistic limits, we bourgeois historians, escaped that particular kind of harness when Voltaire began the process of replacing the religious (or authoritarian) version of history with the enlightened (or rational) version.[1]

Soviet historians, of course, accept as axiomatic that American historians (except the occasional progressive scholar who kicks over the traces to reflect Marx's scientific historical laws) wear an equally limiting, but different, set of blinders. Whatever bourgeois may mean—and the term in Soviet usage is all too often an epithet substituted for "prejudiced" and "reactionary"—as a crit-

GEORGE BARR CARSON, JR. *is professor of history at Oregon State University.*
1. See Gerhard Masur, "Distinctive Traits of Western Civilization: Through the Eyes of Western Historians," *American Historical Review,* LXVII (April, 1962), 591-608, for suggestive discussion of this point.

icism of historical interpretation, the implication is not simply the negative one of neglecting Marxian laws of development but a positive adoption of other laws of development equally rigid but false. For example, a recent historiographical symposium discussed the "Europocentrism" of historical writing in the old world and then added:

If in the countries of the old world the conception of "europocentrism" flowered, then in the USA persistently and consistently the history of the country "formed by God and ourselves," the founding of which was to become the highest point in the progressive growth of mankind, has been canonized. The doctrine of "natural rights," founded in the "age of enlightenment," on American soil assumed a unique, messianic coloring. In the United States natural rights received the name of the theory of "manifest destiny." John Jay in 1777 wrote that the Americans were the first people singled out by God and given an opportunity to choose rationally a form of government and, consequently, the right of interpretation of what "is included in the concept of the great and equal rights of man." This premise is the starting point for the American falsifying conception that what was granted to them was the high mission of the chosen defenders of the rights of all mankind.[2]

Granted our respective (as Soviet and as American historians) blinders, the foregoing shows roughly how we look to each other. Under such conditions is it possible for us to look at any historical question with any degree of agreement on its interpretation? As a test case I have selected Denis Diderot. There has been substantial scholarly publication about him both in the United States and in the USSR in the last decade, and he is regarded as an important and original thinker in both countries. These are, in brief, indispensable areas of agreement for a common point of departure. As a test topic I have selected natural rights. It involves the concept of government and its basis, and it involves the issue of property; these are areas of profound disagreement between writers in the United States and in the USSR. How do American and Soviet scholars, under these conditions, treat a historical phenomenon arising in a third country and antedating either of their national existences?

Every English, every American, and every French schoolboy

2. USSR Academy of Sciences, Institute of History, *Protiv fal'sifikatsii istorii*, ed. V. G. Trukhanovskii *et al.* (Moscow, 1959), pp. 54-55.

knows the essentials of the doctrine of natural rights in its modern form because at a crucial point in his country's history some significant application or exposition of it appeared. John Locke's treatises on civil government are perhaps the most fundamental statement on natural rights; Jefferson's (in the Declaration of Independence) the most felicitous; the French Revolution's Declaration of the Rights of Man and of the Citizen the most succinct: "The end of every political association is the protection of the natural and imprescriptible rights of man: these are liberty, property, security, and resistance against oppression." The elucidation of the doctrine of natural rights, and the theory of social contract related to it, is a commonplace in the historical treatment of seventeenth-century revolution against absolute monarchy, eighteenth-century colonial revolt against mercantilist imperialism, and middle-class revolution against French absolute monarchy and feudal aristocracy. The elucidation in English, American, and French historical literature is not normally dependent upon the anachronism of Marxian historical analysis. What of Soviet literature?

In a 1949 textbook, *The Theory of the State and Law,* published for the Ministry of Higher Education by the USSR Academy of Sciences Institute of Law,[3] the treatment is fairly standard cliché. The book gives very little attention to Locke individually but reviews "bourgeois" methods of jurisprudence in class-conflict terms. A major criticism is that "bourgeois" writers look at any legal institution or governmental form separately from the complex of its environmental conditions. This juridical approach, for example, may be used to discuss political freedom wholly apart from the ruling role of capital in society. The institution of elections in bourgeois democratic states is portrayed in juridical terms as the voluntary assent of equal electors, segregating the issue from the facts: i.e., the power relationships of classes in society, the economic and political domination of the bourgeoisie, monopolistic oppression, and bureaucratic corruption. "The result is a 'juridical conception,' or a 'purely juridical design' of these institutions."[4] The eighteenth-century

3. USSR Academy of Sciences, Institute of Law, *Teoriia gosudarstva i prava* (Moscow, 1949).
4. *Ibid.,* p. 30.

French materialists—of whom Diderot is an outstanding example—attempted to explain the state of nature in materialistic terms, but their approach to the state of society and to the state and law remained idealistic. "The origin and transformation of the character of the state and law they [French materialists] explained by spiritual (*dukhovnie*) factors and processes, making them [state and law] dependent upon the growth of this or that idea, concept, opinion, etc."[5] Actually, they could not give "correct" answers in studying problems of the state and of law because they retained this erroneous base. The same textbook summarizes, patronizingly but accurately, the essence of the social-contract, natural-rights theory, emphasizing its metaphysical character. And of course the text points out that the theory served as a weapon in promoting a bourgeois revolution, which was at the time (eighteenth century) a progressive and positive role for the bourgeoisie.[6]

In the last decade another treatment of the same theory shows evidence of considerably greater sophistication. *The Theory of the State and Law* was open to the same criticism it had leveled against bourgeois theorists, that of ignoring the setting in which the theory developed. The charge is hardly true of a more recent work on modern and contemporary social and political theory by A. M. Deborin, published by the USSR Academy of Sciences.[7] Volume I is primarily concerned with the eighteenth-century French "Bourgeois" Revolution and its antecedents. Part 3 ("The English Revolution of the Seventeenth Century and Its Political Ideas") has a substantial section on Locke. The tone of the section is perhaps indicated fairly at the beginning: "If one discards the religious conceptions of Locke, which are the basis of his political thought...," then his borrowings from the Levellers account for most of his democratic views.[8] This does not make Locke sound very original; he was the apologist par excellence for the English bourgeois revolution and the compromise of 1688 be-

5. *Ibid.*, p. 42.   6. *Ibid.*, pp. 70-72.
7. A. M. Deborin, *Sotsial'no-politicheskie ucheniia novogo i noveishego vremeni,* Vol. I (Moscow, 1958). *Teoriia gosudarstva i prava* (n. 3) was first published in an edition of 100,000 copies, Deborin in an edition of 4,500 copies. The nature of the treatment of a subject may well differ, of course, with whether a book is a text for wide use in schools or a monograph for limited use. American historical publications often reflect a similar differential between textbook and monographic literature, the former lagging behind the latter by twenty years or more.
8. Deborin, p. 195.

tween the landowning and the merchant-industrial groups in England.

Deborin, as does *The Theory of the State and Law*, criticizes bourgeois theorists for not distinguishing between state (*gosudarstvo*) and society (*obshchestvo*), and Locke falls into this pit. The criticism of Locke—and of eighteenth-century theory on the state of nature and natural rights generally—is that Locke viewed mankind atomistically, individualistically, each man as an independent and private entity. Such a view is incompatible with *society*, which to a Soviet writer means mankind in association. Man, under the latter circumstances, must be assumed to have quite different characteristics from those presumed in Locke's scheme of things. Locke is called a nominalist. The Soviet critic is not likely to recognize as valid and "natural" characteristics that presume man can be separated from society. If he is, or could be, he has no government, nor needs any. But as he does *not* exist in individual isolation, the nature of government is not properly explained by postulating him in that condition.[9]

According to Locke, in the pregovernmental state of nature the resources of nature are the common possession of man, or as Deborin puts it: "In the 'state of nature' the law of everything for all prevails, that is, community property." What converts the public property of mankind in a state of nature to the private property of man in a state of government (or society, since as noted above the two are interchangeable to "bourgeois" theorists including Locke) is the individual labor of men. It is the protection of this individually created private property that is the first function of government—a protection that did not exist prior to the establishment of government.[10] Locke's logic is based on the concept that in the state of nature, as every individual has a proprietary right in his own person, he is chiefly concerned with what is needed to preserve his existence; hence, he has a proprietary interest in what his own labor produces to insure survival. Although Deborin recognizes this basis of Locke's interest in the property concept, he goes off on the familiar tangent that Locke is defending bourgeois property; Locke's government defends the proprietors (who are a minority) against the nonproprietors.[11]

9. *Ibid.*, pp. 196-197.   10. *Ibid.*, pp. 202-203.
11. *Ibid.*, p. 206.

In the end, quoting Marx, Deborin writes that for Locke "the bourgeois rationale was the normal rationale for humankind."[12]

Deborin's narrow view of Locke's theoretical principles ("The whole political theory of Locke consists of nothing more than a tract on methods of protecting private property") may perhaps be due to the emphasis placed upon associating him with the English political settlement of 1688, and the historical fact that the governmental system thereafter developed was, and continued to be, dominated by well-defined class interest. This emphasis is characteristic, of course, of Soviet (and Marxist) monism. That proprietary rights can be created and secured by political organization in anything except the means and instruments of production, narrowly defined by Marx as bourgeois property in industrial society, is never admitted, despite the theoretical possibility of applying Locke's concepts in a more extended fashion. The much-maligned bourgeois juridical approach might help here. Modern society in the United States in many ways makes efforts to defend as proprietary (natural) rights those things needed by any individual for his particular survival and does so in the name of liberty and equality. Government not only can protect the farmer in his ownership of land, the factory owner and his plant, but the worker in his tenure of job rights, and the pensioner in the security of his savings. These different individuals in contemporary society are not equally property owners—i.e., egalitarian in income or possessions—but can be equally protected in the security of their peculiar property—i.e., their means of subsistence. Indeed, the possibility that the propertyless can acquire property, implied throughout Locke's system by his theory that what creates private property is individual labor, is ignored in Soviet commentary. "The bourgeoisie," Deborin writes concerning the Declaration of the Rights of Man and the Citizen,

naturally, could not at this period, when it needed the backing of the masses of the people, demand liberty and equality only for itself. But it protected its class interests, embodying them in the Constitution of 1791 and in the Declaration of the Rights of Man and the Citizen wherever those documents spoke of the inviolability and the sanctity of property. Here a deep gulf was opened between *man* and *citizen,* a gulf that in future would be further widened and deepened.[13]

12. *Ibid.,* p. 209.   13. *Ibid.,* p. 525.

For the Soviet critic property right is something bourgeois, denied to any non-bourgeois and to the propertyless (i.e., any who do not have "bourgeois" property). In short, the famous French "Civil Code" should have been called the "Property Code."

If Locke, whose ideas on natural rights were the principal source of eighteenth-century thinking on the subject, suffers from rather patronizing treatment at the hands of Soviet writers, Diderot on the whole fares much better. To the Soviet as well as to the non-Soviet scholar, Diderot is an original genius and a precursor of revolutionary change. Since the doctrine of natural rights permeated eighteenth-century thinking, Diderot could not escape it and its emphasis on private property, as the Soviet scholar will admit. But any shortcomings in Diderot's ideas on private property were offset by his outstanding contribution to materialist philosophy.

For more than a generation the standard Soviet work on Diderot was I. K. Luppol's *Denis Diderot: An Outline of His Life and Ideas* (*mirovozzrenie*: world view, in sociological terminology), first published in 1924, and in a second edition in 1934. The author's preface to the second edition enumerated some interesting reasons for the re-publication: in the first place the book, kindly received by critics, was out of print and 1934 was the one hundred and fiftieth anniversary of Diderot's death. A second edition provided opportunity for making some desirable changes— correcting factual error, noting newly published works on Diderot or works not known to the author at time of first writing, and so on. More significantly perhaps, the book had been used as an aid for the study of French eighteenth-century materialism in a seminar at the Moscow Institute of Red Professors. There the author had learned of ideological mistakes, chiefly stemming from his attribution to Diderot of an excessively close approximation of dialectical materialism. Although Diderot was an outstanding materialist, Luppol had gone too far, and for this he blamed his youth and inexperience at the time the book was written. The second edition corrected the faults in historical perspective but was not a new book. In 1960 the USSR Academy of Sciences, Institute of Philosophy, republished the second edition; the editor's preface asserted that it was the first important and still the only

Soviet monographic research study on French eighteenth-century materialism.[14]

To Luppol the importance of Diderot was plainly that he was a forerunner of dialectical materialism and of scientific socialism. Luppol is therefore interested in Diderot's ideas on state and society because they help explain his ideas on virtue, morality, and happiness, areas of major concern in the study of Diderot's philosophy. Virtue, morality, and happiness are characteristics that do not exist in man except among men in association; hence, the need to study man in his social environment.[15]

Diderot, according to Luppol, found the first beginnings of society in the conflict between man and nature, an emphasis that distinguished him from other theorists of his age. Diderot was concerned with the conflict between man and nature because it led to the union of men against nature, i.e., to the formation of society—and government, since Luppol also takes the position common to other Soviet writers about the eighteenth century that Diderot and his age did not distinguish between them. " 'Isolated man,' " Luppol quotes Diderot, " 'had only one adversary, nature. Man in society had two—man and nature.' "[16] With the formation of government, Diderot's thought adopted the typical eighteenth-century social-contract concept of the natural-rights theory. The structural details of government, Luppols avers, did not interest Diderot. Diderot was concerned with the philosophical problem of virtue, which he considered the basis of society, and this enables Luppol to take off again on Diderot's sensistic and materialist philosophy, which are Luppol's chief concern.

For all Luppol's concern with the philosophical problems of ethics, he cannot abstract Diderot's thought wholly from problems of state and law. According to Diderot, the supreme desire of man is to be happy; man has " 'only one obligation, to be happy; only one virtue—justice.' "[17] As a materialist, Diderot recognized the primacy of self-interest but believed that a true concept of self-interest, given man in society with the dual adversaries of man and nature, led to altruism. Otherwise, man had gained little in forming a union against nature. Contract was perhaps not the

---

14. I. K. Luppol, *Deni Didro; ocherki zhizni i mirovozzreniia* (Moscow, 1960).
15. *Ibid.*, p. 243.   16. *Ibid.*, p. 247.
17. *Ibid.*, p. 248.

"initium" of society, as in Hobbes or Rousseau, but the "princi-
pium." Virtue and the general temper in the last analysis depended upon the organization of the state and upon legislation;
the eighteenth century could not get around the hypothesis of
contract.[18]

The Marxian framework of Luppol's approach shows through
when, in attributing to Diderot the attitude that moral basis was
sufficient to change political structure, he adds: "If that [the idea
that changing man's political organization or laws could improve
society—a common, if quaint, eighteenth-century idea] seems
naïve, one must remember Diderot in the light of his own
times."[19] The thesis that political organization is superstructure,
a function of the stage of development of productive forces, had
not yet been revealed in Diderot's day.

Luppol's study of Diderot as a revolutionary precursor of
dialectical materialism is nearly four decades old in conception,
and three in execution, facts which are not changed by the recent
reissue under the imprimatur of the Academy of Sciences. In the
same year that Luppol's work again was made available, the
Moscow Social and Economic Literature Press published a new
study by A. I. Kazarin, *The Economic Thought of Denis Diderot*.[20] Kazarin's study cites some recent work on Diderot outside
the Soviet Union, including Arthur M. Wilson's *Diderot: The
Testing Years, 1713-1759*,[21] probably the most significant new
work on Diderot published in any language in the last quarter-
century. Since Wilson's and Kazarin's works were published
within a few years of each other, they invite comparison with
each other and contrast with Luppol.

Kazarin, to be sure, opens with the customary nod to the
gods when his first sentence states "Denis Diderot was Karl Marx's
favorite author,"[22] to be followed by the statement that Marx,
Engels, and Lenin regarded Diderot as an outstanding representative of eighteenth-century materialist philosophy. Kazarin, like
Wilson, seems to consider Diderot "the" *philosophe*, not just
another member of that somewhat amorphous group of French

18. *Ibid.*, p. 244.   19. *Ibid.*, pp. 251-252.
20. A. I. Kazarin, *Ekonomicheskie vozzreniia Deni Didro* (Moscow, 1960).
21. Arthur M. Wilson, *Diderot: The Testing Years, 1713-1759* (New York, 1957).
22. Kazarin, p. 3.

reformers and literary men. To both Wilson and Kazarin, Diderot is an important revolutionary figure. Wilson makes quite a point throughout his work of the fact that Diderot represented new ideals in society—those of the bourgeois and his virtues—and worked toward their recognition and realization. Kazarin finds Diderot's thought a background for the laws of society formulated by Marx and Engels in the 1840's, and argues Diderot recognized that material production is the base for social organization, a classic Marxian tenet. Of course, Diderot was an eighteenth-century thinker, living in an age when Marxists admit the revolutionary character of the bourgeoisie, to which Diderot belonged; Kazarin insists, however, that Diderot "was able to treat critically not only the bourgeoisie as a class, but also bourgeois ideals."[23] Diderot, in short, embodied the contradictions of his age and was thus a notable example of the dialectic principle in the eighteenth century.

The most striking contrast between Kazarin and Luppol, and at the same time an interesting parallel between Kazarin and Wilson, is the attention Kazarin gives to Diderot's environment. Kazarin's effort to set the stage for his study of Diderot's ideas, to describe the climate of opinion in which they evolved, is hardly distinguishable from the similar approach characteristic of any good modern "bourgeois" historian. For example, Kazarin stresses the Austrian war of the 1730's, the pattern of hunger, epidemic, and famine in the same decade, and the repressive administration of Cardinal Fleury. All this could not but have affected the formation of the young Diderot's "world view" and his attitude toward church and state and their role in *ancien régime* society. "Politics," writes Kazarin, "spontaneously dug itself into his life."[24] The heavy emphasis on this *mise en scène*, rather than on the dicta of Marx, Engels, and Lenin, is well illustrated by Kazarin's statement: "All this is very important for understanding Diderot's character, without account of which it is impossible to understand his world view and the idealogical content of his creative work."[25] If, as some scholars assure us, "the Soviets, after all, have given up the 'class character' of a number of disciplines,

23. *Ibid.*   24. *Ibid.*, p. 16.
25. *Ibid.*, p. 18.

beginning, under Stalin, with linguistics and certain aspects of economics, [and] later extending a new scientific freedom . . . ,"[26] perhaps we have in Kazarin a tentative similar tendency in history.

The eighteenth-century view of natural rights gave pre-eminence to property because other rights followed from it. Property was a means of self-preservation, but also a guarantee of liberty—i.e., lack of dependence upon or subjection to others—and of equality to the extent that society was or could be organized to enable all citizens to hold some property. Kazarin depicts Diderot basically as a proponent of this view, although he was, like many of his contemporaries, a student of Montesquieu and strongly influenced by him and his historical approach to the study of laws. Diderot, according to Kazarin, agreed with Montesquieu that in a republic property was the most important guarantee of general welfare and that without private property, trade, industry, or agriculture could not develop. Like other figures of the eighteenth-century Enlightenment, Diderot shared with Montesquieu the "juridical illusion" that only on the basis of strengthening private property was it possible to prepare the way for progress and provide conditions for a happy life. Diderot was persuaded that all people equally had the right to be private proprietors, that a rational society could not be built without private property. To reconstruct society, one must begin, according to Diderot, with the establishment of a new system of laws corresponding to natural law.[27] And since the time of Locke natural law and its use to sanction rational government had been heavily dependent on the idea of property as the most important of man's natural rights.

Kazarin takes care to note, although emphasizing Diderot's ideas on private property, that Diderot thought all should become private proprietors without too great inequality in proprietary possessions. The author quotes from Mercier's dictionary of 1802 the definition of "capitalist" (a word rarely used in the eighteenth century), saying it is simply a paraphrase of Diderot's definition:

26. Gerhart Niemeyer, reviewing Herbert S. Dinerstein, *War and the Soviet Union*, in *Slavic Review*, XX (Dec., 1961), 720-721.

27. Kazarin, pp. 24-25.

Capitalist—this is something known only in Paris. It signifies the possessor of a monstrous fortune, a man with a heart of bronze, having affection only for metal. As for land tax, he has nothing to do with it, for he owns not an inch of land. How tax him? Like the Arabs of the desert, robbing caravans and caching gold in the earth from fear of others, the capitalists buried our money.[28]

Actually, Kazarin's purpose here is to show that Diderot was hospitable to new currents in economic thought and sometimes invented new terms or gave new meaning to old ones. But of course Diderot could not foresee the commanding position capitalists, still rare in his day, would obtain in the economy of the future. He continued to regard land as the chief form of property and the business of agriculture as one of the most respectable, expounding in his *Encyclopédie* the thesis: " 'Man has no worth without land, and land has no value without man.' "[29] In thus reflecting the natural-rights theory of property as a means of self-preservation, Diderot did not intend that all urban inhabitants should engage in agriculture; rather he was insisting upon the right of everyone wanting to do so to work the land with his own labor and to acquire the ownership of land in consequence. He who did not work the land with his own labor, and did not want to, should not be its proprietor but must renounce it.

In the decade of the 1750's Diderot's ideas seemed very close to those of the utopian communists (Rousseau and others; Kazarin's term). From Diderot's study of natural law and his philosophical materialism, which encouraged the concept of physical equality and the essential similarity of men, was derived not only the idea of juridical equality, but social equality and equality of needs and property. In fact, Kazarin argues that if Diderot felt it necessary to publish Rousseau's article on "Political Economy" in 1757 in Volume VII of the *Encyclopédie*, it was because the article largely corresponded to his own ideas.[30] Luppol probably would not agree; he says it is sometimes difficult to find Diderot's true opinions in the *Encyclopédie*, citing the articles "Autorité politique" and "Société" (written after 1757). In the latter article one runs into God every two or three lines; plainly this does not sound like the notoriously atheistic Diderot.[31] Luppol and

28. *Ibid.*, p. 52.
30. *Ibid.*, p. 66.
29. *Ibid.*, p. 53.
31. Luppol, p. 245.

GEORGE BARR CARSON, JR.

Kazarin ignore altogether the problem of censorship in mid-eighteenth-century France, about which Wilson has much to say. But Diderot did adhere to the ideal of social equality, even while admitting the difficulty of achieving this ideal in actual practice. Only democratic governmental structure, he believed, provided adequate conditions for its achievement, and some inequality of property and needs would prevail even in democratic states. The expansion of these inequalities might lead to the downfall of democracy unless such expansion were kept under tight rein.[32] Diderot did not, however, believe one could build society on the basis of eliminating ideas of wealth and power, that is, by trying to approach more closely to natural man, who lacked these concepts. Once out of the forest and into society, man had those ideas around him and governments must reckon with them. In the end, Kazarin says, "his [Diderot's] sober intellect could not reconcile itself to utopias."[33]

Turning from the Soviet to the "bourgeois" historian, let us consider Arthur Wilson's work on Diderot, which was described in that archetype of "bourgeois" historical journals, the *American Historical Review,* as "easily the most complete, the most impartial, and the most carefully documented biography of Diderot in any language."[34] Does Wilson's work present a picture of Diderot substantially opposed to that presented by Kazarin, or one which would be fundamentally unacceptable to Kazarin on the evidence of his own work? I think not. Consider some passages from Wilson's chapter, "Diderot's Thoughts on the Interpretation of Nature." The author has been discussing Diderot's interest in biological researches and how they illuminated problems of theology and metaphysics, particularly Diderot's striking approach to the theory of evolution.

Here [Wilson writes] we have the thinker who was aware of time and change, who had an intimation of the role of *process* in the elaboration of organic life, and who grappled with the concepts of the dynamic and the genetic.... But whenever one begins to think, as Diderot did, in terms of concepts in which time and the changes brought about by time make all the difference—process, adaptation, development—one needs a new kind of logic to supplement the old

32. Kazarin, pp. 58-59.   33. *Ibid.,* p. 191.
34. *American Historical Review,* LXIII (Oct., 1957), 106.

logic of the Aristotelian syllogism, which takes no account of time. Diderot was a precursor of the nineteenth-century philosophers and scientists who, following Hegel, adopted the mode of logic represented by the dialectic of thesis, antithesis, and synthesis. Marxist writers in particular are appreciative of the dialectical character of Diderot's thought. Karl Marx himself once referred to Diderot as his favorite prose writer. . . .[35]

Not only do we have concurrence between Kazarin and Wilson on the dialectical quality of Diderot's thought and its appeal to Marx, but on the issue of natural rights there is appeal to the same evidence—a particular selection of Diderot's *Encyclopédie* articles—and similar conclusion. "In his article on 'Political Authority,'" writes Wilson, "Diderot stated his opinions very plainly. . . . This article did indeed sound like one by John Locke or Thomas Jefferson. 'No man,' he wrote, 'has received from nature the right of commanding others. Liberty is a present from Heaven, and every individual of the same species has the right to enjoy it as soon as he enjoys reason.' "[36] Wilson describes in detail the relationship between Diderot and Rousseau, both personal and intellectual. The strong interest of both men in the Academy of Dijon's prize contest subject, "What is the origin of inequality among men, and is it authorized by natural law?," resulted in one of Rousseau's most famous works. Wilson cites the evidence for Diderot's considerable influence on the essay and emphasizes the close correspondence between Diderot's and Rousseau's ideas at this time (1750's).[37] In Wilson's chapter "Changing the General Way of Thinking," Diderot's mirroring of the intellectual current of his times is clearly evident in the discussion of Volume V of the *Encyclopédie*. Of Diderot's essay on natural rights, the author says: "This was a subject in the vein of the great natural lawyers of the preceding century, men like Grotius and Pufendorf, so that a highly competent political philosopher [George H. Sabine] has been able to say with some justification of Diderot's article that it was 'a rhetorical flourish with conventional ideas.' "[38] Further:

His article, being in the tradition of the natural law school, contributed to keeping concepts current that later provided the inspira-

35. Wilson, p. 194.
37. *Ibid.*, p. 225.
36. *Ibid.*, p. 142.
38. *Ibid.*, p. 233.

tion for documents like the Declaration of Independence and the Declaration of the Rights of Man and of the Citizen. Diderot wrote of man's dignity and—in 1755—of his "inalienable rights," and frequently referred to "the general will." This phrase has become so deeply associated with Jean-Jacques Rousseau and his idea of the social contract that Montesquieu's earlier use of the term in *L'Espirit des lois* seems to have become generally forgotten. In Volume V of the *Encyclopédie* both Diderot, in his article on *"Droit naturel,"* and Rousseau, in his on "Economy," used the term with some of the identical overtones of meaning that are found in the *Social Contract* seven years later.[39]

The same articles that attracted Kazarin's interest are the focus here; "Authority" (by Diderot, Vol. I), "Natural Right" (Diderot, Vol. V), "Political Economy" (Rousseau, Vol. V), "Natural Equality" (De Jaucourt, Vol. V).

The eighteenth century's obsession with natural rights perhaps is taken more for granted than explicitly paraded in Wilson, but then both lay and scholarly readers of Wilson already have heard a lot about natural rights. It is evident in every chapter of Wilson's work that he has studied Diderot more thoroughly than any contemporary publishing on the subject; he has taken infinite pains in research, and (in subjective vein) his book is well written. He has style, as did Diderot. In fairness to Kazarin, it should be added that a substantial part of his work is devoted to Diderot's ideas and plans for Russia presented to Catherine the Great, a subject not dealt with in Wilson. But the main point is that, whether or not Kazarin borrowed from or was directly influenced by Wilson's work in forming his own picture of Diderot, he has treated his subject in the basically scholarly pattern "bourgeois" historians expect in a monograph. Kazarin is not in essential disagreement with Wilson on the content or the nature of Diderot's thought.

The original question was whether it is possible for Soviet and "bourgeois" historians to look at any historical question with any degree of agreement on its interpretation. The answer is yes in the case of Diderot. Why then do Soviet and "bourgeois" historians appear so different to each other? One reason is probably the highly polemical character of most Soviet criticism of non-

39. *Ibid.,* pp. 233-234.

Soviet historical writing. Periodically a new Soviet historiographical symposium on foreign history appears under some such title
as that published in 1959 by the USSR Academy of Sciences,
Institute of History, cited at the beginning of this paper. One is
likely to be put off at the start by the crudeness of the title (*On
Falsifications of History*) that implies falsification is a trait peculiar to foreign histories, but the articles themselves are sometimes
much more sophisticated. The opening paper in this recent collection provides a useful example; the title is "History in a
'Changing World' (On Certain Conceptions in Contemporary
Bourgeois 'World History')."[40] A considerable section is given
over to a discussion of the two-volume history of world civilization edited by Professor Max Savelle.[41] The pertinent criticism
here is that although the book emphasizes that the world is now
"a close community of peoples" and essays to "present the *whole*
of human civilization" the authors are unable to approach the
subject except in terms of two camps, West and East, at any given
period, ancient or modern; the titles of the parts are alleged to
show the division.[42]

The Soviet historians are saying that bourgeois historians may
say, but do not really *think,* "world"; they think "East and West."
When eighteenth-century thinkers wrote about the rights of man
they meant exactly what they said—not "Western" man or "Eastern" man, but man. Thus if we avoid thinking "East and West,"
which would be irrelevant and inapplicable to the age of natural
rights and the social contract, the Soviet view of Diderot is probably not far from the American, but with somewhat more emphasis on his materialism than his bourgeoisness. Even that minor
caveat may be superfluous. The editor of the 1960 edition of
Luppol wrote that Diderot stands as an "always intelligent, far-
seeing, and implacable battler of the young and at the time revolutionary French bourgeoisie."[43] In that judgment Soviet and
non-Soviet scholars concur.

Another reason why Soviet and "bourgeois" historians look
so different to each other is probably what appears to the "bour-

40. *Protiv fal'sifikatsii istorii*, pp. 3-67.
41. Max Savelle *et al., A History of World Civilization* (2 vols.; New York, 1957).
42. *Protiv fal'sifikatsii istorii*, p. 63.
43. Luppol, p. 4; from the preface by M. Grigor'ian.

geois" historian to be the Soviet historian's abysmal ignorance of much contemporary research. Professor Alexander Gershenkron, in an excellent review of a recent Soviet book, *Essays in the History of Economic Sciences in Russia in the 18th Century,* gives an illuminating picture of the state of Soviet historical scholarship when he points to the absence of foreign influences upon the Soviet author. "All modern literature on mercantilism seems quite unknown to him. At any rate, he writes as though nothing has been said on the subject since the days of Marx, thus providing striking evidence for the intellectual isolation in which Soviet historians find themselves."[44] Kazarin on Diderot suggests at least faintly that the isolation may break down in individual cases; Kazarin has at least glimpsed the authority of Wilson on the subject. Perhaps it is no longer so much the blinders of Marxism that restrict the horizon of Soviet historians, but to some extent the more common ones of provincial research everywhere—lack of sources.[45]

44. Alexander Gershenkron, reviewing N. K. Karataev, *Ocherki po istorii ekonomicheskikh nauk v rossii XVIII veka,* in *American Historical Review,* LXVII (Jan., 1962), 414.

45. One remarkable distinction between Soviet and non-Soviet study of Diderot is that the latter usually reflects painstaking research in France while the former obviously does not. Of course, as is well known, Diderot's personal library found its way to Russia, thanks to the largesse of the Empress Catherine II, but this does not give Russian scholars any material advantage over other scholars working in France insofar as the eighteenth-century French *philosophes* and their milieu are concerned. Kazarin's citations reflect the Soviet scholar's problem of sources. He includes only one reference to work in English; p. 12, n. 1 (appended to a statement that Diderot *père* employed hired labor in his shop) reads: "Sm. [See] Franco Venturi, *Jeunesse de Diderot,* Paris, 1939; A. M. Wilson, *The Testing Years, 1713-1753* [sic], Oxford, 1957." Some of Kazarin's citations of Diderot's works are from the French. (Kazarin does not identify the edition; it appears to be the *Œuvres complètes de Diderot,* ed. Assézat and Tourneux [Paris, 1875-1879], which was used by Luppol.) Most of his references, however, are to the collected works of Diderot in Russian, published in Moscow, 1935-1947. There are references to only Russian editions of the works of Turgot and Quesnay, and to a Russian edition (1902) of Félix Rocquain, *L'Esprit révolutionnaire avant la révolution, 1715-1789* (Paris, 1878); the one reference to John Morley, *Diderot and the Encyclopedists* (2 vols.; London, 1878) is general and lists the Russian translation (1882). These are representative. The reference to the definition of capitalist in Mercier's dictionary (see n. 28, above) is taken from P. Lafarg, *Sobstvennost' i eë proiskhozhdenie [Property and Its Origin]* (Moscow, 1959), p. 41 (see Kazarin, p. 51 n. 1). The following is a complete list of non-Russian twentieth-century works cited by Kazarin in that portion of his book covering the same period as Wilson's book: Venturi and Wilson, listed above; Jean Oestreicher, *La pensée politique et économique de Diderot* (1936); "Un inédit de Diderot," *La Pensée. Revue du rationalisme moderne,* no. 55 (1954 Mai-Juin); Jean Luc, *Diderot l'artiste et le philosophe* (Paris, 1938); LeGras, *Diderot et la Encyclopédie* [sic] (Amiens, 1928); Jacques Proust, "La documentation technique de Diderot dans l'Encyclopédie," *Revue d'histoire littéraire de la France* (1957), no. 3, pp. 335-352; Jacques Proust, *Le* [sic] *pensée de*

Finally, both the Soviet and the "bourgeois" historian obviously believes the other is not really free to write scientific history. Admittedly the compulsion upon the Soviet writer to follow a particular line of interpretation, whatever the sources, is a grievous one. I am not trying to explain away the fact of Soviet "party-line" historical writing. On the other hand there is certainly merit in the charge (see n. 2 above) that Americans act and talk as though they knew better than others what were best for the peoples of the world. True, the compulsion upon the American writer, self-imposed or otherwise, to follow a particular line of interpretation seems so intangible as to be different in kind rather than in degree.[46] But the restrictions on historians' interpretations are by no means altogether external, arbitrary, or irrational. On the question of individual proprietary rights in means of production there is simply no common ground between the Russian and the Lockean heritage. Russian theory and practice, even before the Soviet regime, has no precedent for property in Locke's sense, as a right generally recognized, or one that ought to be. The most ancient and the most persistent Russian tradition is that of the state (prince or tsar) or the community (household, *volost, mir*, at various epochs) as proprietor. The principal exception is only partial: eighteenth-century recognition of proprietary rights in land or industrial enterprise in the Roman civil law sense applied only to a small class and was never applied to or accepted by peasants en masse. The attempt to extend the concept of individual proprietary rights in land during the last years of the imperial regime proved abortive. The Soviet regime abandoned the concept at the outset.

In Soviet and "bourgeois" writing about Diderot and natural

Diderot de 1753 à 1769; Français [sic] Quesnay et la physiocratie (Paris, 1958); *Le Mouvement physiocratique en France de 1756 à 1770* (2 vols.; Paris, 1910). To one accustomed to the rigorous standards in footnote citation imposed by such compendiums as the University of Chicago Press's *Manual of Style*, Kazarin's references are at best slovenly.

46. Professor Donald W. Treadgold of the University of Washington argued this point forcefully in discussion at the 1962 meeting of the Pacific Coast Branch, American Historical Association (Aug. 29, 1962, Loyola University of Los Angeles), pointing out that adherence to a specified interpretation sometimes has been literally a life or death matter in the Soviet Union. Since no such final sanctions apply in the United States, he took exception to my position that historians in *both* countries work against consciously or unconsciously recognized societal compulsions.

rights two major sets of ideas appear to be at work: commonly accepted standards in scholarly search for historical truth, and diverging ideological attitudes toward property and the causes of events. Soviet and "bourgeois" historians, having scrutinized the evidence concerning Diderot according to approved procedures of historical research, can agree to certain facts about his life and thought. The limit of agreement is reached in examining the implications of natural rights as an idea in history. To the Soviet school the concept of natural rights was valid only as a weapon in the particular case of a middle-class political movement in France. To the "bourgeois" school the concept of natural rights ought to be valid as a universal principle supporting rights against the state anywhere and any time. As any historian should know, the most successful revolutionary movements always have claimed universality for their principles. Since both the Soviet and the "bourgeois" historian claim to be the heirs of revolutionary movements, agreement on the universality of a principle still peculiar to one is perhaps expecting too much.

Does that provide an answer to the question implied at the outset—whether historians of the two schools can learn from each other? I think the answer is a qualified yes. At least, we can learn from them, since we are of course dispassionate and open-minded —in examining such problems as the doctrine of natural rights.

CONCLUSION

Richard Herr

Early in the incubation of this collection of essays, the authors and editors exchanged lengthy letters in search of the proper kind of volume to honor Louis Gottschalk. We concluded that a volume of essays, if it were to be of interest and use to historians—and what kind of homage to a dean of our profession would a book be that was not of use and interest?—should focus on a problem that currently concerns historians. At the same time it should be related to Professor Gottschalk's work and the instruction he gave us. Out of this exchange of views emerged the theme—"the role of ideas in history." We also decided that the most promising way to attack the problem was to let each author approach it within the framework of a concrete historical situation on which he had done research. The essays were thus to be case studies, not theoretical discussions. Finally the plan called for a conclusion to summarize the different solutions that had been given, point out the general lessons that might emerge, and suggest lines of future investigation and speculation.

The most striking characteristic of these essays is undoubtedly the multiplicity of approaches and solutions that they furnish to the problem. They reflect one of the enviable features of American historical scholarship (if one may, without offense, apply the term "American" to a collection that includes the work of two Canadian authors), its lack of dogmatism and subservience to one, or even two or three, schools of thought. Fourteen scholars, all of whom feel they owe a debt to one professor, have gone off in almost as many directions, yet none of them considers himself a rebel—eloquent evidence both of the gifts of the teacher and of the intellectual climate. The editor who has to summarize such variety finds himself perplexed by how to proceed.

He might try pointing out the common conclusions of the authors about ideas in the past. He might, for instance, take Karl Weintraub's study of the opposing attitudes of Voltaire and Con-

dorcet toward the common man and set it beside Gertrude Himmelfarb's portrait of Bentham. In the one case we have two
leading *philosophes,* mutual admirers, who were poles apart in
their feelings toward true popular sovereignty: the aged panegyrist
of Louis XIV, believer in a proper social pecking order with enlightened roosters at the top and docile cocks to mind them, and
the egalitarian revolutionary, enemy of bourgeois aristocracy, for
whom public salvation could come only through universal education. In the other case, a "father of democracy" who dreamed of
himself as Big Brother, closer to the elitist spirit of Voltaire than
to the democratic one of Condorcet. Then the editor could show
how Ezio Cappadocia's distinction between liberals and Liberals
follows the same pattern. For the Liberals admired the common
people and decried Madame de Staël's praise of aristocracy and
the British constitution, while the liberals admired liberty but
saw in the common people only Jacobins. In all these examples
we seem to have a chronological extension of the familiar Jeffer-
son-Hamilton debate that R. R. Palmer has looked at in greater
geographical extension. Together, these studies suggest a need
to consider the parturition of modern democracy in a new
conceptual framework. A possible starting point is Weintraub's
observation: "Most of the program of the French Revolution
could have been accomplished by men with Voltaire's outlook;
for the vaster revolution, which put the world into the hands of
the common man and his rising expectations, one had to follow
Condorcet" (p. 62). After this sally, the editor could turn to
a comparison of the lessons of Edward Tannenbaum, Richard
Herr, and John Fagg for nineteenth-century monarchism, or of
George Carson and Georg Iggers for the relation between societies
and historical philosophies. But such a conclusion to the volume
in the long run could not avoid becoming pedantic and boring.
The reader, settled back in his chair and looking forward to
coffee and brandy, would hardly relish cold abstracts of the meal
he has just enjoyed.

No, the conclusion must be something else. In search of a
better solution, we look through the essays and hit upon the statement made at the outset by Palmer. Musing on the meaning of
the role of ideas in history, he says:

"Ideas" may mean images in individual minds, or climates of opinion characteristic of whole generations or periods. They may refer to concepts, beliefs, doctrines, and programs consciously formulated in words; or to vague *états d'âme,* emotions, attitudes, or purposes, colorations of personality, moods and feelings, incentives and drives, predispositions to thought and behavior arising from the depths of the unconscious (pp. 4-5).

Here, we notice, is a twofold scale by which to judge an idea; one measures the number of people who hold it, the other locates it in a gamut running from consciously formulated beliefs to vague *états d'âme.* We can turn these scales into a two dimensional table on which we can locate the various kinds of ideas described by the essays in the hope that some lessons will emerge from the process.

Glancing through the essays, we are aware at once that simple polar categories will not do them justice. Neither the term "individual" nor "whole generation" on the scale of persons holding an idea will fit Iggers' German historians or Palmer's American farmers. We must interpose another term. "Group" will do, meaning a number of individuals who have something in common, most especially an idea that does not have universal acceptance. We note also that none of our authors has chosen to study all mankind in thirty pages. Therefore let us substitute for "whole generations" the term "society," assigning a vague geographic instead of a vague chronological limit to our largest unit.

So much for the Subject axis. The Idea axis also needs elaborating. The type "concepts, beliefs, doctrines, and programs consciously formulated in words" seems clear enough, and we can assign it the term "concept," remembering that it includes programs or calls to specific action. At the other end, the kind of idea described as "vague *états d'âme,* emotions, attitudes or purposes, colorations of personality, . . . predispositions to thought and behavior arising from the depths of the unconscious" is somewhat less clear, but it may take on meaning as we use it. Let us call it for short "predisposition." Again, however, an intermediary species is needed, for in the essays we frequently see ideas that are neither "concept" nor "predisposition" but crude representations of a reality that the subject does not perceive directly.

They are presumably, but not necessarily, distortions of reality. For want of a better name, we can borrow one already overworked by sociologists and purveyors of public relations (we are not the first historians to do so) and call these representations "images." If "concepts" are comparable to Descartes's "clear and distinct ideas," "images" correspond to Kant's "phenomena."

Now we have our table (below), and we can turn to our first

SUBJECT	IDEA		
	Concept	Image	Predisposition
Individual	Individual—Concept	Individual—Image	Individual—Predisposition
Group	Group—Concept	Group—Image	Group—Predisposition
Society	Society—Concept	Society—Image	Society—Predisposition

task, to fix the ideas described by the essays into the table. The first box is labeled "Individual—Concept." Several authors have dealt with this kind of idea. Weintraub describes Voltaire's and Condorcet's views on society and history. Voltaire holds the concept: the history of human progress is the actions of great men and creative elites; Condorcet: the history of human progress is the extension of rationality and the perfection of the common man. In Gordon McNeil's essay the ideas of Robespierre on the legislative system belong in this category too. Even if they are not always consistent, they are given clear expression in speeches and pamphlets. One must also include the concepts of Rousseau, which of course continue in existence after the death of their author and had an effect on Robespierre. Gertrude Himmelfarb's "Haunted House of Jeremy Bentham" has many stories, but the top floor consists of his expressed views on prison reform, and they belong here too.

Moving down our table to concepts held by groups of people, we find that a large number of our authors furnish cases to put in this square. "The principles of the French Revolution, which can still be summarized as Liberty, Equality, and Fraternity," that Palmer discovers among bourgeois Europeans and American farmers (pp. 8-9) fit here. So do Leslie Tihany's utopias. Although he studies individual authors, he sees them as forming a group united by their utopian mentality. (He also studies the ideas of one individual in the case of Morelly's influence on Babeuf.) Geoffrey Adams, in describing the *philosophes'* campaign for religious toleration, gives as clear an example of this category as one could desire. Harold Parker does too when he says French scientists in the eighteenth century held "the conviction that science should be immediately useful to industry" (p. 93). The essays of Cappadocia, Carson, and Iggers deal with the ideas on history of identifiable groups. For Cappadocia the groups are the two kinds of Restoration liberals, and their concepts consist of views on Madame de Staël's interpretation of the French Revolution. Iggers breaks down the historical tradition held by German historians for over a century into three basic "concepts" (his word) of "individuality," "identity," and "the primacy of the state" (pp. 290-293). And Carson deals with two groups, Soviet and bourgeois historians (he used individual authors as representatives of groups), and their "concepts" (again his word) of natural rights, property, and government, as well as their specific views on Diderot.

We jump next to the bottom square in this column, "Society —Concept." To our surprise, after the crowded one we just left, we discover no one here at all. Tihany does open with a reference to Russia and America as the present day utopias of Chinamen or noble savages, but these utopias are surely "images" rather than clearly verbalized "concepts." On consideration, the dearth of "society—concepts" may not be entirely fortuitous. Individuals obviously have clear concepts, and all members of a group selected because of the similarity of their ideas by definition hold the same concept, but it is hard to imagine a whole society agreeing on a well defined and intellectual idea.

As we move to the Image column, our first impression on looking at the top category, "Individual—Image," is again of empty space. No author appears to have bothered about images held by mere individuals. And yet there is at least one exception: the exalting image that Robespierre had of the people, who "alone are good, just, and magnanimous." Associated with it are his images of his political opponents as evil "particular wills," and

RICHARD HERR

of Rousseau, who "loved the people more than anyone else." These certainly fit the category of distorted representations of realities, even though McNeil does not call them images (pp. 143, 146). Their importance in understanding Robespierre's varying proposals makes us suspect that his case is not unique. The first suggestion to come out of this survey is therefore that historians pay more explicit attention to the effect of this kind of idea on the actions of leading historical figures.

We go on to the next square, wondering by now if we have not, like Alice, inadvertently walked through a looking glass. Here we see a near-perfect example of this category, "Group— Image," in Parker's study of the interrelations of French administrators, scientists, and artisans. Eschewing the unscholarly temptation to analyze in a few pages eighteenth-century French industry (the reality), he says, "One can describe, however, the French industrial world as it appeared in the administrative reports, and hence, in the minds of French administrators" (p. 89). (We begin to observe that several of our authors have operated in more than one square, and this observation encourages us to believe that our journey will not be entirely fruitless.) This seems to be all there is here, and we are about to cross into the next square, when we come upon a magnificent growth, one that spreads in all directions but whose trunk looks rooted here. This is the "myth" of Edward Tannenbaum. Image? Evidently, for it provides man with a "global 'image' of himself" and reappears in different directions as "global motivating images" and "image-beliefs." Although held by vast numbers of people, it belongs in the rank "group" rather than "society," for French counterrevolutionaries and revolutionaries had different myths. But, when Tannenbaum's "image-beliefs" call for re-establishment of the social and political roles of the church and aristocracy, they reach out toward our column "Concept"; and when the myths include a "religious base," they extend in the other direction toward "Predisposition." There is a unique interpenetration of levels in Tannenbaum's analysis with which our scheme is not particularly suited to deal.

By comparison, the next square, "Society—Image," is relatively clear and orderly. Palmer shows us in one corner the "images and ideas" that Americans obtained of the French Revolution through their reliance on British sources of information (pp. 16-17). In another, Raymond Rockwood places the "legend" of Voltaire. Although partisans and enemies of the Revolution disagreed violently in their attitude toward the *philosophe*, the legend is properly here, not in "Group—Image." Both sides agreed that he was *le chef des incrédules*, or at least of the anticlericals, and that was the essential feature of the legend. In Herr's essay, the images of Fernando and Godoy as personifications of good and evil were also held by the entire society. (Even if *everyone* did not hold them, active disbelievers were only a small group.) In a similar fashion Fagg explains the fate of Isabel II in terms of the popular images of the Spanish rulers. For a long time public wrath was diverted from the queen, at least outside Madrid, by the conception of her mother and General Narváez as the authors of evil, much as Godoy had been for an earlier generation. But when they disappeared, the public relations of Isabel herself broke down, and the role of Good was filled now by an imaginary woman, *La gorda*, the Revolution. Perhaps Spaniards are more given to imagery than other peoples, but there is much in Fagg's account that recalls Tannenbaum's myth: the faith in monarchy in the face of the obvious inadequacy of the monarchs, the need felt for a symbol of national unity and someone to embody it. As with Tannenbaum, all levels of the popular ideas Fagg describes seem best classified as "images."

A difficulty of a different order appears when we turn to the third, or "predisposition," column. "Predispositions" (vague *états d'âme,* colorations of personality, and the other attributes for this phenomenon) appear in many essays, often cloaked under different terms. Thus Weintraub finds the explanation for the discordant views of Voltaire and Condorcet on the role of the common man in their "divergences of world view, personality, interest, and temperament" (p. 42). McNeil is less explicit, but the factor is also present in his analysis of Robespierre's thought. The serene self-confidence with which Robespierre reversed his positions, one moment echoing and the next contradicting his alleged mentor, Rousseau, stemmed from his predisposition to deem himself virtuous. More than his colleagues, he was close to the people

("Je suis peuple moi-même," p. 143). Bentham would have shuddered at the suggestion that he was *peuple lui-même*, he who was entitled by his intellect to be people's jailer, but his ideas, like those of the Incorruptible, rose out of megalomania. Himmelfarb, McNeil, and Weintraub are intimately concerned with that kind of predisposition known as personality, which they all agree in seeing as a cause molding the ideas of their subjects.

Predispositions also appear at the levels group and society. Tihany finds two types of utopian mentality, empirical and non-empirical, which produce distinct utopian ideas. Parker shows that French artisans, administrators, and scientists, after a century of collaboration, developed "habitual attitudes, ideas, and actions" that determined their reactions in the face of a new situation (p. 101). In the more generalized category of "Society—Predisposition" we can place Fagg's popular desire in Spain for a symbol of national unity. Palmer's "integration" is an even clearer case: "The demand for equality of treatment and social participation, whether it be called a principle or a psychological need, goes beyond the differences between races, classes, or countries." "The role of ideas," he adds, "is undoubtedly to meet human needs." Evidently, even for Palmer, such a predisposition as the psychological need for integration is less properly an idea than a fountain of ideas (p. 19). Tannenbaum says a myth objectifies men's social experiences and serves "to reduce the tensions between themselves and the physical and social milieu in which they are called upon to live. In short, it gives them their *raison d'être* [without which, presumably, men find life unbearable]" (p. 267). Here too a psychological need lies beneath the idea. The readiness that Herr discovers in the Spanish people (and by inference in other societies at other times) to believe that their fate is determined by a struggle between forces of good and evil is another example of this category. The images of Fernando and Godoy were in some respects patently absurd, and yet they were given credence because of this predisposition. Thus at all levels our authors uncover "predispositions." None of them, however, has labeled the predisposition he describes an "idea in history." This realization raises doubts in our mind about the correctness of

calling it a type of idea and including it in our table. Let us
leave the question open for the nonce.

To sum up, we can fill in our table, listing under each category of ideas the essays that deal with it. (Italics indicate the
major emphasis of the essay, parentheses that the essay has no
explicit discussion of that category.)

SUBJECT	IDEA		
	Concept	Image	Predisposition
Individual	*Weintraub* *McNeil* *Himmelfarb* Tihany	(McNeil)	Weintraub (McNeil) (Himmelfarb)
Group	*Palmer* *Cappadocia* *Tihany* *Iggers* *Adams* Carson Parker	*Parker* *Tannenbaum*	Tihany Parker
Society		*Rockwood* *Herr* *Fagg* Palmer	Palmer Herr Tannenbaum (Fagg)

We can now use this classification as a basis for a systematic
look at the solutions given to the problem of the role of ideas
in history. The authors made no attempt to agree on a definition
for the word "role," and it is clear that they do not all treat
an identical problem. Most address themselves partly or wholly
to the effect of ideas. Most also try to determine their origin,
while some do only one or the other. Thus Weintraub's essay
does not assess the effect (or "influence") of Voltaire's and
Condorcet's ideas about the common man (unless we call the
place of the common man in their historical writing an effect,
but this would beg the question). The other authors to treat
"Individual—Concept," McNeil, Himmelfarb, and Tihany, do
take up the issue. All three have serious doubts about the effect
on historical events of the ideas put forward by individuals.
Bentham's contemporaries rejected his projects and later generations misunderstood them. Himmelfarb therefore denies him the

rank of father of reform (but she does leave open the possibility that he fathered less commendable developments) (p. 238). The doctrines of Rousseau had less weight on Robespierre's proposals for the legislative power than did the latter's view of the policies called for by the situation, even though Robespierre considered himself a disciple of Rousseau (see McNeil, pp. 135, 156, and *passim*). Babeuf, on the other hand, was a loyal follower of his mentor Morelly, or as he thought, Diderot. He concocted a conspiracy to put Morelly's *Code de la nature* in force, but the only material result was to place one more neck beneath the guillotine. Lenin's is a different case, partly no doubt because, like Robespierre, he knew how to respond to the needs of the situation, or, as Tihany puts it, he had an empirical utopian mentality (pp. 34 and 35-37). In all these cases personality seems to determine what ideas are accepted and how consistently, but the doctrines of Marx, Morelly, or Rousseau do not directly affect events.

The pendulum has made a full swing since the days when Voltaire and Rousseau could be held responsible for the French Revolution. Mindful of the unwarranted claims made for the influence of great thinkers on following generations, we have since the days of Becker systematically discredited such claims. We are now close to saying that no thinker or writer ever had any influence, at least none that can be singled out. Gottschalk has already reached a similar verdict. After considering carefully the role of the *philosophes,* he has written: "The significance of the intellectual thus does not lie in his being a creator. He is only a critic. He does not father new intellectual attitudes but works upon the raw material of independent hostility that he finds in the general atmosphere around him."[1] Despite the negative cast to this conclusion, however, it contains a positive assertion that we are in danger of overlooking: an intellectual does work upon the raw material in the atmosphere around him. The importance of this role has been suggested by Daniel Mornet, who spent his life investigating the ideas of the French Enlightenment. In his early studies he concluded that while intellectual figures famous in their own day do not propound new ideas that become forces

1. Louis Gottschalk, "Philippe Sagnac and the Causes of the French Revolution," *Journal of Modern History,* XX (1948), 142.

in history, they do, through the popularity of their writing, bring to the fore one of several tendencies already present.[2] Here is one kind of influence that deserves more thought and research. Now that the excessive allegation of direct influence by individual thinkers on historical events has been discredited, the nature of their indirect influence should be explored realistically but imaginatively.

Of course, any intellectual influence can be ascribed a significant role in history only if one feels that general trends of thought do affect historical developments. Whether or not they do is a major issue of debate among those of our authors who deal with concepts held by groups. Their conclusions run the range from skepticism to affirmation. Tihany, except in the case of Babeuf, finds it impossible "to establish a documented causal connection between French revolutionary action and utopian stimulation" (p. 32). Cappadocia maintains that the ideas on history expressed by the Liberals during the Restoration (specifically, their reaction to Madame de Staël's *Considérations*) stemmed from the political exigencies of the moment, their need for Bonapartist support, not from intellectual beliefs (pp. 196-198). (One is reminded of McNeil's conclusions about Robespierre's political motivation. But would either McNeil or Cappadocia deny that some ideal determined the political position of their subjects in the first place?) Not everyone is so negative. Parker, dealing with a different kind of concept, credits it with some effect: "All this activity on the part of the [eighteenth-century French] scientists—the steady appraisal of thousands of inventions, the encyclopedic description of industrial processes, the individual treatises—was sustained [caused? prolonged?] by the conviction that science should be immediately useful to industry" (p. 93). During the early years of the Revolution this and similar ideas "helped to maintain the direction adopted" (p. 108). Adams shows how an active campaign by a heterogeneous group of *philosophes*, Calvinist pastors, and enlightened royal ministers, who were inspired by the common ideal of religious toleration,

2. Daniel Mornet, *Le Sentiment de la nature en France de Jean-Jacques Rousseau à Bernardin de Saint-Pierre* (Paris, 1907) and *Les Sciences de la nature en France au XVIIIe siècle* (Paris, 1911). These works study the influence of Rousseau and Buffon.

eventually brought about a relaxation of the laws against Protestants. Practical considerations no doubt weighed with the royal government too. Going a step further, Iggers credits German classical historism with influencing "not only historiographical practice but also political decisions, and in this way [it] helped to transform political and social institutions or to preserve them in the face of changing economic and social conditions" (p. 327). These are the kinds of difference of opinion among the authors as to the effectiveness of concepts. One suspects that they are partly due to the different natures of the cases studied, but one would not be surprised if the authors, given each other's evidence to review, should reach conflicting interpretations. We are brought back to the heterogeneity of American historical scholarship.

No such disaccord exists among the authors who discuss images. They agree that images have some influence on action. In the simplest form, Parker indicates that the image of French industry held by royal administrators led them to seek the advice of scientists on technical matters (p. 92). (He adds that established practice also encouraged this policy.) Rockwood shows how, in a somewhat different way, the legend of Voltaire, once it became a political issue by the transfer of his remains to the Pantheon, pinpointed the clergy as the enemies of reform and thereby strengthened the anticlericalism of the Revolutionaries. Both Herr and Fagg believe that the images Spaniards had of their rulers directed their political actions in moments of crisis. Tannenbaum's myth has a similar if more all-embracing role. It determined the action (or lack of action, the acceptance of the *politique du pire*) of the counterrevolutionaries after 1871. "For them only a miracle could make the myth a reality. This patient hoping for a miracle expressed the abiding influence of the myth on its believers" (p. 285).

Images and, to an extent on which there is less agreement, concepts appear to determine the nature of the actions taken. The effects of predispositions are different. We have described them already when we sought to discover what the term "predisposition" represented in our essays. We found that the authors used it primarily to explain why certain concepts and images are held.

Personality and temperament account for the divergent ideas of individuals (Weintraub, McNeil, Himmelfarb); mass psychological needs lie behind the images, myths, and principles which groups and societies accept (Palmer, Herr, Fagg, Tannenbaum). Predisposition thus plays a different role from image and concept. Concepts and images define or influence the specific form action will take; predispositions define or explain the concepts and images. This difference serves to augment our doubts about calling predispositions "ideas."

A question not yet broached is that of the relation between images and concepts. Is one the outgrowth of the other? Can both be products of the same predisposition? Is there any difference in the way they define action? Or are they merely different degrees of the same phenomenon? The examples provided by Palmer and Rockwood lead us to suspect that images and concepts are not of the same order. Americans had roughly the same image of the French Revolution; they held opposing concepts as to what policy one should adopt toward it. Clericals and revolutionaries agreed more or less in their image of Voltaire; they were at swords' points about the transfer of his remains to the Pantheon. Tannenbaum draws a similar distinction between myth and ideology. Myths, even in their most specific form as "image-beliefs," never get beyond an imprecise idea of what action is desirable; but "an ideology is a program of ideas whose purpose is to promote a specific path of action." Ideologies are temporary trappings for myths (pp. 267-270). These three instances suggest that a concept (program) does frequently intervene between image and action and that definition may take place on two levels, with diametrically opposed inclinations sometimes arising from the same image. None of our essays has tackled these questions directly, so they do not provide much insight into them. The problem deserves more thought.

Up to now our analysis has very likely read more into the essays than the authors always intended, or has described their conclusions in terms they may not entirely admit. When they wrote, none was aware of the categories that have been used here. There is one feature, however, that is common and explicit in the essays. This is a general agreement on the complexity of historical causation, on the difficulty of singling out the effect of ideas from that of other factors present in a situation. To quote Palmer again: "The antithesis of ideas and conditions seems like the antithesis of heredity and environment; it may be a useful tool of analysis, but it is difficult to employ since neither term of the antithesis is ever observed without the other" (pp. 5-6).

In this antithesis, "conditions" no more has one single meaning than does "ideas." Our essays point to several factors that operate in conjunction with ideas and can properly be called conditions. The previous experiences of individuals are one. Cappadocia credits prejudices arising out of personal experiences before the Restoration with determining some of Madame de Staël's doctrines, notably her anti-Bonapartism (p. 183). Weintraub's main thesis is the importance of personality in fashioning the ideas of Voltaire and Condorcet, but he agrees with the latter that Voltaire's lack of democratic spirit came from his belonging to an earlier generation. The ideas of these two *philosophes* were in part a reaction to their lives (pp. 41-44, 62-64).

Political circumstances are another form of "conditions" that complement ideas as historical causes. Political exigencies determined the vagaries of Robespierre's policies as they did the reception given by various parties to Madame de Staël's *Considérations* (McNeil and Cappadocia). Political developments discredited both Godoy and Isabel II and helped prepare their downfall (Herr and Fagg). Adams shows that the *philosophes'* campaign for Protestant toleration was affected by the political upheavals and fiscal penury of the reign of Louis XVI (pp. 81-83). In Iggers' essay the interaction becomes more complex. German historism helped fashion political reality—the liberals' acceptance of Bismarck's solution to the German question—and in turn the Bismarckian state helped historism survive into the twentieth century. Historism went down with the state in the cataclysm of 1945 (pp. 326-327). Rockwood centers his attention even more explicitly on the interplay of political events with an idea, the legend of Voltaire. The combination of the struggle over the Civil Constitution, Louis XVI's flight to Varennes, and the apotheosis of Voltaire sharpened the picture of Voltaire as the enemy of the Church and as the champion of equality and liberty. The

CONCLUSION 363

effect was to revive religious issues of the mid-century Enlightenment that had been dormant in recent decades. Anticlericalism became strong in the Revolutionary spirit, as it had not been previously, and it was joined by incipient republicanism.

When historians speak of the "antithesis of ideas and conditions," however, what they usually mean by the second term is social and economic conditions. Several of our authors have studied the antithesis in this light. Tannenbaum's myth operates in a social and political setting and is modified by the evolution of the real world (pp. 272-273). Palmer makes the problem central to his essay: are certain ideas the expression of a class viewpoint? The immediate conclusion is that they are not, at least in the Atlantic world of the French Revolutionary era, if social class is understood in commonly accepted terms. The Revolutionary ideals of the European bourgeoisie frightened American merchants, while they found ardent supporters among American farmers. But by considering the ideals as embodying not the specific aims of the bourgeoisie but the desires of any class that feels segregated, he returns to the belief that ideas can be associated with levels of society. Carson extends the problem still further and asks if censorship is the only cause for the differences between Russian and American interpretations of a past age. The answer is that other factors are also present. Historians as members of a society tend, not always consciously, to glorify the ideals of the society. The material environment of the historian also enters in, as when he interprets the historical significance of the demand for the "right of property" according to the nature of the property he has known (p. 347).

In searching for an explanation of the difference between Babeuf's failure and Lenin's success, Tihany points to a complicated interplay of factors. Lenin was inspired by Marx's empirical *Manifesto*, whereas Babeuf had only Morelly's non-empirical *Code de la nature*. This change in utopia (idea) resulted from a transformation in utopian mentality following the French Revolution (a factor we have placed under the heading predisposition), which in turn was brought about by new conditions, the political events and economic transformations of the nineteenth century ("the fuller unfolding of the Industrial Revolution, . . . the failure of

European working-class revolutions," p. 34). Nor is this all. In the end, Tihany finds it necessary to stress the importance of the political situation in which Babeuf and Lenin operated, the different organizations at their disposal, and the relative strength of the governments they faced.

The most careful study of a multiplicity of factors working over an extended period is Parker's. In it we see individuals (scientists and members of the Bureau of Commerce) entering a situation (the French industrial world) with certain ideas and attitudes (which in this case came down from the previous century—that scientists should aid industrial progress and that government should stimulate productivity). These ideas and attitudes shaped their perception of the situation. They devised solutions that seemed to work and were repeated until they became habit. But the solutions also modified the situation. As they were carried by new men into slightly new situations, they were elaborated. "Since the Revolution did not offer new problems in this area before the war, the old solutions continued to be used by the old personnel. No one was prompted to think of doing anything else ... There were thus interlocking and sustaining continuities of people, resources, machines, problems, organization, documents, administrative practice, and ideas" (pp. 108-109).

In all these cases there is concurrent action of ideas and conditions. If we look closely, however, it appears that ideas and conditions are usually presented as different types of historical causes. The authors use conditions to explain the origin of ideas, their continuity, or their change. In the case of individuals previous experiences clearly help determine what ideas are held (one's ideas are the products of one's experiences). In a less obvious way the same holds true for groups and societies. Political circumstances are a form of collective experience, and so are social and economic conditions. Herr's essay illustrates this point. Unpopular political policies, natural disasters, economic hardships, and social instability provided the experiences of Spaniards at the time they were accepting the images of Fernando and Godoy.

Conditions thus appear as a factor molding ideas. We have already seen that the same holds true for predispositions. The consensus of the essays is that ideas arise from two sources: the predispositions (personality, psychological needs, propensity) of individuals and groups, and the conditions (past and present experiences and environment) of the individuals and groups. Action is defined directly by ideas—concepts and images—and so indirectly by predispositions and conditions. This being the case, let us definitely remove the tag "idea" from "predisposition" and consider it a separate factor causally prior to ideas, just as environment is. Two species of ideas remain: concepts and images.

At this point one might legitimately raise the question: if ideas are the products of predispositions and environment, does this not solve the problem of their role by eliminating it? Are they not simply effects, superstructure, the middle dominoes in a row serving to knock down those ahead of them when they are pushed over from behind by the real causes, interesting to observe perhaps but of little use for understanding the forces that make history click? To this objection we can answer pragmatically that no one has so far demonstrated that certain conditions and predispositions always produce the same idea; and until someone does (which is unlikely, the mysteries of the human mind being what they are), the role of ideas will have to be probed as an at least partially independent variable. Indeed predispositions can be discerned more readily from ideas than vice versa, and to a certain extent so can conditions. More than a row of dominoes, historical causes are like passengers on a subway, shoving each other back and forth in no predictable pattern.

This jostling becomes more evident as soon as we consider history not arbitrarily as single actions but realistically as sequences of interrelated actions. Each new action taken because of certain ideas modifies conditions and perhaps predispositions and thus modifies succeeding ideas and actions. Given the resources of historical documentation and the human mind, it would be impossible to analyze each action of a complex historical development for ideas, predispositions, and conditions, just as it is impossible to study individually the motivation of all persons involved in any historical event. In certain individuals and at certain times, and thus in certain actions, predisposition will count more than previous experience (conditions), images more than programs (concepts), and in others less. But since predispositions are relatively stable, and conditions and ideas (both concepts and images) do not usually change overnight, the three terms appear to form a helpful apparatus for analyzing long historical processes, like the relaxation of French laws against Protestants, as well as single events, like the apotheosis of Voltaire. Although some of our essays stress one term and others another, the three terms together, predisposition, conditions, and ideas (each covering a number of different factors), appear sufficient to fit all the essays.

Is this consensus entirely fortuitous? This editor thinks not. Rather it is evidence of our own tradition and environment. American historiography, for all its diversity, does seem to have common features. The Russians, Carson tells us, accuse us of remaining idealistic after Marx demonstrated the truth of historical materialism. Like the eighteenth-century philosophers, we still make state and law and other historical developments "dependent upon the growth of this or that idea, concept, opinion, etc." (quoted by Carson, p. 333). The Russians are not alone in insisting on the primacy of social and economic factors; it is a historical philosophy widespread in Europe. The French school founded by Marc Bloch and Lucien Febvre and revolving around the journal *Annales: économies, sociétés, civilisations* has been the focus of much of this thinking. Iggers points out its recent influence in Germany (p. 323), but Italy and Spain present similar cases. Among these groups, social, economic, and demographic history is ascendant. The words *structures sociales* and *conjoncture* have become their Open, Sesame! If *conjoncture* ever stood for a precisely defined idea, the coincidence of certain economic factors to bring about specific effects, it has risen above it to the symbol of a faith. In the words of one of its leading exponents, *l'histoire conjoncturelle* can "establish the most profound social history possible, that of classes in the interplay (*dynamique*) of their contradictions, and finally enlighten the origin and development, not only of economic movements, but of thoughts, doctrines, institutions, events . . . approaching *total* history. . . ."[3] (As usual the lines have been drawn more sharply than the founders of the movement intended. One need only recall Bloch's *Les*

3. Pierre Vilar, *La Catalogne dans l'Espagne moderne: recherches sur les fondements économiques des structures nationales* (Paris, 1962), I, 17 (italics in the original).

Rois thaumaturges and Febvre's *Le Problème de l'incroyance au XVIᵉ siècle* to be aware of their belief in the seminal role of ideas.) The adepts of this movement ridiculed mercilessly Mornet's *Les Origines intellectuelles de la Révolution française,* and they have tended, *sotto voce,* to disparage American historians who have not followed their lead.

It is precisely their emphasis on social and economic factors as the sole ultimate cause of history that Palmer and Iggers attack here. "While it is important to study the 'social structures,' as French historians of the Revolutionary period so frequently insist," Palmer says, "it is well to do so with both caution and open-mindedness, and to avoid reducing politics, ethics, or psychology to a form of sociology with a class angle" (p. 18). Palmer represents a widespread attitude in our fraternity. J. H. Hexter, for example, has criticized the British historical tradition of this century which has sought to explain the triumph of British parliamentary democracy through the rise of the middle class. Hexter counters that faith in ideals was the essence of the seventeenth-century struggle and dares anyone to call this Whig history.[4] In our country the socio-economic interpretation was championed by Charles Beard for a generation. The keystone of his argument was his *An Economic Interpretation of the Constitution of the United States.* Recently Edmund S. Morgan has rewritten the story of the American Revolution for a popular series. He dismisses as baseless Beard's charges that the authors of the Constitution worked with their minds on their portfolios. (Morgan is able to draw on the investigations of Robert Brown and Forrest McDonald.) The founders of our nation, he says, in fighting for their rights were motivated simultaneously by material interests and genuine principles.[5]

Without claiming any systematic knowledge of current American historiography, this editor believes that these examples represent a wide, though of course far from universal, trend of recent decades. Its emergence can be observed in the writings of Louis Gottschalk, who has devoted much thought to the relative impor-

4. J. H. Hexter, *Reappraisals in History* (New York, 1963), especially the essays "The Myth of the Middle Class in Tudor England" and "Storm over the Gentry."
5. Edmund S. Morgan, *The Birth of the Republic, 1763-89* (Chicago, 1956), pp. 51-53, 131-135.

tance of ideas in historical causation. As we have already seen, a major theme of his writing seems to support those historians who relegate ideas as causes to the scrap heap of historical theories. He once stated that his own work and that of several students— all but one of whom have essays in this volume—indicates that the revolutionary spirit at the close of the Old Regime would not have been significantly different without the *philosophes*.[6] "For all their importance to the historian, thoughts . . . are products rather than producers of their age. . . . They are effects rather than causes."[7]

These statements show their author riding the downswing of the pendulum away from earlier claims made for intellectuals and abstract ideas. But they do not reveal the entire man. He adds:

In other words, a revolution must arise out of the total cultural pattern if it is not to be abortive. The *philosophes*, of course, belonged to their cultural pattern. Their minds were fitted, and in turn they helped to fit the minds of other men, to the great change that began to come in 1789, but they alone did not make the change.[8]

In this quotation, ideas as a factor in history cease to be bottled up within the writings of a small group called intellectuals and are expanded to become "the total cultural pattern." This enables them to be more than simply products of an age, a social class, or a *conjoncture*. The full significance of the change comes out in Gottschalk's interpretation of the causes of revolutions, which he published after being immersed in the problem for more than two decades. He sees three causes, briefly (1) demand for change, consisting of widespread dissatisfaction with existing conditions and solidified public opinion, (2) hopefulness of success based on public familiarity with programs of reform and trusted leaders, and (3) the weakness of the conservative forces, which arises partly from the same conditions that produce (1) and (2).[9] It takes only a change in terminology to restate major aspects of the first two causes as images and concepts, the two types of idea

6. Gottschalk, *loc. cit.*, p. 143.   7. *Ibid.*, p. 145.
8. *Ibid.*, p. 143.
9. Louis Gottschalk, "Causes of Revolution," *American Journal of Sociology*, L (1944), 1-8. See also his *The Place of the American Revolution in the Causal Pattern of the French Revolution* (Easton, Pa., 1948).

we have defined here. The role of ideas as historical causes is reborn in a new form. We should not be misled by Gottschalk's insistence that ideas arise from social and political conditions:

If this [the significance of the American Revolution in creating the principles of 1789] is part of the history of ideas, it is a part that shows that ideas are often *results* and not causes, and results of *events* and not of intellectualism.[10]

or his assertion that many agents besides intellectuals spread new ideas:

In providing programs the intellectuals play their major role. To be sure, they also help to create that general awareness of dissatisfaction, that solidified public opinion, which was described above as necessary to create effective demand for revolutionary change. They are aided in that regard, however, by many factors not exclusively intellectual, such as law courts, pulpits, schools and colleges, newspapers, political rallies, salons, and theaters.[11]

Our essays have said the same. Because these passages were written in the forties, they were directed at opponents that have ceased to worry us. But his thinking opened up paths along which we are traveling. To return to our earlier metaphor, the pendulum reached the end of the swing and started back again.

If the essays in this volume, in reasserting the importance of ideas in a complex social process, reflect a general American tendency, whence has it come? One might suggest that the present authors received it from Gottschalk, and he in turn from Becker, who focused attention on "the state of mind that conditioned . . . events." Without denying the share of these teachers in the final result, we can dismiss this explanation as inadequate. It recalls the now discredited variety of intellectual history which traced the inheritance and elaboration of ideas from thinker to thinker, as if such a chain sufficed to understand the place of ideas in history. In any case such an explanation will not account for an extensive American school of thought. A sounder one may emerge if we look at the thinking of American social scientists on the question.

On the basis of what even the best disposed critic would have

10. Gottschalk, "Sagnac," *loc. cit.*, p. 146 (italics in the original).
11. Gottschalk, "Causes," *loc. cit.*, pp. 5-6.

to term a superficial acquaintance with theories that are more disparate than those of historians, this editor ventures to assert that some general lines of thought about individual and social motivation can be detected among the behavioral scientists. For instance, many would agree that environment influences ideas and prejudices. Thus the eminent sociologist Paul F. Lazarsfeld can refer to it as a "fact" that in the United States "the poor, the urban residents, and the Catholics are more likely to vote the Democratic ticket, while the well-to-do, the Protestants, and the rural dwellers are more frequently found in the Republican camp."[12] Environment, it will be noted, is taken to be not just economic class but also collectivities such as church (and, though not explicit in this quotation, ethnic, professional, and social groups) as well as ecology (urban versus rural is only the most obvious distinction). But environment is not all; the personality of the individual and the psychic state of societies have received increasing attention of late. One study has probed the character-istics of "authoritarian personalities," whose existence is held to abet the spread of fascism.[13] The social psychologist David C. McClelland, who has investigated the connection between the content of folk tales and children's stories and the economic achievement of societies, urged social scientists to direct their at-tention "away from an exclusive concern with the external events in history to the 'internal' psychological concerns that in the long run determine what happens in history."[14] The effects of person-ality and environment on individuals have been combined by Robert K. Merton and others into the theory of the "social role." "*Social role* is the part played by an individual in response to an understanding shared by members of a group as to the attitudes and behavior that should normally follow from his occupation of a given position or status" (the effect of environment). When an individual chooses his social group in the first place and then determines how far and in what way he will follow the role ex-pected of him, "consciously or unconsciously he tries to satisfy

12. Paul F. Lazarsfeld, Bernard Berelson, and Hazen Gaudet, "The Process of Opinion and Attitude Formation," in Lazarsfeld and Morris Rosenberg (eds.), *The Language of Social Research* (Glencoe, Ill., 1955), pp. 234-235.
13. T. W. Adorno *et al., The Authoritarian Personality* (New York, 1950).
14. David C. McClelland, *The Achieving Society* (New York, 1961), p. 105.

what psychoanalysts might call 'the imperatives of his super-ego' "
(the effect of personality).[15]

Those behavioral scientists who adopt these views assume that
environment and personality (conditions and predisposition, as
we have called them here) produce lasting points of view, prejudices, or ideas which will influence the subject's reaction in a new
situation. Behavior in a wave of anti-Semitism, in an integration
crisis, or in the face of an appeal to overthrow democratic institutions will be determined less by the immediate statement of the
issues (or the recent price of bread) than by longstanding attitudes toward minority groups or outside authority that come from
personality and the various aspects of environment. The task of
the behavioral scientist becomes that of finding, usually through
questionnaires and interviews, the relationship between views on
immediate questions and longstanding attitudes and between
these attitudes and the environment and personality that produced
them. In doing so, they make use of the further assumption that
the study of a properly selected set of individuals will give results
that can be generalized by statistical procedures into more or less
trustworthy statements about a whole population.

To judge from our essays, historians have a basically similar
view of human motivation. There are concepts and images that
are molded by conditions and predispositions, and these concepts
and images determine the form of action in a specific situation.
Historians seem more prone than sociologists to emphasize the
conditions immediately preceding an event (an economic depression, for instance), but the reason may be simply that historians
have available the sources to study the immediate background,
which a contemporary observer often lacks, while they have difficulty in obtaining evidence to establish a relation between the
actions of participants in an event and their early experiences.
And historians, by the nature of their subject, usually study a
wider variety of developments over a longer period than do most
behavioral scientists.

This similar understanding of motivation can be partially explained as a conscious adoption by historians of the approaches

15. Thomas C. Cochran, "The Historian's Use of Social Role," in Louis Gottschalk (ed.), *Generalization in the Writing of History* (Chicago, 1963), pp. 103, 107-
108.

of the social scientist. We have, some willy and others nilly, followed the injunction of Turner and his contemporaries to make
use of the procedures and knowledge of related disciplines. It
is a practice recently championed by Gottschalk and the committee of historical analysis of the Social Science Research Council
in their volume *Generalization in the Writing of History*.

Nevertheless, this is hardly the full explanation. Something
more fundamental is at work, influencing both historians and
social scientists. We might call it a philosophy of human behavior
held in common by American scholars, the present stage of a long
tradition that has its roots in the epistemology of Locke, the
pedagogy of Rousseau, the psychoanalysis of Freud, and the prag-
matism of William James, as well as the economics of Adam
Smith and Marx. This tradition does not offer us a doctrine, a
new monistic interpretation, but a pragmatic sense of the entire
social process with its many elements. It includes a realization
that the process is shot through with ideas at every point. Ideas
affect perception of the situation, of possible courses of action, of
the action as it is proceeding, and of the new situation. The approach also flexibly recognizes that the importance of ideas—and
of conditions and predispositions—differs from instance to instance
—from the activity of Vico to that of Garibaldi, from the Boston
Tea Party to the Constitutional Convention. No one thinks that
the last word has been said on the problem. On the contrary,
we can hope that the heterogeneity of American scholarship, its
international orientation and permanent inducement to discover
new insights, will continue to modify our theoretical framework
and produce more satisfying accounts of human behavior.

The final task envisaged for this conclusion was to provide suggestions for the future. Some have already been made: that historians pay more attention to the influence of images on the
actions of leading individuals; that we investigate the relation
between images and concepts, the interaction of different kinds
of ideas, an all but neglected subject; and that we reconsider the
influence of widely known intellectuals, particularly in determining which of various available paths public ideas will follow. The
pattern of analysis used here to draw common lessons from these
essays also carries with it the implicit suggestion that it or some

similar scheme may be of use for further study of ideas in history. As developed here it consists first of a breakdown of ideas by type (concepts and images) and by the number of persons holding them (individual, group, society). There follows the location of the place of ideas in the historical process by a projection of the analysis in two directions: toward the major causes discovered for the content of ideas, that is, predispositions (personality, psychological need) and conditions (environment, past experience); and toward the effect of ideas in defining historical action. Elaboration of the pattern through interplay of the various factors is possible, and indeed necessary as soon as an extended time span is considered.

Our consideration of the American scholarly tradition leads to two further suggestions. The one that comes out most forcefully is almost trite: that historians take counsel more frequently with social scientists, since the latter study the springs of human activity more systematically than historians are trained to do. These essays suggest various points at which we could turn to our behavioral colleagues. At the start of this conclusion, we observed two distinct reactions among those persons favorable to democracy in the French Revolutionary era that could be represented by Voltaire and Condorcet. One might ask if these reactions did not have their origin partly in two distinct personality types, as studied by modern psychoanalysts. Or another case, when Parker says that French scientists had "the conviction that science should be immediately useful to industry" (p. 93, see Conclusion, p. 353), is he not describing a "social role" and should he not formulate questions about their activity in the light of sociological studies of role behavior? Should not Palmer consult social psychologists before asserting that a demand for integration is a basic psychological need and not, let us say, simply the manifestation of an economic drive? And should Herr not provide evidence that individuals have a tendency to political Manichaeism before assuming that whole societies do? As Palmer says, "The problem of the role of ideas in history turns into a series of problems of epistemology and of psychology, problems of human nature and human behavior, which are by no means limited to history, and

with which the historian is not especially well-equipped to deal"
(p. 5).

There is another suggestion, which has the merit of being
fresher. It concerns our understanding of historical causation.
Apart from the usual specialization of historians by countries and
epochs, we have chosen to define our fields by their relationship
to other disciplines in which we have acquired more than ordinary
interest and expertise. Thus intellectual history is the province
of persons with a penchant for philosophy and literature (we have
ceased to be surprised by scholars in these fields who decide to
become intellectual historians), and economic history has been in
the hands of trained economists. Political science engenders political and diplomatic history; sociology, social history; the natural
sciences, history of science, to list other obvious instances. The
development has had various effects, some good, others questionable. The most evident is all to the good, for history has acquired
that richness of texture that Turner, Becker, and James Harvey
Robinson preached. But the process has also tended to inhibit
historians from taking a broad view of their subject. Can one
who has chosen to become an intellectual historian offer a theory
about social and economic developments without risking the verdict of superficiality and ignorance? Suffering from this inhibi-
tion and still eager to serve a useful function, or perhaps simply
through careless terminology, intellectual historians have labeled
their conclusions the "intellectual causes" of history, economic
historians call theirs "economic causes," and so on through social,
political, and other causes (of the French Revolution, for example). What higher contributions can a historian be expected
to make than to illuminate a full-fledged cause? By a spontaneous
and unpremeditated process, historical causation has become sub-
divided along lines that parallel surprisingly the divisions of our
higher education, as if there were some real relation between the
haphazard ramification of the departments of a modern American
university, itself a phase of the development of Western culture,
and the forces behind human evolution. We have given the result our blessing and sanctified it under the infallible dogma of
"multiple causation." And this when university departments are

growing more and more uncertain as to what terrain is rightly theirs![16]

It is clear from these essays that by the study of ideas in history the authors mean something more than "intellectual history." This is no accident. The more one looks at the accepted terms, the more irrelevant they appear to the way historians analyze causation in practice. To give one example, there is a current controversy over the reasons for France's slow economic development in the nineteenth century. Lack of capital and natural resources says one side, lack of entrepreneurial spirit says the other. Are these both best described as "economic causes" of French evolution, or is one understood better as "conditions" and the other as a "predisposition"? If we set aside the misleading labels, we shall see more clearly our real assumptions. Louis Gottschalk has already shown us how. Before he could construct a meaningful pattern of the causes of revolution, he was forced to dismiss the old-fashioned intellectual causes of the French Revolution. In his causal pattern ideas reappeared properly integrated with other factors. A similar investment of thought and effort should earn us rich dividends. It will make us more conscious of the theoretical framework within which we operate and thus clarify our understanding of the nature of history. It may even make us more daring in tackling kinds of history in which we have not been "properly trained." A historian will always have to limit his objectives and acquire needed specialized abilities if he is to undertake meaningful research. But he need not fall into a rut. A fresh look at the nature of historical causation should smooth the road leading to significant conclusions. If these studies encourage such a look, they will have achieved their aim of being useful to the profession.

16. This explanation is more than the whim of one mind. It has already been advanced, in much more telling and urbane fashion, by J. H. Hexter (*Reappraisals in History*, pp. 197-198). My explanation had been reached and this paragraph written before I read his essay. Hexter generously attributes the responsibility for the meaningless multiplication of causes to the members of the outside disciplines, but he does not allow historians to escape scot free. He sees the same result coming from our propensity for working in one kind of archive at a time. His whole discussion deserves serious meditation (*ibid.*, pp. 194-201).

WRITINGS OF
LOUIS GOTTSCHALK

BOOKLETS

The Life of Jean Paul Marat. Girard, Kansas: Haldeman-Julius Co., 1923.

The Ancient Regime (France Before the Revolution). Girard, Kansas: Haldeman-Julius Co., 1924.

The Fall of Louis XVI. Girard, Kansas: Haldeman-Julius Co., 1924.

The First French Republic. Girard, Kansas: Haldeman-Julius Co., 1924.

The Consulate of Napoleon Bonaparte. Girard, Kansas: Haldeman-Julius Co., 1925.

The Empire of Napoleon. Girard, Kansas: Haldeman-Julius Co., 1925.

Restoration and Reaction in France, 1814-1815. Girard, Kansas: Haldeman-Julius Co., 1925.

Franklin and Lafayette. Washington: Institut français de Washington, 1939.

The Place of the American Revolution in the Causal Pattern of the French Revolution. Easton, Pa.: American Friends of Lafayette, 1948. Also in H. Ausubel, ed., *The Making of Modern Europe.* New York: Dryden Press, 1951; and in Peter Amann, ed., *The Eighteenth-Century Revolution—French or Western?* ("Problems in European Civilization.") Boston: D. C. Heath and Co., 1963.

The United States and Lafayette. Les États-Unis et Lafayette. ("Augustana Library Publications: Occasional Paper," No. 3.) Rock Island, Ill.: Augustana Library, 1958.

BOOKS

Jean Paul Marat: A Study in Radicalism. New York: Greenberg, Publisher, Inc., 1929. French edition, 1929. Italian edition, 1961.

The Era of the French Revolution (1715-1815). Boston: Houghton Mifflin Company, 1929.

Lafayette Comes to America. Chicago: The University of Chicago Press, 1935.

Lafayette Joins the American Army. Chicago: The University of Chicago Press, 1937.

Lady-in-waiting: The Romance of Lafayette and Aglaé de Hunolstein. Baltimore: Johns Hopkins University Press, 1939.

Lafayette and the Close of the American Revolution. Chicago: The University of Chicago Press, 1942.

(Editor). *The Letters of Lafayette to Washington, 1777-1799.* New York: Privately printed by Helen Fahnestock Hubbard, 1944.

(With Clyde Kluckhohn and Robert Angell). *The Use of Personal Documents in History, Anthropology, and Sociology.* ("Social Science Research Council Bulletin," No. 53.) New York: Social Science Research Council, 1945.

Lafayette between the American and the French Revolution (1783-1789). Chicago: The University of Chicago Press, 1950.

Understanding History: A Primer of Historical Method. New York: Alfred Knopf, 1950.

(With Donald Lach). *Europe and the Modern World.* 2 vols. Chicago: Scott, Foresman, and Company, 1951, 1954.

(Co-author and editor). *Generalization in the Writing of History: A Report of the Committee on Historical Analysis of the Social Science Research Council.* Chicago: The University of Chicago Press, 1963.

UNESCO, *History of Mankind: Cultural and Scientific Development.* Volume IV. In press.

ARTICLES

"The Radicalism of Jean Paul Marat," *Sewanee Review,* XXIX (1921), 155-170.

"J.-P. Marat et la Journée du 14 Juillet 1789," *La Révolution française,* new ser. No. 17 (1923), pp. 13-18.

"Communism during the French Revolution, 1789-1793," *Political Science Quarterly,* XL (1925), 438-450.

"Du Marat Inédit," *Annales historiques de la Révolution française,* III (1926), 209-216.

"A Letter of Benjamin Franklin," *The American Printer* (January 20, 1926), p. 46.

"The Criminality of Jean Paul Marat," *South Atlantic Quarterly,* XXV (1926), 154-167.

"Marat a-t-il été en Angleterre un criminel de droit commun?" *Annales historiques de la Révolution française* (1926), pp. 111-126. Translated from *South Atlantic Quarterly,* XXV (1926), 154-167.

"Revolutionary Analogies," *The History Quarterly* [of the Filson Club and the University of Louisville], I (1926-27), 8-23.

"The Importance of Albert Mathiez," *Nation,* CVII (1928), 619-621.

"L'Affaire Marat," *Annales historiques de la Révolution française,* VI (1929), 600-601.

"Professor Aulard," *Journal of Modern History,* I (1929), 85-86.

"Lafayette," *Journal of Modern History*, II (1930), 281-287.

"Lazare N. M. Carnot"; "Marquis de Lafayette"; "Jean Paul Marat"; and "Comte Albert Vandal," in *Encyclopedia of the Social Sciences*, 1930.

"Lafayette as a Commercial Expert," *American Historical Review*, XXXVI (1930-1931), 561-564.

"The French Revolution: Conspiracy or Circumstance?" in *Persecution and Liberty: Essays in Honor of George Lincoln Burr*. New York: The Century Company, 1931.

"L'Influence d'Albert Mathiez sur les études historiques aux États-Unis," *Annales historiques de la Révolution française*, IX (1932), 457-460.

"La Lettre de Carnot du 10 Thermidor An II," *Annales historiques de la Révolution française*, IX (1932), 457-460.

"Albert Mathiez," *Journal of Modern History*, IV (1932), 231.

"Studies since 1920 of French Thought in the Period of the Enlightenment," *Journal of Modern History*, IV (1932), 242-260.

"The Peasant in the French Revolution," *Political Science Quarterly*, XLVIII (1933), 589-599.

"Potentialities of Comparative History," *Bulletin of the Society for Social Research*, XV (1936), 1 and 6.

(With Janet L. MacDonald), "Letters on the Management of an Estate during the Old Regime," *Journal of Modern History*, VIII (1936), 64-81.

"Quelques études récentes sur Marat," *Annales historiques de la Révolution française*, XIII (1936), 97-122.

"Leon Trotsky and the Natural History of Revolutions," *American Journal of Sociology*, XLIV (1938), 339-354.

"A Critique of Sorokin's Social and Cultural Dynamics," *Bulletin of the Society for Social Research*, XVII (1939), 9-10.

"The Attitude of the European Officers in the Revolutionary Armies toward George Washington," *Journal of the Illinois State Historical Society*, XXXII (1939), 20-50.

"Revolutionary Traditions and Analogies," *University* [of Kansas City] *Review*, VI, (1939-1940), 19-25.

"The Evaluation of Historical Writings," in Louis Wilson, ed., *The Practice of Book Selection, Papers Presented before the Library Institute of the University of Chicago, July 31 to August 13, 1939*. Chicago: The University of Chicago Press, 1940.

"The Scope and Subject Matter of History," *University* [of Kansas City] *Review*, VIII (1941-42), 75-83.

"The Charles XV Collection," *Augustana Bulletin*, Series 37, No. 3 ("Publication of the Augustana Swedish Culture Institute," No. 5.) (March 1942), pp. 4-5.

"Darlan, Here You Are," Chicago Council on Foreign Relations, *Foreign Notes,* XIX, No. 20 (Dec. 18, 1942).

"Peace Congresses: Past and Future," *The Chicago Jewish Forum,* I (Winter, 1942-43), 3-8.

"Lessons of Modern History for World Peace," in Lyman Bryson *et al.,* eds., *Approaches to World Peace.* Fourth Symposium of the Conference on Science, Philosophy and Religion. New York: Harper, 1944.

"Causes of Revolution," *American Journal of Sociology,* L (1944), 1-8.

"French Parlements and Judicial Review," *Journal of the History of Ideas,* V (1944), 105-112.

(With Milancie Hill Sheldon), "More Letters on the Management of an Estate during the Old Regime," *Journal of Modern History,* XVII (1945), 147-152.

"Some Recent Countersocialistic Literature," *Journal of Modern History,* XVII (1945), 221-225.

"Propositions," in *Theory and Practice in Historical Study: A Report of the Committee on Historiography.* (Social Science Research Council, Bulletin 54.) New York, 1946.

"Carl Becker: Skeptic or Humanist?", *Journal of Modern History,* XVIII (1946), 160-162.

(With Josephine Fennell), "Duer and the Conway Cabal," *American Historical Review,* LII (1946-1947), 87-96.

"Philippe Sagnac and the Causes of the French Revolution," *Journal of Modern History,* XX (1948), 137-148.

"Our Vichy Fumble," *Journal of Modern History,* XX (1948), 47-56.

"How to Evaluate the Russian Revolution," *Common Cause,* III (1949-50), 434-439.

"Possible Readjustments by the Scholar," in Pierce Butler, ed., *Librarians, Scholars, and Booksellers at Mid-Century.* Chicago: The University of Chicago Press, 1953.

"A Professor of History in a Quandary," *American Historical Review,* LIX (1954), 273-286.

"The Historian's Use of Generalization," in Leonard D. White, ed., *State of the Social Sciences.* Chicago: University of Chicago Press, 1956. Arabic translation, prepared for the Social Sciences Section of the UNESCO Middle East Science Cooperation Office, in *Readings in the Social Sciences,* No. 3 (1959).

"Reflections on Burke's Reflections on the French Revolution," *Proceedings of the American Philosophical Society,* C (1956), 418-429.

"The Revolutionary Tradition," in Roger P. McCutcheon, ed., *The Present-Day Relevance of Eighteenth-Century Thought.* Washington: American Council of Learned Societies, 1956.

"Year of the Sputnik: '57 in Perspective—Historian's View," *Chicago Sun-Times*, December 29, 1957.

"Report on the Work of the Council's Committee on Historical Analysis," in Social Science Research Council, *Items*, XII (1958), 25-27.

"Mankind Will Survive," *Context, a University of Chicago Magazine*, I (1961), 26-28.

"Hillel's Tasks—from the Perspective of the University," in B'nai B'rith Hillel Foundations, *Changing Patterns of Jewish Life on the Campus*. Washington, 1961, pp. 68-74.